WOMEN'S LIVES
IN MEDIEVAL EUROPE

Women's Lives in Medieval Europe

A Sourcebook

Edited by

Emilie Amt

Routledge

New York • London

Published in 1993 by

Routledge
An imprint of Routledge, Chapman and Hall, Inc.
29 West 35th Street
New York, NY 10001

Published in Great Britain by

Routledge
11 New Fetter Lane
London EC4P 4EE

Library of Congress Cataloging in Publication Data

Women's lives in medieval Europe : a sourcebook / edited by Emilie
Amt.
        p.   cm.
    Includes bibliographical references.
    ISBN 0-415-90627-X. — ISBN 0-415-90628-8 (pbk.)
    1. Women—History—Middle Ages, 500–1500—Sources. 2. Europe—
History—Sources.   I. Amt, Emilie,   .
    HQ1143.W65   1993
    305.4'094'0902—dc20   92-12815
                                                              CIP

ISBN 0-415-90627-X (HB)
ISBN 0-415-90628-8 (PB)

Contents

Acknowledgments

I have incurred many debts in the preparation of this book. For hours of discussion of the Middle Ages, medieval women and the teaching of women's history, I would like to thank my students at both Washington College and the Oxford Centre for Medieval and Renaissance Studies, and my friends and colleagues, especially S. J. Allen, Susan Fischler, Elizabeth Baer, Ellen Klein and Elizabeth Amt. I am grateful to Dr. Maryann Brink and Dr. Jacqueline Murray for reading and commenting on the entire manuscript; the faults that remain are of course my own. A generous Faculty Enhancement Grant from Washington College in 1990 aided in the collection of documents for the volume. For help in assembling the collection, my thanks are due to Jacklin Wheeler, Rachel Demma and the staff of the Clifton M. Miller Library, especially Lois Kuhn.

I am grateful to the authors and presses which have generously allowed me to reprint their translations of medieval documents here. Every effort has been made to trace copyright holders, although that has not been possible in every case.

Introduction

This book is a collection of primary sources for the study of women's lives in Europe during the Middle Ages, from about 500 to about 1500 A.D. Its purpose is to present firsthand information about women's everyday lives and activities and the conditions in which they lived, and to show the reader on what sorts of evidence historians base their conclusions about these aspects of history. For readers who have little background in medieval history, some general information about medieval Europe may be helpful.

Until the fifth century A.D., much of western Europe lay within the Roman Empire, a vast collection of terrritories including parts of the Middle East and North Africa. In Europe itself during the centuries of Roman rule, much of the native Celtic population had become highly Romanized in its culture, political allegiance and legal practices. In the last few centuries of the Roman Empire, the Germanic tribes which had long lived on the eastern fringes of the European provinces moved into the Romanized lands in large numbers. This wave of "barbarian" invasions, along with severe political and economic problems, gradually killed off the Roman Empire, which was replaced by a number of Germanic successor kingdoms, including those of the Franks in Gaul (modern France), the Visigoths in Spain, the Ostrogoths in Italy, the Burgundians in and around what is now Switzerland, and the Anglo-Saxons in England.

The Germanic tribes brought with them a very different society from that of Rome. Whereas Roman civilization was highly urbanized, for example, the Germans had until then seldom settled even in villages. The Romans had a long history of written legislation; the Germans used a system of customary law which had not yet been written down. Different practices regarding marriage and family can be seen in the extracts from Roman and Germanic law in this book (8, 10–11).[1] Centuries of contact between the Germans and the empire, however, had wrought changes on both sides, and now, as the Germans settled in what had long been Roman territory, further mingling of the two cultures occurred. The Germanic kingdoms which were established inside the old boundaries of the now defunct empire were by no means entirely Germanic in their ethnic makeup or their culture.

---

1. Numbers in parentheses refer to readings.

Even more influential than Roman tradition in this process of change was the religion of the late Roman Empire. Christianity had originated in Palestine, where a small group of Jews believed that the Jewish carpenter Jesus, who had been executed by the Roman authorities early in the first century A.D., was the "Christ," the son of God and savior of humanity. Although Christians were persecuted at first by both the Jewish religious authorities and the Roman government, their religion survived and spread. In the year 313 it achieved official sanction from the Roman emperor Constantine, and in the late fourth century it became the official religion of the empire. The cultural initiative of the late Roman Empire passed from pagan writers to Christian theologians such as St. Jerome (4) and St. Augustine of Hippo (5), who explored the details of Christian belief and laid the foundation for church law. It was the Christian church, too, which filled the vacuum in leadership during the fifth century, as the Roman world faced widespread military, political and economic crises and the Roman government crumbled. Bishops began to provide the services for which the government had once been responsible; in particular, the bishop of Rome came to assume a prominent role in Italy, so much so that as the "pope" he was eventually recognized as the leader of the church throughout the western Mediterranean regions. Clergymen and monks also preserved what ancient learning survived the fall of the Roman Empire in the west, and throughout most of the Middle Ages the church maintained a near monopoly on literacy and education.

The church was eager to convert the pagan Germans to Christianity. It accomplished this through intensive mission work and through alliances with Germanic kings, queens and nobles, who saw advantages to themselves in allying with the existing authority in their new territories. Christian beliefs, including ideas about women, marriage and family, had already mingled with Roman traditions. Now Christian views were adopted by the Germanic settlers as well. Thus the three main ingredients of medieval European civilization had come together: the Roman, the Germanic and the Christian. Part I of this book presents examples of these three traditions. The rest of the book is about the new civilization that arose from their combination.

The period from the fifth century to the eleventh is often designated the "Early Middle Ages." This is the time sometimes known as the "Dark Ages"—in part because of the collapse of Roman civilization, with the loss of much classical knowledge, but also because relatively few historical sources remain to tell us of the events of these years. The documents which do survive include the laws which the Germanic kings were now having written down (10–11) and the works of historians such as Gregory of Tours (29, 43). Much of the essential character of medieval Europe was already apparent in this early period, especially in religious matters. Monasteries and convents, for example, came to play a key role in economic and cultural life, and many noble families dedicated sons and daughters to the religious life, in which they lived according to a monastic "rule" such as that of Caesarius of Arles (61). Women were encouraged to be nuns, but their other options in the church—serving as deaconesses or in partnership with husbands who were priests—were closed off by the decisions of church councils (60). These councils established "canon law" or church law, which regulated the lives of members of the clergy and many aspects of private life for lay people. For most of the laity, canon law was enforced by the local priest, who heard one's confession regularly and assigned penance for one's sins. Thus the church gradually succeeded in imposing on secular society its standards of behavior in areas such as marriage.

The political face of early medieval Europe was dominated by the Franks, and in the eighth century the Frankish kingdom under Charlemagne (768–814 A.D.) and his descendants conquered and ruled many neighboring kingdoms. The resulting "Carolingian Empire" included much of what is now France, Germany and Italy. Among their other activities, the emperors promulgated new rules for the administration of the empire and their own estates, some of which survive to inform us about everyday life in Carolingian Europe (44). In this new realm cultural energy reached a height unknown since the days of Roman power. The rich intellectual life of the royal court produced many of the written works of the period, but relatively isolated individuals such as the noblewoman Dhuoda could also be well educated (30).

While the Carolingian Empire flourished, however, the west was beginning to suffer invasions by three new groups: the Scandinavian Vikings, the Muslim "Saracens" from North Africa, and the Asian Magyars. Under these onslaughts and other stresses in the ninth and tenth centuries, imperial government once again collapsed, and Europe entered another period of political fragmentation. This time, the surviving political units were small kingdoms, duchies and counties, ruled by local nobles who could offer some degree of protection to their followers. The bond between a lord and each his followers, or vassals, became an important one in many parts of western Europe in these years. Noblemen put themselves under the lordship of more powerful men who could grant them estates called "fiefs" (from the Latin *feudum*) in return for loyalty and military service. Such "feudal" relationships dominated many aspects of life for the ruling classes in the centuries to follow.

The period from the eleventh century through the thirteenth is often called the "High Middle Ages." Underlying much of the history of these years was a widespread economic revival in Europe which had begun long before the eleventh century in some parts of the continent and continued throughout the High Middle Ages in others. New technology, a slightly improved climate and expanding frontiers gradually raised the standard of living and produced surpluses which formed the basis for a commercial boom. Towns flourished as centers of trade, and the town-dwelling population, which made its living in trade and industry, grew. The use of money as a medium of exchange increased, along with banking and written record-keeping (53–55). Townspeople organized themselves into guilds: the merchant guild, which often served as a sort of town government, included only the wealthiest citizens, while each industry had its own craft guild, which set standards and regulated the industry, and to which all practitioners of that trade belonged (51). Towns were often able to use their wealth to buy a certain amount of independence from their lords.

Christianity in the High Middle Ages was characterized by an increasing variety of activities and outlooks. In the eleventh century the church struggled overtly with secular authorities for ecclesiastical power and independence, and in the twelfth century canon lawyers like Gratian (18) codified church policy and reasserted its pre-eminence in many areas of life. In 1095, the increasingly militant church launched the first of the Crusades, papally sanctioned holy wars against the Muslims of the Holy Land and Spain and against heretics in Europe. The Crusades would last through the thirteenth century, and one of their unintended effects was the widespread persecution of the Jewish minority in Europe (70). Another characteristic of high medieval religion was dissatisfaction with the wealth, worldliness and soft living that critics perceived in many monasteries and convents. New "reform" orders of monks—and less often of nuns—were founded in the late eleventh century, only to become so worldly themselves that a new wave of reform was called for in the early thirteenth century. From this second wave came the Dominican and Franciscan orders, including the Poor Clares (64). Large numbers of Christians also turned to less formal religious movements, such as that of the Beguines (67) and their male counterparts, the Beghards. Mysticism, the direct communication of the soul with God, was practiced by such respected individuals as Hildegard of Bingen (63) and St. Bernard of Clairvaux. Some groups, such as the Waldensians (79), found that their spiritual enthusiasm led them into beliefs and practices condemned by the church; and this upsurge in heresy in the twelfth and thirteenth centuries caused the church to found the Inquisition to deal with Christians who had strayed from the fold (80).

Many of these religious developments centered on towns and cities, and so too did the new forms of higher education. The cathedral schools of the twelfth century and the universities of the thirteenth century were urban institutions. While women participated fully in the religious revival of these years, they were excluded from formal higher education once the university became the standard seat of learning. The universities also guarded their monopoly on certain fields like medicine carefully (25). In other spheres of culture, however, noblewomen played a prominent role, serving as patrons and producers of music and poetry and shaping the codes of chivalry and courtly love, which softened the hard-working and unromantic lives of the nobility.

Medieval writers commonly divided the members of society into three "estates" or "orders": those who fought, those who prayed, and those who worked. While the estates were often described in terms of men only, in reality women belonged to or were attached to each of them. The "fighters" were the knights or noblemen, whose wealth, power and status derived from their lands; for this reason they were willing to swear allegiance to the lords who gave them fiefs and let their heirs inherit them. The women of this estate did not normally fight, but they shared in the other jobs of the nobility, running households and estates; and the concern with land shaped every noblewoman's life in fundamental ways, such as the choice of a husband. The praying estate consisted of the clergy and the monastic community, and while women were excluded from the former, they made up a sizeable and often active portion of the latter. The third estate, the workers, did not mean everyone who worked—for virtually everyone, including nobles, monks and nuns, did work in medieval society— but those whose position in society was defined by their manual labor: artisans, servants and the peasantry. Artisans might work for themselves or as employees; servants worked for employers or their lords. Peasants worked the land, raising their own food and supporting their lords. There were many degrees of social status within the working estate, even among the peasantry. Some peasants were free, but most were serfs or villeins, who were not slaves but were legally bound to the land and required to perform certain work for their lords. Serfs might hope to achieve freedom through manumission (45) or by running away to a town, where the law often granted them freedom if they remained for a set length of time, often a year and a day. Women participated fully in the working life in industry, domestic service and agriculture.

Many aspects of life, culture and institutions were similar across medieval Europe, but there were also important differences from region to region, in agricultural and industrial products, in political and social organization, and in the ethnic and religious makeup of the population. The towns of Italy, for example, tended to be freer of outside control than were most European towns, and some of them specialized in Mediterranean trade, which brought eastern luxury goods to the west. The Iberian peninsula comprised Muslim territories in the south along with a number of small Christian principalities in the north, and the warfare between them was a major factor in shaping Spanish society (14). At the same time, Germans were pushing eastward into the lands of the pagan Slavs, bringing new lands into cultivation, on which grain was grown for much of Europe, and which drew surplus peasants eastward as settlers. The German king also claimed the prestigious title of "Holy Roman Emperor" and lands stretching as far south as central Italy; yet the real power in Germany usually lay with the territorial princes and the bishops, and few emperors were able to assert control in Italy. The kings of France, on the other hand, steadily enlarged their territories and their control over their vassals, forming alliances with rich towns and with the church. Wine was already one of the major products of the thriving French economy, and a new market for French wine was one of the results when a Norman French duke conquered the Anglo-Saxon kingdom of England in 1066 and replaced the old Anglo-Saxon nobility there with French noble families. England's greatest export was raw wool, large amounts of which were sold to the towns of Flanders, a particularly important center for cloth making on the northern French coast. Medieval merchants visited fairs across the continent, and while the vast majority of Europeans probably never traveled far from the place of their birth, pilgrims, scholars and soldiers also helped to spread goods, news and ideas.

The fourteenth and fifteenth centuries, known as the "Later Middle Ages," are best known for the traumas they brought. Population growth had already begun to slow in the early fourteenth century, before the Black Death, or bubonic plague, killed between a quarter and a third of the entire population of Europe in 1347–49 (28). For the next few centuries, this terrifying disease would continue to break out periodically. The initial plague left behind a land surplus and a severe labor shortage, which enabled peasants and workers to win improved legal status, pay and conditions; their lords and employers then attempted to limit such gains through laws controlling wages and prices. Meanwhile, England and France engaged in a long series of wars known collectively as the Hundred Years' War (1337–1453), which battered the French countryside and left England in political disarray. Yet this period of upheaval was also the backdrop to a great deal of cultural activity, such as that in which Christine de Pisan (39) participated at the French royal court, and the literary and artistic developments in fifteenth-century Italy which are known today as the Renaissance.

The materials in this book are, as much as possible, about ordinary women. Although many of them belonged to the nobility, no queens or princesses are represented, and other famous or exceptional women have generally been avoided. Literary or artistic sources are missing here, even though much of what we know or surmise about the lives of medieval women comes from or is influenced by literature and art. Instead, the material in this book is "historical": public and private records, letters, laws, regulations and instructional works, historical and personal narratives, and plans and drawings based on archaeological evidence. Whenever appropriate, women's own writings have been included. Not enough of these survive from the Middle Ages to enable us to build up an accurate picture of life from a purely female perspective, especially because women who wrote were not usually interested in telling us many of the things we most want to know about them. But to hear their occasional voices adds an important dimension to the study of women's lives.

The modern reader may encounter certain difficulties in reading medieval texts. For example, there are strong religious elements and ecclesiastical biases in many of the documents here, which may be alien or frustrating to the reader familiar with a more secular society. This is in part because medieval Europe was indeed a highly religious civilization, and the modern reader must therefore resist the urge to dismiss the true religious feelings and important religious motivations of the men and women who appear in these sources. Miracles and religious visions were accepted as real by many or most people. The church itself was an integral part of the power structure, controlling vast wealth and wielding great political influence and judicial power. Religious differences even defined marginal and persecuted groups within society (Jews, Muslims and heretics). The church's views played a large part in shaping secular laws and social norms, and sex roles and gender constructs are perhaps the areas in which this is most obvious. On the other hand, the religious viewpoint of the sources can sometimes distort our view of even religious subjects. Much of the written material that survives from the Middle Ages was written by churchmen, but this does not mean that churchmen spoke for everyone.

Similarly, the reader should be aware that medieval standards of truth, originality and accuracy were not the same as ours. Supernatural explanations of events were more widely accepted than they are today. Authors of literature and history borrowed freely from other works, and the boundaries between myth, story and history were not clear ones. Literary conventions can also distort the historical record; for example, the writers often invented dialogue freely, and sometimes even the villains speak in biblical quotations. One way to read such sources is to look for clues in accounts as to what might "really" have happened. Another is to study the mind-set of the age, taking the belief itself as an important historical fact. A third is to enter into the mind-set of the age, taking the belief for granted. All three approaches can be illuminating for the student of medieval history.

The sources in this book are grouped thematically and arranged chronologically within those thematic sections. The reader will notice that there are far more documents here from the twelfth and later centuries than from the Early Middle Ages. This is mainly because the more widely literate culture of the High and Later Middle Ages has left us far more written sources, and also because the written evidence from which historians deduce what we know about life in the Early Middle Ages tends to be more fragmentary and lends itself less well to selective reading by non-specialists. Once we reach the twelfth and thirteenth centuries, medieval historians find themselves profiting from a virtual explosion of written source materials which illuminate almost all aspects of society. As the reader will find in these pages, those aspects include the daily lives, concerns and occupations of women.

A Note on Money

From the eighth to the thirteenth century, the standard coin of most European countries was the silver penny (plural "pence"). For accounting purposes, twelve pennies made a "shilling," and twenty shillings made a "pound." These units, of course, went by different names in different languages.

English	1 penny	1 shilling (=12 pence)	1 pound (=20 shillings)
symbol/abbreviation	d.	s.	£
Latin	denarius, denarii	solidus, solidi	libra, libre
Italian	denaro, denari	soldo, soldi	lira, lire
French	denier, deniers	sou, sous	livre, livres

Part I

The Heritage of Ideas: Christian Belief, Roman Ideals, and Germanic Custom

It is a commonplace that medieval civilization was a blend of Roman, Christian and Germanic elements. The readings in this section examine the condition of women in these three traditions and the ideas about women that were passed on to medieval Europe. Of the documents represented here, the Roman ones have the least direct relevance to the study of medieval women, but they reveal a set of attitudes that are echoed in many other pieces in this book; Roman law was studied and imitated in the High Middle Ages and had a particular effect on canon law. The Germanic documents represent a society as yet little influenced by the church, but they also describe the status and condition of European women in the first few centuries after the conversion of the Germans to Christianity. The Christian writings were the ones that continued to exert the most direct and vital influence on the atmosphere in which Europeans lived and worked throughout the Middle Ages, for the Bible and the Church Fathers were still regarded as having spiritual and practical authority in the fifteenth century and beyond.

A. Christian Belief

1. The Bible: Adam and Eve (1st Millennium B.C.)

The Scriptures of the Hebrews became the Old Testament—the first part—of the Christian Bible. Genesis, the first book of the Old Testament, begins with the story of the creation of the universe, the earth and everything on it. The extracts reproduced here include the two versions given in Genesis of the creation of the first people, and the story of the "Fall" of humankind from a perfect state into one of sin. The Fall created the need for God's eventual salvation of the human race through Jesus Christ.
Source: Genesis 1:24–2:9, 2:15–3:20, from the Revised Standard Version of the Bible. Used by permission of the National Council of the Churches of Christ.

And God said, "Let the earth bring forth living creatures according to their kinds: cattle and creeping things and beasts of the earth according to their kinds." And it was so. And God made the beasts of the earth according to their kinds, and everything that creeps upon the ground according to its kind. And God saw that it was good.

Then God said, "Let us make man in our image, after our likeness, and let them have dominion over the fish of the sea, and over the birds of the air, and over the cattle, and over all the earth, and over every creeping thing that creeps upon the earth." So God created man in his own image, in the image of God he created him; male and female he created them. And God blessed them, and God said to them, "Be fruitful and multiply, and fill the earth and subdue it; and have dominion over the fish of the sea and over the birds of the air and over every living thing that moves upon the earth." And God said, "Behold, I have given you every plant yielding seed which is upon the face of all the earth, and every tree with seed in its fruit; you shall have them for food. And to every beast of the earth, and to every bird of the air, and to everything that creeps on the earth, everything that has the breath of life, I have given every green plant for food." And it was so. And God saw everything that he had made, and behold, it was very good. And there was evening and there was morning, a sixth day.

Thus the heavens and the earth were finished, and all the host of

13

them. And on the seventh day God finished his work which he had done, and he rested on the seventh day from all his work which he had done. So God blessed the seventh day and hallowed it, because on it God rested from all his work which he had done in creation.

These are the generations of the heavens and the earth when they were created.

In the day that the Lord God made the earth and the heavens, when no plant of the field was yet in the earth and no herb of the field had yet sprung up—for the Lord God had not caused it to rain upon the earth, and there was no man to till the ground; but a mist went up from the earth and watered the whole face of the ground—then the Lord God formed man of dust from the ground, and breathed into his nostrils the breath of life; and man became a living being. And the Lord God planted him a garden in Eden, in the east; and there he put the man whom he had formed. And out of the ground the Lord God made to grow every tree that is pleasant to the sight and good for food, the tree of life also in the midst of the garden, and the tree of the knowledge of good and evil. . . .

The Lord God took the man and put him in the garden of Eden to till it and keep it. And the Lord God commanded the man, saying, "You may freely eat of every tree of the garden; but of the tree of the knowledge of good and evil you shall not eat, for in the day that you eat of it you shall die."

Then the Lord God said, "It is not good that the man should be alone; I will make him a helper fit for him." So out of the ground the Lord God formed every beast of the field and every bird of the air, and brought them to the man to see what he would call them; and whatever the man called the living creature, that was its name. The man gave names to all cattle, and to the birds of the air, and to every beast of the field; but for the man there was not found a helper fit for him. So the Lord God caused a deep sleep to fall upon the man, and while he slept took one of his ribs and closed up its place with flesh; and the rib which the Lord God had taken from the man he made into a woman and brought her to the man. Then the man said,

> This at last is bone of my bones and flesh of my flesh;
> she shall be called Woman,
> because she was taken out of Man.

Therefore a man leaves his father and his mother and cleaves to his wife, and they become one flesh. And the man and his wife were both naked, and were not ashamed.

Now the serpent was more subtle than any other wild creature that the Lord God had made. He said to the woman, "Did God say, 'You shall not eat of any tree of the garden'?" And the woman said to the serpent, "We may eat of the fruit of the trees of the garden; but God said, 'You shall not eat of the fruit of the tree which is in the midst of the garden, neither shall you touch it, lest you die.'" But the serpent said to the woman, "You will not die. For God knows that when you eat of it your eyes will be opened, and you will be like God, knowing good and evil." So when the woman saw that the tree was good for food, and that it was a delight to the eyes, and that the tree was to be desired to make one wise, she took of its fruit and ate; and she also gave some to her husband, and he ate. Then the eyes of both were opened, and they knew that they were naked; and they sewed fig leaves together and made themselves aprons.

And they heard the sound of the Lord God walking in the garden in the cool of the day, and the man and his wife hid themselves from the presence of the Lord God among the trees of the garden. But the Lord God called to the man, and said to him, "Where are you?" And he said, "I heard the sound of thee in the garden, and I was afraid, because I was naked; and I hid myself." He said, "Who told you that you were naked? Have you eaten of the tree of which I commanded you not to eat?" The man said, "The woman whom thou gavest to be with me, she gave me fruit of the tree, and I ate." Then the Lord God said to the woman, "What is this that you have done?" The woman said, "The serpent beguiled me, and I ate." The Lord God said to the serpent,

> Because you have done this,
> cursed are you above all cattle, and above all wild animals;
> upon your belly you shall go,
> and dust you shall eat all the days of your life.
> I will put enmity between you and the woman,
> and between your seed and her seed;
> he shall bruise your head,
> and you shall bruise his heel.

To the woman he said,

> I will greatly multiply your pain in childbearing;
> in pain you shall bring forth children,
> yet your desire shall be for your husband,
> and he shall rule over you.

And to Adam he said,

> Because you have listened to your wife,
> and have eaten of the tree of which I commanded you,
> 'You shall not eat of it,'
> cursed is the ground because of you;
> in toil you shall eat of it all the days of your life;
> thorns and thistles it shall bring forth to you;
> and you shall eat the plants of the field.
> In the sweat of your face you shall eat bread
> till you return to the ground,
> for out of it you were taken;
> you are dust, and to dust you shall return.

The man called his wife's name Eve, because she was the mother of all living.

2. The Bible: Model Women in the Gospels (1st c. A.D.)

> The Gospels are early accounts of the life of Jesus Christ, and form part of the New Testament, the second part of the Christian Bible. The events described in these extracts took place in the late first century B.C. and early first century A.D.
> Source: Luke 1:26–49, 7:36–39, 44–48, 50; John 20:1–18, from the Revised Standard Version of the Bible. Used by permission of the National Council of the Churches of Christ.

The Virgin Mary

> In the following passage a young woman learns that she is to become miraculously pregnant with the "Son of God," Jesus Christ—the central figure of the Christian religion. The importance of the Virgin Mary in Christian attitudes toward women is second only to that of Eve. The "Annunciation" also became a favorite subject of medieval artists, playwrights and poets.

In the sixth month the angel Gabriel was sent from God to a city of Galilee named Nazareth, to a virgin betrothed to a man whose name was Joseph, of the house of David; and the virgin's name was Mary. And he came to her and said, "Hail, O favored one, the Lord is with you!" But she was greatly troubled at the saying, and considered in her mind what sort of greeting this might be. And the angel said to her,

> Do not be afraid, Mary, for you have found favor with God. And behold, you will conceive in your womb and bear a son, and you shall call his name Jesus.
> He will be great, and will be called the Son of the Most High; and the Lord God will give to him the throne of his father [King] David, and he will reign over the house of Jacob for ever; and of his kingdom there will be no end.

And Mary said to the angel, "How can this be, since I have no husband?" And the angel said to her,

> The Holy Spirit will come upon you, and the power of the Most High will overshadow you; therefore the child to be born will be called holy, the Son of God. And behold, your kinswoman Elizabeth in her old age has also conceived a son; and this is the sixth month with her who was called barren. For with God nothing will be impossible.

And Mary said, "Behold I am the handmaid of the Lord; let it be to me according to your word." And the angel departed from her.

In those days Mary arose and went with haste into the hill country, to a city of Judah, and she entered the house of Zechariah and greeted Elizabeth. And when Elizabeth heard the greeting of Mary, the babe leaped in her womb; and Elizabeth was filled with the Holy Spirit and she exclaimed with a loud cry, "Blessed are you among women, and blessed is the fruit of your womb! And why is this granted me, that the mother of my Lord should come to me? For behold, when the voice of your greeting came to my ears, the babe in my womb leaped for joy. And blessed is she who believed that there would be a fulfillment of what was spoken to her from the Lord." And Mary said,

> My soul magnifies the Lord,
> and my spirit rejoices in God my Savior,
> for he has regarded the low estate of his handmaiden.
> For behold, henceforth all generations will call me blessed;
> for he who is mighty has done great things for me,
> and holy is his name.

Mary Magdalene

Although the woman in the first story below is not named, she is elsewhere identified as a "Mary," and she was believed in the

Middle Ages to be the same person as Mary Magdalene, one of
Jesus' followers, "from whom seven devils had been driven out"
(Luke 8:2). Mary Magdalene's close relationship with Jesus is
shown in the second story below, where she is the first to see
him after his resurrection from the dead. Thus Mary Magdalene
became an important model for repentant sinners, and particularly
for prostitutes.

One of the Pharisees[2] asked [Jesus] to eat with him, and he went
into the Pharisee's house, and sat at table. And behold, a woman of
the city, who was a sinner, when she learned that he was sitting at
table in the Pharisee's house, brought an alabaster flask of ointment,
and standing behind him at his feet, weeping, she began to wet his
feet with her tears, and wiped them with the hair of her head, and
kissed his feet, and anointed them with the ointment. Now when the
Pharisee who had invited him saw it, he said to himself, "If this man
were a prophet, he would have known who and what sort of woman
this is who is touching him, for she is a sinner." And Jesus answering
said to him, ". . . Do you see this woman? I entered your house, you
gave me no water for my feet, but she has wet my feet with her tears
and wiped them with her hair. You gave me no kiss, but from the
time I came in she has not ceased to kiss my feet. You did not anoint my
head with oil, but she has anointed my feet with ointment. Therefore I
tell you, her sins, which are many, are forgiven, for she loved much;
but he who is forgiven little, loves little." And he said to her, "Your
sins are forgiven. . . . Your faith has saved you; go in peace."

[The following episode takes place on Easter morning, two days after
the crucifixion and burial of Jesus.]
    Now on the first day of the week Mary Magdalene came to the tomb
early, while it was still dark, and saw that the stone had been taken
away from the tomb. So she ran, and went to Simon Peter and the
other disciple, the one whom Jesus loved, and said to them, "They
have taken the Lord out of the tomb, and we do not know where they
have laid him." Peter then came out with the other disciple, and they
went toward the tomb. They both ran, but the other disciple outran
Peter and reached the tomb first; and stooping to look in, he saw the
linen cloths lying there, but he did not go in. Then Simon Peter came,
following him, and he went into the tomb; he saw the linen cloths
lying, and the napkin, which had been on his head, not lying with

---

2. Pharisees = members of a strict sect in Judaism.

the linen cloths but rolled up in a place by itself. Then the other disciple, who reached the tomb first, also went in, and he saw and believed; for as yet they did not know the scripture, that he must rise from the dead. Then the disciples went back to their homes.

But Mary stood weeping outside the tomb, and as she wept she stooped to look into the tomb; and she saw two angels in white, sitting where the body of Jesus had lain, one at the head and one at the feet. They said to her, "Woman, why are you weeping?" She said to them, "Because they have taken my Lord, and I do not know where they have laid him." Saying this, she turned around and saw Jesus standing, but she did not know that it was Jesus. Jesus said to her, "Woman, why are you weeping? Whom do you seek?" Supposing him to be the gardener, she said to him, "Sir, if you have carried him away, tell me where you have laid him, and I will take him away." Jesus said to her, "Mary." She turned and said to him in Hebrew, "Rabboni!" (which means Teacher). Jesus said to her, "Do not hold me, for I have not yet ascended to the Father; but go to my brethren and say to them, I am ascending to my Father and your Father, to my God and your God." Mary Magdalene went and said to the disciples, "I have seen the Lord"; and she told them that he had said these things to her.

3. The Bible: Epistles of St. Paul (1st c. A.D.)

St. Paul was one of the early converts to Christianity and traveled widely in the ancient world as a Christian missionary. His role in shaping the beliefs and spreading the faith of the early Christian church can hardly be overestimated. His teachings on women—like his teachings on everything else—became important Christian doctrines. The passages below are taken from his letters of advice to the fledgling Christian communities; these passages were often cited by medieval writers and indeed are still cited today.
Source: Revised Standard Version of the Bible. Used by permission of the National Council of the Churches of Christ.

Marriage and Celibacy

I Corinthians 7:1–14, 25–34

It is well for a man not to touch a woman. But because of the temptation to immorality, each man should have his own wife and each woman her own husband. The husband should give to the wife her conjugal rights, and likewise the wife to her husband. For the wife does not rule over her own body, but the husband does; likewise the husband does not rule over his own body, but the wife does. Do not refuse one another except perhaps by agreement for a season, that you may devote yourselves to prayer; but then come together again, lest Satan tempt you through lack of self-control. I say this by way of concession, not of command. I wish that all were [celibate] as I myself am. But each has his own special gift from God, one of one kind and one of another.

To the unmarried and the widows I say that it is well for them to remain single as I do. But if they cannot exercise self-control, they should marry. For it is better to marry than to be aflame with passion.

To the married I give charge, not I but the Lord, that the wife should not separate from her husband (but if she does, let her remain single or else be reconciled to her husband)—and that the husband should not divorce his wife.

To the rest I say, not the Lord, that if any brother has a wife who is an unbeliever, and she consents to live with him, he should not divorce her. If any woman has a husband who is an unbeliever, and he consents to live with her, she should not divorce him. For the unbelieving husband is consecrated through his wife, and the unbelieving wife is consecrated though her husband. . . .

Now concerning the unmarried, I have no command of the Lord, but I give my opinion as one who by the Lord's mercy is trustworthy. I think that in view of the present distress it is well for a person to remain as he is. Are you bound to a wife? Do not seek to be free. Are you free from a wife? Do not seek marriage. But if you marry, you do not sin, and if a girl marries she does not sin. Yet those who marry will have worldly troubles, and I would spare you that. I mean, brethren, the appointed time has grown very short. . . . For the form of this world is passing away.

I want you to be free from anxieties. The unmarried man is anxious about the affairs of the Lord, how to please the Lord; but the married man is anxious to please his wife, and his interests are divided. And the unmarried woman or girl is anxious about the affairs of the Lord, how to be holy in body and spirit; but the married woman is anxious about worldly affairs, how to please her husband. . . .

A wife is bound to her husband as long as he lives. If the husband dies, she is free to be married to whom she wishes, only in the Lord. But in my judgment she is happier if she remains as she is. And I think that I have the Spirit of God.

Husbands and Wives

Ephesians 5:22–33

Wives, be subject to your husbands, as to the Lord. For the husband is the head of the wife as Christ is the head of the church, his body, and is himself its Savior. As the church is subject to Christ, so let wives be subject in everything to their husbands. Husbands, love your wives, as Christ loved the church and gave himself up for her, that he might sanctify her, having cleansed her by the washing of water with the word, that the church might be presented before him in splendor, without spot or wrinkle or any such thing, that she might be holy and without blemish. Even so husbands should love their wives as their own bodies. He who loves his wife loves himself. For no man ever hates his own flesh, but nourishes and cherishes it, as Christ does the church, because we are members of his body. "For this reason a man shall leave his father and mother and be joined to his wife, and the two shall become one." This is a great mystery, and I take it to mean Christ and the church; however, let each one of you love his wife as himself, and let the wife see that she respects her husband.

Women's Role in the Church

I Corinthians 14:34–35

As in all the churches of the saints, the women should keep silence in the churches. For they are not permitted to speak, but should be subordinate, as even the law says. If there is anything they desire to know, let them ask their husbands at home. For it is shameful for a woman to speak in church.

I Timothy 2:8–15; 3:8–13; 5:1–5, 9–14

I desire then that in every place the men should pray, lifting holy hands without anger or quarreling; also that women should adorn themselves modestly and sensibly in seemly apparel, not with braided hair or gold or pearls or costly attire but by good deeds, as befits women who profess religion. Let a woman learn in silence with all submissiveness. I permit no woman to teach or to have authority over men; she is to keep silent. For Adam was formed first, then Eve; and Adam was not deceived, but the woman was the transgressor. Yet woman will be saved through bearing of children,[3] if she continues in faith and holiness, with modesty.

Deacons[4] . . . must be serious, not double-tongued, not addicted to much wine, not greedy for gain; they must hold the mystery of the faith with a clear conscience. And let them also be tested first; then if they prove themselves blameless let them serve as deacons. The women likewise must be serious, no slanderers, but temperate, faithful in all things. Let deacons be married only once, and let them manage their children and their households well; for those who serve well as deacons gain a good standing for themselves and also great confidence in the faith which is in Christ Jesus. . . .

Do not rebuke an older man but exhort him as you would a father; treat younger men like brothers, older women like mothers, younger women like sisters, in all purity.

Honor widows who are real widows. If a widow has children or grandchildren, let them first learn their religious duty to their own family and make some return acceptable in the sight of God. She who is a real widow, and is left all alone, has set her hope on God and continues in supplications and prayers night and day. . . .

Let no one be enrolled as a widow who is under sixty years of age, or has been married more than once; and she must be well attested for her good deeds, as one who has brought up children, shown hospitality, washed the feet of the saints, relieved the afflicted, and devoted herself to doing good in every way. But refuse to enroll younger widows; for when they grow wanton against Christ they desire to marry, and so they incur condemnation for having violated their first pledge. Besides that, they learn to be idlers, gadding about from house to house, and not only idlers but gossips and busybodies, saying what they should not. So I would have younger widows marry, bear children, rule their households, and give the enemy no occasion to revile us. . . .

Gender and Christ

Galatians 3:26–28

> This short passage is one of the most important in Paul's writings for the more liberal tradition about women's place in the Christian church.

---

3. Alternate translations read: "saved through the Birth of the Child," i.e., the birth of Jesus, or "brought safely through childbirth."
4. Deacons = church officials with administrative and charitable functions.

For in Christ Jesus you are all sons of God, through faith. For as many of you as were baptized into Christ have put on Christ. There is neither Jew nor Greek, there is neither slave nor free, there is neither male nor female; for you are all one in Christ Jesus.

4. St. Jerome: Virginity and Marriage (4th c. A.D.)

One of the most influential theologians of the early church, St. Jerome (c. 340–420) practiced much of his ministry among wealthy and pious women, encouraging them to live as dedicated virgins or widows. Eustochium was one of these. Jovinian was a churchman who asserted that the married life was just as worthy in God's view as the celibate one; Jerome argued against this at length. His reply is famous in part for the passage he quotes from "Theophrastus," an ancient writer known from no other source.

Letter to Eustochium

Source: Reprinted by permission of the publishers and the Loeb Classical Library from *Select Letters of St. Jerome*, translated by F. A. Wright, Cambridge, Mass.: Harvard University Press, 1963.

. . . Some one may say: "Do you dare to disparage wedlock, a state which God has blessed?" It is not disparaging wedlock to prefer virginity. No one can make a comparison between two things, if one is good and the other evil. Let married women take their pride in coming next after virgins. "Be fruitful," God said, "and multiply and replenish the earth" [Gen. 1:28]. Let him then be fruitful and multiply who intends to replenish the earth: but your company is in heaven. The command to increase and multiply is fulfilled after the expulsion from Paradise, after the recognition of nakedness, after the putting on of the fig leaves which augured the approach of marital desire. Let them marry and be given in marriage who eat their bread in the sweat of their brow, whose land brings forth thorns and thistles, and whose crops are choked with brambles. My seed produces fruit a hundredfold.

. . . Eve in Paradise was a virgin: it was only after she put on a garment of skins that her married life began. Paradise is your home. Keep therefore as you were born, and say: "Return unto thy rest, O my soul" [Ps. 116:7]. . . .

I praise wedlock, I praise marriage; but it is because they produce me virgins. I gather the rose from the thorn, the gold from the earth, the pearl from the oyster. Shall the ploughman plough all day? Shall he not also enjoy the fruit of his labour? Wedlock is the more honoured when the fruit of wedlock is the more loved. Why, mother, grudge your daughter her virginity? She has been reared on your milk, she has come from your body, she has grown strong in your arms. Your watchful love has kept her safe. Are you vexed with her because she chooses to wed not a soldier but a King? She has rendered you a high service: from to-day you are the mother by marriage of God. . . .

In the old days, as I have said, the virtue of continence was confined to men, and Eve continually bore children in travail. But now that a virgin has conceived in the womb a child, upon whose shoulders is government, a mighty God, Father of the age to come, the fetters of the old curse are broken. Death came through Eve: life has come through Mary. For this reason the gift of virginity has been poured most abundantly upon women, seeing that it was from a woman it began. As soon as the Son of God set foot on earth, He formed for Himself a new household, that as He was adored by angels in heaven He might have angels also on earth. . . .

Against Jovinian

Source: *St. Jerome: Letters and Select Works*, tr. W. H. Fremantle. *Select Library of Nicene and Post-Nicene Fathers*, Ser. 2, Vol. VI (Edinburgh, 1892).

. . . But you will say: "If everybody were a virgin, what would become of the human race?" Like shall here beget like. If everyone were a widow, or continent in marriage, how will mortal men be propagated? . . . You are afraid that if the desire for virginity were general there would be no prostitutes, no adulteresses, no wailing infants in town or country. Every day the blood of adulterers is shed, adulterers are condemned, and lust is raging and rampant in the very presence of the laws and the symbols of authority and the courts of justice. Be not afraid that all will become virgins: virginity is a hard matter, and therefore rare, because it is hard. "Many are called, few chosen." Many begin, few persevere. And so the reward is great for those who have persevered. If all were able to be virgins, our Lord would never have said (Matt. 19:12): "He that is able to receive it, let him receive it": and the Apostle would not have hesitated to give his advice, (l Cor. 7:25) "Now concerning virgins I have no commandment of the Lord."

. . . A book *On Marriage*, worth its weight in gold, passes under the name of Theophrastus. In it the author asks whether a wise man marries. And after laying down the conditions—that the wife must be fair, of good character, and honest parentage, the husband in good health and of ample means, and after saying that under these circumstances, a wise man sometimes enters the state of matrimony, he immediately proceeds thus: "But all these conditions are seldom satisfied in marriage. A wise man therefore must not take a wife. For in the first place his study of philosophy will be hindered, and it is impossible for anyone to attend to his books and his wife. Matrons want many things, costly dresses, gold jewels, great outlay, maid-servants, all kinds of furniture, litters and gilded coaches. Then come curtain-lectures the live-long night: she complains that one lady goes out better dressed than she: that another is looked up to by all: 'I am a poor despised nobody at the ladies' assemblies.' 'Why did you ogle that creature next door?' 'Why were you talking to the maid?' 'What did you bring from the market?' 'I am not allowed to have a single friend, or companion.' She suspects that her husband's love goes the same way as her hate. There may be in some neighbouring city the wisest of teachers; but if we have a wife we can neither leave her behind, nor take the burden with us. To support a poor wife, is hard: to put up with a rich one, is torture.

"Notice, too, that in the case of a wife you cannot pick and choose: you must take her as you find her. If she has a bad temper, or is a fool, if she has a blemish, or is proud, or has bad breath, whatever her fault may be—all this we learn after marriage. Horses, asses, cattle, even slaves of the smallest worth, clothes, kettles, wooden seats, cups, and earthenware pitchers, are first tried and then bought: a wife is the only thing that is not shown before she is married, for fear she may not give satisfaction. Our gaze must always be directed to her face, and we must always praise her beauty: if you look at another woman, she thinks that she is out of favour. . . . If a woman be fair, she soon finds lovers; if she be ugly, it is easy to be wanton. It is difficult to guard what many long for. It is annoying to have what no one thinks worth possessing. But the misery of having an ugly wife is less than that of watching a comely one. Nothing is safe, for which a whole people sighs and longs. One man entices with his figure, another with his brains, another with his wit, another with his open hand. Somehow, or sometime, the fortress is captured which is attacked on all sides.

"Men marry, indeed, so as to get a manager for the house, to solace weariness, to banish solitude; but a faithful slave is a far better manager, more submissive to the master, more observant of his ways, than a wife who thinks she proves herself mistress if she acts in opposition to her husband, that is, if she does what pleases her, not what she is commanded. But friends, and servants who are under the obligation of benefits received, are better able to wait upon us in sickness than a wife who makes us responsible for her tears (she will sell you enough to make a deluge for the hope of a legacy); who boasts of her anxiety, yet drives her sick husband to the distraction of despair. But if she herself is poorly, we must fall sick with her and never leave her bedside. Or if she be a good and agreeable wife (how rare a bird she is!), we have to share her groans in childbirth, and suffer torture when she is in danger. . . .

"Then again, to marry for the sake of children, so that our name may not perish, or that we may have support in old age, and leave our property without dispute, is the height of stupidity. For what is it to us when we are leaving the world if another bears our name, when even a son does not all at once take his father's title, and there are countless others who are called by the same name. Or what support in old age is he whom you bring up, and who may die before you, or turn out a reprobate? Or at all events when he reaches mature age, you may seem to him long in dying. Friends and relatives whom you can judiciously love are better and safer heirs than those whom you must make your heirs whether you like it or not. Indeed, the surest way of having a good heir is to ruin your fortune in a good cause while you live, not to leave the fruit of your labour to be used you know not how."

5. St. Augustine of Hippo:
On Marriage and Concupiscence (423 A.D.)

Augustine of Hippo (354–430) was the single most influential writer on Christian theology in the "patristic" period, so named for the "Fathers" of the church. His views on most subjects became the accepted position of the medieval church; some of his thoughts on marriage and sex are reproduced here.

Source: *St. Augustin: Anti-Pelagian Writings*, tr. Peter Holmes, Robert Ernest Wallace and Benjamin B. Warfield. *Select Library of Nicene and Post-Nicene Fathers*, Ser. 1, Vol. V (New York, 1893).

The union, then, of male and female for the purpose of procreation is the natural good of marriage. But he makes a bad use of this good who uses it bestially, so that his intention is on the gratification of lust, instead of the desire of offspring. . . . [But] marriage of believers converts to the use of righteousness that carnal concupiscence by which "the flesh lusteth against the Spirit" (Gal. 5:17). For they entertain the firm purpose of generating offspring to be regenerated—that the children who are born of them as "children of the world" may be born again and become "sons of God." Wherefore all parents who do not beget children with this intention, this will, this purpose, of transferring them from being members of Christ, but boast as unbelieving parents over unbelieving children—however circumspect they be in their cohabitation, studiously limiting it to the begetting of children—really have no conjugal chastity in themselves. . . . There is, then, no true chastity, whether conjugal or vidual,[5] or virginal, except that which devotes itself to true faith. For though consecrated virginity is rightly preferred to marriage, yet what Christian in his sober mind would not prefer catholic Christian women who have been even more than once married, to not only vestals, but also to heretical virgins? . . .

It is, however, one thing for married persons to have intercourse only for the wish to beget children, which is not sinful: it is another thing for them to desire carnal pleasure in cohabitation, but with the spouse only, which involves venial sin. For although propagation of offspring is not the motive of the intercourse, there is still no attempt to prevent such propagation, either by wrong desire or evil appliance. They who resort to these, although called by the name of spouses, are really not such; they retain no vestige of true matrimony, but pretend the honourable designation as a cloak for criminal conduct. Having also proceeded so far, they are betrayed into exposing their children, which are born against their will. They hate to nourish and retain those whom they were afraid they would beget. . . . Sometimes, indeed, this lustful cruelty, or, if you please, cruel lust, resorts to such extravagant methods as to use poisonous drugs to secure barrenness; or else, if unsuccessful in this, to destroy the conceived seed by some means previous to birth, preferring that its offspring should rather perish than receive vitality; or if it was advancing to life within the womb, should be slain before it was born. Well, if both parties alike are so flagitious, they are not husband and wife; and if such were their

---

5. Vidual = of widows.

character from the beginning, they have not come together by wedlock but by debauchery. But if the two are not alike in such sin, I boldly declare either that the woman is, so to say, the husband's harlot; or the man, the wife's adulterer. . . .

In matrimony, however, let these nuptial blessings be the objects of our love—offspring, fidelity, the sacramental bond. Offspring, not that it be born only, but born again; for it is born to punishment unless it be born again to life. Fidelity, not such as even unbelievers observe one towards the other, in their ardent love of the flesh. For what husband, however impious himself, likes an adulterous wife? Or what wife, however impious she be, likes an adulterous husband? This is indeed a natural good in marriage, though a carnal one. But a member of Christ ought to be afraid of adultery, not on account of himself, but of his spouse: and ought to hope to receive from Christ the reward of that fidelity which he shows to his spouse. The sacramental bond, again, which is lost neither by divorce nor by adultery, should be guarded by husband and wife with concord and chastity. For it alone is that which even an unfruitful marriage retains by the law of piety, now that all that hope of fruitfulness is lost for the purpose of which the couple married. Let these nuptial blessings be praised in marriage by him who wishes to extol the nuptial institution. Carnal concupiscence, however, must not be ascribed to marriage: it is only to be tolerated in marriage. It is not a good which comes out of the essence of marriage, but an evil which is the accident of original sin. . . .

B. Roman Ideals

6. Funeral Eulogy of Turia (1st c. B.C.)

In the following funeral speech, which was later engraved on a
memorial tablet, a Roman man of the first century B.C. pays
tribute to his wife. She is traditionally known as Turia, but their
actual identities are unknown.
Source: Erik Wistrand, *The So-Called Laudatio Turiae: Introduction,
Text, Translation, Commentary,* Studia Graeca et Latina Gothobur-
gensia, XXXIV (Göteborg: Acta Universitatis Gothoburgensis,
1976).

. . . Why should I mention your domestic virtues: your loyalty,
obedience, affability, reasonableness, industry in working wool, religion without superstition, sobriety of attire, modesty of appearance?
Why dwell on your love for your relatives, your devotion to your
family? You have shown the same attention to my mother as you did
to your own parents, and have taken care to secure an equally peaceful
life for her as you did for your own people, and you have innumerable
merits in common with all married women who care for their good
name. It is your very own virtues that I am asserting, and very few
women have encountered comparable circumstances to make them
endure such sufferings and perform such deeds. Providentially Fate
has made such hard tests rare for women.

We have preserved all the property you inherited from your parents
under common custody, for you were not concerned to make your
own what you had given to me without any restriction. We divided
our duties in such a way that I had the guardianship of your property
and you had the care of mine. . . .

Your generosity you have manifested to many friends and particularly to your beloved relatives. On this point someone might mention
with praise other women, but the only equal you have had has been
your sister. For you brought up your female relations who deserved
such kindness in your own houses with us. You also prepared mar-
riage-portions for them so that they could obtain marriages worthy of
your family. The dowries you had decided upon Cluvius and I by
common accord took upon ourselves to pay, and since we approved
of your generosity we did not wish that you should let your own
patrimony suffer diminution but substituted our own money and gave

our own estates as dowries. I have mentioned this not from a wish to commend ourselves but to make clear that it was a point of honour for us to execute with our means what you had conceived in a spirit of generous family affection. . . .

You provided abundantly for my needs during my flight[6] and gave me the means for a dignified manner of living, when you took all the gold and jewellery from your own body and sent it to me and over and over again enriched me in my absence with servants, money and provisions, showing great ingenuity in deceiving the guards posted by our adversaries.

You begged for my life when I was abroad—it was your courage that urged you to this step—and because of your entreaties I was shielded by the clemency of those against whom you marshalled your words. But whatever you said was always said with undaunted courage.

Meanwhile when a troop of men . . . tried to profit by the opportunities provided by the civil war and break into our house to plunder, you beat them back successfully and were able to defend our home. . . .

Why should I now hold up to view our intimate and secret plans and private conversations: how I was saved by your good advice when I was roused by startling reports to meet sudden and imminent dangers; how you did not allow me imprudently to tempt providence by an overbold step but prepared a safe hiding-place for me, when I had given up my ambitious designs, choosing as partners in your plans to save me your sister and her husband Cluvius, all of you taking the same risk? There would be no end, if I tried to go into all this. It is enough for me and for you that I was hidden and my life was saved. . . .

When peace had been restored throughout the world and the lawful political order reestablished, we began to enjoy quiet and happy times. It is true that we did wish to have children, who had for a long time been denied to us by an envious fate. . . .

When you despaired of your ability to bear children and grieved over my childlessness, you became anxious lest by retaining you in marriage I might lose all hope of having children and be distressed for that reason. So you proposed divorce outright and offered to yield our house free to another woman's fertility. . . . I must admit that I flared up so that I almost lost control of myself; so horrified was I by what you tried to do that I found it difficult to retrieve my composure.

---

6. This and the next few paragraphs describe Turia's actions during a time when her husband was in exile for political reasons.

. . . What desire, what need to have children could I have had that was so great that I should have broken faith for that reason and changed certainty for uncertainty? But no more of this! You remained with me as my wife. For I could not have given in to you without disgrace for me and unhappiness for both of us.

But on your part, what could have been more worthy of commemoration and praise than your efforts in devotion to my interests: when I could not have children from yourself, you wanted me to have them through your good offices and, since you despaired of bearing children, to provide me with offspring by my marriage to another woman. . . .

Fate decreed that you should precede me. You bequeathed me sorrow through my longing for you and left me a miserable man without children to comfort me. I on my part will, however, bend my way of thinking and feeling to your judgements and be guided by your admonitions.

But all your opinions and instructions should give precedence to the praise you have won so that this praise will be a consolation for me and I will not feel too much the loss of what I have consecrated to immortality to be remembered for ever. . . .

I pray that your [spirits] will grant you rest and protection.

7. Seneca: Letter to His Mother (1st c. A.D.)

In this letter to his mother, the Roman philosopher Seneca tries to comfort her in her distress over his exile from Rome. He praises her virtues, which are typical of the ideal Roman matron, by setting them against the faults he saw in many women of his day. He cites as models of behavior Cornelia and Rutilia, mothers famous in Roman history for their virtues.
Source: Reprinted by permission of the publishers and the Loeb Classical Library from *Seneca: Moral Essays*, Vol II, translated by John W. Basore, Cambridge, Mass.: Harvard University Press, 1932.

It is not for you to avail yourself of the excuse of being a woman, who, in a way, has been granted the right to inordinate, yet not unlimited, tears. And so our ancestors, seeking to compromise with the stubbornness of a woman's grief by a public ordinance, granted the space of ten months as the limit of mourning for a husband. They did not forbid public mourning, but limited it; for when you lose one who is most dear, to be filled with endless sorrow is foolish fondness, and to feel none is inhuman hardness. The best course is the mean between affection and reason—both to have a sense of loss and to crush it. There is no need for you to regard certain women, whose sorrow once assumed ended only with their death—some you know, who, having put on mourning for sons they had lost, never laid the garb aside. From you life, that was sterner from the start, requires more; the excuse of being a woman can be of no avail to one who has always lacked all the weaknesses of a woman.

Unchastity, the greatest evil of our time, has never classed you with the great majority of women; jewels have not moved you, nor pearls; to your eyes the glitter of riches has not seemed the greatest boon of the human race; you, who were soundly trained in an old-fashioned and strict household, have not been perverted by the imitation of worse women that leads even the virtuous into pitfalls; you have never blushed for the number of your children, as if it taunted you with your years; never have you, in the manner of other women whose only recommendation lies in their beauty, tried to conceal your pregnancy as if an unseemly burden, nor have you ever crushed the hope of children that were being nurtured in your body; you have not defiled your face with paints and cosmetics; never have you fancied the kind of dress that exposed no greater nakedness by being removed. In you has been seen that peerless ornament, that fairest beauty on which time lays no hand, that chiefest glory which is modesty. You cannot, therefore, allege your womanhood as an excuse for persistent grief, for your very virtues set you apart; you must be as far removed from woman's tears as from her vices. But even women will not allow you to pine away from your wound, but will bid you finish quickly with necessary sorrow, and then rise with lighter heart—I mean, if you are willing to turn your gaze upon the women whose conspicuous bravery has placed them in the rank of mighty heroes.

Cornelia bore twelve children, but Fortune had reduced their number to two . . . Nevertheless, when her friends were weeping around her and cursing her fate, she forbade them to make any indictment against Fortune, since it was Fortune who had allowed the Gracchi to be her sons. Such a woman had right to be the mother of him who exclaimed in the public assembly: "Do you dare to revile the mother who gave birth to me?" But to me his mother's utterance seems more spirited by far . . .

Rutilia followed her son Cotta into exile, and was so wrapped up in her love for him that she preferred exile to losing him; and only her son's return brought her back to her native land. But when, after he had been restored and now had risen to honour in the state, he died, she let him go just as bravely as she had clung to him; and after her son was buried no one saw her shed any tears. When he was exiled she showed courage, when she lost him, wisdom; for in the one case she did not desist from her devotion, and in the other did not persist in useless and foolish sorrow. In the number of such women as these I wish you to be counted. In your effort to restrain and suppress your sorrow your best course will be to follow the example of those women whose life you have always copied.

8. Laws of the Roman Empire (3rd–6th c. A.D.)

Roman civil law evolved over the course of many centuries. The selection below on dowry is from Ulpian's *Rules*, a third-century book of legal commentary; the laws on marriage, divorce and adultery are from the *Corpus Juris Civilis*, a compilation commissioned by the sixth-century emperor Justinian and used in the Middle Ages as a textbook of Roman law.
Source: *The Civil Law*, tr. S. P. Scott (Cincinnati, 1932). Reprinted by AMS Press, New York.

Dowry

A dowry is either given, expressly stated, or promised.

A woman who is about to be married can state her dowry, and her debtor can do so, at her direction; a male ascendant of the woman related to her through the male sex, such as her father or paternal grandfather, can likewise so do. Any person can give or promise a dowry. . . .

When a woman dies during marriage, her dowry given by her father reverts to him, a fifth of the same for each child she leaves being retained by the husband, no matter what the number may be. If her father is not living, the dowry remains in the hands of the husband. . . .

When a divorce takes place, if the woman is her own mistress, she herself has the right to sue for the recovery of the dowry. If, however, she is under the control of her father, he . . . can bring the action for the recovery of the dowry; nor does it make any difference whether it is adventitious or profectitious.

If the woman dies after the divorce, no right of action will be granted to her heir, unless her husband has been in default in restoring her dowry. . . .

Portions of a dowry are retained either on account of children, on account of bad morals, on account of expenses, on account of donations, or on account of articles which have been abstracted.

A portion is retained on account of children, when the divorce took place either through the fault of the wife, or her father; for then a sixth part of the dowry shall be retained in the name of each child, but not more than three-sixths altogether. . . .

A sixth of the dowry is also retained on the ground of a flagrant breach of morals; an eighth, where the offence is not so serious. Adultery alone comes under the head of a flagrant breach of morals; all other improper acts are classed as less serious.

If a husband in anticipation of divorce abstracts anything belonging to his wife, he will be liable to an action for the clandestine removal of property.

Marriage and Divorce

Roman citizens unite in legal marriage when they are joined according to the precepts of the law, and the males have attained the age of puberty and the females are capable of childbirth, whether they are the heads of families or the children of families, if the latter have also the consent of the relatives under whose authority they may be, for this should be obtained and both civil and natural law require that it should previously be secured.

Those who seize the property of a wife on account of a debt of her husband, or because of some public civil liability which he has incurred, are considered to have been guilty of violence. . . .

Marriage is dissolved by divorce, death, captivity, or by any other kind of servitude which may happen to be imposed upon either of the parties . . .

It is not a true or actual divorce unless the purpose is to establish a perpetual separation. Therefore, whatever is done or said in the heat of anger is not valid, unless the determination becomes apparent by the parties persevering in their intention, and hence where repudiation takes place in the heat of anger and the wife returns in a short time, she is not held to have been divorced.

Adultery

The *lex Julia*[7] declares that wives have no right to bring criminal accusations for adultery against their husbands, even though they

---

7. *Lex Julia* = "Julian law," a law against adultery, dating from 18 B.C.

may desire to complain of the violation of the marriage vow, for while the law grants this privilege to men it does not concede it to women. . . .

No one doubts that a husband cannot accuse his wife of adultery if he continues to retain her in marriage. . . . Under the new law, however, he can do so, and if the accusation is proved to be true, he can then repudiate her, and he should file a written accusation against her. If, however, the husband should not be able to establish the accusation of adultery which he brought, he will be liable to the same punishment which his wife would have undergone if the accusation had been proved. . . .

The laws punish the detestable wickedness of women who prostitute their chastity to the lusts of others, but do not hold those liable who are compelled to commit fornication through force, and against their will. And, moreover, it has very properly been decided that their reputations are not lost, and that their marriage with others should not be prohibited on this account. . . .

Where a girl, less than twelve years old, brought into the house of her husband, commits adultery, and afterwards remains with him until she has passed that age, and begins to be his wife, she cannot be accused of adultery by her husband, for the reason that she committed it before reaching the marriageable age; but, according to a rescript of the Divine Severus, which is mentioned above, she can be accused as having been betrothed. . . .

The right is granted to the father to kill a man who commits adultery with his daughter while she is under his control. . . .

Hence the father, and not the husband, has the right to kill the woman and every adulterer; for the reason that, in general, paternal affection is solicitous for the interests of the children, but the heat and impetuosity of the husband, who decides too quickly, should be restrained.

. . . Where the law says, "He may kill his daughter at once," this must be understood to mean that having today killed the adulterer he cannot reserve his daughter to be killed subsequently; for he should kill both of them with one blow and one attack, and be inflamed by the same resentment against both. But if, without any connivance on his part, his daughter should take to flight, while he is killing the adulterer, and she should be caught and put to death some hours afterwards by her father, who pursued her, he will be considered to have killed her immediately.

C. Germanic Custom

9. Tacitus: The Germans (98 A.D.)

Tacitus, a Roman historian who died in 117 A.D., described the Germans in a work which is one of our earliest pieces of information about the Germanic tribes. Disgusted with the corruption he perceived in Roman society, Tacitus is here holding up the "barbarian" Germans as models of virtue; thus many of the things he emphasizes in this account are traditional Roman virtues such as modesty, morality and courage. The term "Germans" refers here to all the Germanic tribes, which would migrate further into western Europe in the centuries after Tacitus; they are the stock from which most western European peoples, including the English and the French, descended.
Source: Tr. Maurice Hutton, in *Tacitus: Dialogus, Agricola, Germania*, Loeb Classical Library (Cambridge: Harvard University Press, 1914).

[The Germans are] a peculiar people and pure, like no one but themselves; whence it comes that their physique, in spite of their vast numbers, is identical: fierce blue eyes, red hair, tall frames, powerful only spasmodically, and impatient at the same time of labour and hard work, and by no means habituated to bearing thirst and heat; to cold and hunger, thanks to the climate and the soil, they are accustomed. . . .

The strongest incentive to courage lies in this, that neither chance nor casual grouping makes the squadron or the wedge, but family and kinship: close at hand, too, are their dearest, whence is heard the wailing voice of woman and the child's cry: here are the witnesses who are in each man's eyes most precious; here the praise he covets most: they take their wounds to mother and wife, who do not shrink from counting the hurts and demanding a sight of them: they minister to the combatants food and exhortation.

Tradition relates that some lost or losing battles have been restored by the women, by the incessance of their prayers and by the baring of their breasts; for so is it brought home to the men that the slavery, which they dread much more keenly on their women's account, is close at hand: it follows that the loyalty of those tribes is more effectually guaranteed from whom, among other hostages, maids of high birth have been exacted.

Further, they conceive that in woman is a certain uncanny and prophetic sense: they neither scorn to consult them nor slight their answers. . . .

For clothing all wear a cloak, fastened with a clasp, or, in its absence, a thorn: they spend whole days on the hearth round the fire with no other covering. The richest men are distinguished by the wearing of under-clothes; not loose, . . . but drawn tight, throwing each limb into relief. They wear also the skins of wild beasts. . . .

The women have the same dress as the men, except that very often trailing linen garments, striped with purple, are in use for women: the upper part of this costume does not widen into sleeves: their arms and shoulders are therefore bare, as is the adjoining portion of the breast.

None the less the marriage tie with them is strict: you will find nothing in their character to praise more highly. They are almost the only barbarians who are content with a wife apiece: the very few exceptions have nothing to do with passion, but consist of those with whom polygamous marriage is eagerly sought for the sake of their high birth.

As for dower, it is not the wife who brings it to the husband, but the husband to the wife. The parents and relations are present to approve these gifts—gifts not devised for ministering to female fads, nor for the adornment of the person of the bride, but oxen, a horse and bridle, a shield and spear or sword; it is to share these things that the wife is taken by the husband, and she herself, in turn, brings some piece of armour to her husband. Here is the gist of the bond between them, here in their eyes its mysterious sacrament, the divinity which hedges it. That the wife may not imagine herself released from the practice of heroism, released from the chances of war, she is thus warned by the very rites with which her marriage begins that she comes to share hard work and peril; that her fate will be the same as his in peace and in panic, her risks the same. This is the moral of the yoked oxen, of the bridled horse, of the exchange of arms; so must she live and so must die. The things she takes she is to hand over inviolate to her children, fit to be taken by her daughters-in-law and passed on again to her grandchildren.

So their life is one of fenced-in chastity. There is no arena with its seductions, no dinner-tables with their provocations to corrupt them. Of the exchange of secret letters men and women alike are innocent; adulteries are very few for the number of the people. Punishment is prompt and is the husband's prerogative: her hair close-cropped, stripped of her clothes, her husband drives her from his house in presence of his relatives and pursues her with blows through the length of the village. For prostituted chastity there is no pardon; beauty nor youth nor wealth will find her a husband. No one laughs at vice there; no one calls seduction, suffered or wrought, the spirit of the age. Better still are those tribes where only maids marry, and where a woman makes an end, once for all, with the hopes and vows of a wife; so they take one husband only, just as one body and one life, in order that there may be no second thoughts, no belated fancies: in order that their desire may be not for the man, but for marriage; to limit the number of their children, to make away with any of the later children is held abominable, and good habits have more force with them than good laws elsewhere.

There then they are, the children, in every house, filling out amid nakedness and squalor into that girth of limb and frame which is to our people a marvel. Its own mother suckles each at her breast; they are not passed on to nursemaids and wet-nurses.

Nor can master be recognised from servant by any flummery in their respective bringing-up: they live in the company of the same cattle and on the same mud floor till years separate the free-born and character claims her own.

The virginity of youth is late treasured and puberty therefore inexhaustible; nor for the girls is there any hot-house forcing; they pass their youth in the same way as the boys: their stature is as tall; when they reach the same strength they are mated, and the children reproduce the vigour of the parents. . . .

10. Laws of the Salian Franks (6th c. A.D.)

The Franks were a Germanic people who migrated into the Roman province of Gaul (modern France) in the fifth century and there became Christians in the course of the sixth and seventh centuries. As in all the Germanic tribes, their "laws" were customary and oral, and were codified only when the tribes came into contact with the literate Romans and adopted or developed written languages. So these laws are not in their primitive form; for example, marriage is a contract here, but the laws contain vestiges of the days when German men had purchased their wives.
Source: *The Laws of the Salian and Ripuarian Franks*, tr. Theodore John Rivers (New York: AMS Press, 1986).

Pact of Salic Laws (Early 6th c.)

10. Concerning abducted slaves . . .

1. If anyone steals another's slave or maidservant, horse or draft horse, and it can be proven that he did this, let him be held liable for 1400 denarii, which make thirty-five solidi, in addition to its value and a fine for the loss of use.

4. If anyone abducts another's maidservant, let him be held liable for 1200 denarii, which make thirty solidi.

6. If anyone seduces a maidservant worth fifteen or twenty-five solidi, if [he is] a swineherd, a vinedresser, a blacksmith, a miller, a carpenter, a groom or any overseer worth twenty-five solidi, let him be held liable, if it can be proven that he did this, for 2880 denarii, which make seventy-two solidi, in addition to her value.

7. If anyone abducts a boy or girl, [both of whom are] domestic servants, let him pay twenty-five solidi for his or her value. Moreover, let him be held liable for 1400 denarii, which make thirty-five solidi, in addition to his or her value and a fine for the loss of his or her use.

13. Concerning abduction of freewomen or wives

1. If three men abduct a girl who is free-born from a house or workshop, let these three be compelled to pay 1200 denarii, which make thirty solidi.

2. Nevertheless, [if] there are more than three [men], let each one of them be held liable for 200 denarii, which make five solidi.

3. Those who carry arrows, let each one of them be held liable for 120 denarii, which make three solidi.

4. For a rapist, let him be held liable for 2500 denarii, which make sixty-two and one-half solidi.

6. But if that girl who is carried off is under the king's protection, then the fredus[8] demanded shall be 2500 denarii, which make sixty-two and one-half solidi.

7. But if a servant of the king or a freedman carries off a freewoman, let him compensate with his life.

8. But if a girl who is free-born of her own will follows any [slave into matrimony], let her lose her freedom.

9. If a freeman takes another's maidservant [for his wife], let him suffer similarly.

---

8. Fredus = fine for wrongdoing, payable to the king and the judge.

11. If anyone is united in an incestuous marriage with his sister or his brother's daughter, or with a cousin of the nearest degree, or with his brother's or uncle's wife, let them be subjected to punishment so that their union will be dissolved. And if they have children, they are not legitimate heirs, but are marked with infamy.

12. But if anyone abducts another's fiancée and unites himself with her in marriage, let him be held liable for 2500 denarii, which make sixty-two and one-half solidi.

13. For the benefit of the bridegroom, whose fiancée she is, let [the abductor] be held liable for fifteen solidi [in addition].

14. If anyone follows a betrothed girl in a wedding procession who is on her way to be married and assaults her on the road and forces her to engage in sex, let him be held liable for 8000 denarii, which make 200 solidi.

15. Concerning homicide of a freeman, or the abduction of another's wife in the lifetime of the husband

1. If anyone kills a freeman or abducts another's wife in the lifetime of the husband, and it can be proven that he did this, let him be held liable for 8000 denarii, which make 200 solidi.

2. If anyone forcibly engages in sex with a free-born girl, and it can be proven that he did this, let him be held liable for 2500 denarii, which make sixty-two and one-half solidi.

3. If anyone secretly engages in sex with a free-born girl [and] both willingly consent, and it can be proven that he did this, let him be held liable for 1800 denarii, which make forty-five solidi.

19. Concerning magic potions or herbs

1. If anyone gives a magic potion or herbs to another to drink, and [the latter] dies, and it can be proven that he did this, let him be held liable for 8000 denarii, which make 200 solidi, or he shall certainly be handed over to fire.

2. If anyone gives a magic potion or herbs to another to drink and he for whom it was prepared lives, let the criminal who is proven to have committed this and is convicted be held liable for 2500 denarii, which make sixty-two and one-half solidi.

3. If anyone throws a magic spell on another wherever he goes, let him be held liable for 2500 denarii, which make sixty-two and one-half solidi.

4. If a woman gives a magic potion to another woman whereby [the

latter] cannot have children, let her be held liable for 2500 denarii, which make sixty-two and one-half solidi.

20. Concerning him who touches a freewoman's hand, arm or finger

1. If a freeman touches a freewoman's or any woman's hand, arm or finger, and it can be proven that he did this, let him be held liable for 600 denarii, which make fifteen solidi.

2. If he presses her arm, let him be held liable for 1200 denarii, which make thirty solidi.

3. If he definitely places his hand above her elbow, and it can be proven that he did this, let him be held liable for 1400 denarii, which make thirty-five solidi.

4. If anyone touches a woman's breast or cuts it so that blood comes forth, let him be held liable for 1800 denarii, which make forty-five solidi.

24. Concerning homicide of young children and women

1. If anyone kills a boy who is free-born and under twelve years of age, but who has not yet completed his twelfth year, and it can be proven that he did this, let him be held liable for 24,000 denarii, which make 600 solidi.

2. But if anyone shears the long hair of a free-born boy without his parents' consent, and it can be proven that he did this, let him be held liable for 1800 denarii, which make forty-five solidi.

3. But if he shears a free-born girl without the parents' consent, and it can be proven that he did this, let him be held liable for 1800 denarii, which make forty-five solidi.

5. If anyone strikes a freewoman who is pregnant [and] if she dies, and it can be proven that he did this, let him be held liable for 28,000 denarii, which make 700 solidi.

6. But if anyone kills a child in its mother's womb or within nine nights before [her child] has a name, and it can be proven that he did this, let him be held liable for 4000 denarii, which make 100 solidi.

8. If anyone kills a freewoman after she has begun to have children, and it can be proven that he did this, let him be held liable for 24,000 denarii, which make 600 solidi.

9. After she can have no more children, let him who kills her be held liable, [if] it can he proven that he did this, for 8000 denarii, which make 200 solidi.

25. Concerning fornication involving maidservants or slaves

1. If a freeman fornicates with another's maidservant, and it can be proven that he did this, let him be held liable to the maidservant's master for 600 denarii, which make fifteen solidi.

2. But if anyone fornicates with a maidservant of the king, and it can be proven that he did this, let him be held liable for 1200 denarii, which make thirty solidi.

5. But if a slave fornicates with another's maidservant and after this crime this maidservant dies, either let this slave pay 240 denarii, which make six solidi, to the maidservant's master, or let him be castrated. In fact, let the slave's master pay the value of what the maidservant is worth to the maidservant's master.

6. But if the maidservant does not die because of this, either let the slave receive 300 lashes upon his back, or let him be compelled to pay 120 denarii, which make three solidi, to the maidservant's master.

7. If a slave unites in marriage with another's maidservant without the master's consent, either let him be whipped, or let him be compelled to pay 120 denarii, which make three solidi, to the maidservant's master.

41. Concerning homicide of freemen

1. But if anyone kills a free Frank or [any] barbarian who is living in accordance with the Salic law, and it can be proven that he did this, let him be held liable for 8000 denarii, which make 200 solidi.

5. But if anyone kills [either] him who is in the king's retinue or a freewoman, and it can be proven that he did this, let him be held liable for 24,000 denarii, which make 600 solidi.

15. If anyone kills a girl who is free-born before she can have children, let him be held liable for 8000 denarii, which make 200 solidi.

16. If anyone kills a freewoman after she has begun to nurse, let him be held liable for 24,000 denarii, which make 600 solidi.

17. But after middle age and after she can have no more children, let him who kills her be held liable for 8000 denarii, which make 200 solidi.

18. If anyone kills a boy who has long hair, let him be held liable for 24,000 denarii, which make 600 solidi.

19. If anyone kills a woman who is pregnant, let him be held liable for 600 solidi.

20. If anyone kills a mother with a child in the womb or before [the child] has a name, let him be held liable for 100 solidi [for the fetus].

21. If anyone kills a freeman inside his house, let him he held liable for 600 solidi.

64. Concerning witches

1. If anyone calls another a witch, that is, a performer of witchcraft, or the latter is said to carry a kettle where witches do their cooking, and it cannot be proven, let him be held liable for 2500 denarii, which make sixty-two and one-half solidi.

2. But if anyone calls a freewoman a witch or prostitute, and it cannot be proven, let him he held liable for 2500 denarii, which make sixty-two and one-half solidi.

3. If a witch eats a man and it can be proven that she did this, let her be held liable for 8000 denarii, which make 200 solidi.

65a. Concerning him who becomes engaged to another's daughter and [later] rejects her

If anyone desires to marry another's daughter in the presence of his and the girl's relatives, and afterwards he rejects her and he is unwilling to take her, let him be held liable for 2500 denarii, which make sixty-two and one-half solidi.

Sixth-Century Legislation

98. Concerning women who marry their slaves

1. If a woman unites in marriage with her slave, let the public treasury acquire all her property and let her be outlawed.

2. If anyone of her relatives kills her, let nothing at all be required from either her relatives or the public treasury for this death. Let that slave endure the worst death by torture, that is, let him be broken on the wheel. But if anyone of the relatives gives food or shelter to this woman [because she has been outlawed], let him be held liable for fifteen solidi.

104. Concerning women who are struck or their hair is untied

1. If anyone unties the hair of a woman, so that her veil falls to the ground, let him be held liable for fifteen solidi.

2. But if he unties her hair band, so that the hair touches her shoulder, let him be held liable for thirty solidi.

3. If a slave strikes a freewoman or unties her hair, either let him lose his hand or let him pay five solidi.

4. If anyone strikes a pregnant freewoman in the stomach or kidneys with his fist or heel and the fetus is not aborted [but] because of this it becomes so ill that it nearly dies, let him be held liable for 200 solidi.

5. If anyone strikes [a woman so that] the fetus is killed and is aborted, let him be held liable for 600 solidi.

6. But if the woman was killed due to this, let him be held liable for 900 solidi.

7. But if the woman who was killed was under the king's protection for some reason, let him be held liable for 1200 solidi.

8. But if the child that was aborted was a girl, let him compensate 2400 solidi.

9. One-half of this compensation is to be observed for maidservants, freedwomen, or Roman women.

10. If anyone aborts the fetus of a maidservant (if she is an ordinary girl), let him compensate sixty-two and one-half solidi, and also one denarius.

11. But if this maidservant is employed in her master's pantry or textile workshop, let him compensate 100 solidi and one denarius for her.

Legislation on Rape (594)

. . . By similar judgment it was agreed on the calends of March [595] when everyone was assembled that whoever attempts to rape [a woman], whereby a dishonorable crime is perpetrated, let him realize that his life is in peril, and let none of our magnates attempt to ask for him, but let each one of them be pursued in such a manner as an enemy of God. But whoever attempts to transgress our edict, in whichever county he is surrendered, that judge by public proclamation may kill the rapist, and no wergeld[9] is required for him. And if he flees to a church, let him be apprehended without any pleading after being surrendered to the bishop, and let him be sent into exile. If perhaps the woman agreed to be seduced, let them both be sent into exile together, and if they flee to a church, let them both be killed together. And let their property be acquired by their lawful relatives and let our public treasury acquire what is owed it.

---

9. Wergeld = an amount of money which a killer was normally required to pay to the victim's family. A person's wergeld varied according to rank, sex and age.

11. Laws of the Burgundians (5th–6th c. A.D.)

The Burgundians were a Germanic tribe who in the fifth century settled in Roman-ruled lands that are now parts of Germany, France and Switzerland. Their laws, like those of the Salian Franks, are examples of Germanic customary law in a later written form, modified by legislation over time. Comparison with the Salian laws reveals some of the most basic ideas of Germanic society about women.
Source: *The Burgundian Code*, tr. Katherine Fischer Drew (Philadelphia: University of Pennsylvania Press, 1972).

XII. Of the stealing of girls

1. If anyone shall steal a girl, let him be compelled to pay the price set for such a girl ninefold, and let him pay a fine to the amount of twelve solidi.

2. If the girl who has been seized returns uncorrupted to her parents, let the abductor compound six times the wergeld of the girl; moreover, let the fine be set at twelve solidi.

3. But if the abductor does not have the means to make the abovementioned payment, let him be given over to the parents of the girl that they may have the power of doing to him whatever they choose.

4. If indeed, the girl seeks the man of her own will and comes to his house, and he has intercourse with her, let him pay her marriage price threefold; if moreover, she returns uncorrupted to her home, let her return with all blame removed from him.

5. If indeed a Roman girl, without the consent or knowledge of her parents, unites in marriage with a Burgundian, let her know she will have none of the property of her parents.

XXX. Of women violated

1. Whatever native freeman does violence to a maidservant, and force can be proved, let him pay twelve solidi to whom the maidservant belongs.

2. If a slave does this, let him receive a hundred blows.

XXXIII. Of injuries which are suffered by women

1. If any native freewoman has her hair cut off and is humiliated without cause (when innocent) by any native freeman in her home or on the road, and this can be proved with witnesses, let the doer of

the deed pay her twelve solidi, and let the amount of the fine be twelve solidi.

2. If this was done to a freedwoman, let him pay her six solidi.

3. If this was done to a maidservant, let him pay her three solidi, and let the amount of the fine be three solidi.

4. If this injury (shame, disgrace) is inflicted by a slave on a native freewoman, let him receive two hundred blows; if a freedwoman, let him receive a hundred blows; if a maidservant, let him receive seventy-five blows.

5. If indeed the woman whose injury we have ordered to be punished in this manner commits fornication voluntarily (i.e., she yields), let nothing be sought for the injury suffered.

XXXIV. Of divorces

1. If any woman leaves (puts aside) her husband to whom she is legally married, let her be smothered in mire.

2. If anyone wishes to put away his wife without cause, let him give her another payment such as he gave for her marriage price, and let the amount of the fine be twelve solidi.

3. If by chance a man wishes to put away his wife, and is able to prove one of these three crimes against her, that is, adultery, witchcraft, or violation of graves, let him have full right to put her away: and let the judge pronounce the sentence of the law against her, just as should be done against criminals.

4. But if she admits none of these three crimes, let no man be permitted to put away his wife for any other crime. But if he chooses, he may go away from the home, leaving all household property behind, and his wife and their children may possess the property of her husband.

XXXV. Of the punishment of slaves who commit a criminal assault on freeborn women

1. If any slave does violence to a native freewoman, and if she complains and is clearly able to prove this, let the slave be killed for the crime committed.

2. If indeed a native free girl unites voluntarily with a slave, we order both to be killed.

3. But if the relatives of the girl do not wish to punish their own relative, let the girl be deprived of her free status and delivered into servitude to the king.

XXXVI. Of incestuous adultery

If anyone has been taken in adultery with his relative or with his wife's sister, let him be compelled to pay her wergeld, according to her status, to him who is the nearest relative of the woman with whom he committed adultery; and let the amount of the fine be twelve solidi. Further, we order the adulteress to be placed in servitude to the king.

LI. [Of inheritance]

3. The mother's ornaments and vestments belong to the daughters without any right to share on the part of the brother or brothers; further, let this legal principle be observed concerning those ornaments and vestments in the case of girls whose mothers die intestate. But if the mother shall have made any disposal of her own ornaments and vestments, there shall be no cause for action thereafter.

4. But if an unmarried girl who has sisters dies, and she has not declared her wishes in writing or in the presence of witnesses, let her portion after her death belong to her sisters and, as has been stated, let her brothers have no share therein.

5. However if the girl dies and does not have a blood sister, and no clear disposition has been made concerning her property, let her brothers become her heirs.

LII. Of betrothed women who, incited by desire, go to consort with others

1. Howsoever often such cases arise concerning which none of the preceding laws have established provisions, it is fitting that the ambiguity of the matter be removed so that the judgment set forth shall have the strength of perpetual law, and the special case shall have general application.

2. Since the deserts of a criminal case which is pending between Fredegisil, our[10] sword-bearer on the one side, and Balthamodus together with Aunegild on the other, have been heard and considered, we give an opinion which punishes this recent crime and imposes a method of restraint for the future.

3. And since Aunegild, after the death of her first husband, retaining her own legal competence, promised herself, not only with the consent of her parents, but also with her own desire and will, to the above-mentioned Fredegisil, and since she had received the greater part of

---

10. The speaker is the king.

the wedding price which her betrothed had paid, she broke her pledged faith, having been aroused by the ardor of her desire for Balthamodus. Furthermore, she not only violated her vows, but repeated her customary shameful union, and on account of this, she ought to atone for such a crime and such a violation of her free status not otherwise than with the pouring forth of her own blood. Nevertheless we command, placing reverence for these holy days before public punishment, that Aunegild, deprived of honor by human and divine judgment, should pay her wergeld, that is three hundred solidi, to Fredegisil under compulsion.

4. Nor do we remove merited condemnation from Balthamodus who presumed to receive a woman due in marriage to another man, for his case deserves death. But in consideration of the holy days, we recall our sentence for his execution, under the condition that he should be compelled to pay his wergeld of one hundred fifty solidi to that Fredegisil unless he offers evident (public) oaths with eleven others in which he affirms that at that time in which he was united with the above-mentioned Aunegild as if by right of marriage, he was unaware that she was pledged to Fredegisil. But if he shall have so sworn, let him suffer neither loss nor punishment. . . .

Given on the 29th of March (517) at Lyons . . .

LIX. Of grandchildren

If the father is dead, let a grandchild with all his possessions be given over to the supervision and care of the grandfather if his mother has decided upon a second marriage. Moreover, if she fails to remarry because she has chosen chastity, let her children with all their property remain in her care (custody) and power.

LXV. Of widows from whom the debts of their husbands are sought

1. If any widow has sons, and if she and her sons have made a cession of the goods of the deceased husband, let them suffer no suit for recovery nor for further claim on account of his debts.

2. If indeed they assume the inheritance, let them also pay the paternal debt.

LXVIII. Of adultery

1. If adulterers are discovered, let the man and the woman be killed.

2. This must be observed: either let him (the injured party) kill both

of them, or if he kills only one of them, let him pay the wergeld of that one according to that customary wergeld which has been established in earlier laws.

LXXIV. Of widows and their children

1. Indeed it has been established in general in a law stated in earlier times that if a woman whose husband has died childless does not enter into a second marriage, she may claim a third of his inheritance for her own use throughout her lifetime; but now after considering more carefully with the nobles of our people all these matters set forth under this same title, it pleases us to limit the general application of the above-mentioned law.

Wherefore we order that any such widow, concerning whom we speak, may receive a portion of the inheritance of her husband if she has not already obtained property from her father or mother, or if her husband has not given her any portion of his property by means of which she can live. . . .

Part II

Conditions of Life:
Law, Marriage, and
Health and Safety

The readings in Part II illustrate some of the general conditions under which medieval women lived—conditions which applied more or less to all women, regardless of social status or occupation. These selections are, however, merely examples; the legal sources, in particular, while they may reflect widespread attitudes toward women, come from specific places at specific times. The documents describing marriage, family life and the perils of warfare and disease generally have a somewhat wider application. Many of the themes and issues raised in a general way in this section will recur later in the book, in the experiences of specific women's lives.

The analysis of these documents requires one to consider why they were written and how accurately they reflect the realities of life. For instance, none of the works in Part II, with the possible exception of Trotula's treatise, was written by a woman. Other cautions apply to any law used as a source: laws are by nature prescriptive (or proscriptive) rather than descriptive; the practices they forbid may in fact be very common ones in the society in question. On the other hand, laws may be anachronistic in forbidding practices that are no longer common.

A. Law

12. Norman Laws (Early 13th c.)

These laws from the French duchy of Normandy deal largely with questions of marriage and inheritance among the nobility, but they also include some laws which apply to the lower classes and some criminal laws. The differing punishments for men and women convicted of the same capital crime (Chapter XXXV, number 6) were a fairly common feature in medieval law codes.

Source: *Coutumiers de Normandie, I: Le Très Ancien Coutumier de Normandie*, ed. Ernest-Joseph Tardif (Rouen, 1881). Tr. E.M.A.

Chapter III. [Concerning Widows and Wards]

1. Widows and wards are under the protection of the church. A widow shall have as her dower[11] up to one third of the inheritance of the donor, except the chief dwelling, which remains to the heir; if indeed another dwelling was given to the widow in dower, she shall have that, except the tower or castle. She shall have her dowry,[12] whatever and as much as was given to her at her betrothal, if the donor was able to give it to her.

2. If, however, the dower or dowry given in this way to the widow is denied to the widow, let them be restored by the oath of men who were present at her betrothal, the relatives and friends of either party; for a betrothal is made by relatives and friends.

Chapter IV. Concerning Mortgages of a Dowry or Dower

1. If the husband of the widow mortgaged the dowry or dower of his wife while she was living, and she abjured [her right], she shall not be held to the command of her husband; but the woman shall have them whole, as they were given to her before the church door.

3. Otherwise, the buyer or mortgage-holder of the dower or dowry of the widow shall have in exchange the equivalent from the inheri-

---

11. Dower = the portion of his goods or land (often one-third) which a man was required to assign to his wife at the time of their marriage. This European-wide custom provided for the widow's support: a woman had a life interest in her dower, but it reverted to her late husband's heirs upon her death.

12. Dowry = the property brought by a woman into her marriage.

tance of the heir of the deceased seller or mortgager; and if the husband had no estate but did have chattels[13] on the day of his death, the money shall be returned to the buyer out of any of these chattels, those of the widow's deceased husband, or of the heir; and if there are none, the buyer will receive nothing from nothing.

Chapter V. Concerning Dowers

1. If anyone has a wife and children, and, while they are living, one of the sons takes a wife, and [the son] gives her as dower part or all of the dowry of his mother, and the father and the sons die, the mother shall have her whole dowry without challenge; and the widowed bride of the son shall receive an equivalent dower from the estate of the father or of the deceased son, and if there is no estate on the part of the deceased husband, the younger widow shall wait for her dower, until her husband's widowed mother, in whose dowry her dower was located, dies.

2. And if the widow was the wife of some rural smallholder, she may have one third of his land in dower; and, if there is only a dwelling without land, the widow shall have her third in the dwelling.

3. For urban properties it shall be the same; for a burgher, if he has but one house, may give a third of it to his wife in dower.

4. If anyone has no estate and has promised silver or gold to his wife in dower, let her dower be taken from their common chattels after the death of her husband; and she may spend that.

5. If a widow wishes to have her own share of the chattels and wishes to have the other portion, belonging to her deceased husband, in dower, she shall have it in this way: that portion shall be put aside in the hands of lawful men, until the land and rent have been obtained, on whose revenues the widow lives, and she shall have the land and rent in dower. This land and rent shall come to the heir after the death of the woman.

6. It is not lawful for a widow to sell the woods in her dower, or to root out thickets.

7. After the death of widows, the dower shall return to the nearer heirs, from whose inheritance the dower was taken. . . .

Chapter IX. Concerning Sisters' Portions

1. All tenements, if they happen to descend to sisters, shall be equally divided, . . . so that the eldest sister shall have the chief dwelling, and her sisters shall hold from her. . . .

---

13. Chattels = movable possessions (as opposed to land).

Chapter X. Concerning the Dowry of Sisters

1. If any heir has a sister, he shall marry her [with a dowry] of part of his father's land, or of money, according to his ability, reasonably, both in kind and in land, unless she forfeits it by living badly and loosely . . . .

Chapter XI. Concerning the Custody of Orphans

1. [The mother shall not] have custody of an orphaned heir, . . . because she will take a husband and have sons by him; those sons, envious of his inheritance, may kill the elder brother or heir, or the husband may kill his stepson, in order to give the inheritance to his own sons.[14] [Nor shall the boy's kinsmen have custody,] lest perhaps desiring his death and coveting his inheritance they abuse the boy. To avoid such faithlessness and cruelty, it has been decreed that an orphan be in the custody of him who was joined to the boy's father by faith through homage and was his companion, . . . the lord of the land, who cannot have that inheritance in demesne; for such heirs of noble family have [custody of] many heirs. . . .

4. An orphan heir may not be married without the consent of his lord, who ought to marry him honorably. The same goes for girls who are heiresses.

5. The sons of . . . a burgher, a peasant or a servant shall not be in custody. . . .

Chapter XIV. Concerning Wards

1. If a male ward has sisters of marriageable age, they shall not wait until their younger brother is of age, but they shall be married by their friends and kinsmen, [with dowries] either of chattels or of land from the estate; whatever the case, they shall have reasonable dowries.

2. And when their brother comes of age, if the dowries were unreasonable, let them be made reasonable either through the courts or through his friends, but, if the dowry has been improved or ploughed or built upon, the value of the improved dowry shall not be counted, but only its value on that day when it was given as dowry at the church door. . . .

---

14. The stepfather had no legal right to the son's inheritance, but the realities of life were such that he might manage to take it anyway.

Chapter XXXV. Concerning Homicide

1. If a father accidentally kills his son, he shall do the penance laid on him by the church, and if he killed him in anger, he shall go into exile, out of the realm of the Duke. His wife shall follow him, but after the death of her husband she may return to her inheritance. And since a son comes from the flesh and blood of the father, a father shall not be punished with death for the killing of his son.

2. If a brother accidentally kills his brother, or a cousin his cousin, or a sister her sister, or a mother her son or daughter, they shall do the penance laid on them by the church.

3. If a brother kills his brother in anger, or a cousin his cousin, or a sister her sister, let them be punished with death; and if they maim them, let them be punished in their limbs.[15]

4. If a mother kills her son or daughter in anger, she shall go into exile from the realm of the Duke, just like the father.

5. If a lord kills his man, let him be punished with death; and, if a man kills his lord, unless it happened by accident, let him be drawn and hanged, and if by accident let him be punished with death.

6. If a son or daughter accidentally kills his or her father or mother, let them do the penance laid on them by the church, and, if in anger, let the son be drawn and hanged, and let the woman be burned to death.

Chapter L. Concerning [Rape]

1. If anyone rapes any maiden, whether she was in a village or in the fields or in the woods, she ought to cry out, if she can, and those nearby ought to hear her. The rapist shall be held, if they can catch him, and the girl, as soon as she can, should hasten to the chief justice of the Duke whom she can find nearby, and he shall have the girl and her injuries examined by good women and law-worthy matrons, who know how to discern the injuries of rape.

2. The rapist who is convicted in this way, by the oaths of good and faithful women, may clear himself of the crime by the trial of water[16] if he wishes, and if he fails it let him be punished in his limbs.

3. And if, before he is convicted of this crime, he wishes to marry

---

15. Punished in his limbs = mutilated.

16. The "trial of water" was a common form of the judicial "ordeal," a traditional means of determining the guilt or innocence of an accused person. In the water trial, the accused was deemed innocent if he or she sank and guilty if he or she floated.

the girl, he may take her to wife; if the girl's parents and the girl are agreeable, this is permitted.

4. But if any woman who is someone's concubine wishes to have her lover as her husband, and therefore she says that he took her by force, and she has been seen by the matrons to have sustained no injuries of deflowering, and no cries were heard by those nearby, and she offers herself to prove this charge by trial, she shall not be heard, but shall be whipped. . . .

5. But if any takes his neighbor's wife by force, the wife shall not prove it [in court], but her husband shall, and he may prove it by a duel, if he wishes. The one who is convicted shall be punished in his limbs; and if the husband loses the duel, he shall give 40 shillings and one penny for having yielded; and the woman shall be whipped. . . .

6. If anyone rapes a widow, and her cries are heard by those nearby, she shall not prove such violence by her own hand; but if she has any man or relative of hers, who saw the crime and was unlawfully wounded, he may accuse the abductor by duel concerning his injury and the crime against the woman. The convicted rapist shall be punished in his limbs; if the other man loses the duel he shall give 40 shillings and one penny for having yielded; the widow shall be whipped.

7. If the widow has no such man, the Duke shall hold the abductor in prison until he is pardoned and released, or he purges himself by trial, even if the crime was noticed by those nearby.

Chapter LI. Concerning [Prostitutes]

2. If anyone takes a prostitute by force and does not give her her price, he shall be in the Duke's mercy for all his chattels, and the prostitute shall have her price, and her damages shall be paid, if her clothes were torn; and if the abductor has no money, he shall do penance in the Duke's custody for eight days. . . .

Chapter LXXIX. Concerning Dowers

1. A woman, after the death of her husband, seeks her dower, either from the estate of her husband, or from someone not related to her. And she may seek only one third of the land of which her husband was seised[17] when he contracted with her at the church door. But if he was not seised of anything, because his father was alive and held

---

17. To be seised of = to be in possession of.

the inheritance, and if the father was present when his heir married the woman, and he consented to the marriage and arranged it, the woman ought to have in dower one third of that part which belonged to her husband, or which would have come to him upon the death of his ancestor.

2. If she was dowered with a certain portion which does not exceed one third of her husband's estate, she ought to be contented with that.

3. If another woman was married to the predecessor of this woman's husband and was dowered on that inheritance, the former shall have one third of the whole inheritance for as long as she lives, and the latter shall have one third of the remaining two thirds of the estate; after the death of the former, one third of her dower shall descend to the latter.

4. If a woman seeks her dower from someone not related to her, he is not required to answer her, except in the presence of the heir and after an inspection. . . . And, while the case is pending, the tenant shall not be robbed, but the heir shall give the woman her whole dower, if he has it, and if he does not have if, she shall have her dower in the land under question, if her husband was seised there when he married her.

5. But if the tenant proves his defense, the woman shall have one third of his tenement, and the heir shall provide him an exchange nearby; and when the woman dies, that tenement shall revert to him who possessed it, and the heir shall have his exchange back.

6. A woman should not be dowered in the chief dwelling if her husband has a tenement in the countryside which is worth one third of his inheritance. But if he does not have such a tenement, she may be dowered with one third of the dwelling. If he has various dwellings, she should have her dower in one which is worth one third [of his whole estate]. If they are of equal value, he should assign her as many as are worth one third [of his whole estate].

7. A man may not do anything with the tenement of which he was in possession when he married his wife, such that the woman will not have her dower after his death. . . .

9. Cases of dower shall allow only one delay for non-appearance [of a party in court], or delay for illness, or more defaults, or other delays, like property cases, because the woman acquires nothing except her own living, and her dower cannot be damaged to the detriment of the heir, and she cannot request her dower in things which her husband acquired after the marriage was contracted. And if the heir says, against the woman seeking dower, that she is in possession of her dower, an inspection should be made.

10. If a woman was dowered with chattels, she should have her dower in chattels after the death of her husband, if there are enough chattels, and this should be counted among the other debts, which are not charged to the woman's part. And if there are not enough chattels, she shall have recourse to the inheritance and the heir, for as much as one third.

11. Questions concerning chattels given in dower belong to the ecclesiastical court; those concerning land belong to the King alone.

12. If a husband loses his inheritance, whether by fraud and collusion, or because of his own offense, so that he is condemned to death or must leave the country, the wife loses her dower, but not that tenement that she has in her own right.

Chapter LXXX. Concerning Women's Dowries

1. When something is given on behalf of a woman to her husband, which is commonly called dowry, if any question arises about it, the ecclesiastical court shall investigate and judge in cases of chattels, and the King's court in cases of land.

2. If anyone gives land as a dowry to his daughter or sister or kinswoman, he may not object to his own deed; but after the donor's death his heirs may revoke whatever was given in excess of the third of the inheritance from which dowries should be given; and this if there is only one daughter or sister.

3. But if there are more, there remains to that married woman and to her heirs only a portion of the third part which belongs to her, because all the sisters cannot have more than a third to be divided thus between them.

4. When a sister arrives at a marriageable age, if her brother or kinsman, whose partner she is in the inheritance, does not wish to provide her with a suitable marriage, and she complains about this, her brother shall be called to the King's court, and a delay of a year and a day shall be given to him. In that period of time he should provide her with a husband, according to her condition and lands, and he should arrange this meanwhile, to the best of his ability. If he does not do this, the King's justice should then supply his default and assign to the woman one third of the inheritance, if she is the only sister, or a part of the third, if there are more, and thus the woman can marry whom she wishes.

5. And as long as she is without a husband, she may run her land just as men do. . . .

7. A woman shall not lose her inheritance on account of her hus-

band's crime; but if he goes into exile, or if he is banished, his wife shall not have possession of her inheritance while he is alive, nor shall she have its profits, but rather the Lord King. But when her husband dies, she may have her inheritance again, unless she, like her husband, was condemned.

13. Laws of Sicily (1231)

The Kingdom of Sicily, which included much of southern Italy, came under the dominion of the Holy Roman Empire in the thirteenth century when the hereditary king of Sicily also became the emperor Frederick II. It was Frederick who had the "Constitutions of Melfi" drawn up—a collection of his own laws for Sicily and those of previous kings.

Source: *The Liber Augustalis, or Constitutions of Melfi, Promulgated by the Emperor Frederick II for the Kingdom of Sicily in 1231,* tr. James M. Powell (Syracuse, NY: Syracuse University Press, 1971).

Book I
Title XX: About rape and violence inflicted on nuns

If anyone presumes to rape nuns or novices, even for the purpose of marriage, he should be punished by death.

Title XXI: About violence inflicted on prostitutes

It is fitting that all persons subject to the scepter of our rule should be governed by the grace of our majesty. We favor the glory of peace by defending one from another, both men and women, from elders, from minors, and from equals and by not allowing force to be used at all.

Therefore, those miserable women who are marked as prostitutes by their quest for shame should rejoice in gratitude for our favor that no one may force them to satisfy his will if they are unwilling. Those acting against this general edict, after they have confessed and been convicted, should be punished by death. The order of consideration should require that if force has been used in places suitable for abode, the cry of the woman oppressed should attract attention as soon as possible after it has been emitted. But it will not appear that force was used if a delay of eight days has ensued, unless it is proved that she was detained against her will for that time.

Title XXII: About those who rape virgins and widows

We order that the capital punishment which the statutes of the divine Augustuses[18] sanctioned against those who rape virgins, widows, wives, or even engaged girls and against their accomplices and supporters should be observed inviolably. Those customs, which obtained in some parts of the Kingdom of Sicily until the present, by which those who raped a woman escaped capital punishment by marrying her or by arranging for another to marry her, should not be permitted at all. . . .

The laws of our predecessors as kings of Sicily permitted the judgment by combat in complaints about violences inflicted on any women at all if the proclamation of these violences was proved within the period assigned by the same constitutions. But by our holy foresight, we order the removal not only of the judgment by combat but also of the penalty of forfeiture both in this case and in all other crimes except for treason and secret murder.

For there is a very great risk for those accusers who can hardly or never prove their accusations by common proofs since crimes of this kind are hidden from the observations of men who are able to provide testimony of the truth. Therefore, when common proofs fail and when extraordinary proofs, like the judgment by combat . . . , have been removed by our law, cases of this kind are left without remedy. Since we are unwilling to dismiss such great crimes unpunished for lack of proof, we have decreed that, if any persons have been accused by violences of this kind by their own confessions as a result of a guilty conscience, or if they have been accused by witnesses who have found the accused in the very acts of sexual intercourse—which cannot happen very often—they should be convicted. Even if we were not consulted, they would be subject to capital punishment both by earlier constitutions and our own. But if the real truth of the matter cannot be proved, but it is only proved that a woman or another in her behalf has three times denounced someone for tampering with her chastity by his actions or in some other way to keep him from repeating this illegal presumption of his, and if he is later found with the woman who is crying out and calling for the help of others with her screams, and if he is found in a struggle, or in flight, or even in or near the house of this woman, or if he holds the woman violently beneath him while he opens the guard of her virginity and corrupts her or attacks her after she has been corrupted, while she is crying out, we order

18. Augustuses = the Roman emperors.

that his case should be remitted to the knowledge of our highness after a full discussion and the aforesaid and similar proofs so that from the opinion of our inspiration, which we shall receive from the hand of God, the case may reach a just decision. But, in the meantime, the accused should be handed over to the custody of his pledges or to jail.

Title XXIII: If anyone should not help a woman suffering violence and crying out

We desire that whoever hears a woman who is being attacked calling out should hasten to run to her assistance when he hears her. But if he does not go to her assistance, he should pay four *augustales* as a penalty to our treasury for such serious neglect. No one should be able to pretend about hearing the screams to escape the penalty if he was under the same roof and in the same place where the voice could be heard and if he is not proved to be deaf or crippled by a severe pain or otherwise ill, or if he is not proved to have been sleeping at the time of the screams.

Title XXIV: About the penalty for women who complain unjustly

We curtail the very evil and abhorrent ground for an accusation, which has prevailed until now to the serious expense of our subjects, whereby a woman who had not suffered the violence or injury of rape made accusations about some persons untruthfully. And thus the accused, for fear of the accusation which would be brought or could be brought or which was already brought, insofar as they were afraid of the contest of the law courts and the outcome of the affair, chose unequal marriages.[19] Sometimes, also, these women obtained black-mail from their victims for concealing the aforesaid accusations. We desire and command that if any woman should in the future be convicted of such false calumny, she should know that she has been caught in a trap of death and that she has fallen into the pit that she was preparing for the downfall of another, if she had proved what she had given information about. If, at the time for punishment, she is found to be pregnant, we, persuaded by our kindness, desire to postpone the punishment until forty days after the delivery. After she has been delivered of the child, we order that it should be reared at our expense by our officials who are then in charge of those regions

---

19. A man could escape a rape charge by marrying the accusing woman.

unless she has next of kin, relatives, or even in-laws whom she may persuade to rear the child with the affection of a relation.

Book II
Title II: A commune which has been accused and a married woman can appoint a procurator in criminal cases

. . . We . . . permit and order, too, that syndics[20] should be appointed in criminal cases and capital accusations as in civil cases which are brought against communes by private persons or by communes against other communes or private persons. . . . We also extend this favor of our majesty to married women. They should be able to appear in judgments in criminal and capital cases through their husbands and others whom they desire as legitimate and sufficiently instructed procurators, if they desire, whether they are the plaintiffs or the defendants. . . .

Title VIII: About the wives and parents of those who have been exiled

We desire that the innocent should avoid punishment and that the guilty should be punished. Therefore, by this general law, we decree that the wives and mothers of those exiled should not be molested in any way in their business, dowries, wedding gifts, and in the dower quarter by reason of the aforementioned exile or condemnation. Rather, they should hold all these goods in full and free of all molestation. But they and the sons or parents of the one exiled should not dare to provide for him in any way at all from the goods which were saved for them by the kindness of our piety. For we want him to be needy and we do not want him to expect sustenance from anyone. But if they do provide for him, we order that they should be deprived of the favor they seem to abuse, and their goods should be added to our treasury.

Title XLI: About the full restitution of legal status to women

We settle the equity of the laws for women who have been injured because of the weakness of their sex by ordering that they should be aided both by us and by our officials to the best of their ability as is decent and necessary.

---

20. Procurators and syndics = representatives of parties in a legal case.

Title XLIV: About the full restitution of the legal status of women

In order to clarify the obscurity of the law that the divine King Roger, our grandfather, promulgated about the restitution of legal status for women, we order that women who live by the law of the Lombards or the Franks should be restored to their former legal status in judicial proceedings only when they are proved to have been injured grossly through the negligence or fraud of their guardians or procurators and when they cannot be preserved from injury from the aforesaid guardians and procurators because those persons are not solvent. The same is the case if they should incur a great loss because of the excessive simplicity[21] of their protectors. For, though the simplicity of the prescribed matters may excuse them, still their simplicity should not result in a loss for the women. However, we do not see that it is necessary for women to have help with contracts, at which they cannot only be present but also have the presence of judges and guardians and procurators, unless perhaps they are shown to have promised or to have agreed by fraud or because of the weakness of their sex to an excessive dowry beyond their patrimony or beyond the capabilities of their patrimony. We also maintain the validity of those cases where the ancient laws aided the rights of women who lacked knowledge: if through error, they illegally withdraw an accusation before the penalty has been handed down; if they commit the crime of incest through ignorance of the law; or if, through ignorance on account of the weakness of their sex, they fail to draw up documents that must be drawn up. They should also receive help if they are found to have been deceived through ignorance of the law in making satisfaction to a creditor in the public courts. Likewise, if they pay as a result of mediation without knowing that they are protected by the benefit of the Velleian *Senatusconsultum*,[22] they should receive help. We desire that all these provisions and others, if the proved antiquity of the law has introduced them, should remain valid.

Book III
Title XIII: How a [dower] should be established in fiefs and *castra*

If any baron or knight marries a wife and he has three fiefs, he may legally establish one of the three fiefs as a [dower] for his wife. But if he has fewer, we permit him to establish a [dower] in money de-

---

21. Simplicity = foolishness, lack of sophistication.
22. The Velleian *Senatusconsultum* = an ancient Roman law which prohibited creditors from suing a woman for another person's debts.

pending on the nature and the number of the fiefs. However, if he has more than three, he may legally establish a [dower] out of the part that has been determined to be greater. Moreover, a count or baron who holds *castra*[23] can establish a [dower] from these *castra*, but he cannot establish the *castrum* from which the barony or county takes its name as a [dower].

Title XV: On [dowers]

We also grant permission for barons and knights to establish a [dower] from two fiefs, and if one of them has only one and a half fiefs, he can establish a half-fief [dower]. But if any of these barons or knights have only one, he should know that he will be allowed the right to establish a [dower] for his wife in the future only in money and not in land, depending on the nature of the fief.

Title XVI: How [dowers] ought to be established

After the death of her husband, a woman who has a dower in land is required to promise fealty for the dower to the heir or to the lord of the barony for his life, his members, and the capture of his body. She should also promise that she will not seek by guile or ingenuity the means whereby the aforesaid dower may be withdrawn from the barony or county, always with the reservation of the mandate of the higher lord. But a woman is not required to promise fealty to the [illegitimate] sons of a common marriage. At the request of the lord, a woman who holds a dower is required to be present at service of the court. If she should not be present, she should be disseized after three warnings by the lord. Also, if unjust burdens are inflicted on the men by the dowers, the woman is required to correct them by the lord of the barony or the fief. The men ought to promise fealty to the lady of the dower, always with the reservation of the right of the lord, count or baron. They are also required to promise fealty to the count or baron, with the reservation of the right of the aforesaid lady of the dower.

Title XVII: About brothers who obligate part of a fief for the dowries of their sisters

We permit brothers to obligate part of a fief for the dowries of their sisters if they do not have movable property or heritable tenancies.

---

23. *Castra* = castles.

Also, if they have three or more fiefs, they can grant one of them as a dowry for their sister. However, in all the aforesaid matters, if a fief is alienated, obligated, or established as a dowry, the marriage itself should be contracted by our special license. Otherwise, all agreements will have no force.

Title XXII: How marriages should be contracted

By the present law, we order that all the men of our kingdom and especially the nobles who desire to contract marriage must have the marriage celebrated solemnly and publicly, with due solemnity and a priestly blessing, after the betrothal has been solemnized. Otherwise, they should know that, if they die, they would be acting against our royal edict and would have no legitimate heirs either by will or by intestacy among those who were procreated from a clandestine and illegal marriage against our law. Women should also know that they would have no legal right to the dowers due other wives. We relax the rigor of this law to all those who have already contracted marriage at the time of its promulgation. We also relax the chain of this necessity for all widows who desire to marry a husband.

Title XXIII: A wife should not be married without license of the court

In order to preserve the honor due to our crown, we order by the present constitution that no count, baron, or knight, or anyone else who holds in chief[24] from us baronies or fiefs registered in the records of our diwan, should dare to marry a wife without license. They should not dare to marry off their daughters, whom they can and should arranges marriages for, or to marry off their sons with movable or immovable property, notwithstanding the contrary custom which is said to have been observed in some parts of the kingdom.

Title XXX: About the right of wardship

We provide in an imperial manner for minors who cannot be helped by the judgment of their age. We order that if our serenity grants the wardship of male or female youths to someone's administration, they should render account of the administration of the wardship in the presence of the justiciar of the region or another to whom we have

---

24. To hold in chief = to hold directly, without an intermediate lord.

ordered this especially delegated, after they have relinquished the wardship with the arrival of puberty. After the amount which should be given to the court for this wardship has been deducted, as is the custom, and also after just and moderate expenses (which it will be established that this guardian has paid out for his sustenance and dress and which he has made for the person or property of the child or for the service due our court from the property of the minor) have been deducted, the remainder must be handed over in full to the orphan. But if it has been proved that the guardian has administered the property of the child fraudulently, he must repair his entire loss as a result of this fraud, whatever it may be, from his own property and pay that amount to our sacred treasury. We abolish for the future the evil custom that, until now, exempted guardians from making accountings.

Title XXXIV: About male and female slaves

We order generally that no male or female slaves should be seized by anyone unless they restore them to their lord as quickly as possible. If they do not know the lord, they should hand them over to the bailiffs of our court. The bailiffs should sent them to our great court. They should know that whoever dares to seize any slave or handmaiden in any way from now on, or to detain them in any way whatever, will, with all his goods, be subject to the penalty of the court. Unless bailiffs send them to our great court, they will undergo the same penalty.

Title XXXVI: About fugitive slaves

We order that fugitive slaves, which a royal commission ordered to be sent to our great court and did not decide their further disposition, should be kept for a year for the convenience of their lords. If, within a year, he who can prove by legitimate documents that he is the owner appears, we order that the aforesaid slaves should be returned to him save for the right which from ancient usage, according to circumstances, belongs to our court. But if the owners do not appear, the slaves should be collected for our private purposes. . . .

Title LXXIV: About adulteries and about procuring

The harshness of the laws has been softened. The penalty against adulterers who attack the wives of others must no longer be the sword. Rather we introduce the penalty of confiscation of their property if they have no legitimate children from the violated marriage or another. For it is most unjust that children should be defrauded of their inheritance if they were born at a time when the law of the marriage was legally observed. But a woman must not be handed over to her husband who would rage against her until he killed her. Instead, the slitting of her nose, which is more severely and more cruelly introduced, should pursue the vengeance of the violated marriage. But if her husband is unwilling to give her a punishment, we will not allow such a crime to go unpunished but will order her to be publicly flogged.

Title LXXVII: Lascivious women must be removed from association with good women

A woman who has exhibited her body for sale far and wide cannot be accused of adultery. But we prohibit violence to be done to her, and we forbid her to dwell among women of good reputation.

Title LXXXI: About the penalty for a wife caught in the act of adultery

If a husband catches his wife in the very act of adultery, he may kill both the adulterer and his wife, but without any further delay.

Title LXXXIV: About madams

We order that madams, who solicit the shame of wives, daughters, sisters, and finally virgins and honest women that some good man has within the walls of his house, should be punished by the slitting of their noses as are adulteresses according to the statutes of our grandfather, King Roger. But we order that those who attract the minds of women, who, since they have lived freely and were under no one's protection, have given themselves to the wills and pleasures of men at any time (though it is not really believable that they would desire to give themselves for the first time), should be beaten after they have been convicted by legitimate proof of committing such acts, and they should be marked on the forehead in recognition of the crime they have attempted. Such madams should know for sure that if they attempt to repeat what they have done again, they will certainly and without doubt be subjected to the slitting of their noses.

Title LXXXV: About the penalty for a mother
who prostitutes her daughter publicly

We order that mothers who publicly prostitute their daughters
should be subject to the penalty of having their noses slit, which was
established by the divine King Roger. But we believe that it is not only
unjust but cruel for other mothers, who give their consent, and for
their daughters, who may not be able to marry a husband because of
their poverty but who also cannot even sustain life, to be subject to
this penalty when they expose themselves to the pleasures of some
man who gives them sustenance for life and other favors.

14. Spanish Laws (13th c.)

From the eighth to the eleventh century, most of the Iberian
peninsula was controlled by Muslims. The Spanish Muslims were
known as "Moors." In the eleventh century, Christian rulers in
northern Spain began a slow "reconquest" of the peninsula. The
laws of these Christian kingdoms reflect their frontier mentality
and the uneasy coexistence of the two societies, Christian and
Muslim. The following extract is from *Las Siete Partidas*, a well-
known law code compiled in the thirteenth century under King
Alfonso X of Leon and Castile. (For Muslim documents from
Spain, see Part VI below.)
Source: Colin Smith, *Christians and Moors in Spain* (Warminster,
England: Aris & Phillips Ltd., 1989).

Christians Captured by Moors

If a woman is pregnant when captured and gives birth in enemy
territory, later being able to return home, the son or daughter that has
been born should enter into ownership of the property which is due
to come to him or her from the father or mother; and should enjoy his
or her rights in all things just as if born in the parental home. If it
should happen that father and mother are captured together, and
that the woman should become pregnant by her husband while in
captivity, and if they afterwards leave captivity bringing their son or
daughter with them, that child should have his or her rights in all
things too, just as if he or she had been conceived and born in Christian
lands. If the child should leave captivity with one parent only, the
father or the mother, the child shall inherit the property of that parent

with whom he or she is living, and has all his or her rights over such property guaranteed; but the child has no concern with the property of the parent who remains a captive, unless that other parent later leaves captivity and both parents acknowledge the child as theirs. There remains a further way in which ancient authorities held that the child could inherit his father's property. This is when the man who is held captive comes to believe that those at home who should be trying to secure his release are not making any effort to do so, and he in his desperation to be free has a child by some woman of the [Muslim] faith who has promised to help him to freedom: if after such a promise she manages to achieve this, and comes home with the man, the son or daughter accompanying her or without her, provided the man so freed acknowledges the child as his and converts him or her to Christianity and is able to prove that the other heirs did nothing to secure his release even though they were in a position to do so. . . .

Christian Women and Moorish Men

If a Moor should lie with a Christian virgin, he should be stoned to death for it; and she, the first time, should lose one half of her property, this passing to her father or mother, or to her grandfather or grandmother if they are alive; if they are not alive, the property passes to the Crown. For the second offense she should forfeit all that she has, the property passing to the persons aforementioned, if alive, and if they are not, it passes to the Crown; and she should be put to death. The same applies to a widow who acts in this way. If a Moor lies with a married Christian woman he should be stoned to death, and she should be placed in the hands of her husband, who may burn her to death, or set her free, or do with her whatever he wishes. If the Moor lies with a prostitute who makes herself available to all, for the first offense they should be tied together and whipped through the town, and for a second offense they should both be killed.

15. Customs of Magdeburg (13th c.)

In 1261 the city of Magdeburg, on the German-Polish border, sent this version of its laws to another town which had asked for them as a model. Towns usually had their own laws, either in addition to or instead of the laws of the kingdom in which the town lay.

Women were not usually considered "citizens" of a town, but their rights were safeguarded in urban law just as they were in feudal law and local and manorial custom. One difference was that land was not necessarily the most important element of an inheritance in an urban family.

Source: Oliver J. Thatcher and Edgar H. McNeal, *A Source Book for Mediæval History* (New York: Charles Scribner's Sons, 1907).

1. When Magdeburg was founded the inhabitants were given such a charter as they wished. They determined that they would choose aldermen every year, who, on their election, should swear that they would guard the law, honor, and interests of the city to the best of their ability and with the advice of the wisest people of the city. . . .

14. If a man dies leaving a wife, she shall have no share in his property except what he has given her in court, or has appointed for her dower. She must have six witnesses, male or female, to prove her dower. If the man made no provision for her, her children must support her as long as she does not remarry. If her husband had sheep, the widow shall take them.

15. If a man and woman have children, some of whom are married and have received their marriage portion, and the man dies, the children who are still at home shall receive the inheritance. Those who have received their marriage portion shall have no part of [the inheritance]. Children who have received an inheritance shall not sell it without the consent of the heirs. . . .

18. No one, whether man or woman, shall, on his sick-bed, give away more than three shillings' worth of his property without the consent of his heirs, and the woman must have the consent of her husband. . . .

55. When a man dies his wife shall give [to his heirs] his sword, his horse and saddle, and his best coat of mail. She shall also give a bed, a pillow, a sheet, a table-cloth, two dishes and a towel. Some say that she should give other things also, but that is not necessary. If she does not have these things, she shall not give them, but she shall give proof for each article that she does not have it.

56. If two or more children inherit these things, the oldest shall take the sword and they shall share the other things equally.

57. If the children are minors, the oldest male relative on the father's side, if he is of the same rank by birth, shall receive all these things and preserve them for the children. When they become of age, he shall give them to them, and in addition, all their property, unless he

can prove that he has used it to their profit, or that it has been stolen
or destroyed by some accident without any fault of his. He shall also
be the guardian of the widow until she remarries, if he is of the same
rank as she is.

58. After giving the above articles the widow shall take her dower
and all that belongs to her; that is, all the sheep, geese, chests, yarn,
beds, pillows, cushions, table linen, bed linen, towels, cups, candle-
sticks, linen, women's clothing, finger rings, bracelets, headdress,
psalters, and all prayer-books, chairs, drawers, bureaus, carpets, cur-
tains, etc., and there are many other trinkets which belong to her,
such as brushes, scissors, and mirrors, but I do not mention them.
But uncut cloth, and unworked gold and silver do not belong to her.

16. London Records:
Crimes and Punishments (14th c.)

The following accounts, from the municipal records of London,
show female criminals before the city officials. Male criminals
faced the same officials and the same or similar penalties; but
some of the crimes described below are particularly female ones.
Source: *Memorials of London and London Life in the XIIIth, XIVth,
and XVth Centuries*, ed. and tr. Henry Thomas Riley (London:
Longmans, Green and Co., 1868).

A Strumpet (1311)

Margaret de Hontyngdone, Marion de Honytone, and Henry le
Beste, were attached in the Ward of Bradstrete by Richard le Kissere,
serjeant of the same Ward, on the Friday next before the Feast of St.
Vincent [9 June] . . . and put into the Tun,[25] because the said Margaret
had before been driven out from the Ward aforesaid as a common
strumpet, and had afterwards harboured men of bad repute, etc. And
William de Louthe, servant of the Company of the Friscobaldi, and
William Sailleben, became sureties for the said Henry, that in future
he would well and trustily behave himself. And the women aforesaid
made oath that they would behave themselves properly in like
manner.

---

25. The Tun = a London prison.

A Curfew-Breaker (1320)

Emma, daughter of William [the Wiredrawer], of York, was taken by William [the] Official, serjeant of the Ward of Chepe, and put into the Tun, on the night of Sunday next before the Feast of St. Martin [11 November], . . . because she was found wandering about after curfew rung at the place assigned, namely, at St. Martin's le Grand, together with a certain fardel of cloths.

Afterwards, on Tuesday the Feast of St. Martin, she was brought to the Guildhall before the Mayor, and was told that she must find security as to keeping the peace; and she was accordingly delivered to the said William [the] Official, that he might take pledge of her for so doing.

A Thief (1337)

Desiderata de Toryntone was taken at the suit of John Baret, of Bydene, in the County of Barkshire, for a certain robbery committed upon him in the hostel of the Bishop of Sarum in Fletestrete, in the suburb of London, on [6 May], . . . of 30 dishes and 24 salt-cellars of silver, belonging to the Lady Alice de Lisle, mistress of him, the same John Baret, value £40; being then in his keeping, and out of the same stolen; as to which he accused her, and of which number, 14 dishes and 12 salt-cellars were found upon her. His sureties that he would prosecute her for felony, were William de Toppesfeld and Reynald de Thorpe.

The jurors say . . . that the said Desiderata is guilty of the felony aforesaid. Therefore she is to be hanged. Chattels she has none.

A Child-Stealer (1373)

On Monday, the Feast of St. Benedict the Abbot [21 March], . . . Alice de Salisbury, a beggar, was adjudged to the pillory called the "thewe," for women ordained, by award of the Mayor and Aldermen, there to stand for one hour in the day; for that, on the Sunday before, she had taken one Margaret, daughter of John Oxwyke, grocer, in the Ropery, in London, and had carried her away, and stripped her of her clothes, that she might not be recognized by her family; that so, she might go begging with the same Alice, and gain might be made thereby etc. As to the which, the same Alice was convicted before the Mayor and Aldermen.

A Scold (1375)

Alice Shether was brought before the Mayor, on Tuesday the 4th of September, . . . for that at the Wardmote of John Haddele, Alderman of Tower Ward, she was indicted for being a common scold; and for that all the neighbours, dwelling in that vicinity, by her malicious words and abuse were so greatly molested and annoyed; she sowing envy among them, discord, and ill-will, and repeatedly defaming, molesting, and backbiting many of them, sparing neither rich nor poor; to the great damage of the persons and neighbours there dwelling, and against the Ordinance of the City.

Wherefore, upon the complaint of the said Alderman, and of many of her neighbours in the same Ward . . . the said Alice was questioned on the matters aforesaid, and it was enquired of her how she would acquit herself thereof; whereupon, she said she was in no way guilty of the things aforesaid, and put herself upon the country as to the same, etc.

The jury . . . said upon their oath,—that she is guilty of all the things above charged against her. Therefore it was awarded that she should have punishment of the pillory, called the "thewe," for women ordained, there to stand for one hour. And precept was given to the Sheriffs to have proclamation made of the nature of her offence.

17. Sumptuary Laws (13th–14th c.)

Sumptuary laws have been common in many societies; they enforce various social distinctions by regulating consumption and display, especially in terms of clothing. Medieval society considered it improper for people to dress above their station in life, as for example when wealthy merchants dressed more richly than nobles who were their social superiors but might be poorer than some members of the bourgeoisie. Sumptuary laws were also used to distinguish between prostitutes and "respectable" women. (Further examples of sumptuary laws can be found in the section on Jewish women in Part VI.)

Venice (1299)

Source: *Lo statuto inedito delle nozze veneziane emanato nell'anno 1299*, ed. C. Foucard (Venice: Tipografia de commercio, 1858). Tr. E.M.A.

1. It has been decreed in the Council, by a vote of 27, that henceforth at weddings or on the occasions of weddings in the city of Venice, no one may send or receive presents, or gifts, or even goblets, by any method or means, under penalty of 20 *soldi di grossi* for each time, except that goblets may be sent to the home of the bride, and also to the home of the bridegroom, on those days when it is customary to send them, and also to the priest, as is the custom.

2. And that the bride may not be accompanied, either when going to her husband or when returning home, by more than eight ladies, and the bridegroom may not have at the wedding banquet more than twenty lords and twenty ladies in all. And similarly the attendants on the part of the bride may not be more than the said number at the banquet, on the day of the wedding. A lady thirteen years old or younger shall not be held to be a lady, unless she is married, and if she has been married and is now a widow she shall be held to be a lady; and a man twenty years old or younger shall not be held to be a lord. . . .

5. Item, that no bride may carry, or cause to be carried, more than four [new] dresses [in her trousseau], under penalty of 20 *soldi di grossi*. . . .

6. Item, that henceforth no man or woman or lady may wear borders of pearls, under penalty of 20 *soldi di grossi*, except that brides, if they wish, may have borders of pearls on their wedding dress a single time, and similarly one headpiece of pearls; and they may not place the aforesaid borders on any gown other than the wedding gown. And the aforesaid borders, which are placed on the wedding dress and cloak, may not be worth more than 20 *soldi di grossi* altogether, under the aforesaid penalty.

7. And that no person may wear an embroidered border beyond the value of five *lire di piccoli*; and no person may place any embroidered border on a cloak or on a fur. Strings of pearls for the hair are totally forbidden and prohibited, so that no woman or lady may wear them henceforth, under penalty of 100 *soldi* for each time she is found contravening this law. And also she may not have more than one row of gold or amber buttons worth more than 10 *soldi di grossi*, under the aforesaid penalty of 100 *soldi*, nor any hair ornament of pearls worth more than 100 *soldi*, under the aforesaid penalty. . . .

8. Item, that henceforth no man or lady or woman may have more than two cloaks of vair or other fur, and if any now have more they may not wear more than two of them from now on, under penalty of 20 *soldi di grossi* for each time.

9. Item, that a lady or woman may wear only one cloak lined with

silk under the aforesaid penalty. Except that if she ought to wear another silk-lined cloak for mourning, she may do so. . . .

10. Item, that henceforth no woman's tunic may have a train of more than one arm's length trailing on the ground or an underdress train of more than half an arm's length, under the aforesaid penalty. Except that a bride may have whatever sort of train she wishes a single time, on her wedding tunic. And the garments which exist today may remain as they are, however many trains they have, and henceforth they may not be manufactured except as stated above, under penalty of 20 *soldi di grossi*. . . .

11. Item, that ladies are exempted and excepted from these orders, when they are going to or coming from the palace, and may wear those things and ornaments which they bring from the palace, but afterwards they may not do otherwise than others may, under the aforesaid penalty of 20 *soldi di grossi*. . . .

England (1363)

> Source: *Statutes of the Realm*, Vol. I (1810). Reprinted with the permission of the Controller of Her Britannic Majesty's Stationery Office. Spelling and punctuation modernized.

8. Item, for the outrageous and excessive apparel of divers people, against their estate and degree, to the great destruction and impoverishment of all the land, it is ordained, that grooms, as well servants of lords, as they of mysteries,[26] and artificers, shall be served to eat and drink once a day of flesh or of fish, and the remnant of other victuals, as of milk, butter, and cheese, according to their estate. And that they have clothes for their vesture, or hosing, whereof the whole cloth shall not exceed two marks, and that they wear no cloth of higher price, of their buying, nor otherwise, not nothing of gold or silver embroidered, aimeled,[27] nor of silk, nor nothing pertaining to the said things; and their wives, daughters, and children shall be of the same condition in their clothing and apparel, and they shall wear no veils passing 12 pence a veil.

9. Item, that people of handicraft, and yeomen, shall take not wear cloth of an higher price for their vesture or hosing, than within forty shillings the whole cloth, by way of buying, nor otherwise; nor stone, nor cloth of silk nor of silver, nor girdle, [knife, button,] ring, garter,

---

26. Mysteries = regulated crafts.
27. Aimeled = enamelled.

nor owche,[28] ribbon, chains, nor no such other things of gold nor of silver, nor no manner of apparel embroidered, aimeled, nor of silk by no way, and that their wives, daughters, and children be of the same condition in their vesture and apparel; and that they wear no veil of silk, but only of yarn made within the Realm, nor no manner of fur, nor of budge, but only of lamb, cony, cat, and fox.

10. Item, that esquires and all manner of gentlemen, under the estate of a knight, which have no land nor rent to the value of an hundred pounds by year, shall not take nor wear cloth for their clothing or hosing of an higher price, than within the price of four marks and a half the whole cloth, by way of buying nor otherwise; and that they wear no cloth of gold, nor silk, nor silver, nor no manner of clothing embroidered, ring, buttons, nor owche of gold, ribband, girdle, nor none other apparel, nor harness,[29] of gold nor of silver, nor nothing of stone, nor no manner of fur; and that their wives, daughters, and children be of the same condition, as to their vesture and apparel, without any turning up or purfle,[30] and that they wear no manner of apparel of gold, or silver, nor of stone. But that esquires, that have land or rent to the value of 200 marks by year and above, may take and wear cloths of the price of five marks, and cloth of silk and of silver, ribband, girdle, and other apparel reasonably garnished of silver; and that their wives, daughters, and children may wear fur turned up of miniver, without ermines or letuse, or any manner of [gem]stone, but for their heads.

11. Item, that merchants, citizens and burgesses, artificers, people of handicraft, as well within the city of London, as elsewhere, which have clearly goods and chattels, to the value of 500 pounds, and their wives and children, may take and wear in the manner as the esquires and gentlemen which have land to rent to the value of 100 pounds by year; and that the same merchants, citizens, and burgesses, which have clearly goods and chattels, to the value of 1000 pounds and their wives and children may take and wear in the manner as esquires and gentlemen, which have land and rent to the value of 200 pounds by year: and no groom, yeoman, or servant of merchant, artificer or people of handicraft shall wear otherwise in apparel than is above ordained of yeomen of lords.

12. Item, that knights, which have land or rent within the value of 200 pounds shall take and wear cloth of 6 marks the whole cloth, for

28. Girdle = belt; owche = ornamental collar or brooch.
29. Harness = armor.
30. Purfle = ornamental border.

their vesture, and of none higher price; and that they wear not cloth of gold, nor cloths, mantle, nor gown furred with miniver nor of ermines, nor no apparel broidered of [gem]stone, nor otherwise; and that their wives, daughters, and children be of the same condition; and that they wear no turning up of ermines, nor of letuses, nor no manner of apparel of [gem]stone, but only for their heads. But that all knights and ladies, which have land or rent over the value of 400 marks by year, to the sum of 1000 pounds, shall wear at their pleasure, except ermines and letuses, and apparel of pearls and [gem]stone, but only for their heads. . . .

14. Item, that carters, ploughmen, drivers of the plough, oxherds, cowherds, shepherds . . . and all other keepers of beasts, threshers of corn, and all manner of people of the estate of a groom, attending to husbandry, and all other people, that have not forty shillings of goods, nor of chattels, shall not take nor wear no manner of cloth, but blanket, and russet [wool] of twelve-pence; and shall wear the girdles of linen according to their estate; and that [they come to eat and drink] in the manner as pertaineth to them, and not excessively. And it is ordained, that if any wear or do contrary to any of the points aforesaid, that he shall forfeit against the king all the apparel that he hath so worn against the form of this ordinance.

B. Marriage

18. Gratian:
Canon Law on Marriage (12th c.)

Marriage was one of the areas in which church courts, rather than secular courts, had jurisdiction over medieval Christians. The rules and precedents with which ecclesiastical courts worked in such cases were complex and at times contradictory. From the twelfth century on, the standard collection of these "canons" was Gratian's *Decretals*, a massive compilation of excerpts from Christian writers and church council decisions illustrating every aspect of Christian life, organized into series of hypothetical cases and their component "questions." The text below consists mainly of Gratian's summary statements; most of the explanatory quotations which make up the bulk of Gratian's book have been omitted here.

Source: *Corpus Juris Canonici*, ed. E. Friedberg (1959). Tr. E.M.A.

Case 27, Question II

1. [According to John Chrysostom:] "Coitus does not make a marriage; consent does; and therefore the separation of the body does not dissolve it, but the separation of the will. Therefore he who forsakes his wife, and does not take another, is still a married man. For even if he is now separated in his body, yet he is still joined in his will. When therefore he takes another woman, then he forsakes fully. Therefore he who forsakes is not the adulterer, but he who takes another woman."

2. . . . When therefore there is consent, which alone makes a marriage, between those persons, it is clear that they have been married.

20. A woman who has been sent to a monastery without the consent of her husband is not prohibited from returning to live with him. . . .

21. He who has become a monk without his wife's consent must return to her. . . .

22. A man may not make a monastic vow without his wife's consent. . . .

If any married man wishes to join a monastery, he is not to be accepted, unless he has first been released by his wife, and she makes a vow of chastity. For if she, through incontinence, marries another

79

man while he is still living, without a doubt she will be an adulteress. . . .

23. A husband and a wife may not turn to the religious life without the knowledge of their bishop. According to the synod of Pope Eugenius, "If a husband and wife have agreed between themselves to turn their life to religion, by no means let this be done without the knowledge of their bishop, so that they may be individually and properly examined by him. For if the wife is not willing, or indeed the husband, the marriage is not dissolved, even for such a reason."

24. A husband is not permitted to be celibate without his wife's consent. . . .

26. A wife is not permitted to take a vow of celibacy, unless her husband chooses the same way of life.

27. A girl who is betrothed is not prohibited from choosing the monastery. [According to Pope Eusebius:] "Parents may not give a betrothed girl to another man; but she herself may choose a monastery."

29. If a woman proves that her husband has never known her carnally, there may be a separation. . . .

35. Marriage is initiated in the betrothal. . . .

36. The union of the couple completes the marriage. For according to St. Ambrose, "In all marriage the union is understood to be spiritual, and it is confirmed and completed by the bodily union of the couple."

50. One man may not take [in marriage] a girl betrothed to another man. . . .

51. If a man plights his troth to any woman, he is not permitted to marry another. . . .

Case 30, Question II

Betrothals may not be contracted before the age of seven. For only the consent is contracted, which cannot happen unless it is understood by each party what is being done between them. Therefore it is shown that betrothals cannot be contracted between children, whose weakness of age does not admit consent. This same is attested by Pope Nicholas: before the time of consent a marriage cannot be contracted. He says, "Where there is no consent from either party, there is no marriage. Therefore those who give girls to boys while they are still in the cradle, and vice versa, achieve nothing, even if the father and mother are willing and do this, unless both of the children consent after they have reached the age of understanding."

Case 30, Question V

1. Clandestine marriages should not be made. . . .
2. It is not permitted to perform a marriage in secret. . . .
6. No one shall marry a wife without a public ceremony. . . .

Case 31, Question I

10. So that the peril of fornication may be avoided, a second marriage is allowed. . . .
11. Neither a second nor a third nor successive marriages shall be condemned. . . .

Case 31, Question II

1. A girl whose own agreement has never been shown is not required by the oath of her father to marry. . . .
3. Those who are to be of one body ought also to be of one spirit, and therefore no woman who is unwilling ought ever to be joined to anyone. . . .

Case 32, Question I

Many authorities and arguments show that an immoral woman should not be taken to wife. For she who is found guilty of adultery is not supposed to be kept in marital fellowship except after the completion of penance. John Chrysostom said this:
1. He who does not wish to forsake his adulterous wife is a protector of vice. "Just as the man who forsakes a chaste woman is cruel and unjust, so he who keeps an immoral woman is foolish and unfair. For he who conceals the crime of his wife is a protector of vice."
2. A man may forsake his wife because of her fornication, but he may not marry another. . . .
4. Let him who does not wish to forsake his adulterous wife do penance for two years, if she pays her conjugal debt[31] to him. . . .
5. After penance for adultery the man may receive his wife. . . .
But it is another thing to marry an immoral woman, or to keep an adulterous wife, whom you dress in your own habits, your chastity and your modesty . . .
14. It is no sin to marry an immoral woman. . . .

---

31. Pay the conjugal debt = have sexual relations with one's spouse.

Case 32, Question II

1. Childbirth is the sole purpose of marriage for women. . . .
3. Immoderate conjugal union is not an evil of marriage, but a venial sin, because of the good of marriage. . . .
7. Those who obtain drugs of sterility are fornicators, not spouses. . . .

Case 32, Question V

19. A man is not permitted to forsake his wife except because of fornication. . . .
21. Let a man who forsakes his wife for a cause short of fornication be deprived of communion. . . .
23. Adultery in either sex is punished in the same way. . . .

Case 32, Question VI

1. A fornicator cannot forsake his wife for fornication. . . .
4. Men are to be punished more severely for adultery than women. . . .

Case 32, Question VII

1. The bond of marriage cannot be dissolved by fornication. . . .
2. Once a marriage has been proved to have begun, it cannot be dissolved for any reason. . . .
3. If a man leaves his wife, or a woman her husband, on account of fornication, he or she is not permitted to marry another. . . .
5. Let a man forsaken by his wife, or a woman forsaken by her husband, be brought to penitence, unless they wish either to live continently or be reconciled to each other. . . .
6. He who dares to wed a woman forsaken by her husband is a fornicator. . . .
8. A faithful wife who leaves her adulterous husband may not marry another. . . .
10. He who forsakes his wife on account of fornication and marries another is proved a fornicator. . . .
14. Unnatural acts are more filthy and disgraceful than fornication or adultery. . . .
25. A marriage cannot be dissolved because of a bodily infirmity or wound. . . .

26. A madman or a madwoman cannot contract marriage. . . .

27. No man may forsake an infertile wife and marry another for her fertility. . . .

Case 33, Question II

1. No man may forsake his wife, unless the reason for forsaking her is first demonstrated to the church. . . .

2. Divine law forbids a man to forsake his wife, except on account of fornication. . . .

3. A woman forsaken by her husband without an inquiry into the cause shall be restored to all her rights. . . .

4. No judgment is to be made between the man and his wife concerning their marriage contract or the crime of adultery, except after such restitution. . . .

5. Marriage is completely forbidden to men who have killed their wives. . . .

6. No man may kill his adulterous wife. . . .

19. Liturgy for the Marriage Service (11th–16th c.)

The medieval church struggled for centuries to assert its authority over marriage; only gradually did it succeed in making the marriage ceremony itself a religious one. A couple might consent to have the ceremony at the church door, for example, but not the Mass inside the church afterwards. Thus the liturgy of the service represents, in a way, an ideal—the church's idea of how a marraige should be solemnized, rather than the way most marriages were necessarily performed. As canon law acknowledged, a marriage need not even be performed by a priest (or in front of witnesses) in order to be valid.

Wedding liturgy, like most liturgy, differed from place to place and changed over time; this example is from Salisbury in England, and was in use there from the mid-eleventh century on. The Sarum liturgy gradually spread throughout the British Isles. Although the service is condensed here, the complete text contains no blessings of the bridegroom comparable to those of the bride. Source: *The Sarum Missal in English*, tr. Frederick E. Warren (London: Alexander Moring Ltd., 1911). Adapted.

The Church Wedding

The man and the woman are to be placed before the door of the church, or in the face of the church, in the presence of God, and the priest, and the people. The man should stand on the right hand of the woman, and the woman on the left hand of the man, the reason being that she was formed out of a rib in the left side of Adam. Then shall the priest ask the banns, and afterwards he shall say in the vulgar tongue,[32] in the hearing of all,

"Brethren, we are gathered together here, in the sight of God, and his angels, and all the saints, and in the face of the Church, to join together two bodies, to wit, those of this man and this woman,"—here shall the priest look upon both persons—"that henceforth they may be one body; and that they may be two souls in the faith and law of God, to the end that they may earn together eternal life; and whatsoever they may have done before this,"

Then let a charge be made to the people in the vulgar tongue, thus—

"I charge you all by the Father, and the Son, and the Holy Ghost, that if any of you know any cause why these persons may not be lawfully joined together in matrimony, he do now confess it."

The same charge shall be made to the man and woman; so that if aught hath been done by them secretly, or if they have made any vow, or know aught in any way concerning themselves, why they may not lawfully contract matrimony, they may then confess it. If anyone shall wish to allege any impediment, and shall give security for proving it, the marriage must be deferred until the truth of the matter be ascertained. If, however, no impediment be alleged, the priest is to enquire about the dower of the woman. The priest shall not betroth, or consent to a betrothal between a man and a woman, before the third publication of banns. Banns ought to be asked on three distinct holy days, so that at least one week-day intervene between each of such holy days. After this, the priest shall say to the man, in audience of all, in the vulgar tongue,

"N[ame] wilt though have this woman to thy wedded wife, wilt thou love her, and honour her, keep her and guard her, in health and in sickness, as a husband should a wife, and forsaking all others on account of her, keep thee only unto her, so long as ye both shall live?"

The man shall answer, "I will."

Then shall the priest say unto the woman, "N[ame] wilt thou take

---

32. In the vulgar tongue = not in Latin, but in the vernacular language.

this man to thy wedded husband, wilt thou obey him, and serve him, love, honour, and keep him, in health and in sickness, as a wife should a husband, and forsaking all others on account of him, keep thee only unto him, so long as ye both shall live?"

The woman shall answer, "I will."

Then let the woman be given by her father or a friend; if she be a maid, let her have her hand uncovered; if she be a widow, covered; and let the man receive her, to be kept in God's faith and his own, as he hath vowed in the presence of the priest; and let him hold her by her right hand in his right hand. And so let the man give his troth to the woman, by word of mouth, presently, after the priest, saying thus:

"I N. take thee N. to my wedded wife, to have and to hold from this day forward, for better, for worse, for richer, for poorer, in sickness, and in health, till death us do part, if holy church will ordain it: And thereto I plight thee my troth" (withdrawing his hand).

Then the woman shall say, after the priest,

"I. N. take thee N. to my wedded husband, to have and to hold from this day, for better, for worse, for richer, for poorer, in sickness, and in health, to be gentle and obedient, in bed and at board, till death us do part, if holy church will ordain it: And thereto I plight thee my troth" (withdrawing her hand).

Then shall the man lay gold, or silver, and a ring upon a dish or book; and then the priest shall ask whether the ring have been previously blessed or not; if it be answered not, then shall the priest bless the ring, thus,

V. The Lord be with you.[33]

R. And with thy spirit.

"Let us pray. O creator and preserver of mankind, giver of spiritual grace, bestower of eternal salvation, do thou, O Lord, send thy blessing †[34] upon this ring, that she who shall wear it may be armed with the strength of heavenly defence, and that it may be profitable unto her eternal salvation. Through etc." R. Amen.

"Let us pray. Bless, O Lord, this ring, which we bless in thy holy name; that whosoever she be that shall wear it, may abide in thy peace, and continue in thy will, and live, and increase, and grow old in thy love; and let the length of her days be multiplied. Through etc."

Then let holy water be sprinkled over the ring. If, however, the ring

---

33. "V." (versicle) indicates the priest's part; "R." is the congregation's spoken response.
34. The crucifix symbol indicates that the priest makes the sign of the cross at this point.

shall have been previously blessed, then immediately after the man has placed the ring upon the book, the priest shall take up the ring, and deliver it to the man. The man shall take it in his right hand with his three principal fingers, holding the right hand of the bride with his left hand, and shall say, after the priest,

"With this ring I thee wed, and this gold and silver I thee give: and with my body I thee worship, and with all my worldly chattels I thee honor."

Then shall the bridegroom place the ring upon the thumb of the bride, saying, "In the name of the Father"; then upon the second finger, saying, "and of the Son"; then upon the third finger, saying, "and of the Holy Ghost"; then upon the fourth finger, saying, "Amen," and there let him leave it, . . . because in that finger there is a certain vein, which runs from thence as far as the heart; and inward affection, which ought always to be fresh between them, is signified by the true ring of the silver. Then, while they bow their heads, the priest shall pronounce a blessing upon them. [A blessing, a Psalm, the Gloria, the Kyrie, a litany and two more blessings are said at this point.]

Here they shall all go into the church, as far as the step of the altar; and the priest, together with his ministers, shall say, as they are going, the Psalm "Blessed are all they etc." . . .

Then the bridegroom and bride kneeling before the step of the altar, the priest shall ask the bystanders to pray for them . . . [A litany, or responsive prayer, is then said.]

"Let us pray. The Lord bless you out of Sion, that ye may behold Jerusalem in prosperity all the days of your life, and that ye may see your children's children, and peace upon Israel. . . .

"Let us pray. O God of Abraham, God of Isaac, and God of Jacob, bless these young persons, and sow the seed of eternal life in their hearts, that whatsoever they shall profitably learn, they may indeed fulfil the same. Through Jesus Christ thy Son, the restorer of mankind. Who with thee etc." R. Amen.

"Let us pray. Look down, O Lord, from heaven, and bless † this compact; and as thou sentest thy holy angel Raphael to Tobias, and to Sarah, the daughter of Raguel; so vouchsafe, O Lord, to send thy blessing † upon these young persons; that they abiding in thy will, and continuing under thy protection, may both live, and grow, and grow old in thy love; that they may be both worthy and peaceful, and that the length of their days may be multiplied. . . .

"Look down, O Lord, mercifully upon this thy servant and upon thy handmaid; that in thy name they may receive heavenly blessing

✝, and that they may see the sons of their sons and daughters, to the third and fourth generation, in safety, and that they may ever remain stedfast in thy will, and hereafter attain to the kingdom of heaven. . . .

"The almighty and merciful God, who by his power did create our first parents Adam and Eve, and did knit them together by his own sanctification, himself sanctify and bless your souls and bodies, and join you together in the union and love of true affection. Through etc."

Then he shall bless them, saying thus:

"God almighty bless ✝ you with all heavenly blessing, and make you worthy in his sight; pour upon you the riches of his grace, and teach you with the word of truth, that ye may be able to please him both in body and soul." R. Amen.

These prayers being finished, they shall be brought into the presbytery, that is to say, between the quire and the altar, on the south side of the church, and the woman being placed on the right hand side of the man, that is to say, between him and the altar, there shall be begun the Mass of the Trinity. . . . [The preliminary portions of the Mass are said.]

"Accede, O Lord, to our supplications, and be pleased mercifully to accept this oblation, which we offer unto thee on behalf of thy servants whom thou has vouchsafed to bring to mature life, and to the day of their espousals."

. . . After the Sanctus the bridegroom and bride shall prostrate themselves in prayer at the step of the altar, a pall being extended over them, which four clerks in surplices shall hold at the four corners, unless one or both shall have been previously married and blessed, because in that case the pall is not held over them, nor is the sacramental blessing given. . . .

"Be favourable, O Lord, unto our supplications, and of thy goodness assist the ordinances whereby thou hast ordained that mankind should be increased; that they who are joined together by thy authority may be preserved in thy help. . . .

"O God, who by thy mighty power hast made all things out of nothing, who after other things set in order in the world didst create for man, made after thine own image, the inseparable assistance of woman; that out of man's flesh woman should take her beginning, teaching that what thou has been pleased to make one, it should never be lawful to put asunder. . . .

"O God, who hast consecrated the state of matrimony to such an excellent mystery, that in it is signified the sacramental and nuptial union betwixt Christ and Church;

"O God, by whom woman is joined to man, and the union, instituted in the beginning, is gifted with that blessing †, which alone has not been taken away either through the punishment of original sin, or through the sentence of the deluge, look graciously, we beseech thee, on this thy handmaiden, who now to be joined in wedlock, seeketh to be guarded by thy protection. May the yoke of love and peace be upon her; may she be a faithful and chaste wife in Christ, and abide a follower of holy matrons. May she be as amiable to her husband as Rachel, wise as Rebecca, long-lived and faithful as Sara. Let not the father of lies get any advantage over her through her doings; bound to thy faith and thy commandments may she remain united to one man; may she flee all unlawful unions; may she fortify her weakness with the strength of discipline. May she be bashful and grave, reverential and modest, well-instructed in heavenly doctrine. May she be fruitful in child-bearing, innocent and of good report, attaining to a desired old age, seeing her children's children unto the third and fourth generation; and may she attain the rest of the blessed, and to the kingdom of heaven. Through etc." [The remainder of the Mass follows.]

Blessing the Marriage Chamber

On the following night, when the bridegroom and bride have gone to bed, the priest shall approach and bless the bed-chamber, saying:
V. The Lord be with you.
R. And with thy spirit.
"Let us pray. Bless †, O Lord, this chamber and all that dwell therein, that they may be established in thy peace and abide in thy will, and live and grow in thy love, and that the length of their days may be multiplied. Through etc."
Blessing over the bed only.
V. The Lord be with you.
R. And with thy spirit.
"Let us pray. Bless †, O Lord, this sleeping-chamber, who neither slumberest nor sleepest; thou who watchest over Israel watch over these thy servants who rest in this bed, guarding them from all phantasies and illusions of devils, guard them waking that they may meditate upon thy commandments; guard them sleeping that in their slumber they may think of thee; and that here and everywhere they may ever be defended by the help of thy protection. Through etc."
Then shall this blessing be said over them in bed:
"Let us pray. God bless † your bodies and souls; and bestow his

blessing † upon you, as he blessed Abraham, Isaac, and Jacob." R. Amen.

Another blessing over them.

"Let us pray. May the hand of the Lord be over you; and may he send his holy angel, to guard and tend you all the days of your life." R. Amen.

Another blessing over them.

"Let us pray. The Father, and the Son, and the Holy Ghost bless † you, triune in number, and one in name." R. Amen.

This done, the priest shall sprinkle them with holy water, and dismissing them in peace, so depart.

20. The Book of Vices and Virtues: Blessings of Marriage (13th–14th c.)

The following description of marriage comes from a fourteenth-century English version of a thirteenth-century French work. It is a handbook intended for the use of priests when instructing their parishioners in the basics of Christian belief and Christian life. Source: *The Book of Vices and Virtues*, ed. W. Nelson Francis (London: The Early English Text Society, 1942). Spelling and vocabulary modernized.

The third branch [of the tree of chastity] is the state and the bond of marriage, for [husband and wife] should keep themselves for each other, cleanly and truly, without any wrongdoing by the one to the other; and the law of marriage asks that the one hold truth and faith of his body to the other. For after they are knit together in the flesh, they are all one body and one soul, as Holy Writ says, and therefore should each of them love the other as himself. For as they are one body, they should be of one heart by true love, and nevermore depart in heart nor in body while they live; wherefore they should keep their bodies cleanly and chastely, without their own harm, and therefore Saint Paul says that women should love their husbands and honor them, and keep themselves chaste and sober: chaste, to keep their bodies from all others than their lords; sober in eating and drinking, for of too much eating and drinking comes much quickening of the fire of lechery.

And also should men keep their bodies chaste, that they not give anything to another woman than their own.

Marriage is a state that men should well cleanly and holily keep for many reasons. For it is a state of great authority. God set it and made it in Paradise on earth in the state of innocence, before ever any man did sin. And . . . it is a sacrament of holy church and betokens the marriage that is between Jesus Christ and holy church, and between God and the soul, wherefore the state of marriage is so holy and so honest that the deed that was previously deadly sin outside of marriage is without sin in marriage, and not only without sin, but in many cases greatly approved by God [as a means] to win the life without end, and it is well to know that in three ways you may do the deed of wedlock without sin and have great merit to the soul.

The first is when men do that deed in hope to have children to serve with God, and with such meaning was first marriage made and ordained principally.

The second case is when the one yields to the other his debt when it is asked . . . ; wherefore if the one refuses the other and will not allow [him or her] to have his [or her] right when it is asked or prayed, whether by mouth, or by sign, as many women do that are shamefaced to ask such things, he or she that refuses the other that bids, is sinning. For he [or she] does him or her wrong of thing that is his by right, for that one has a right in that other's body. But he that yields that which he owes does well and rightfully when he does it with that intent, and deserves approval from God, for righteousness drives him thereto and not lechery.

The third case is when a man bids of his wife such thing to keep her from sin, and namely when he sees that she is so full of shame that she would never bid her lord of such a thing, and therefore dreads that she might fall lightly in sin unless he bed her thereof. Whoso prays in that intent and yields his debt, he does not sin, but deserves great approval from God, for compassion moves him to do that.

21. Holy Maidenhood:
A Debate on Marriage (13th c.)

Holy Maidenhood is a treatise on virginity; its purpose is to convince young women to become nuns, dedicating themselves to chastity for religious purposes. The author clearly shares the views of St. Jerome on the desirability of celibacy. But he is not above using other arguments to persuade his female audience against marriage. While the goal is to portray married life in as negative a light as possible, arguments in favor of marriage are quoted so that they can be refuted, and this is also an interesting piece of writing for its emphasis on the physical as well as spiritual welfare of women. This version is a modern paraphrase of the original Middle English.

Source: Adapted from *Hali Meidenhad: An Alliterative Homily of the Thirteenth Century*, ed. F. J. Furnivall (Early English Text Society, 1922; repr. New York: Greenwood Press, 1969).

But observe more exactly, as we before told thee, what the wedded suffer. . . . Now thou art wedded, and from so high estate alighted so low: . . . into the filth of the flesh, into the manner of a beast, into the thraldom of a man, and into the sorrows of the world. See now, what fruit it has, and for what purpose it chiefly is: All for that, or partly for that, be now well assured, to cool thy lust with filth of the body, to have delight of thy fleshly will from man's intercourse: before God, it is a nauseous thing to think thereon, and to speak thereof is yet more nauseous. . . .

"Nay," thou wilt say, "as for that filth, it is nought; but a man's vigour is worth much, and I need his help for maintenance and food; of a woman's and man's copulation, worldly welfare arises, and a progeny of fair children, that give much joy to their parents." Now thus hast thou said, and thinkest that thou sayest the truth. But I will show you that this is all made smooth with falsehood. But first of all, now, whatsoever welfare or joy come out of it, it is too expensively bought, for which thou soilest thyself, and surrenderest thine own dear body to be given up to ill usage, and dealt with so shamefully, with so irrecoverable a loss as the grace of maidenhood is . . . .

Thou sayest that a wife hath much comfort of her husband, when they are well consorted, and each is well content with the other. Yea. But 'tis rarely seen on earth. But suppose it is so: wherein is their comfort and delight for the most part, but in the filth of the flesh or worldly vanity, which turns all to sorrow and care in the end? Not only in the end, but ever and anon; for many things shall anger and vex them, and make them worry, and sorrow and sigh for each other's ills. Many things shall separate and divide them, which annoy loving persons: and the dint of death at the end sever one from another. So it cannot but be that that vigour must end in misery; and the greater their satisfaction together was, the sorer is the sorrow at parting. . . .

Thus, woman, if thou hast a husband, . . . yet shall need happen to thee. And what if things be lacking to thee, so that thou have neither thy will with him, nor prosperity either, and must groan without goods within waste walls, and in want of bread must breed thy offspring; and still further, lie under the most hateful man, who, though thou hadst all wealth, will turn it to sorrow; for, suppose now, that riches were rife with thee, and thy wide walls were proud and well supplied, and suppose that thou hadst many under thee, domestics in thy hall, and thy husband were angry with thee, and should become hateful to thee, so that each of you two shall be exasperated against the other; what worldly good can be joy to thee? When he is out, thou shalt await his homecoming with all sorrow, care, and dread. While he is at home, all thy wide dwellings seem too narrow for thee; his looking on thee makes thee aghast; his loathsome mirth and his rude behaviour fill thee with horror. He chideth and jaweth thee, as a lecher does his whore; he beateth thee and mauleth thee as his bought thrall and patrimonial slave. Thy bones ache, and thy flesh smarteth, thy heart within thee swelleth of sore rage, and thy face outwardly burneth with vexation. What shall be the copulation between you in bed? But those who best love one another often quarrel there, though they make no show thereof in the morning; and often from many a slight, though they love each other ever so much, they each bitterly grieve by themselves. She, much against her will, must suffer his will, often with great misery, though she loves him well. All his foulnesses and his indecent playings,—be they even accompanied with filthiness, especially in bed—she shall, whether she wishes to or not, suffer them all. May Christ shield every maiden from inquiring or wishing to know what these be! for they that try them most, find them most odious . . .

Look around, happy maiden, if the knot of wedlock be once knotted, let the man be an idiot or a cripple, be he whatever he may, thou must keep to him. If thou art fair, and with good cheer fairly salutest all, in no wise shalt thou protect thyself against slander and evil blame. If thou art of no great esteem and ill-tempered, thou mayest, both to others and to thy husband, become of still less esteem. If thou become of small esteem to him, and he of as little to thee, or if thou love him much and he regards thee little, it will grieve thee so strongly that, quick enough, thou wilt, as many cursed women have done, make poison, and give evil in place of remedy. Or whosoever will not act so, may deal with witches, and, to draw his love towards her, forsake Christ and her Christianity, and true faith.

. . . If she cannot breed, she is called barren. Her lord loveth and respects her less; and she, as one that is very bad, weepeth at her fate, and calleth them glad and happy that breed a family.

But now suppose it all happen that she have her wish of offspring, as she pleases, and then let us see what amount of joy arises therefrom.

In begetting thereof, is her flesh first torn with foulness. . . . In the gestation, is heaviness and hard pain every hour; in the actual birth is the strongest of all pangs, and occasional death; in the nourishing the child, many a miserable moment. As soon as it appears in this life, it bringeth with it more care than joy, specially to its mother; for if it is a misshapen birth, as often happens, and if it lacks any of its limbs, or if it somewhat be amiss, it is a sorrow to her, and a shame to all its kindred, a reproach in an evil mouth, a talk among all men. If it is wellshapen and seemeth likely to live, a fear of the loss of it is instantly born along with it; for she is never without fear lest it go wrong, till one or other of the two lose the other. And often it occurs that that child most loved, and most bitterly purchased, most sorrows and disturbs its parents at last. Now what joy hath the mother? She hath, from the misshapen child, sad care and shame, both; and for the thriving one, fear, till she lose it for good. . . .

Now let us proceed! Consider we what joy ariseth afterwards from gestation of children, when the offspring in thee quickeneth and groweth. How many miseries immediately wake up therewith, that work thee woe enough, fight against thine own flesh, and with many sorrows make war upon thine own nature. Thy ruddy face shall turn lean, and grow green as grass. Thine eyes shall be dusky, and underneath grow pale; and by the giddiness of thy brain thy head shall ache sorely. Within thy belly, the uterus shall swell and strut out like a water bag; thy bowels shall have pains, and there shall be stitches in thy flank, and pain rife in thy loins, heaviness in every limb. The burden of thy breast on thy two paps, and the streams of milk which trickle out of thee. All thy beauty is overthrown with a withering. Thy mouth is bitter, and nauseous is all that thou chewest, and whatever thy stomach disdainfully receives, with lack of appetite, it throws up again. With all thy pleasure, and thy husband's joy, thou art perishing. Ah, wretch! the anxiety about the throes of thy torment depriveth thee of the night's sleep. When it cometh to that at last, there is the sore sorrowful anguish, the strong piercing pang, the comfortless ill, the pain upon pain, the wandering lamentation. While thou art in trouble therewith, in thy fear of death, shame there is in addition to that sorrow, at all the old wives' indelicate skill, who are skilled in that time of woe, and whose help thou must have, no matter how unbecoming. . . . [W]e reproach not women with their sufferings, which the mothers of us all endured at our own births; but we exhibit them to warn maidens, that they be the less inclined to such things. . . .

After all this, there cometh from the child thus born, a crying and a weeping, that must about midnight make thee to waken, or her that holds thy place, for whom thou must care. And what of the cradle foulness and the constant giving of the breast? to swaddle and feed the child for so many unhappy moments. And consider his late growing up, and his slow thriving; and that thou must ever have an anxiety in looking for the time when the child will perish, and bring on his mother sorrow upon sorrow. Though thou be rich, and have a nurse, thou must, as a mother, care for all that to the nurse belongeth to be done. . . .

Little knoweth a maiden of all this same trouble of wives' woe, in her relation to her husband; nor of their work so nauseous that they in common work; nor of the pain, nor of the sorrow and the filth in the bearing and birth of a child; nor of a nurse's watches, nor of her sad trials in the child's fostering: how much she must at once put into its mouth, neither too much nor too little; though these things be unworthy to be spoken of, yet they show all the more in what slavery wives be, that must endure the like, and in what freedom maidens be, that are free from them all. And what if I ask besides, though it may seem silly, how the wife stands, that heareth, when she cometh in, her child scream, sees the cat at the meat, and the hound at the hide? Her cake is burning on the stone and her calf is sucking all the milk up, the pot is running into the fire, and the churl is scolding. Though it be a silly tale, it ought, maiden, to deter thee more strongly from marriage, for it seems not silly to her that trieth it. . . .

C. Health and Safety

22. Simeon of Durham: Accounts of Warfare (11th c.)

Medieval chronicles are full of accounts of warfare—descriptions of great battles and sieges, treaties and diplomacy, and the rise and fall of generals and kings. Relatively little of this written material describes the effects of war on noncombatants, including women, but the common people suffered a great deal from the movement of armies, the recruitment of troops, the sacking of cities and the devastation of the countryside, all of which were common activities during wartime. Even when the side effects of warfare are described, as in the following excerpts, the sufferings of the people are not the real point of the work, and the descriptions are much influenced by literary conventions. Still, such set pieces do remind us of the prevalence of warfare in this age. The writer is a monk living in northern England in the early twelfth century.

Source: Simeon of Durham, tr. J. Stevenson in *The Church Historians of England* (1858).

At last, between the Nativity of St. Mary [8 Sept. 1011] and the feast of St. Michael [29 Sept.], surrounding Canterbury, [the Danes] besieged it. And on the twentieth day of the siege, through the treachery of Almer the archdeacon, . . . part of the city was burnt, the army entered, and took the town. Some were killed with the sword, some perished in the flames, many were thrown headlong from the walls, and some died, being suspended by the privy members. Matrons dragged by the hair through the streets of the city, at last were thrown into the flames and perished. Infants torn from the mother's breast were carried on pikes, or crushed to pieces by a wagon driven over them. Meanwhile the archbishop Alfege was taken, bound, imprisoned, and tormented in various ways. . . . There were taken Godwin, bishop of Rochester, Leofruna, abbess of the monastery of St. Mildryth, Elfred, the king's steward; also monks and clerics, and innumerable people of both sexes. Then Christ Church was plundered and burnt; the band of monks and the entire population, as well men as women and children, was decimated. Nine were put to death, the tenth was kept alive. Of these tenths the number consisted of four monks and eight hundred men. . . .

A.D. 1013. . . . Suane, king of the Danes . . . made an expedition against the southern Mercians; and crossing Watling-street, issued his orders that they should devastate the land, burn the towns, plunder the churches, put to death (regardless of pity) all of the male sex who might fall into their hands, preserve the females for the gratification of their lust, and perpetrate all the evil they could. . . .

A.D. 1069. . . . In consequence of the Normans having plundered England . . . so great a famine prevailed that men, compelled by hunger, devoured human flesh, that of horses, dogs, and cats, whatever custom abhors; others sold themselves to perpetual slavery, so that they might in a way preserve their wretched existence; others, while about to go into exile from their country, fell down in the middle of their journey and gave up the ghost. It was horrific to behold human corpses decaying in the houses, the streets, and the roads, swarming with worms, while they were consuming in corruption with an abominable stench. For no one was left to bury them in the earth, all being cut off either by the sword or by famine, or having left the country on account of the famine. Meanwhile, the land being thus deprived of any one to cultivate it for nine years, an extensive solitude prevailed all around. There was no village inhabited between York and Durham; they became lurking places to wild beasts and robbers, and were a great dread to travellers. . . .

A.D. 1070. . . . [King Malcolm of Scotland] ordered his troops no longer to spare any of the English nation, but either to smite all to the earth, or to carry them off captives under the yoke of perpetual slavery. Having received this licence, it was misery even to witness their deeds against the English. Some aged men and women were beheaded with the sword; others were thrust through with pikes, like swine destined for food; infants snatched from their mother's breasts were thrown high into the air, and in their fall were received on the points of lances and pikes thickly placed in the ground. The Scots, more savage than wild beasts, delighted in this cruelty, as an amusing spectacle. These children of the age of innocence, suspended between heaven and earth, gave up their souls to heaven. Young men also and maidens, and whoever seemed fit to toil and labour, were bound and driven before the face of their enemies, to be reduced in perpetual exile to slaves and bondmaids. Some of these females, worn out by running in front of their drivers further than their strength would bear, falling to the earth, perished even where they fell.

Seeing these things, Malcolm was not yet moved to pity by tears, nor groans of the unhappy wretches; but, on the contrary, gave orders that they should be still further pressed onward in the march. Scotland was, therefore, filled with slaves and handmaids of the English race; so that even to this day, I do not say no little village, but even no cottage, can be found without one of them.

23. Liturgy for Mothers (11th–16th c.)

These extracts come from the liturgy for two short church services, one a Mass on behalf of pregnant women and those in labor, and the other for the "churching" of women—the blessing of women who have recently given birth and are attending church for the first time after the delivery.
Source: *The Sarum Missal in English*, tr. Frederick E. Warren (London: Alexander Moring Ltd., 1911).

Prayers for Women Pregnant and in Labor

Kind virgin of virgins, holy mother of God, present on behalf of thy devoted handmaidens their earnest prayers to the Son, thou that art the benign assister of women in travail. . . .

Hearken, O most merciful Father, to the entreaty of thy servant on behalf of thy poor handmaidens who are now, or who shall be hereafter, in labour; most humbly entreating thy majesty, that as by thy providence thou hast ordered that they do conceive, so by thy blessing thou wouldest go before them, and bring matters to a speedy and successful issue, to the honour of thy holy name, through the intercession of the glorious virgin. . . .

Poor women, labouring with child, flee to thy succour, O Mary; whom I entreat thee that thou despise not in the hour of their necessity, but deliver them from all dangers, virgin ever blessed. . . .

Hail, Mary, consoler of women in labour, full of grace, helper of infants; because the Lord is with thee, be their protector; that thou mayest be blessed above women, and that the fruit of thy womb may be extolled by all Christians as blessed above all. . . .

Blessing of a Woman after Childbirth

[The service begins outside the church.]
[Priest:] "O God, who hast delivered this woman thy servant from the peril of childbirth, and hast made her to be devoted to thy service; grant that when the course of this life hath been faithfully finished,

she may obtain eternal life, and rest under the wings of thy mercy.
. . ."

Then shall the woman be sprinkled with holy water by the priest,
saying, "Thou shalt purge me, O Lord, with hyssop."

Then shall the the priest lead her by the right hand into the church,
saying, "Enter into the temple of God, that thou mayest have eternal
life, and live for ever and ever."

24. Trotula of Salerno:
The Diseases of Women (11th–13th c.)

Trotula probably practiced medicine in the Italian city of Salerno
sometime between the mid-eleventh and the early thirteenth century. She was unusual in being a female writer about medicine,
but not unusual in being a female practitioner; much of the health
care of women, particularly in gynecological matters, was provided by midwives and other women. Salerno was famous for its
medical school, with a faculty of learned men, and many historians
have doubted whether Trotula really existed, arguing that the
works attributed to her were more likely written by male aca-
demics.

Source: Trotula of Salerno, *The Diseases of Women*, tr. Elizabeth
Mason-Hohl (The Ward-Ritchie Press, 1940).

Gynecology and Obstetrics

Prologue

Since God, the author of the universe, in the first establishment of
the world, distinguished the individual natures of things each according to its own kind, He differentiated the human race above the
other creatures by means of extraordinary dignity. To it, beyond the
condition of other animals, He gave freedom of reason and of intellect.
Moreover, desiring its generation to subsist perpetually, He created
it male and female in different sexes that by means of their fertile
propagation future offspring may never cease to come forth. Blending
their embraces with a pleasing mixture, He made the nature of the
male hot and dry and that of the female cold and wet so that the excess
of each other's embrace might be restrained by the mutual opposition

of contrary qualities.[35] The man's constitution being hot and dry might assuage the woman's coldness and wetness and on the contrary her nature being cold and wet might soothe his hot and dry embrace. Likewise that the male having the stronger quality might pour seed into the woman as into a field and the woman endowed with a weaker quality, subject as it were to the function of the man, might naturally take unto her bosom the poured out seed. Since then women are by nature weaker than men it is reasonable that sicknesses more often abound in them especially around the organs involved in the work of nature. Since these organs happen to be in a retired location, women on account of modesty and the fragility and delicacy of the state of these parts dare not reveal the difficulties of their sicknesses to a male doctor. Wherefore I, pitying their misfortunes and at the instigation of a certain matron, began to study carefully the sicknesses which most frequently trouble the female sex. Since in women not so much heat abounds that it suffices to use up the moistures which daily collect in them, their weaknesses cannot endure so much exertion as to be able to put forth that moisture to the outside air as in the case of men. Nature herself, on account of this deficiency of heat, has assigned for them a certain specific purgation namely the menses, commonly called flowers. . . . Now a purgation of this sort usually befalls women about the 13th or 14th year or a little earlier or later according to whether heat or cold abounds in them more. It lasts up to about the 50th year if she is lean; sometimes up to the 60th or 65th if she is moist; in the moderately fat up to about the 45th. If such purgations have been of normal time and regularity, Nature sufficiently unloads women of superfluous moisture. If the menstruation has taken place too copiously various sicknesses arise from it. The appetite for food and drink is diminished, sometimes vomiting occurs, and often they have an appetite for earth, coals, chalk, and the like. At times from the same cause they feel pain around the neck, the back, and around the head. There may be acute fever, sharp pains in the heart, dropsy, and dysentery. These conditions appear either because the menstrual periods are missing for a long time or because they do not have them at all. For this latter reason not only dropsy, dysentery, and heart attacks but also other more serious illnesses occur. . . . Sometimes a woman's periods are lacking because the blood is clotted in the body or it is emitted through other parts as through the mouth in the spit, through the nostrils, or through hemorrhoids. Sometimes the periods fail be-

---

35. This explanation of the nature of the human body had originated with the ancient Greeks and was a basic component of medieval medical theory.

cause of excessive grief or anger or excitement or fear. If they have ceased for a long time there is a suspicion of serious future illness. Often the urine is changed into a red color or into a color like the washings from fresh meat; sometimes the woman's appearance is changed into a gray or leaden color, or into the color of grass.

Chapter II. Concerning scantiness of menses

There are women who, when they come to the time of the menses, have none or a very slight amount. These patients we help in this way: take the red roots of willow, the kind of which baskets are woven and crush them after cleaning them well of their outer bark. When crushed blend them by cooking with wine or water and the next day give a warm draught of the decoction for drinking. If she is suffering very severely you will give her food prepared in the following way: grate a rather large carrot and a mallow, mix with barley flour and whites of eggs, and of all this make small curls or noodles. . . . If women have scanty menses and emit them with pain, take one dram[36] each of betonica, pennyroyal, centonica, and wormwood; let them be cooked down to one-half in wine or water. Strain this through a cloth and let it be drunk steaming hot. If the menses have been absent for a long time, make a powder of two drams of rhubarb and one dram each of wormwood and pepper; let her take this morning and evening for three days and let her cover herself so that she sweats. Also take one dram each of mint, pennyroyal, and rue, four drams of grain salt, five drams of red caulis, and three heads of leek. Cook all of these together in a clean pot and let her drink it in her bath. . . . Also take tansy, clover, and wormwood cooked with butter and place over the navel. A certain doctor in the region of Francia did this: he took leaves of laurel and ginger and ground them together in a clean pot; he put this mixture over live coals under a perforated seat and over this he let the woman sit. She took in the smoke from below and thus made the menses begin. It may be necessary to do this thrice or more times. However let the woman who habitually practices fumigations of this sort anoint her vulva inside with cold ointments lest she be irritated. For the aforementioned fumigation the following are also efficacious: ciminum, fennel, dill, calmento, mint, and nettle either all mixed together or one alone. For bringing on the menses massage is helpful,

---

36. Dram = a small unit of measurement, equal today to one-eighth of an ounce.

and likewise coitus. However, bloodletting[37] is injurious. Let her eat, if she be without fever, leeks, onions, pepper, garlic, ciminum, and scaly fish. Let her drink strong wine, if she be without pain in the head and without weakness of muscles and without fever, because in all fever wine is injurious.

Chapter III. On excessive flow of menses

There are also other women the opposite to those mentioned, who have extraordinarily copious periods. These you may help in the following ways: Either pulverize old leather and cook it with leaves of laurel to make a suffumigation or take hot ashes mixed with red wine and blended together to form a soft paste. Make it into a small wedge, wrap it in a new linen cloth and insert it in the vagina while it is still hot. Or take sage and camphor, grind vigorously, make little curls of wine, cook over a hot brick and give it to the patient for the purpose of curbing the menses. Or make a powder of the seeds of nettle and the horn of a stag and give it with wine to the patient as a drink. Another remedy which restricts menses is made in this way: Take a stag's horn pulverized with the ashes of dried nettle, blend with rain water and give it to her to drink, not omitting the aforementioned fumigation because this comforts cold wombs. . . .

Chapter VIIII. On ulcers of the womb

Sometimes the womb is ulcerated by strong medicines or by instruments. This is recognized from its beginning through a discharge coming out, by pain, and by puncture of the womb. If there are sores from the discharge or from corrosion of veins the discharge tends somewhat towards blackness with a horrible fetid odor. Cleansing agents ought to be applied first to the discharging area and things given to alleviate pain such as the juice of mulberry and plantain with oil of roses, white of egg with woman's milk, and with juice of parsley or lettuce all of which are of a cold nature. Let the diet be cold. Bathe the woman in water wherein has been cooked roses, myrtles, chick peas, psyllia, lentils, oak-galls, wild pomegranate blossoms, and the like. If the veins have become rotted, let snake's blood be given or myrrh, mushroom, incense, or long birthwort. Of these separately or

---

37. Bloodletting, or bleeding, was believed to remove unhealthy substances and "humors" from the body, and was a common medical practice into the nineteenth century.

all together make a clyster or pessary. No less is acacia helpful injected with flax as a suppository.

Chapter XI. On the hindrances to conception . . .

. . . "Note," says Galen,[38] "that women who have narrow vulvas and tight wombs ought not to have husbands lest they die if they conceive." But since they cannot all abstain they need our help. If one of them for fear of death dare not conceive[39] let her carry on her naked flesh the womb of a she-goat which has never had offspring. A certain stone is found called Galgates which, worn on the neck or even tasted, prevents conception. Also remove the testicles from a weasel and let it be left alive. Let the woman carry these testicles with her on her bosom tied in the skin of a goose or in some other skin and she will not conceive. If she has been injured in childbirth and for fear of death does not wish to conceive again, let her lay on the last afterbirth as many grains of cataputia or of barley as the years which she desires to remain sterile. If she wishes to remain barren forever let her lay on a handful.

Chapter XV. On regulations for pregnant women

When a woman is first pregnant care must be taken that nothing be named in her presence which cannot be had because if she shall ask for it and it not be given to her she has occasion for miscarrying. But if she should seek to have potter's earth or chalk or coals, let beans cooked with sugar be given to her. When the time for parturition is imminent the woman should be bathed often; anoint her abdomen with olive oil or oil of violets and let her eat light and digestible foods. If her feet have swollen, let them be anointed with oil of roses and with vinegar. Instead of heavy foods let her eat quickly digested things like citrons and pomegranates. If her abdomen is distended with flatulence take three drams each of parsley seed, *amoes*, mint, mastic, *garyophyllons*, cardamon, roots of carrots, coffee, *galangale*, iris, and five drams of sugar; make a very fine powder and cook it all with honey; give three scruples[40] to her with wine for this substance removes flatulence and prevents abortion if properly taken.

---

38. Galen, a second-century Greek physician, was revered as a medical authority.
39. In the eyes of the medieval church, the use of contraception was a sin; therefore Trotula is careful to explain the circumstances in which it might perhaps be excused.
40. Scruple = one-third of a dram.

Chapter XVI. On the regulations for the woman about to give birth

When the time for giving birth is imminent, let the woman prepare herself as the custom is, and the midwife likewise. Let sneezing be done with great caution, holding tightly the nostrils and the mouth, in order that the greatest part of the strength and spirits may tend toward the womb. . . . Above all things let her guard herself from cold. Let an aromatic fumigation be made below the nostrils; it can also safely be applied at the mouth of the womb because then a fragrant womb follows and an ill smelling one is avoided. For this purpose fragrant kinds of substances avail as musk, amber, wood of aloe and the like for rich patients, and fragrant herbs as mint, pennyroyal, calamentum, wild marjoram and the like for the poor. It is to be noted that there are certain physical remedies whose virtues are obscure to us, but which are advanced as done by midwives. They let the patient hold a magnet in her right hand and find it helpful. Likewise they let her drink a powder of ivory or they find that coral suspended on the neck is helpful. In similar fashion that white substance which is found in the dung of an eagle, when given in drinks is advantageous. Likewise give the dung of baby birds which is found in the swallow's nest. Washings of this are serviceable for this and for many other purposes.

Chapter XVII. On difficulty of parturition

There are, however, certain women so narrow in the function of childbearing that scarcely ever or never do they succeed. This is wont to happen for various reasons. Sometimes external heat comes up around the internal organs and they are straightened in the act of giving birth. Sometimes the exit from the womb is too small, the woman is too fat, or the foetus is dead, not helping nature by its own movements. This often happens to a woman giving birth in winter. If she has by nature a tight opening of the womb, the coldness of the season constricts the womb still more. Sometimes the heat all goes out of the woman herself and she is left without strength to help herself in childbearing.

In the first place and above all things when there is difficulty in childbirth one must have recourse in God. Descending then to lower means, it is helpful to the woman in difficult labor to be bathed in water in which has been cooked mallow, chick peas, flaxseed, and barley. Let her sides, abdomen, hips, and flanks be rubbed with oil of roses or oil of violets. Let her be rubbed vigorously and let vinegar and sugar be given her as a drink, and powdered mint and a dram of absinth. Let sneezing be provoked by placing dust of incense in the nostrils, or powder of candisium, or pepper or euphorbia. Let the woman be led with slow pace through the house. Do not let those who are present look in her face because women are wont to be bashful in childbearing and after the birth. If the child does not come forth in the order in which it should, that is, if the legs or arms should come out first, let the midwife with her small and gentle hand moistened with a decoction of flaxseed and chick peas, put the child back in its place in the proper position. If the child be dead take rue, mugwort, absinth, and black pepper and give this pulverized in wine or in water in which lupins have been cooked. Or let savory be mashed and bound over the abdomen and the foetus, whether dead or alive, will come forth. . . . Also those who are in difficult labor must be aided in the following manner: Let a bath be prepared and the woman put in it; after she has come out let a fumigation be made of wheat and similar aromatics for comforting and relaxing. Let sneezes be produced with white hellebore well reduced to powder. Colphon[41] says to let the limbs be shaken to break the bag of water and in this way the foetus will come forth. Thus also those may be aided who are laboring much to bring forth a dead foetus: Let the patient be placed in a linen cloth stretched by four men at the four corners with the patient's head somewhat elevated. Let the four corners be strongly drawn this way and that by the opposite corners and she will give birth immediately, God favoring her. If the afterbirth has remained within there is need of haste that it shall come out. Let sneezing be provoked with mouth and nostrils shut. Or take lye made from ash tree ashes and mix it with one dram of powdered mallow seed. Give this to the woman to drink and she will immediately vomit. Or give mallow seed powder alone in a drink of hot water and if she vomits it will be a good thing. Also let her be fumigated below with bones of salted fish or with horses hoofs, or with the dung of a cat or lamb. These things bring out the afterbirth. Also let those things be done which have been mentioned before for bringing forth menstruation. If difficulty in child-birth should result from tightness of the mouth of the womb, the cure of this is more difficult than anything else therefore we subjoin this advice: let the woman take care the last three months in her diet that she so use light and digestible foods that through them the limbs may be opened. Such foods are egg yolks, the meat and juice of chickens and small birds—partridges and pheasants, and scaly fish of good

---

41. Colphon = another medical authority.

flavor. Let her often take a bath in fresh water to which has been added herbs of softening character such as matura and the like. Let her avoid a bath tinctured with copper and calcium. When she comes out of the bath, let her be anointed with hot ointment such as oil of laurel, oil of flaxseed, or the grease of goose, duck, or hen. Let this anointing be done from the navel down.

Chapter XVIIII. On the choice of a wet nurse[42]

The nurse ought to be young and have a pink and white complexion. Let her be not too near to prospective parturition nor too far removed from preceding parturition. Let her not be dirty. She should have neither weak nor too heavy teats, but breasts full and generous, and she should be moderately fat. Let her not eat salt, sharp, acid or styptic things—leeks, onions, nor the other kinds of things that are mixed with foodstuffs such as pepper, garlic and colewort. Especially have her avoid garlic. Let her beware of anxiety and guard herself during menstruation. If the milk is diminished, let pap be made of bean flour or rice flour and a bread containing milk and sugar be given to her to eat. The milk will be increased if a decoction of the seeds of fennel be drunk. If however the milk becomes thick, the nurse's nourishment will have to be made lighter. Compel her to exercise and she should be given vinegar syrup and light wines. If the milk becomes too thin let her nourishment be thick and substantial and have her rest more. If the child's bowels be loose, let foods which cause constipation be given to the nurse.

General Health Care

Chapter XLIIII. On lice

For lice originating in the armpits and in the pubic hair, we mix ashes with oil and anoint these parts. For general lice around the eyes and head we make this ointment sufficiently strong for expelling them: Take aloes one ounce, white lead five ounces, olibanum, and bacon with grease—the bacon finely divided. Pulverize the other ingredients and make an ointment with the grease.

---

42. Wet nurse = woman hired to breast-feed another woman's child.

Chapter LII. On foulness of the breath

For foulness of the breath owing to a fault of the stomach, let tops of myrtle be grated and cooked in wine until reduced to one half. Let this wine be drunk on an empty stomach.

Chapter LIIII. On worms of the hands and feet

For ejecting worms from the hands and feet, that condition which is called *sirones*, take a heated brick and a vessel of water. Place seed of henbane upon the hot brick and have the patient hold his feet over the steam and you will see the worms like hairs falling into the water. Also for this condition take oat straw and burn it to ashes. Pour water over the hot ashes and have the patient hold his feet in this until it becomes cold. Then strain off the water and if you look through the ashes you will find worms like threads which have been drawn out by the steam of the henbane. Worms of the hands will fall by the same treatment. Note that if a place has been gnawed by worms, take straw and burn it to ashes; put the ashes into very hot water and let the patient immerse the parts in this hot solution and the worms will come out. Afterwards dress the wound as you would any other sore.

Chapter LV. For deafness of the ears

For deafness take the cooked fat of fresh eels, juice of caprifolium, juice of Jove's beard, and a handful of ant's eggs. Grind, strain, and mix them with oil and cook. After cooking add vinegar or wine in sufficient quantity to make it more penetrating. Pour it into the sound ear and stop up the defective ear, letting [the patient] lie partly on the sound ear. In the morning he must be careful of drafts. For some time let him lie on the sound ear and then on the defective ear.

Chapter LVI. On the tonsils

Mugwort grated, heated, and placed over tonsils, dissolves them. Also this ingredient mixed with wine and cooked in honey and placed over the face and neck modifies, ripens, and diminishes the tonsils.

Chapter LVIII. On toothache

For toothache and for comforting the mouth after extractions take two drams of sal ammoniac, fourteen drams of costrum, four drams of pepper, and two drams of green leaves. Mix thus: put sal ammoniac into a pot and burn until charred; when it is cold mix it with spices.

Reduce it all to a very fine powder, and with it rub the teeth and the ulcerated areas. Pimpinella or its juice whitens the teeth very well and its foliage bruised and applied remedies a tumor of the gums.

Chapter LX. On roughness of the hands

For healing roughness of the hands take sour sorrel and smoke of earth mixed with pork grease and butter made in May to make an ointment. Anoint the hands with this.

Cosmetics

Chapter LXI. On adornment and whitening of the face

. . . To make an ointment for whitening the face take two ounces of the best white lead. After it has been ground fine sift it through a cloth, add rain water, and cook it until almost all of the water has boiled off. Chill it and add the rose water. Again boil it until it becomes thick and firm so that minute pills can be formed of it. When you wish the patient to be anointed with it, take a pill and liquify it in the hands with a little water. Rub the face with this allowing it to dry on. Rinse with pure water and it will last eight days.

For reddening the face, take a root of a certain little vine, clean it, cut it up fine, and dry it. Afterwards pulverize, mix it with rose water, and use a very fine linen cloth for applying it to the face. For a woman too white, if she lacks redness, we make a red color. A ruddy color as if natural, may be applied to disguise the appearance of whiteness.

For the wrinkles of the face of an old woman, take a broad leaf of sword plant, extract the juice, and in the morning anoint the face. The next morning the skin will be raised and broken. This we treat with the aforesaid ointment in which the root of a lily is mixed. We cover the skin with powder and after washing it appears fine enough.

For freckles of the skin, which are from accident, take a root of dragonwort reduced to a powder, also bones of cuttlefish and olibanum. After powdering these mix them with water. With this smear the parts by rubbing it in with rose or bran water, or by rubbing the freckles with a crumb of bread until they disappear. Another remedy is to put into very sharp vinegar seven whole eggs and leave them there until the shells soften into the likeness of a thin skin. Mix this with four ounces of powdered mustard and anoint the face frequently.

Likewise for removing red spots from the face, we put blood suckers of various kinds in a reed, the place where the blood suckers are to be suck, being previously washed with wine—that is around the nostrils and the ears on either side. Also we put cupping glasses[43] on the shoulder blades.

25. University of Paris Records: Case of a Woman Physician (1322)

> Most trades and professions were regulated in medieval towns; with the rise in the thirteenth century of university education, from which women were excluded, the medical profession came to be increasingly controlled by medical faculties. The case below documents the clash between a woman who continued to provide health care and the academic community. Jacoba's arguments were eventually rejected by the authorities.
>
> Source: *Chartularium universitatis parisiensis*, eds. H. Denifle and E. Chatelain (Paris: Delalain, 1891). Tr. E.M.A.

The dean and masters who preside over the faculty of medicine of Paris intend to prove the following against the lady Jacoba Felicie, the defendant:

1. That the said Jacoba has visited many sick people suffering from serious illness, in Paris and in the suburbs, often examining their urine both jointly and separately, taking their pulse, and feeling, palpating and holding their bodies and limbs.

2. That, after such examination of urine and such touching, she has said to those sick people, "I shall heal you, God willing, if you have faith in me," making an agreement with them to cure them, and receiving money for this.

3. That, when the agreement had been made between the said defendant and the patients or their friends, for the cure of their internal illness or of the wound or external abcess appearing on the bodies of the said patients, the said defendant often has visited and visits the said patients, constantly and continually examining their urine in the manner of physicians and doctors, taking their pulse, and touching and holding their bodies and limbs.

4. And that, after these touchings and actions, she has given and gives the said patients syrups to drink, pain relievers, laxatives and digestives, both liquid and nonliquid, as well as aromatic, and other

---

43. Cupping glass = a tool used for bloodletting.

potions, which they take and drink by mouth in the presence of the said defendant, who herself ordered and gave them.

5. That, in these actions, she has often exercised and continues to exercise a medical practice in Paris and its suburbs, that she has practiced and practices it from day to day, although she has not been approved in any official school in Paris or elsewhere, and that she does this without the license of the chancellor of the church of Paris and of the said dean and masters.

6. That she does this in violation of the law, by which she was not and has not been approved, and that she was warned by order of the venerable man the official of Paris, under pain of excommunication and sixty Parisian pounds, that henceforth she might not practice in Paris or in the suburbs, as mentioned above, and she is liable to the aforesaid penalties, since she is neither licensed nor approved by the aforesaid chancellor, dean and masters, and since a special warning had even been given to her that she might not from henceforth [practice]. . . .

7. That, ignoring the warning and prohibition that were given her, the said defendant, neither approved nor licensed by the said persons, as mentioned above, has practiced and practices in Paris and in its suburbs, continually visiting the sick and giving them the aforesaid potions and examining their urine, and diagnosing their illnesses, as has been said. . . .

Clemence de Belvaco, a maker of pewter pots, who lives in front of the king's palace, [produced and sworn as a] witness . . . and asked what she knew of the charges, etc., answers on oath that she knew nothing, except that when she herself was suffering a heat sickness and was in the hands of the physicians, her husband had heard Jean de St. Omer say that he and others had been cured by the said Jacoba, with God's help, of the illnesses which they suffered. And then her husband sent for the said Jacoba. When she came, the same Jacoba inspected her urine and took her pulse, saying nothing to her. And when she had done this, the same Jacoba had a certain drink made of many herbs . . . , and when the said drink had been made and [Clemence] had seen it, she did not want to drink from it, because it was so horrible, and her husband and her physicians had kept her, she says, from drinking from that potion. Asked if she knows whether [Jacoba] had visited other sick people in Paris and in the suburbs and whether she herself had been present at those visits, etc., she answers that she knows nothing beyond what she has already said. . . .

Joanna, wife of Denis Bilbaut, living in the street of the ironmongers in Paris, [produced and sworn as a] witness, . . . and asked [what she knew of the charges], etc., answers on oath that when, around the the previous feast of St. Christopher, she was afflicted with a feverish illness, and very many physicians had visited her in this illness, including a certain brother from Cordelis, Master Herman, Mainfred and many others, she was so oppressed with this sickness that on a certain Wednesday around this feast day she could not speak, and the aforesaid physicians consigned her to death. And so it would have been for her, had not the said Jacoba intervened, at her own request to her. When she arrived, she examined her urine and palpated her pulse, and soon she gave her a certain clear water to drink, and she gave her another syrup to cause her to go to the privy. And she worked so well on her that, with God's grace helping, she arose cured of her illness. And she has been asked whether she saw the said Jacoba visit other invalids. She answers that she saw no visits to other sick people besides herself, but she says that she had heard it said that [Jacoba] had cured other invalids, including Jean de St. Omer and many others whom she did not know, in the city of Paris and in villages and suburbs. Asked whether [Jacoba] had visited her for money or for free, she answers that she never paid anything to the said Jacoba for curing her, but she freely offered to give money which the same Jacoba refused to accept. . . .

Joanna de Monciaco, a mercer[44] living in the street called "Quiquempoix," a widow, produced [and sworn] as a witness [and] asked what she knew concerning the charges, etc., answers that she had recently suffered from a certain sickness around her kidneys, for which she had been for eleven days at [the hospital of] St-Sulpice near St-Germain-des-Prés, near Paris, and for which illness the physicians Masters Guilbert, Herman, Mainfred and Thomas sought a cure as best they could, but for which they could do nothing, as she told it. And when she had seen this, and was disturbed by it, she heard tell of the said Jacoba and of her cures, and she immediately sent for her to come to her. When [Jacoba] arrived, she examined her and took her pulse and examined her urine. And immediately when she had done this, she told Joanna that with the grace of God she would put Joanna in a good state. Joanna answered that she wished this. And then Jacoba visited her for many days, and often gave her a certain very clear water to drink, by virtue of which, and with God's help, she was cured, as she says. Asked whether she knows of what the said water was composed, she says she does not know. Asked whether Jacoba

---

44. Mercer = dealer in textiles.

visited her in the manner of physicians, she says she does not know, except as she has already said. Asked whether Jacoba made an agreement with her to cure her and whether Jacoba received money from her for this, she replied that she did not, and that she wished to have nothing. . . .

These are the arguments which the said Jacoba makes and proposes. . . .

. . . Jacoba says that if the said deans and master have issued any statute, decree, warning, prohibition or excommunication, which they now try to use against her, they did so at the time merely because of and against idiots and fatuous ignorant ones, fools totally ignorant of the art of medicine and its precepts and usurping practical office, from whose number the said Jacoba is exempted, being experienced in the art of medicine and learned in the precepts of that art. For which reasons the aforesaid statute, decree, warning, prohibition and excommunication are not and cannot be binding on her. . . .

And [she argues that] the said statute and decree, etc., were made because of and against the aforesaid idiots, fools and usurpers and those who then were in Paris practicing medicine, who now are dead or else so old and decrepit that they cannot exercise the said office, as appears from the tenor of the said statute and decree, etc., which were enacted one hundred and two years ago, and Jacoba was not alive at that time, nor for sixty years afterwards, in the nature of things; rather she is young, inasmuch as she is about thirty years old, as is shown by her appearance. . . .

And [she argues that] it is better and more suitable and proper that a woman wise and experienced in the art should visit sick women, and that she should examine them and inquire into the secrets of nature and its hidden things, than that a man should do so, to whom it is forbidden to see and inquire into the aforesaid things, nor to touch women's hands, breasts, belly and feet, etc.; rather a man ought to avoid and shun the secrets of women and the intimate things associated with them as much as possible. And it used to be that a woman allowed herself to die, rather than reveal her secret illnesses to a man, because of the modesty of the female sex, and because of the shame which she would have suffered in revealing them. And for these reasons many women and even men perished in their illnesses, not wanting to call in doctors, lest they see their private parts. . . .

And supposing, for the sake of argument, that it were bad for a woman to visit, cure and examine, as has been said, etc., nevertheless it is less bad that a wise woman, discreet and experienced in the aforesaid matters, should practice in the aforesaid matters, because the sick of either sex, who have not dared to reveal their private parts to men, do not wish to die. Therefore the laws say that lesser evils should be permitted, so that greater ones may be avoided. And therefore, since the said Jacoba is experienced in the art of medicine, it is better for her to visit, that she might practice medicine, than that the sick should die, especially because she cures and heals everyone in her care, and it ought to be permitted.

And it has been ascertained and so proved, that some sick people of either sex, afflicted with many grave illnesses and laboring through the work of many experienced masters of the art of medicine, have not been able to recover from their illnesses at all, despite all the care and diligence which they could give them, which sick people the said Jacoba, when she was called in afterwards, cured in a short time. . . .

26. London Records:
Sanitary Conditions (14th c.)

The following proclamations by the mayor and aldermen of London and by the English king belong to a long series of efforts to control the problem of waste disposal.
Source: *Memorials of London and London Life in the XIIIth, XIVth, and XVth Centuries*, ed. and tr. Henry Thomas Riley (London: Longmans, Green and Co., 1868).

1309

Seeing that the people in the town do cause the ordure that has been collected in their houses, to be carried and placed in the streets, and in the lanes of the City, whereas they ought to have it carried to the [River] Thames, or elsewhere out of the town; and that thereby the streets and lanes are more encumbered than they used to be;—we do forbid, on the King's behalf, that from henceforth any person shall have the ordure that has been collected in his house, carried into the King's highways; but let them cause the same to be carried to the Thames, or elsewhere out of the City, whither it used to be carried. And if anyone shall do so, he shall be amerced, for the first time, in 40 pence, and afterwards, in half a mark each time; and nevertheless, he shall have the same removed at his own charges. And the same penalty shall be incurred by those before whose houses dung shall be found, if, after the dung has been placed there, they shall not immediately have their Alderman told by whom such dung has been so brought there. Also, no person shall have any dung raked or removed to the front of the houses of others; but he must immediately have it carried from thence to within his house, [there to be kept] a day and a night, on pain before-mentioned.

1357

The King to the Mayor and Sheriffs of our City of London, greeting. Considering how that the streets, and lanes, and other places in the city aforesaid, and the suburbs thereof, in the times of our forefathers and our own, were wont to be cleansed from dung, laystalls, and other filth, and were wont heretofore to be protected from the corruption arising therefrom, from the which no little honour did accrue to the said city, and those dwelling therein; whereas now, when passing along the water of Thames, we have beheld dung, laystalls, and other filth, accumulated in divers places in the said city, upon the bank of the river aforesaid, and have also perceived the fumes and other abominable stenches arising therefrom; from the corruption of which, if tolerated, great peril, as well to the persons dwelling within the said city, as to the nobles and others passing along the said river, will, it is feared, ensue, unless indeed some fitting remedy be speedily provided for the same;—We, wishing to take due precaution against such perils, and to preserve the honour and decency of the same city, in so far as we may, do command you, that you cause as well the banks of the said river, as the streets and lanes of the same city, and the suburbs thereof, to be cleansed of dung, laystalls, and other filth, without delay, and the same when cleansed so to be kept; and in the city aforesaid, and the suburbs thereof, public proclamation to be made, and it on our behalf strictly to be forbidden, that any one shall, on pain of heavy forfeiture unto us, place or cause to be placed dung or other filth to be accumulated in the same. And if any persons, after proclamation and prohibition so made, you shall find doing to the contrary thereof, then you are to cause them so to be chastised and punished, that such penalty and chastisement may cause fear and dread unto others of perpetrating the like. . . .

1379

. . . the Ordinance made heretofore as to the cleansing of streets and lanes of all manner of dung, filth, rubbish, and shavings, shall be strictly kept in all points. And . . . no one shall throw dung, filth, or rubbish, into the kennels of the City in time of rain, that it may float away with the water, on the peril that awaits the same. And . . . every officer of the said city shall have power to take the carts that bring thither [loam], sand, or gravel, and to load them at their departure with the filth and dung gathered from the kennels; but those carts only, and no others, on the peril that awaits the same.

27. Royal Proclamation: Exclusion of Lepers (1346)

Leprosy was a particularly frightening disease to the medieval world; its victims suffered horrific symptoms and often lost fingers, noses or limbs before eventually dying. The affliction was thought to be highly contagious. Here King Edward III of England continues the long medieval tradition of forbidding lepers contact with healthy members of society; but there was also a long tradition of establishing charitable institutions to care for those with leprosy.
Source: *Memorials of London and London Life in the XIIIth, XIVth, and XVth Centuries*, ed. and tr. Henry Thomas Riley (London: Longmans, Green and Co., 1868).

. . . Forasmuch as we have been given to understand, that many persons, as well of the city [of London], as others coming to the said city, being smitten with the blemish of leprosy, do publicly dwell among the other citizens and sound persons, and there continually abide; and do not hesitate to communicate with them, as well in public places as in private; and that some of them, endeavoring to contaminate others with that abominable blemish, (that so, to their own wretched solace, they may have more fellows in suffering,) as well in the way of mutual communications, and by the contagion of their polluted breath, as by carnal intercourse with women in stews[45] and other secret places, detestably frequenting the same, do so taint persons who are sound, both male and female, to the great injury of the people dwelling in the city aforesaid, and the manifest peril of other persons to the same city resorting;—We, wishing in every way to provide against the evils and perils which from the cause aforesaid may unto the said city, and the whole of our realm, arise, do command you, strictly enjoining, that, immediately on seeing [this decree], you

---

45. Stews = bathhouses.

will cause it to be publicly proclaimed on our behalf in every Ward of the city aforesaid, that all persons that have such blemish, shall, within fifteen days from the date of [this decree], quit the City and the suburbs aforesaid, on the peril which is thereunto attached, and betake themselves to places in the country, solitary, and notably distant from the said city and suburbs, and take up their dwelling there; seeking their victuals, through such sound persons as may think proper to attend thereto, wheresoever they may deem it expedient. And that no persons shall permit such leprous people to dwell within their houses and buildings in the City, and in the suburbs aforesaid, on pain of forfeiture of their aforesaid houses and buildings, and more grievous punishment on them by us to be inflicted, if they shall contravene the same. And further, taking with you certain discreet and lawful men who have the best knowledge of this disease, all those persons, as well citizens as others, of whatever sex or condition they may be, whom, upon diligent examination in this behalf to be made, within the city and suburbs aforesaid you shall find to be smitten with the aforesaid blemish of leprosy, you are to cause to be removed from the communion of sound citizens and persons without delay, and taken to solitary places in the country, there, as stated above, to abide. And this, as you shall wish to keep yourselves scatheless, and to avoid our heavy indignation, you are not to delay doing; and as to that which you shall have done herein, you are distinctly and openly to certify us in our Chancery under your seals, within the fifteen days next ensuing herefrom. . . .

28. Boccaccio: The Plague in Florence (1348)

The bubonic plague, or Black Death, first appeared in Europe in 1347–9, killing up to a third of the continent's population. The Italian writer Giovanni Boccaccio prefaced his famous collection of stories, the *Decameron*, with his own eyewitness account of the effects of the plague on his native city of Florence.
Source: *The Decameron of Giovanni Boccaccio*, tr. Frances Winwar (New York, 1955).

In the year of Our Lord 1348 the deadly plague broke out in the great city of Florence, most beautiful of Italian cities. Whether through the operation of the heavenly bodies or because of our own iniquities which the just wrath of God sought to correct, the plague had arisen in the East some years before, causing the death of countless human beings. It spread without stop from one place to another, until, unfortunately, it swept over the West. Neither knowledge nor human foresight availed against it, though the city was cleansed of human filth by chosen officers in charge and sick persons were forbidden to enter it, while advice was broadcast for the preservation of health. Nor did humble supplications serve. Not once but many times they were ordained in the form of processions for the propitiation of God by the faithful, but, in spite of everything, toward the spring of the year the plague began to show its ravages in a way short of miraculous.

It did not manifest itself as in the East, where if a man bled at the nose he had certain warning of inevitable death. At the onset of the disease both men and women were afflicted by a sort of swelling in the groin or under the armpits which sometimes attained the size of a common apple or egg. Some of these swellings were larger and some smaller, and all were commonly called boils. From these two starting points the boils began in a little while to spread and appear generally all over the body. Afterwards, the manifestation of the disease changed into black or livid spots on the arms, thighs and the whole person. In many these blotches were large and far apart, in others small and closely clustered. Like the boils, which had been and continued to be a certain indication of coming death, these blotches had the same meaning for every person on whom they appeared.

Neither the advice of physicians nor the virtue of any medicine seemed to help or avail in the cure of these diseases. Indeed, whether the nature of the malady did not suffer it, or whether the ignorance of the physicians could not determine the source and therefore could take no preventive measures against it, the fact was that not only did few recover, but on the contrary almost everyone died within three days of the appearance of the signs—some sooner, some later, and the majority without fever or other ill. Moreover, besides the qualified medical men, a vast number of quacks, both men and women, who had never studied medicine, joined the ranks and practiced cures. The virulence of the plague was all the greater in that it was communicated by the sick to the well by contact, not unlike fire when dry or fatty things are brought near it. But the evil was still worse. Not only did conversation and familiarity with the diseased spread the malady and even cause death, but the mere touch of the clothes or any other object the sick had touched or used, seemed to spread the pestilence. . . .

Let alone the fact that one man shunned the other and that nobody had any thought for his neighbor; even relatives visited their folks little or never, and when they did, they communicated from a distance. The calamity had instilled such horror into the hearts of men and women that brother abandoned brother, uncles, sisters and wives left their dear ones to perish and, what is more serious and almost incredible, parents avoided visiting or nursing their own children, as though these were not their own flesh.

As a result, the only help that remained to the many men and women who sickened was either the mercy of friends, who were rare, or the covetousness of servants who agreed to nurse them at the prospect of ridiculously exorbitant wages. Even at that, however, these servants were scarce and of the run of coarse-grained men and women, unused to such services and whose chief duty was perhaps to reach the patients whatever they called for, or to watch them die. Often their occupation brought them to perdition, together with their profits. From this neglect of the sick by neighbors, relatives and friends, and from the scarcity of servants, an almost unprecedented custom arose. Once sick, no woman, however charming, beautiful or well-born, hesitated to engage a man in her service, no matter whether he was young or old, high-born or low, or to reveal any part of her naked body to him if the disease required it, as if he had been of her own sex—all of which later resulted in immodesty in those who were cured. It followed also that many who might perhaps have lived if they had been tended, perished of this neglect. So great was the multitude of those who died in the city night and day, that it was terrible to hear of, and worse still to see. Out of sheer necessity, therefore, quite different customs arose among the survivors from the original laws of the townspeople. . . .

More wretched still were the circumstances of the common people and, for a great part, of the middle class, for, confined to their homes either by hope of safety or by poverty, and restricted to their own sections, they fell sick daily by thousands. There, devoid of help or care, they died almost without redemption. A great many breathed their last in the public streets, day and night; a large number perished in their homes, and it was only by the stench of their decaying bodies that they proclaimed their death to their neighbors. Everywhere the city was teeming with corpses. A general course was now adopted by the people, more out of fear of contagion than of any charity they felt toward the dead. Alone, or with the assistance of any bearers they could muster, they would drag the corpses out of their homes and pile them in front of the doors, where often, of a morning, countless bodies could be seen. Biers were sent for. When none was to be had, the dead were laid upon ordinary boards, two or three at once. It was not infrequent to see a single bier carrying husband and wife, two or three brothers, father and son, and others besides.

Times without number when a couple of priests were walking, carrying a cross before a corpse, they were soon followed by two or three sets of porters with their respective biers. And, where holy men had thought to be burying one man, they found seven or eight on their hands, sometimes more. Nor were these dead shown the respect of candles, tears or mourners. Death had become so common that no more attention was given to human lives than would be given to goats brought to slaughter nowadays. . . . So many bodies were brought to the churches every day that the consecrated ground did not suffice to hold them, particularly according to the ancient custom of giving each corpse its individual place. Huge trenches were dug in the crowded churchyards and the new dead were piled in them, layer upon layer, like merchandise in the hold of a ship. A little earth covered the corpses of each row, and the procedure continued until the trench was filled to the top.

But I shall not linger over the details of our city's past afflictions, for while such bitter times were upon it, the country round about was not spared. In the castles which were as miniature cities compared to the large towns, through the scattered hamlets and in the fields the wretched, poverty-stricken peasants and their families died helpless and unattended. On the wayside, in the tilled fields, about their houses, indifferently by day or night they fell dead, more like animals than human beings; whereupon those who remained, growing lax in their habits like the city folk, and careless of their duties, lived as if every day were their last. . . .

To go back to the city—what more can be said? Such was the cruelty of heaven and to a great degree of man, that between March and the following July it is estimated more than a hundred thousand human beings lost their lives within the walls of Florence, what with the ravages attendant upon the plague and the barbarity of the survivors toward the sick. . . .

Part III

The Noble Life

This section is about the lives of women of high social rank: the nobility and, in the Later Middle Ages, the gentry or knightly class. What primarily set the members of this small group (perhaps five percent of the population) apart from their social inferiors was their status as landowners, or more correctly, landholders. These are the people who lived in castles and manor houses, with peasants to work the land for them. But the nobles themselves did not lead lives of leisure; a noblewoman was responsible for the smooth running of a household that might include large numbers of servants, retainers and relatives, and she was often expected to look after the whole estate—and even defend it in her husband's absence.

Throughout much of Europe in the High and Later Middle Ages the members of this class were linked to each other in complex networks of lordship and vassalage, the relationships known today as "feudal" ones because they were based on the possession of a "fief" (*feudum*). A noble lady could inherit a fief, but it then passed to her husband. Rarely was she herself considered either a lord or a vassal, and never was she allowed to run her estates as an unmarried woman. Virtually the only single women in this social class were those who became nuns, even though wives showed themselves perfectly capable of overseeing their husbands' properties. Widows, however, were often allowed a great deal of latitude in ruling their own lands.

Because literacy was somewhat more widespread among the upper classes and because they had both literate staffs and more contacts with the highly literate world of the church, we have far more written evidence about the lives of noble women than about their lowlier contemporaries, and we have more personal glimpses from an earlier date than we generally do for the working classes.

29. Gregory of Tours: The Story of Ingitrude and Berthegund (6th c.)

The author and narrator of this story is Bishop Gregory of Tours, who took a particular interest in these events because the nunnery which Ingitrude had founded was located on the grounds of his church.
Source: Gregory of Tours, *The History of the Franks*, tr. O. M. Dalton (Oxford: Oxford University Press, 1927). Reprinted by permission of Oxford University Press.

The matter between Ingitrude and her daughter I think it well to relate from its beginning. When, some years before, Ingitrude founded the convent [in the city of Tours], . . . she sent a message to her daughter, to the following effect: "Leave thy husband, and come to me, that I may make thee abbess of this flock which I have assembled." Her daughter, on receiving this foolish advice, came with her husband to Tours, where she entered her mother's nunnery, saying to him: "Return hence and look after our property and our children; I shall not go back with thee. For none that is joined in wedlock shall behold the kingdom of God." But the husband sought me out and told me all that his wife had said. Thereupon I went to the nunnery and there read aloud those canons of the Nicene Council in which it is said: "If a woman abandon her husband, and spurn the nuptial state in which she hath lived with honour, on the plea that she who hath been joined in wedlock shall have no part in the glory of the celestial kingdom, let her be accursed." When she heard this, Berthegund was afraid of excommunication at the hands of the bishops of God; she therefore quitted the convent and returned home with her husband. But after three or four years her mother again sent her a message, entreating her to come to her. Thereupon she loaded vessels with her own goods and those of her husband, who was away from home, took one of her sons with her, and came to Tours. But her mother could not keep her there on account of the husband's obstinate pursuit; she also feared to become involved in the charge to which her daughter had exposed them both by her dishonesty. She therefore sent her to Bertram, bishop of Bordeaux, her own son, and brother of Berthegund. The husband following her, the bishop said to him: "She shall no longer be thy wife, because thou didst wed her without the assent of her parents." At this time, be it said, they had been married nearly thirty years. The husband came several times to Bordeaux, but the bishop always refused to give her up. On the occasion of King Guntram's visit to Orleans, of which I have written above, this man bitterly accused the bishop, saying: "Thou hast taken from me my wife, together with her servants; and behold thou hast done that which ill beseemeth a bishop, for thou hast sinned with her handmaids, and she with servants of thy household." The king at this was furious, and forced the bishop to promise the restoration of the wife to her husband. "She is my kinswoman," he said; "if she hath committed any evil in her husband's house, I will punish her; but if she hath not, why should the husband be exposed to all manner of humiliation, and his wife be taken from him?" Then Bishop Bertram gave his promise, saying: "Certainly my sister came to me, after the lapse of many years, and I kept her with me as long as she cared to stay, out of my affection and love for her. She hath now left me; let him seek her and take her whither he will; I shall not stand in his path." Although he made this statement, he sent her a private message to put off her secular garb, do penance, and withdraw to the church of the holy Martin; which things she straightway did. Her husband then came with a following of many men to remove her from the sacred place. She was in the habit of a nun, and declared that she was vowed to penitence; she therefore refused to go with him. Meanwhile Bishop Bertram died at Bordeaux. She now came to her senses and said: "Woe is me, that ever I hearkened to the advice of a wicked mother. My brother is dead; I am forsaken by my husband and separated from my children. Whither shall I go in my misery; what shall I now do?" After reflecting for a while, she decided to go to Poitiers; and though her mother [wished] to keep her with her, she altogether failed in this. In consequence enmity arose between them and they were always coming before the king in a dispute about property, the daughter claiming that which came to her from her father, the mother her part in the estate of her late husband. Berthegund produced a deed of gift from her brother Bertram, saying: "This and this my brother bestowed upon me." But her mother would not recognize the deed, seeking to secure all for herself, and sent emissaries to break into her daughter's house and take her effects, the deed among them. At a later time she was proved in the wrong as to this action, for she was forced to restore some of these effects upon her daughter's demand. The king sent letters to my brother, Bishop Maroveus, and myself urging us to bring about a reconciliation. When Berthegund came to Tours and appeared in our court, we compelled her, as far as we could, to listen to reason. But we were unable to bend her mother, who betook herself in bitter dudgeon to the king with the object of disinheriting her daughter from all share in her father's property. When she had stated her case before him in her daughter's absence, judgement was given that the said daughter should receive a quarter, and that the remaining three-quarters should pass to herself and to her grandsons, the children of another son. The priest Theuthar . . . came by the royal command to make the division. But the daughter resisting, no division was made, and the quarrel was not appeased. . . .

Ingitrude . . . now began to fail in health, and appointed her niece abbess in her stead. The community murmured at this act, but upon our reprimand contention ceased. Ingitrude was on bad terms with her daughter, who had taken her property from her; and she now adjured us that this daughter should not be suffered to offer prayers either in the monastery which she had founded, or at her tomb. She departed this life I believe, in the eightieth year of her life, and was buried on the eighth day of March. Nevertheless, her daughter Berthegund came to Tours, and not being received, went to King Childebert, begging him [for] permission to succeed her mother in the government of the monastery. The king had forgotten the decision which he had formerly given in favour of the mother, and now granted her a new diploma, signed by his own hand, to the effect that she might have possession of all that had belonged to her father and her mother, and take all that Ingitrude had left to the nunnery. Armed with this order she came back, and stripped the place so bare of all its furniture that she left nothing within but bare walls. She then assembled a motley crowd of scoundrels, ready for any lawless act, to carry off all the produce of any other lands given to the monastery by the devout. So many wicked things she did, that it were scarce possible to set them down in order. When she had possessed herself of all that I have described, she returned to Poitiers, venting false accusations against the abbess, notwithstanding that she was her nearest kinswoman.

30. Dhuoda: Manual for Her Son (841–43)

Dhuoda was a ninth-century noblewoman who married a high-ranking official at the court of the king of the Franks. While nuns in the Early Middle Ages were often better educated than they

were in later centuries, a lay female author was a great rarity. The book that Dhuoda wrote for her son while she was her husband's virtual prisoner is our only source for the rather sad and somewhat mysterious facts of her life. Most of the work is taken up with moral and religious teachings; the parts reproduced below are the autobiographical sections and some of those which illustrate, however sketchily, Dhuoda's relationship with her child. The italicized phrases are biblical quotations.
Source: *Handbook for William: A Carolingian Woman's Counsel for Her Son*, tr. Carol Neel (Lincoln, NB, and London: University of Nebraska Press, 1991).

In the name of the Holy Trinity

In the name of the Holy Trinity, here begins the handbook of Dhuoda, which she sent to her son William.

I am well aware that most women rejoice that they are with their children in this world, but I, Dhuoda, am far away from you, my son William. For this reason I am anxious and filled with longing to do something for you. So I send you this little work written down in my name, that you may read it for your education, as a kind of mirror. And I rejoice that, even if I am apart from you in body, the little book before you may remind you, when you read it, of what you should do on my behalf. . . .

Here begins the Prologue

Things that are obvious to many people often escape me. Those who are like me lack understanding and have dim insight, but I am even less capable than they. Yet always there is he at my side who *opened the mouths of the dumb, and made the tongues of infants eloquent.* I, Dhuoda, despite my weakness of mind, unworthy as I am among worthy women—I am still your mother, my son William, and it is to you that I now address the words of my handbook. From time to time children are fascinated by dice more than all the other games that they enjoy. And sometimes women are absorbed in examining their faces in mirrors, in order then to cover their blemishes and be more beautiful, for the worldly intention of pleasing their husbands. I hope that you may bring the same care, burdened though you may be by the world's pressures, to reading this little book addressed to you by me. For my sake, attend to it—according to my jest—as children do to their dice or women to their mirrors.

Even if you eventually have many more books, read this little work of mine often. May you, with God's help, be able to understand it to your own profit. You will find in it all you wish to know in compact form. You will find in it a mirror in which you can without hesitation contemplate the health of your soul, so that you may be pleasing not only in this world, but to him who formed you out of dust. What is essential, my son William, is that you show yourself to be such a man on both levels that you are both effective in this world and pleasing to God in every way.

My great concern, my son William, is to offer you helpful words. My burning, watchful heart especially desires that you may have in this little volume what I have longed to be written down for you, about how you were born through God's grace. I shall best begin there.

Preface

In the eleventh year of the imperial rule of our lord Louis, who then reigned by Christ's favor—on the twenty-ninth of June 824—I was given in marriage at the palace of Aachen to my lord Bernard, your father, to be his legitimate wife. It was still in that reign, in its thirteenth year on the twenty-ninth of November, that with God's help, as I believe, you were born into this world, my firstborn and much-desired son.

Afterward, as the wretchedness of this world grew and worsened, in the midst of the many struggles and disruptions in the kingdom, that emperor followed the path common to all men. For in the twenty-eighth year of his reign, he paid the debt of his earthly existence before his time. In the year after his death, your brother was born on the twenty-second of March in the city of Uzès. This child, born after you, was the second to come forth from my body by God's mercy. He was still tiny and had not yet received the grace of baptism when Bernard, my lord and the father of you both, had the baby brought to him in Aquitaine in the company of Elefantus, bishop of Uzès, and others of his retainers.

Now I have been away from you for a long time, for my lord constrains me to remain in this city. Nonetheless I applaud his success. But, moved by longing for both of you, I have undertaken to have this little book—a work on the scale of my small understanding—copied down and sent to you. Although I am besieged by many troubles, may this one thing be God's will, if it please him—that I might see you again with my own eyes. I would think it certain that I would, if God were to grant me some virtue. But since salvation is far from me, sinful woman that I am, I only wish it, and my heart grows weak in this desire.

As for you, I have heard that you father, Bernard, has given you as a hostage to the lord king Charles. I hope that you acquit yourself of this worthy duty with perfect good will. Meanwhile, as Scripture says, *Seek ye therefore the kingdom of God . . . and all these things shall be added unto you*, that is all that is necessary for the enjoyment of your soul and your body.

So the preface comes to an end. . . .

Cautionary words . . .

And so I urge you, O my handsome and beloved son William, that you not be distracted by the mundane cares of this earthly world from acquiring many volumes. In these books you should seek out and learn from the wise men of the church, the holiest of masters, more and greater things about God your creator than are written here. Beseech the Lord, cherish him, and love him. If you do this, he will be your guardian, your leader, your companion, and your country— *the way, and the truth, and the life*—endowing you most generously with prosperity in this world. He will bring all your enemies to peace. As for you, as is written in Job, *Gird up thy loins like a man*. Be humble of heart and chaste in body. *Set thyself up on high, and be glorious*, and *clothe thyself with beauty*.

What more can I say? I, Dhuoda, am always with you to encourage you. In the future, should I fail you by my absence, you have this little moral work as a reminder, so that as you read in spirit and body and as you pray to God you may be able to look upon me as if in a mirror. Then you may clearly see your duty to me. My son, my firstborn son— you will have other teachers to present you with works of fuller and richer usefulness, but not anyone like me, your mother, whose heart burns on your behalf.

Read the words I address to you, understand them and fulfill them in action. And when your little brother, whose name I still do not know, has received the grace of baptism in Christ, do not hesitate to teach him, to educate him, to love him, and to call him to progress from good to better. When the time has come about that he has learned to speak and read, show him this little volume gathered together into a handbook by me and written down in your name. Urge him to read it, for he is your flesh and your brother. I, your mother Dhuoda, urge you, as if I even now spoke to both of you, that you "hold up your heart" from time to time when you are oppressed by the troubles of this world, and "look upon him who reigns in heaven" and is called God. May that all-powerful one whom I mention frequently even in my unworthiness make both of you, my sons—along with my lord and master Bernard, your father—happy and joyful in the present world. May he make you successful in all your undertakings, and after the end of this life may he bring you rejoicing to heaven among his saints. Amen. . . .

Returning to myself, I grieve

The sweetness of my great love for you and my desire for your beauty have made me all but forget my own situation. I wish now, *the doors being shut*, to return to my own self. But because I am not worthy to be numbered among those who are mentioned above,[46] I still ask that you—among the innumerable people who may do so—pray without ceasing for the remedy of my soul on account of your special feeling for me, which can be measured.

You know how much, because of my continual illnesses and other circumstances, I have suffered all these things and others like them in my fragile body—according to the saying of a certain man, *in perils from my own nation, in perils from the Gentiles*—because of my pitiful merits. With God's help and because of your father, Bernard, I have at last confidently escaped these dangers, but my mind still turns back to that rescue. In the past I have often been lax in the praise of God, and instead of doing what I should in the seven hours of the divine office, I have been slothful seven times seven ways. That is why, with a humble heart and with all my strength, I pray that I may take my pleasure in continually beseeching God for my sins and my transgressions. May he deign to raise even me into heaven, shattered and heavy though I am.

And since you see me as I live in the world, strive with watchful heart—not only in vigils and prayer but also in alms to the poor—that I may be found worthy, once I am liberated from the flesh and from the bonds of my sins, to be freely received by the good Lord who judges us.

Your frequent prayer and that of others is necessary to me now. It will be more and more so in time to come if, as I believe, my moment is upon me. In my great fear and grief about what the future may bring me, my mind casts about in every direction. And I am unsure how, on the basis of my merits, I may be able to be set free in the end.

---

46. Dhuoda has listed relatives for whom William ought to pray.

Why? Because I have sinned in thought and in speech. Ill words themselves lead to evil deeds. Nevertheless I will not despair of the mercy of God. I do not despair now and I will never despair. I leave no other such as you to survive me, noble boy, to struggle on my behalf as you do and as many may do for me because of you, so that I may finally come to salvation.

I acknowledge that, to defend the interests of my lord and master Bernard, and so that my service to him might not weaken in the March and elsewhere—so that he not abandon you and me, as some men do—I know that I have gone greatly into debt. To respond to great necessities, I have frequently borrowed great sums, not only from Christians but also from Jews. To the extent that I have been able, I have repaid them. To the extent that I can in the future, I will always do so. But if there is still something to pay after I die, I ask and I beg you to take care in seeking out my creditors. When you find them, make sure that everything is paid off either from my own resources, if any remain, or from your assets—what you have now or what you eventually acquire through just means, with God's help.

What more shall I say? As for your little brother, I have above directed you time and again concerning what you should do for him. What I ask now is that he too, if he reaches the age of manhood, deign to pray for me. I direct both of you, as if you were together here before me, to have the offering of the sacrifice and the presentation of the host made often on my behalf.[47]

Then, when my redeemer commands that I depart this world, he will see fit to prepare refreshment for me. And if this transpires through your prayers and the worthy prayers of others, he who is called God will bring me into heaven in the company of his saints.

This handbook ends here. Amen. Thanks be to God. . . .

I ask that you write this epitaph on my grave

When I too have reached the end of my days, see to it that my name as well be written down among the names of those dead persons. What I wish and what I yearn for with all my might, as though it were happening now, is that you order the following verses to be cut in the stone of the place where I am buried, on the slab that hides my body. Then those who see this epitaph on my burial place may pour out worthy prayers to God for my unworthy self.

---

47. I.e., that they have masses said for her soul.

And as for any other who may someday read the handbook you now peruse, may he too ponder the words that follow here so that he may commend me to God's salvation as if I were buried beneath these words.

> Find, reader, the verses of my epitaph:
> Formed of earth, in this tomb
> Lies the earthly body of Dhuoda.
>> Great king, receive her.
> The surrounding earth has received in its depths
> The flimsy filth of which she was made.
>> Kind king, grant her favor.
> The darkness of the tomb, bathed with her sorrow,
> Is all that remains to her.
>> You, king, absolve her failings.
> You, man or woman, old or young, who walk back and
>> forth
> In this place, I ask you, say this:
>> Holy one, great one, release her chains.
> Bound in the dark tomb by bitter death,
> Closed in, she has finished life in earth's filth.
>> You, king, spare her sins.
> So that the dark serpent
> Not carry away her soul, say in prayer:
>> Merciful God, come to her aid.
> Let no one walk away without reading this.
> I beseech all that they pray, saying:
>> Give her peace, gentle father,
> And, merciful one, command that she at least be enriched
> With your saints by your perpetual light.
> Let her receive your amen after her death.

Return frequently to this little book. Farewell, noble boy, and always be strong in Christ. This little book was begun in the second year after the death of Louis, the late emperor, two days before the Kalends of December, on the feast of St. Andrew, at the beginning of the holy season of the Lord's Advent. With God's help it was finished four days before the Nones of February, the feast of the Purification of the holy and glorious Mary, always virgin, under the favorable reign of Christ and in the hope for a God-given king.

Reader, if you are found worthy to see Christ in eternal happiness, pray for that Dhuoda who is mentioned above.

31. Anglo-Saxon Wills (10th–11th c.)

"Anglo-Saxon" is the general term used today for the various
Germanic tribes (including Angles and Saxons) who settled the
southern and central parts of the island of Britain in the fifth and
sixth century, setting up kingdoms which collectively became
known as "England" ("Angle-land"). About seventy Anglo-Saxon
wills survive today in some form, many of them made by women;
the women's wills are similar to those of men because Anglo-
Saxon law allowed women to own land and leave it to heirs of their
own choice. (Later in the Middle Ages, women's testamentary
powers were often limited to the disposition of their clothing and
other personal belongings.) In the pieces below, elipses indicate
places where words are missing or indecipherable because of
damage to the manuscripts.
Source: *Anglo-Saxon Wills*, ed. and tr. Dorothy Whitelock (Cambridge, 1930). Reprinted by permission of Cambridge University
Press.

The Will of Wynflæd (c. 950)

Wynflæd declares how she wishes to dispose of what she possesses,
after her death. She bequeathes to the church her offering—. . . . and
the better of her offering-cloths, and her cross; and to the refectory
two silver cups for the community; and as a gift for the good of her
soul a mancus[48] of gold to every servant of God, and besides that one
mancus to Ceolthryth and Othelbriht and Elsa and Æthel. . .th; and
one pound to the community at Wilton and one mancus to Fugel.

And she bequeathes to her daughter Æthelflæd her engraved brace-
let and her brooch, and the estate at Ebbesborne and the title-deed as
a perpetual inheritance to dispose of as she pleases; and she grants to
her the men and the stock and all that is on the estate except what
shall be given from it both in men and stock for the sake of her soul.
And at Charlton, also, she grants her the men and the stock except
the freedmen, and except that a gift for her soul to the value of half a
pound be supplied for Milborne from the stock at Charlton, and from
Chinnock a gift for her soul to the value of half a pound for Yeovil.

And to Eadmær [she grants] the estates at Coleshill and Inglesham,
and she grants to him also the estate at Faccombe, which was her
marriage-gift, for his lifetime, and then after his death, if Æthelflæd

---

48. Mancus = a type of coin.

survive him, she is to succeed to the estate at Faccombe, and after her death it is to revert to Eadwold's possession. And if it is God's will that Eadwold be old enough in his father's lifetime to hold land, then I ask Eadmær to relinquish to him one of two estates, either Coleshill or Adderbury, and after his lifetime, both. And at Inglesham she wishes that there be furnished on her behalf for Wantage a gift for her soul worth half a pound, and [the same] at Coleshill; and that from the stock the equivalent of sixty pence be supplied for Shrivenham, sixty for Coleshill and sixty for Childrey.

And Wulfwaru is to be freed, and she is to serve whom she pleases, and . . . ttryth also. And Wulfflæd is to be freed on condition that she serve Æthelflæd and Eadgifu. And she bequeathes to Eadgifu a woman-weaver and a seamstress, the one called Eadgifu, the other called Æthelgifu. And Gerburg is to be freed, and Miscin and Hi. . . . and the daughter of Burhulf at Chinnock, and Ælfsige and his wife and elder daughter, and Ceolstan's wife. And at Charlton Pifus and Eadwyn and . . . .'s wife are to be freed. And at Faccombe Eadhelm and Man and Johanna and Sprow and his wife and En. . . . and Gersand and Snel are to be freed. And at Coleshill Æthelgyth and Bica's wife and Æffa and Beda and Gurhann's wife are to be freed; and Wulfwaru's sister, Brihtsige's wife, and . . . . the wright, and Wulfgyth, Ælfswith's daughter are to be freed. And if there be any penally enslaved man besides these whom she has enslaved, she trusts to her children that they will release him for her soul's sake.

And [she grants] to Ælfwold her two buffalo-horns and a horse and her red tent. And she bequeathes to Eadmær a cup with a lid, and another to Æthelflæd, and prays that between them they will furnish two fair goblets to the refectory for her sake, or augment her own ornamented cups. . . . worth one pound. Then she would like half a pound of pence to be put into each cup, and that Eadwold should be given back his own two silver cups. And she bequeathes to him her gold-adorned wooden cup in order that he may enlarge his armlet with the gold, or that he may receive sixteen mancuses of red gold in exchange; that amount has been put on it. And she bequeathes to him two chests and in them a set of bed-clothing, all that belongs to one bed.

And Eadmær is to pay to Eadwold as much stock and as many men as he (?) has bequeathed to him at Avon, and he afterwards [is to pay] to his father what he wishes. And with regard to the estate at Chinnock, the community at Shaftesbury possess it after her death, and she owns the stock and the men; this being so, she grants to the community the peasants who dwell on the rented land, and the bondmen she grants to her son's daughter Eadgifu, and also the stock, except the gift for her soul which must be rendered to Yeovil; and she wishes that six oxen and four cows with four calves be allowed to remain on the estate. And of the bondmen at Chinnock she bequeathes to Eadwold, Ceolstan, Eadstan's son, and Æffa's son, and Burhwyn [and] Martin and Hisfig; and in their place she bequeathes to Eadgifu, Ælfsige the cook and Ælfwaru, Burga's daughter, and Herestan and his wife, and Ecghelm and his wife and their child, and Cynestan and Wynsige and Brihtric's son and Eadnyn and Bunele's son and Ælfhere's daughter.

And she bequeathes to Æthelflæd, daughter of Ealhhelm, Ælfhere's younger daughter, and her double badger-skin(?) gown, and another of linen or else some linen cloth. And to Eadgifu two chests and in them her best bed-curtain and a linen covering and all the bed-clothing which goes with it, and . . . . and her best dun tunic, and the better of her cloaks, and her two wooden cups ornamented with dots, and her old filagree brooch which is worth six mancuses. And let there be given to her four mancuses from her . . . . and a long hall-tapestry and a short one and three seat coverings. And she grants to Ceolthryth whichever she prefers of her black tunics and her best holy veil and her best headband; and to Æthelflæd the White her . . . . gown and cap and headband, and afterwards Æthelflæd is to supply from her nun's vestments the best she can for Wulfflæd and Æthelgifu and supplement it with gold so that each of them shall have at least sixty pennyworth: and for Ceolwyn and Eadburg it shall be thirty pennyworth. And there are two large chests and a clothes' chest, and a little spinning box and two old chests.

Then she makes a gift to Æthelflæd of everything which is unbequeathed, books and such small things, and she trusts that she will be mindful of her soul. And there are also tapestries, one which is suitable for her, and the smallest she can give to her women. And she bequeathes to Cynelufu her share of the untamed horses which are with Eadmær's. And to Æthelflæd she grants her . . . . and the utensils and all the useful things that are inside, and also the homestead if the king grant it to her as King Edward granted it to Brihtwyn her mother. And Eadwold and his sister are to have her tame horses in common. . . .

The Will of Wulfwaru (984–1016)

I, Wulfwaru, pray my dear lord King Ethelred, of his charity, that I may be entitled to make my will. I make known to you, Sire, here in this document, what I grant to St Peter's monastery at Bath for my poor soul and for the souls of my ancestors from whom my property and my possessions came to me; namely then, that I grant to that holy place there an armlet which consists of sixty mancuses of gold, and a bowl of two and a half pounds, and two gold crucifixes, and a set of mass-vestments with everything that belongs to it, and the best dorsal that I have, and a set of bed-clothing with tapestry and curtain and with everything that belongs to it. And I grant to the Abbot Ælfhere the estate at Freshford with the produce and the men and all the profit which is obtained there.

And I grant to my elder son Wulfmær the estate at Claverton, with produce and with men and all profits; and the estate at Compton with produce and men and all profits; and I grant him half the estate at Butcombe with produce and men and all profits, and half of it I grant to my younger daughter Ælfwaru, with produce and men and all profits. And they are to share the principal residence between them as evenly as they can, so that each of them shall have a just portion of it.

And to my younger son Ælfwine I grant the estate at Leigh, with produce and men and all the profits; and the estate at Holton, with produce and men and all profits; and the estate at Hogston, with produce and men and all profits; and thirty mancuses of gold.

And I grant to my elder daughter, Gode, the estate at Winford, with produce and men and all profits; and two cups of four pounds; and a hand of thirty mancuses of gold and two brooches and a woman's attire complete. And to my younger daughter Ælfwaru I grant all the women's clothing which is left.

And to my son Wulfmær and my second son Ælfwine and my daughter Ælfwaru—to each of the three of them—I grant two cups of good value. And I grant to my son Wulfmær a hall-tapestry and a set of bed-clothes. To Ælfwine my second son I grant a tapestry for a hall and tapestry for a chamber, together with a table-cover and with all the cloths which go with it.

And I grant to my four servants Ælfmær, Ælfweard, Wulfric and Wulfstan, a band of twenty mancuses of gold. And I grant to all my household women, in common, a good chest well decorated.

And I desire that those who succeed to my property provide twenty freedmen, ten in the east and ten in the west; and all together furnish a food-rent for Bath every year for ever, as good as ever they can afford, at such season as it seems to all of them that they can accomplish it best and most fittingly. Whichever of them shall discharge this, may he have God's favour and mine; and whichever of them will not discharge it, may he have to account for it with the Most High, who is the true God, who created and made all creatures.

The Will of Wulfgyth (1046)

Here in this document it is made known how Wulfgyth grants after her death the things which Almighty God has allowed her to enjoy in life.

First to my lord his due heriot.[49] And I grant the estate at Stisted, with the witness of God and my friends, to Christchurch for the sustenance of the monks in the community, on condition that my sons Ælfketel and Ketel may have the use of the estate for their lifetime; and afterwards the estate is to go to Christchurch without controversy, for my soul and for my lord Ælfwine's and for the souls of all my children: and after their lifetime half the men are to be free. And I grant to the church at Stisted, besides what I granted during my life, [Eldeme's] land and in addition so much that in all there shall be after my death fifty acres of woodland and of open land.

And I grant to my sons Ulfketel and Ketel the estates at Walsingham and at Carleton and at Harling; and I grant to my two daughters, Gode and Bote, Saxlingham and Somerleyton. And to the church at Somerleyton sixteen acres of land and one acre of meadow. And to my daughter Ealdgyth I grant the estates at Chadacre and at Ashford, and the wood which I attached to the latter. And I grant Fritton to Earl Godwine and Earl Harold.

And I grant to Christ's altar at Christchurch a little gold crucifix, and a seat-cover. And I grant to St Edmund's two ornamented horns. And I grant to St Etheldreda's a woollen gown. And I grant to St Osyth's half a pound of money, and that my children shall give. And I grant to St Augustine's one dorsal.[50]

And he who shall detract from my will which I have now declared in the witness of God, may he be deprived of joy on this earth, and may the Almighty Lord who created and made all creatures exclude him from the fellowship of all saints on the Day of Judgment, and may he be delivered into the abyss of hell to Satan the devil and all his accursed companions and there suffer with God's adversaries, without end, and never trouble my heirs.

Of this King Edward and many others are witnesses.

---

49. Heriot = payment owed to one's lord upon one's death.
50. Dorsal = an ornamental hanging for a chair or altar.

A Will of Siflæd (10th or 11th c.)

Here in this document it is made known how Siflæd granted her possessions when she went across the sea.[51]

First, to the village church in Marlingford five acres and one homestead and two acres of meadow and two wagonloads of wood; and to my tenants their homesteads as their own possession: and all my men [are to be] free. And I grant to each of my brothers a wagonload of wood. And I grant to Christchurch at Norwich four head of cattle, and two to St Mary's, and one to my. . . . And I grant to St Edmund's all that may happen to be left of my property, that is house and homestead in Marlingford, with wood and open land, meadow and live stock.

And if I come home, then I wish to occupy that estate for my life; and after my death the will is to take effect. And whosoever alters this, may God turn away his face from him on the Day of Judgment, unless he repent it here.

The Will of Ulf and Madselin (ca. 1067)

This is the agreement which Ulf and his wife Madselin made with [God] and with St Peter when they went to Jerusalem. That is, the estate at Carlton to Peterborough after their death for the redemption of their souls; and the estate at Bytham to St. Guthlac's; and the estate at Sempringham to St. Benedict's at Ramsey.

And to Bishop Ealdred the estates at Lavington and Hardwick as a complete purchase, and the estates at Skillington and Hoby and Morton, on which the Bishop has a mortgage of eight marks of gold; and if they return home, the Bishop is to be paid his gold; but if neither of them return, the Bishop is to supply for their souls' sake as much as the land is worth above that gold. And if it should go other than well with the Bishop, the Abbot Brand is to succeed on these same terms.

And I have granted the estate at Manthorpe to the Abbot Brand. And I have granted the estate at Wilby to my kinsman Siferth. And she has granted the estate at Stoke to her kinswoman Leofgifu. And she has granted the estate at Stroxton to Ingemund, and he [has granted] to her in return the west hall at Winterton.

And the estate at Overton is to be sold, and [the money] employed

---

51. It was common practice to make a will before going on a pilgrimage or other long journey.

for the souls of both of us. And I have granted two estates to my mother, namely Kettleby and Keelby Cotes, and she has granted to me Messingham and Kettleby. And if I do not come home Ingemund is to have the estate at Kirmington. And I have granted the estate at Claxby to my brother Healden: and the estate at Ormsby and all that I possessed there to St Mary's monastery. And my servants are to have Limber if I do not come home; and the estate at Lohtun which she has there [is to go] to Thorney.

32. The Life of Christina of Markyate: Christina's Rebellion (12th c.)

Christina of Markyate was born in England at the end of the eleventh century. Her family was a noble Anglo-Saxon one, as her biographer tells us; thus she belonged to the same group as the women whose wills precede this reading. But the Anglo-Saxon nobility was being depressed into a lower status by the French Normans who had conquered England in 1066, bringing with them a somewhat different way of life; thus the details of Christina's daily life were part of a vanishing culture. Christina's biography was written because she was a renowned holy woman—a local saint. "Saints' lives" were a common form of narrative writing throughout medieval Europe; the writer of such a work presented the holy figure as capable of miracles and worthy of veneration.

Christina's struggle did not end with the episcopal decision described below; after this a bribe from Autti caused the bishop to reverse his ruling, and Christina eventually had to run away from home to enter the religious life. She died sometime between 1155 and 1166.

Source: Reprinted from *The Life of Christina of Markyate, a Twelfth Century Recluse*, edited and translated by C. H. Talbot (1959), by permission of Oxford University Press. Reprinted in the Oxford Medieval Texts series, 1987.

In the town of Huntingdon there was born into a family of noble rank a maiden of uncommon holiness and beauty. Her father's name was Autti, her mother's Beatrix. The name which she herself had been given in baptism was Theodora, but later on, through force of circumstance, she changed it to Christina.

. . . Autti and Beatrix brought their daughter Christina with them to our monastery of the blessed martyr St. Alban, where his sacred bones are revered, to beg his protection for themselves and for their child. When the girl therefore had looked carefully at the place and observed the religious bearing of the monks who dwelt there, she declared how fortunate the inmates were, and expressed a wish to share in their fellowship. . . . Thenceforward she lost all interest in worldly ostentation and turned to God with all her heart, and said, "Lord, my desire is before Thee, and my groaning is not hid from Thee. . . . Grant me, I beseech Thee, purity and inviolable virginity whereby Thou mayest renew in me the image of Thy Son: who lives and reigns with Thee in the unity of the Holy Spirit God for ever and ever, Amen."

After she had returned to Huntingdon she revealed to Sueno [her spiritual advisor] what she had vowed and he, who was considered in those parts as a light of God, confirmed the virgin's vow before God.

. . .

After this the aforesaid young man [Burthred] called on her father and mother to arrange his betrothal with the girl who they had promised should be his wife. When they spoke to her about preparations for the wedding, she would not listen. And when they asked the reason, she replied: "I wish to remain single, for I have made a vow of virginity." On hearing this, they made fun of her rashness. But she remained unmoved by it: therefore they tried to convince her of her foolishness and, despite her rejections, encouraged her to hurry on the marriage preparations. She refused. They brought her gifts and made great promises: she brushed them aside. They cajoled her; they threatened her; but she would not yield. At last they persuaded one of her close friends and inseparable companions, named Helisen, to soothe her ears by a continuous stream of flattery, so that it would arouse in her, by its very persistence, a desire to become the mistress of a house. . . . But she was quite unable to extort one word signifying her consent even though she had spent a whole year trying out these stratagems. Some time later, however, when they were all gathered together in the church, they made a concerted and sudden attack on her. To be brief, how it happened I cannot tell. All I know is that by God's will, with so many exerting pressure on her from all sides, she yielded (at least in word), and on that very day Burthred was betrothed to her.

After the espousal the maiden returned once more to her parents' home whilst her husband, though he had houses elsewhere, built her a new and larger dwelling-place near his father-in-law. But although she was married, her former intentions were not changed, and she freely expressed her determination not submit to the physical embraces of any man. The more her parents became aware of her persistence in this frame of mind, the more they tried to break down her resistance, first by flattery, then by reproaches, sometimes by presents and grand promises, and even by threats and punishment. And though all her friends and relatives united forces together in this purpose, her father Autti surpassed them all in his efforts, whilst he himself was outclassed by the girl's mother, as will become evident later on. After they had tried out many methods without result, they finally hit on this subterfuge. Putting her under strict and rigorous guard, they prevented any religious god-fearing man from having any conversation with her: on the other hand they freely invited to the house people given to jesting, boasting, worldly amusement, and those whose evil communications corrupt good manners. . . . [And] they took her with them, against her will, to public banquets, where divers choice meats were followed by drinks of different kinds, where the alluring melodies of the singers were accompanied by the sounds of the zither and the harp, so that by listening to them her strength of mind might be sapped away and in this way she might finally be brought to take pleasure in the world. But their wiles were outwitted at all points and served but to emphasize her invincible prudence.

See finally how she acted, how she behaved herself at what is called the Gild merchant, which is one of the merchants' greatest and best-known festivals. One day, when a great throng of nobles were gathered together there, Autti and Beatrix held the place of honour, as being the most important among them. It was their pleasure that their daughter Christina, their eldest and most worthy daughter, should act as cup-bearer to such an honourable gathering. Wherefore they commanded her to get up and lay aside the mantle which she was wearing, so that, with her garments fastened to her sides with bands and her sleeves rolled up her arms, she should courteously offer drinks to the nobility. They hoped that the compliments paid to her by the onlookers and the accumulation of little sips of wine would break her resolution and prepare her body for the deed of corruption. Carrying out their wishes, she prepared a suitable defence against both attacks. Against the favours of human flattery she fixed in her memory the thought of the Mother of God. . . . Against the urge to drunkenness, she opposed her burning thirst. . . .

But as her parents had been outwitted in this, they tried something else. And at night they let her husband secretly into her bedroom in order that, if he found the maiden asleep, he might suddenly take her by surprise and overcome her. But even through that providence to which she had commended herself, she was found dressed and awake, and she welcomed the young man as if he had been her brother. And sitting on her bed with him, she strongly encouraged him to live a chaste life, putting forward the saints as examples. . . . When the greater part of the night had passed with talk such as this, the young man eventually left the maiden. When those who had got him into the room heard what had happened, they joined together in calling him a spineless fellow. And with many reproaches they goaded him on again, and thrust him into her bedroom another night, having warned him not to be misled by her deceitful tricks and naïve words nor to lose his manliness. Either by force or entreaty he was to gain his end. And if neither of these sufficed, he was to know that they were at hand to help him: all he had to mind was to act the man.

When Christina sensed this, she hastily sprang out of bed and clinging with both hands to a nail which was fixed in the wall, she hung trembling between the wall and the hangings. Burthred meanwhile approached the bed and, not finding what he expected, he immediately gave a sign to those waiting outside the door. They crowded into the room forthwith and with lights in their hands ran from place to place looking for her, the more intent on their quest as they knew she was in the room when he entered it and could not have escaped without their seeing her. . . . Then the maiden of Christ, taking courage, prayed to God, saying: "Let them be turned backward, that desire my hurt;" and straightaway they departed in confusion, and from that moment she was safe. . . .

Whilst her parents were setting these and other traps for her they fixed a day for the marriage with their son-in-law several times. For they hoped that some occasion would arise when they could take advantage of her. For what woman could hope to escape so many snares? And yet, with Christ guarding the vow which his spouse had made, the celebration of the wedding could nohow be brought about. Indeed, when the day which they had fixed approached and all the necessary preparations for the marriage had been arranged, it happened first that all the things prepared were burned by an unexpected fire, and then that the bride was taken with a fever. In order to drive away the fever, sometimes they thrust her into cold water, at other times they blistered her excessively. . . .

Her father brought her [to the priory of Huntingdon] another time, and placing her before Fredebertus, the reverend prior, and the rest of the canons of the house, addressed them with these words: "I know, my fathers, I know, and I admit to my daughter, that I and her mother have forced her against her will into this marriage and that against her better judgement she has received this sacrament. Yet, no matter how she was led into it, if she resists our authority and rejects it, we shall be the laughing-stock of our neighbours, a mockery and derision to those who are round about. Wherefore, I beseech you, plead with her to have pity on us: let her marry in the Lord and take away our reproach. Why must she depart from tradition? Why should she bring this dishonour on her father? Her life of poverty will bring the whole of the nobility into disrepute. Let her do now what we wish and she can have all that we possess." When Autti had said this, Fredebertus asked him to leave the assembly and with his canons about him he began to address the maiden with these words: "We are surprised, Theodora, at your obstinacy, or rather we should say, your madness. We know that you have been betrothed according to ecclesiastical custom. We know that the sacrament of marriage, which has been sanctioned by divine law, cannot be dissolved, because what God has joined together, no man should put asunder. . . . [He quotes several passages from the Bible about marriage and about children's duty of obedience to parents.] Nor should you think that only virgins are saved: for whilst many virgins perish, many mothers of families are saved, as well we know. And since this is so, nothing remains but that you accept our advice and teaching and submit yourself to the lawful embraces of the man to whom you have been legally joined in marriage."

To these exhortations Christina replied: "I am ignorant of the scriptures which you have quoted, father prior. But from their sense I will give my answers thereto. My father and mother, as you have heard, bear witness that against my will this sacrament, as you call it, was forced on me. I have never been a wife and have never thought of becoming one. Know that from my infancy I have chosen chastity and have vowed to Christ that I would remain a virgin: this I did before witnesses, but even if they were not present God would be witness to my conscience continuously. This I showed by my actions as far as I was allowed. And if my parents have ordered me to enter into a marriage which I never wanted and to break the vow which I made to Christ which they know I made in my childhood, I leave you, who are supposed to excel other men in the knowledge of the scriptures, to judge how wicked a thing this is. If I do all in my power to fulfil the vow I made to Christ, I shall not be disobedient to my parents. What I do, I do on the invitation of Him whose voice, as you say, is heard in the Gospel: 'Every one who leaves house or brothers or sisters or father or mother or wife or children or possessions for My name's sake shall receive a hundredfold and possess eternal life.' Nor do I think that virgins only will be saved. But I do say, and it is true, that if many virgins perish, so rather do married women. And if many mothers of families are saved, which you likewise say, and it is true, certainly virgins are saved more easily."

Fredebertus, astonished at the common sense and answers of Christina, asked her, saying, "How do you prove to me that you are doing this for the love of Christ? Perhaps you are rejecting marriage with Burthred in order to enter a more wealthy one?" "A more wealthy one, certainly," she replied. "For who is richer than Christ?" Then said he, "I am not joking. I am treating with you seriously. And if you wish us to believe you, take an oath in our presence that, were you betrothed to him as you have been to Burthred, you would not marry even the king's son." At these words the maiden casting her eyes up to heaven and with a joyful countenance replied: "I will not merely take an oath, but I am prepared to prove it, by carrying red-hot iron in these my bare hands.[52] For, as I have frequently declared, I must fulfil the vow which through the inspiration of His grace I made to the only Son of the Eternal King, and with the help of this same grace I mean to fulfil it. And I trust to God that the time is not far off when it will become clear that I have no other in view but Christ."

Fredebertus then called in Autti and said to him: "We have tried our best to bend your daughter to your will, but we have made no headway. We know, however, that our bishop Robert will be coming soon to his vill at Buckden, which is near this town. Reason demands that the whole question should be laid before him. Let the case be put into his hands after he comes and let her take the verdict of the bishop, if of no other. What is the point of tearing your vitals and suffering to no purpose? We respect the high resolution of this maiden as founded on impregnable virtue." To which Autti replied, "I accept your advice. Please seek the bishop on this affair." He agreed, and so Autti brought back his daughter and placed her under the usual restraint.

In the meantime he heard that the bishop had come out to Buckden. Fredebertus immediately sought him out, being sent by Autti: and with him went the most noble citizens of the town, who thought that, as the marriage had already been performed, the bishop would immediately order the betrothed woman to submit to the authority of her husband. Hence they laid before him in detail and without delay all the facts which they knew pertained to the business in hand, namely what Christina had done, what others had done to her, begin-

---

52. The ordeal of the hot iron was a common procedure for determining guilt or innocence in Germanic law. If the burns healed cleanly, the subject was judged to be telling the truth.

ning with her childhood and bringing it up to the present day. At last they brought forward the proposal . . . that since neither adversity not prosperity could bring her to it she should be forced to accept her marriage at least by episcopal authority. After weighing the evidence minutely, the bishop said: "I declare to you, and I swear before God and His blessed Mother that there is no bishop under heaven who could force her into this marriage, if according to her vow she wishes to keep herself for God to serve Him freely and for no man besides."

33. Autobiography of Guibert de Nogent: Life of His Mother (11th–12th c.)

> Guibert de Nogent was born into a noble French family in the 1060s. His father died during Guibert's infancy, leaving a young widow. Guibert eventually became a monk and served as Abbot of Nogent for twenty years. His autobiography, written in 1115, is unusual both because it is a rare medieval example of this genre and because Guibert says so much in it about his mother, giving us what is presumably an informed narrative account of her life, albeit from a rather limited viewpoint. The book is addressed to God.
>
> Source: *The Autobiography of Guibert of Nogent, Abbot of Nogent-sous-Coucy*, tr. C. C. Swinton Bland (London and New York, 1925).

Her Character

. . . First and above all, therefore, I render thanks to Thee for that Thou didst bestow on me a mother fair, yet chaste, modest and most devout. . . .

Thanks to Thee therefore, O God, that Thou didst infuse her beauty with virtue; for the seriousness of her manner was such as to make evident her scorn for all vanity; her rare speech and her tranquil features gave no encouragement to light looks. Thou knowest, Almighty God, Thou didst put into her in earliest youth the fear of Thy Name and into her Heart revolt against the allurements of the flesh. Take note that hardly anywhere was she to be found in the company of those who made much of themselves, and as she was temperate herself, so was she sparing in blame of those who were not, and when sometimes a scandalous tale was told by strangers or those of her own household, she would turn away herself and take no part in it, and was as much annoyed by such whisperings as if she had been slandered in her own person. . . .

Of this woman most true, as I hope and believe, I was by Thy favour born, the worst of all that she begat. In two senses was I her last child, for whereas my brothers and sisters have passed away in good hope of salvation, I alone am left in utter despair. . . .

Childbirth

Almost the whole of Good Friday had my mother passed in excessive pain of travail, (in what anguish, too, did she linger, when I wandered from the way and followed slippery paths!) when at last the eve of Easter dawned.

Racked, therefore, by pains long-endured, and her tortures increasing as her hour drew near, when she thought I had at last in natural course come to the birth, instead I was returned within the womb. By this time my father, friends, and kinsfolk were crushed with dismal sorrowing for both of us, for whilst the child was hastening the death of the mother, and she her child's in denying him deliverance, all had reason for compassion. It was a day on which with the exception of the special anniversary service celebrated at its own time the regular offices[53] for the household were not taking place. And so they ask[ed] counsel in their need and [fled] for help to the altar of the Lady Mary, and to her (the only Virgin to bear a child that ever was or would be) this vow was made and in the place of an offering this gift laid upon the Gracious Lady's altar: that should a male child come to the birth, he should be given up to the service of God and of herself in the ministry, but if one of the weaker sex, she should be handed over to the corresponding calling. At once was born a weak little being, almost an abortion, and at that timely birth there was rejoicing only for my mother's deliverance, the child being such a miserable object. In that poor mite just born there was such a pitiful meagreness that he had the corpse-like look of one born out of due time. . . . On that same day, when I was put into the cleansing water,[54] a certain woman—as I was told in joke when a boy and young man—tossed me from hand to hand saying, "Can such a child live, think you, whom nature by a mistake has made almost without limbs, giving him something more like a line than a body?"

---

53. Offices = church services.
54. Put into the cleansing water = baptized.

Raising a Son

Although [my teacher] crushed me by such severity, yet in other ways he made it quite plain that he loved me as well as he did himself. With such watchful care did he devote himself to me, with such foresight did he secure my welfare against the spite of others and teach me on what authority I should beware of the dissolute manners of some who paid court to me, and so long did he argue with my mother about the elaborate richness of my dress, that he was regarded as exercising the guardianship not of a master, but of a parent, and not over my body only, but my soul, too. . . . Certainly this same master and my mother, when they saw me paying to both alike due respect, tried by frequent tests to see whether I should dare to prefer one or the other on a definite issue.

At last, without any intention on the part of either, an opportunity occurred for a test which left no room for doubt. Once I had been beaten in school—the school being no other than the dining-hall in our house, for he had given up the charge of others to take me alone, my mother having wisely required him to do this for a higher emolument and a better position. When, therefore, at a certain hour in the evening, my studies, such as they were, had come to an end, I went to my mother's knees after a more severe beating than I had deserved. And when she, as she was wont, began to ask me repeatedly whether I had been whipped that day, I, not to appear a tell-tale, entirely denied it. Then she, whether I liked it or not, threw off the inner garment which they call a vest or shirt, and saw my little arms blackened and the skin of my back everywhere puffed up with the cuts from the twigs. And being grieved to the heart by the very savage punishment inflicted on my tender body, troubled, agitated and weeping with sorrow, she said: "You shall never become a clerk,[55] nor any more suffer so much to get learning." At that I, looking at her with what reproach I could, replied: "If I had to die on the spot, I would not give up learning my book and becoming a clerk." Now she had promised that if I wished to become a knight, when I reached the age for it, she would give me the arms and equipment.

But when I had, with a good deal of scorn, declined all these offers, she, Thy servant, O Lord, accepted this rebuff so gladly, and was made so cheerful by my scorn of her proposal, that she repeated to my master the reply with which I had opposed her. Then both rejoiced that I had such an eager longing to fulfill my father's vow. . . .

---

55. Clerk = member of the clergy.

At length my mother tried by every means to get me into a church living.[56]

Early Married Life

After these reasonings at length I return to Thee, my God, to speak of the conversion of that good woman, my mother. She, when hardly of marriageable age, was given to my father, a mere youth, by provision of my grandfather. . . .

Now it so happened that at the very beginning of that lawful union conjugal intercourse was made ineffective through the bewitchments of certain persons. For it was said that their marriage drew upon them the envy of a step-mother, who, having nieces of great beauty and nobility, was plotting to entangle one of them with my father. Meeting with no success in her designs, she is said to have used magical arts to prevent entirely the consummation of the marriage. His wife's virginity thus remaining intact for three years, during which he endured his great misfortune in silence, at last, driven to it by his kinsfolk, my father was the first to reveal the facts. Imagine how my kinsmen tried hard in every way to bring about a divorce, and their constant pressure upon my father, young and raw, to become a monk. . . . This, however, was not done for his soul's good, but with the purpose of getting possession of his property. But when their suggestion produced no effect, they began to hound the girl herself, far away as she was from her kinsfolk and harassed by the violence of strangers, into voluntary flight out of sheer exhaustion under their insults, and without waiting for divorce. Meanwhile she endured all this, bearing with calmness the abuse that was aimed at her, and, if out of this rose any strife, pretending ignorance of it. Besides certain rich men perceiving that she was not in fact a wife, began to assail the heart of the young girl; but Thou, O Lord, the builder of inward chastity, didst inspire her with purity stronger than her nature or her youth. . . .

O God, Thou knowest how hard, how almost impossible it would be for women of the present time to keep such chastity as this; whereas there was in those days such modesty, that hardly ever was the good name of a married woman smirched by ill report. Ah! how wretchedly have modesty and honour in the state of maidenhood declined from those times to these, and both the reality and the show of a mother's

---

56. Living = position or sinecure in the church to support a clerk, usually as a parish priest.

guardianship shrunk to naught! Therefore coarse mirth is all that may be noted in their manners and naught but jesting heard, with sly winks and ceaseless chatter. Wantonness shews in their gait, only silliness in their behaviour. So much does the extravagance of their dress depart from the old simplicity that in the enlargement of their sleeves, the straitness of their skirts, the distortion of their shoes of Cordovan leather with their curling toes, they seem to proclaim that everywhere shame is a castaway. A lack of lovers to admire her is a woman's crown of woe. On her crowds of thronging suitors rests her claim to nobility and courtly pride. There was of old time, I call God to witness, greater modesty in married men, who would have blushed to be seen in the company of such women, than there is now in married women; and men by such shameful conduct are emboldened in their amours abroad and driven to haunt the market-place and the public street. . . .

When, therefore, that bewitchment was brought to naught with the aid of a certain old woman, my mother submitted to the duties of a wife as faithfully as she had kept her virginity when assailed by so many reproaches. Happy as she was in all else, she laid herself open to the chance, if not the certainty, of endless misery when she, whose goodness was ever growing, begat [me]. . . . Yet Thou knowest, Almighty One, with what purity and holiness in obedience to Thee was my upbringing, what care of nurses in infancy, of masters and teachers in boyhood, she gave me, with no lack even of fine clothes for my little body, putting me on an honourable equality with sons of princes and nobles. . . .

O God, Thou knowest what warnings, what prayers she daily poured into my ears not to listen to corrupting words from anyone. She taught me, as often as she had leisure from household cares, how and for what I should to pray to Thee. Thou alone knowest with what pains she travailed that the sound beginning of a happy and honourable childhood guarded by Thee, might not be ruined by an unsound heart. . . .

A Missing Husband

Now whilst the young girl was still living a married life, something befell which gave no slight impulse to the amendment of her life. The French in the time of King Henry were fighting with much bitterness against the Normans and their Count William, who afterward conquered England and Scotland, and in that clash of the two nations it was my father's fate to be taken prisoner. It was the custom of this

Count never to hold his prisoners for ransom, but to condemn them to life-long captivity. The news being brought to his wife . . . , she abstained from food and drink, and sleep was still more impossible through her despairing anxiety, the cause of this being not the amount of his ransom, but the impossibility of his release.

In the dead of that night, as, full of deep anxiety, she lay in her bed, since it is the habit of the Devil to invade souls weakened with grief, suddenly whilst she lay awake, the Enemy himself rushed upon her and by the burden of his oppression almost crushed the life out of her. As she choked in agony of spirit and lost all use of her limbs, being unable to make a single sound, having only her reason free, in utter silence she awaited aid from God alone. Then behold, from the head of her bed, a spirit, no doubt a good one, [called on the Virgin Mary, overcame the evil spirit] . . . and said, "Take care to be a good woman." But the attendants, alarmed by the sudden uproar, rose to see how their mistress did, and found her half-dead, with bloodless face and all the strength of her body beaten down; they questioned her about the noise and thereupon were told the causes of it, and hardly were they able by their presence and talk and by lighting of a lamp to revive her.

Widowhood

Now after the death of my father, although the beauty of her face and form remained undimmed, and I, scarce half a year old, was enough cause for anxiety, she resolved to continue in her widowhood. With what spirit she ruled herself, what an example of modesty she set, may be gathered from the following instance. When my kinsmen, eager for my father's fiefs and possessions, strove to take them by the exclusion of my mother, they fixed a day for advancing their claims [in court]. The day came and the nobles were in council prepared to act in despite of all justice. My mother, being assured of their greedy intentions, had retired to the church and was repeating her regular prayers before the image of the crucified Lord. One of my father's kinsmen, having the same views as the others and instructed by them, came to request her presence to hear their decision, as they were waiting for her. Whereupon she said, "I will do nothing in the matter but in the presence of my Lord." "Whose lord?" said he. Then, stretching out her hand towards the image of the crucified Lord, she replied, "This is my Lord, this is the advocate through whom I will plead." At that saying the man reddened and, not being very subtle, put on a wry smile to hide his evil intent and went off to tell his friends what he had heard. And they too, being covered with confusion at such an answer, and knowing they had no just occasion against her utter honesty, ceased to trouble her.

Soon one of the chief men of that place and province, a nephew of my father, as greedy as he was powerful, attacked the woman in the following terms: "Since, mistress," said he, "you have sufficient youth and beauty, it is meet that you should marry, that your life in the world may be more pleasant; and the children of my uncle should be placed under my care to be trustily brought up by me, his possessions finally coming into my hands, as is right they should." "But," said she, "you know that your uncle was of very noble descent. Since God has taken him away, Hymen[57] shall not repeat his rites over me, unless a marriage with some much greater noble shall offer." Now with craft did the woman speak of getting for husband a greater noble, knowing that could hardly, if at all, come to pass, so that, as he misliked talk of a higher noble, she, who was wholly set against noble and mean alike, might forthwith put an end to all hope of a second marriage. And he setting down to overmuch pride her talk of a greater noble, she rejoined, "Certainly a greater noble, or none at all." He perceiving the resolution with which the lady spoke, desisted from his designs, and never again required of her anything of the kind.

In much fear of God, then, and with like love of all her kin and, most of all, the poor, this woman wisely ruled us and ours, and that loyalty which she had given her husband in his lifetime she kept unbroken and with double constancy to his spirit, with no loosening of the ancient union of their bodies by substitution of other flesh on his departure, almost every day striving to relieve him by the offering of the life-bringing sacrifice.[58] Friendly to all the poor in general, to some in her abounding pity she was generous and bountiful to the full extent of her means. The sting of remembering her sins could not have been sharper if she had been given up to all kinds of wickedness, and if she had dreaded the punishment of every ill deed that is done. In plainness of living there was nothing that she could do, for her delicacy and her sumptuous rearing did not admit of a meagre diet. In other matters no one knew what self-denial she practised. With these eyes I have seen and made certain by touch that whereas over all she wore garments of rich material, next to her skin she was covered with the roughest haircloth, which she wore not only in the daytime,

---

57.   Hymen = Greek god of marriage. The use of classical allusions, even to pagan gods, was common in medieval literature.

58.   The life-bringing sacrifice = a mass said for the benefit of his soul.

but, what was a great hardship for a delicate body, she even slept in it at night.

The night offices she hardly ever missed, being as regular at the services attended by all God's people in holy seasons; in such fashion that scarcely ever in her house was there rest from the singing of God's praises by her chaplains, who were always busy at their office.

So constantly was her dead husband's name on her lips, that in prayer, in almsgiving, in the midst of ordinary business, she continually spoke of him, because he was for ever in her mind. For with love of whom the heart is full, to his name shapeth the tongue in speech, whether it will or no.

Retirement to Religious Life

About twelve years after my father's death, I am told, during which the widow managed house and children under worldly garb, she now made haste to bring to happy birth a resolve with which she had long been in labor. . . . [S]he resolved to retire to the monastery of [Fly]. Having therefore built a little house built near the church through the agency of my master, at last she came forth from the place where she was staying, and knowing that I should be utterly an orphan with no one on whom to depend—for great as was my wealth of kinsfolk and connections, yet there was none to give me the loving care a little child needs at such an age, for with no lack of food and clothing I [still] suffered from the loss of all those precautions for the helplessness of tender years that only a woman can provide—knowing I say, that I should be exposed to such want of care, yet the love and fear of God hardened her heart, but in her journey to this convent having to pass through the town in which I was living, the sight of the castle gave intolerable anguish to her lacerated heart stung with the bitter remembrance of what she had left behind. . . .

A few years before her death she conceived a strong desire to take the sacred veil. When I tried to dissuade her, putting forward as authority the passage where it is written, "Let no prelate attempt to veil widows," saying that her most chaste life would be sufficient without the external veil, as Anselm, too, abbot of Bec, . . . had of old time forbidden, yet so much more was she inflamed and by no reasoning could be driven from her resolve. So she prevailed, and when taking the veil in the presence of John, the Abbot of that place, gave satisfactory reasons for this act, and in the end she proved that . . . her consecration was invited by signs from heaven.

34. Alexander Neckham:
A Country House (12th c.)

While the bedchamber described here belonged to the owners of
the home, any woman who worked in the kitchen of a wealthy
household such as this one was likely to be a servant rather than
the mistress of the house. The garden provided the household
with herbs for both cooking and for health care, and some of the
plants mentioned here are the same ones recommended by Trotula
(Part II, above).
Source: U. T. Holmes, *Daily Living in the Twelfth Century, Based on
the Observations of Alexander Neckham in London and Paris* (Madison:
University of Wisonsin Press, 1952).

The Bedroom

In the bedchamber let a curtain go around the walls decently, or a
scenic canopy, for the avoiding of flies and spiders. From the style or
epistyle of a column a tapestry should hang appropriately. Near the
bed let there be placed a chair to which a stool may be added, and a
bench nearby the bed. On the bed itself should be placed a feather
mattress to which a bolster is attached. A quilted pad of striped cloth
should cover this on which a cushion for the head can be placed. Then
sheets of muslin, ordinary cotton, or at least pure linen, should be
laid. Next a coverlet of green cloth or of coarse wool, of which the fur
lining is badger, cat, beaver, or sable, should be put—all this if there
is lacking purple and down. A perch should be nearby on which can
rest a hawk. . . . From another pole let there hang clothing. . . .

The Kitchen

In a kitchen there should be a small table on which cabbage may be
minced, and also lentils, peas, shelled beans, beans in the pod, millet,
onions, and other vegetables of the kind that can be cut up. There
should be also pots, tripods, a mortar, a hatchet, a pestle, a stirring
stick, a hook, a cauldron, a bronze vessel, a small pan, a baking pan,
a meathook, a griddle, small pitchers, a trencher, a bowl, a platter, a
pickling vat, and knives for cleaning fish. In a vivarium let fish be
kept, in which they can be caught by net, fork, spear, or light hook,
or with a basket. The chief cook should have a cupboard in the kitchen
where he may store away aromatic spices, and bread flour sifted
through a sieve—and used also for feeding small fish—may be hidden

away there. Let there be also a cleaning place where the entrails and feathers of ducks and other domestic fowl can be removed and the birds cleaned. Likewise there should be a large spoon for removing foam and skimming. Also there should be hot water for scalding fowl.

Have a pepper mill, and a hand mill. Small fish for cooking should be put into a pickling mixture, that is, water mixed with salt. . . . There should be also a garde-robe[59] pit through which the filth of the kitchen may be evacuated. In the pantry let there be shaggy towels, tablecloth, and an ordinary hand towel which shall hang from a pole to avoid mice. Knives should be kept in the pantry, an engraved saucedish, a saltcellar, a cheese container, a candelabra, a lantern, a candlestick, and baskets. In the cellar or storeroom should be casks, tuns, wineskins, cups, cup cases, spoons, ewers, basins, baskets, pure wine, cider, beer, unfermented wine, mixed wine, claret, nectar, mead, . . . pear wine, red wine, wine from Auvergne, clove-spiced wine for gluttons whose thirst is unquenchable. . . .

The Garden

It should be ornamented with roses and lilies, the heliotrope, violets, and mandrakes. One should have also parsley, costus, fennel, southernwood, coriander, sage, savory, hyssop, mint, rue, dittany, celery, pyrethrum, lettuce, cress, and peonies. There should be made beds for onions, leeks, garlic, pumpkins, and shallots. A garden is distinguished when it has growing there cucumbers, the soporific poppy, daffodils, and acanthus. There should not be lacking pot vegetables such as beets, dog's mercury, orach, sorrel, and mallows. Anise, mustard, white pepper, and absinthe give usefulness to any garden. A noble garden will show you also medlars [very similar to persimmons], quinces, bon chretien pears, peaches, pears of St. Regulus, pomegranates, lemons, oranges, almonds, dates which are the fruit of palm trees, and figs.

. . . Colewort and ragwort excite love, but the marvelous frigidity of psyllium seed offers a remedy for that affliction. Myrtle too is a friend of temperance. . . . Those who are experienced in such matters distinguish between the heliotrope and our "heliotrope" which is called calendula, and between mugwort and our native "mugwort" which is feverfew. It happens that the wool-blade is one shrub and the silverleaved wool-blade is another. The gladiolus bears a yellow

---

59. Garde-robe = normally, a privy; in this case, a chute for kitchen waste.

one; but the burweed has no flower. Other noted herbs are hore-hound, hound's-tongue or *cynoglossa,* parsley, *macedonium,* bryony, groundsel, wild myrrh or angelica, regina, coriander—three heaven-gazing species.

35. Matilda of Stickney: Land Grants (ca. 1170–98)

The most common kind of written evidence from much of medi-eval Europe is not narrative but documentary: formal agreements, records of transactions, accounts kept by institutions or individu-als, and so on. Charters, a very common type of document, most often record land grants or sales, many of which were made to the church. Most charters record the actions of men, and the witnesses to the actions, whose names are recorded at the end, were also usually men, the rare female witness generally being the wife of the grantor. Still, sufficient numbers of women's names and actions appear in the vast body of charter evidence to make this kind of document useful to the historian of women, particu-larly in tracing women and their lands within families.

Matilda of Stickney and her husband belonged to the lower end of the landed class of medieval England; they may not even have been of knightly status, but their charters are typical in most ways of the documents left to us by the lower nobility.

Source: "Some Revesby Charters of the Soke of Bolingbroke," ed. Dorothy M. Owen, in *A Medieval Miscellany for Doris Mary Stenton,* eds. Patricia M. Barnes and C. F. Slade (London: Pipe Roll Society, 1962). Tr. E.M.A.

To all sons of the holy mother the church, William of Stickney and Matilda his wife [send] greeting. Know that we have given and granted to God and St. Mary and the monks of St. Lawrence [i.e., Revesby Abbey, Lincolnshire], in perpetual alms, (1) whatever they hold be-tween the causeway[60] which goes from the door of the grange[61] toward Stickney and Margaret's meadow which is next to Torendic, and be-tween the yard of the grange and their sheepfold, and (2) meadowland three perches[62] in width, along the western side of Nordike causeway, contiguous with the causeway, and in length from a certain piece of land in Stickney to Smalna, and (3) whatever they have inside their

---

60. The region was characterized by marshes.
61. Grange = barn.
62. Perch = measure of land, roughly 5 yards.

ditch, from the eastern corner of the garden to the western corner of the orchard, from the northern part of the causeway which goes from the grange toward Stickney. All these things we have granted them in perpetual alms, free and quit from all earthly service and secular exaction, and whatever is owed to the king or to any man for this land, we and our heirs shall do, and we and our heirs guarantee this land and this donation to the same monks against all men. Witnesses: Robert, son of Ernisius; Ralph Travers; William de Agerni; William, the clerk of Robert son of Ernisius; Torald, dean of Edlington; Robert his brother; Robert Calf; Geoffrey of Enderby; Adam of Enderby; Alan his brother; Gilbert de Cauz.

To all sons of the holy mother the church, William of Stickney [sends] greeting. Know that I, for my health and that of all my ancestors, have granted to the monks of St. Lawrence that they may have the common pasture and all its easements in all places which are called "Wythage". This common and these easements I have granted and given them in perpetual alms, with the consent and good will of Matilda my wife and of Alan my heir, free and quit of all earthly service and secular exaction and absolved by me and my heirs. Witnesses: Thorald, dean of Horncastle; Ralph, clerk of Baumber; Andrew, son of John of Edlington; Warin of Edlington; William Tisun; Master William of Newark; Robert of Enderby; Reiner de Belleland; Gilbert of Bolingbroke.

To all sons of the holy mother the church, Matilda daughter of Roger of Huditoft, wife of William of Stickney, [sends] greeting. Know that I have granted and given to God and Saint Mary and the monks of St. Lawrence, for the health of my own soul and my husband William's, and those of all my ancestors and heirs, in perpetual alms, that whole toft[63] which Alice, sister of Hugh Habba, held in Stickney. This land, with all its appurtenances within the village and outside, I have given to the same monks free and quit by me and my heirs, and absolved of all earthly service and secular exaction, except that those monks shall give to me and to my heirs ten and a half pence annually, that is, five pence at Christmas and five and a half pence at the feast of St. Botolph. And whatever service is owed for this land to the king or to any man, I and my heirs will do, and we will guarantee it against all men. Witnesses: Alan, priest of Stickney; Roger the cleric; Geoffrey le Neucumen; William the cleric; Eustace; Godfrey and Simon; Lady Margaret; and Elena, wife of Roger the clerk.

---

63. Toft = a homestead with its farmland.

To all sons of the holy mother the church, Matilda, daughter of
Roger of Huditoft of Stickney, [sends] greeting. Know that I have
granted and given to God and St. Mary and to the monks of St.
Lawrence, in perpetual alms, half a bovate[64] of land in the territory of
Stickney, that is, that half a bovate which Alan le Neucumen held in
that village. I have given this land free and quit by me and my heirs,
and absolved of all earthly and secular exaction, with all its appurtenances in tofts and crofts,[65] in meadows and pastures, in arable land
and marshland. And whatever is owed for this land to the king or to
any man, I and my heirs will do, and we will guarantee this land
with all its appurtenances to the same monks, against all men. This
donation I made to them in the time of my widowhood, with the
consent and good will of Alan, my son and heir, and of my other
heirs. These were the witnesses: Robert, the deacon of Bolingbroke;
Robert, the priest of Mareham; Roger of Benniworth; Gilbert de Bou-
logne; Nicholas del Keene; Alard of Hoiland; William, son of Hem-
ming; Richard, cleric of Mareham; Geoffrey and Adam of Enderby.
These were also witnesses: Christiana, wife of Henry of Claxby; and
Eda, wife of Richard, the clerk of Mareham.

36. The Roll of Ladies and Boys and Girls (1185)

In 1185 King Henry II of England had an investigation made and
a document drawn up listing the women and children under his
direct feudal control: the widows, daughters and minor sons of
his deceased feudal tenants. Under feudal custom, the widows
and unmarried children were his to give in marriage (generally
for a fee), and the lands were his to exploit until their rightful
heirs came of age. The partial results of this inquiry survive today;
this is an unusual document, but it illustrates a very common
situation: noble women and children whose feudal lords had great
power over their lives and lands. The information provided about
the individuals here is sketchy, but illuminating all the same—
especially as these are people about whom we otherwise would
know little or nothing.

Source: *Rotuli de Dominabus et Pueris et Puellis de XII Comitatibus,*

---

64. Bovate = measure of land, based on what one ox could plow in a season; roughly
10 to 20 acres.
65. Croft = small holding of farmland.

ed. John Horace Round (London: The Pipe Roll Society, 1913; repr. Kraus, 1966). Used with the permission of the Controller of Her Britannic Majesty's Stationery Office. Tr. E.M.A.

Rohese de Bussy, who was the daughter of Baldwin fitzGilbert and the wife of William de Bussy, is in the gift of the Lord King, and is 50 years old; and she has two daughters, of whom John de Builli has the elder and Hugh Wake has the second. Her inheritance in Morton is worth £15 per year, with stock of three plow-teams[66] and 200 sheep. The land which she now has there is worth £4; her two daughters and the other men who hold by their service have the rest. . . .

The wife of Walter Furmage, who was the daughter of Thomas de Nevill, is in the gift of the Lord King, and is 24 years old, and she has a daughter who is the heir, who is not yet a year old. She has half a plow-team of land in Crosholm, for which she pays 5s. annually, and it could be put to farm with a mill for 2 marks [i.e., 13s. 4d.]. The same woman has four bovates[67] of land in Sinterby, which she holds in demesne, and she cultivates them with one plow, and they are her dowry from her father's fief, and the land is worth 12s. per year.

The wife of Simon de Crevequer, who was the daughter of Robert fitzErnisius, and daughter of the daughter of John Ingelram, is in the gift of the Lord King, and is 24 years old; and she has two sons, the elder of whom is five years old, the younger four. Her land in Haneworth is worth 100s. annually, and it cannot be worth more. . . .

Margaret Engaine has been in the gift of the Lord King for the past eight years; and Geoffrey Brito married her, it is said, without a license from the King; and this was previously shown to the justices. Geoffrey Brito found pledges that he would answer at the exchequer, three weeks after Michaelmas, for the aforesaid Margaret whom he married; they were Thomas de Hale and Alan de Hale and John of Southwick. . . . Margareta Engaine, whom Geoffrey Brito married, as is told above, has six pounds' worth of land in Pytchley; and she is 50 years old, and her heir is Richard Engaine. And she was the daughter of Richard fitzUrse. . . .

Alicia, who was the wife of Fulk de Lusors and the sister of William d'Auberville, is in the gift of the Lord King; and she has two sons who are knights and two others and six married daughters and three unmarried daughters, who are in the custody of their mother. Her land in Glaptorn is worth 100s. annually with the following stock: two

---

66. Plow-team = either the team itself or the amount of land it can cultivate.
67. Bovate = a measure of land, equal to one-eighth of a plow-team.

plow-teams and six cows and one bull and 30 pigs and 40 sheep. Her land in Abiton, which is her dower and is in Spelho Hundred, is worth £14 annually.

Alicia, who was the wife of Thomas de Bellofago and the daughter of Waleran d'Oiri, is in the gift of the Lord King, and is 20 years old. She has in Ashley one and a half knights' fees, which Peter of Ashley and Robert de Watervill hold from her; their service was given as dower to the aforesaid lady. She has one son who is three years old and is in the custody of Nigel fitzAlexander.

Beatrice, who was the wife of Robert Mantel, the Lord King's servant in the Honor of Nottingham, is in the gift of the Lord King, and she is 30 years old. Her land in Roade, which she has in dower, is worth 30s. per year with stock of one plow-team, and there are six virgates[68] there. She has three sons and one daughter; the eldest son is 10 years old and is in the custody of Robert de Salcey, it is said, on the King's orders. The other children are with their mother. . . .

Mary de Traili, who was the wife of Geoffrey de Trailli, is in the gift of the Lord King, and she is 40 years old, and was the kinswoman of Earl Simon. Walter de Trailli was her son and heir, and besides him she has another son who is a monk, and one married daughter, and another who is a nun. Her land, Northill, is worth £14 annually. . . .

Beatrice, who was the wife of Richard Gubiun, is in the gift of the Lord King, it is believed, because she has her dower in Northampton; and she is more than 40 years old and has seven sons and six daughters. She has 18 pounds' worth of land in Flete Hundred in the fief of Simon de Beauchamp. . . .

Matilda Malherbe is in the gift of the Lord King and is 40 years old; and she has a son and heir who is a knight, and also sons and daughters besides him, but the jurors do not know how many. Half of the village of Hockliffe, which is her dowry, and which she holds from Robert Malherbe her brother, is worth £4 15s. 4d. annually, with the one plow-team which is there; and if 100 sheep were added, it would be worth £5 15s. 4d. . . .

William of Windsor, son of William of Windsor the elder, is in the custody of the Lord King. And by [the King's] orders he is and has been in the custody of his mother Hawise of Windsor, for nine years, along with his lands, Horton and Eton. The aforesaid William is 18 years old. . . .

Hawise of Windsor is in the gift of the Lord King, and, besides the

---

68. Virgate = a measure of land, equal to one-fourth of a plow-team.

above-named heir, she has seven daughters; two of them are overseas, two are nuns, and three are in the gift of the Lord King. The age of the aforesaid lady is not known to the jurors, because she was born overseas. . . .

Basilia, who was the wife of David Pinel . . . and is 18 years old, and was the daughter of Robert Taillard of Merlawe, is in the gift of the Lord King, and she has two thirds of the aforementioned half hide[69] of land, with her children, that is, one son and one daughter, who are in the custody of their mother . . . , and the son is three years old, and the daughter is two. . . .

Cecily of Bowthorpe is in the gift of the Lord King; she has had two husbands, Hugh de Scotcia and Eustace of Leyham. By Hugh she had three sons, and by Eustace two sons and two daughters. Reginald, her firstborn son and heir, is 24 years old; his father Eustace was of the family of the count of Meulan and a kinsman of Robert fitzHumfrey. The aforesaid Cecily is of the family of the Earl de Redvers, and she is 50 years old. Her land in Bowthorpe is worth £8 with regular stock. In the same manor Roger of Hoo holds a quarter of a knight's fee from the same Cecily, beyond the land worth £8. The aforesaid Reginald her son has a wife, the niece of the sheriff Wimer, whom, according to Wimer, he received from the King.

She who was the wife of John de Bidun the younger, Matilda by name, is in the gift of the Lord King, and she is 10 years old and was the daughter of Thomas fitzBernard. Her land in Kirkby is worth £6, with stock of one plow-team, and it cannot be worth more.

37. Cristina Corner: Petition for Exemption from Sumptuary Laws (15th c.)

See Part II above for sumptuary laws of the sort that Cristina Corner is challenging here by petitioning the pope. Her petition was granted for a period of three years, for a fee.
Source: *Lo statuto inedito delle nozze veneziane emanato nell'anno 1299,* ed. C. Foucard (Venice: Tipografia de commercio, 1858). Tr. E.M.A.

Most blessed father: Since in the city of Venice there has been from ancient times . . . an edict, law or statute, by which it is decreed

---

69. Hide = fiscal measurement of land, roughly 80 to 120 acres.

that women of that city may not wear in public caps, circlets, rings, necklaces, garments, or ornaments of gold and silver, precious stones, gems or jewels, or other precious jewelry or ornaments, under certain penalties, therefore your devoted Cristina, daughter of Andrew Corner of Venice, dares not wear her many jewels and ornaments, although she is known to have them. Wherefore she, who comes from a noble family, beseeches Your Holiness that she be permitted to wear publicly the aforesaid circlets, rings, necklaces, garments, and ornaments of gold and silver, pearls, gems, precious stones or jewels, and other jewelry and precious ornaments, in honor of her parents, and of her own beauty, and that she, who has previously complied with this law, according to the tradition and custom in the said city, shall in these matters live freely and lawfully, as she can and is able. Deign from your special grace to grant and permit this, the aforesaid law and statute or any others to the contrary notwithstanding.

38. Leonor López de Córdoba: Autobiography (14th–15th c.)

Leonor López was a Spanish woman of very high rank, as she carefully explains in this work, which is one of the earliest known pieces of female autobiography. She was only eight years old when, as she tells us, she was imprisoned with the rest of her family for political reasons. After the events described below, she rose once more to a powerful position at the royal court, but she had to retire in disfavor in 1412, and it was after this that she had the story of part of her life written down in her own words.
Source: Amy Katz Kaminsky and Elaine Dorough Johnson, "To Restore Honor and Fortune: 'The Autobiography of Leonor López de Córdoba,'" in The Female Autograph: Theory and Practice of Autobiography from the Tenth to the Twentieth Century, ed. Domna C. Stanton (University of Chicago Press, 1987).

. . . Therefore, know all who see this document, how I, Doña Leonor López de Córdoba, daughter of my Lord Grand Master Don Martín López de Córdoba and Doña Sancha Carrillo, to whom God grant glory and heaven, swear by this sign † which I worship, that all that is written here is true for I saw it and it happened to me, and I write it to the honor and glory of my Lord Jesus Christ, and of the Holy Virgin Mary his mother who bore him so that all creatures that suffered might be certain that I believe in her mercy, that if they commend themselves from the heart to the Holy Virgin Mary she will console and succor them as she consoled me. And so that whoever might hear it [might] know the tale of my deeds and miracles that the Holy Virgin Mary showed me, it is my intention that it be left as a record. I ordered it written as you see before you. I am the daughter of the aforesaid Grand Master of Calatrava, in the time of Lord King Don Pedro, who bestowed the honor of giving him the Commandery of Alcantara, and at last of Calatrava, and that Grand Master my father was a descendant of the House of Aguilar and nephew of Don Juan Manuel, son of a niece of his, a daughter with a brother. And he rose to very high rank, as can be found in the *Chronicles of Spain*.

As I have said, I am the daughter of Doña Sancha Carrillo, niece and maid of the most illustriously remembered Lord King Don Alfonso (whom God grant Holy paradise), father of the aforementioned Lord King Don Pedro. My mother died very young, and so my father married me at the age of seven years to Ruy Gutiérrez de Henestrosa, son of Juan Ferrández de Henestrosa, High Chamberlain of Lord King Don Pedro and his High Chancellor of the Secret Seal, and High Steward of Queen Doña Blanca his wife, who married Doña María de Haro, Lady of Haro and los Cameros. My husband inherited many goods from his father and many offices. And his men on horseback numbered three hundred, and forty skeins of pearls as fat as chickpeas, and five hundred Moors, men and women, and two thousand marks of silver in tableware, and the jewels and gems of his household you could not write down on two sheets of paper. And his father and his mother left all this to him because they had no other son or heir. To me, my father gave twenty thousand gold coins upon marriage. And my husband and I resided in Carmona with the daughters of Lord King Don Pedro, and my brothers-in-law, husbands of my sisters, and a brother of mine whose name was Don Lope López de Córdoba Carrillo. . . .

. . . And Lord King Don Enrique seeing himself King of Castile came to Seville and . . . ordered that they cut off my father's head in the Plaza de San Francisco in Seville, and that his property be confiscated, and that of his son-in-law, defenders, and servants. . . .

The rest of us were kept prisoner for nine years until Lord King Enrique died. Our husbands had sixty pounds of iron each on their feet, and my brother Don Lope López had a chain on top of the irons, in which there were seventy links. He was a child of thirteen years, the most beautiful creature there was in the world. And they singled out my husband to be put in the hunger tank, where they held him for six or seven days without food or drink because he was a cousin of the lady princesses, daughters of Lord King Don Pedro. At this juncture a plague came, and my two brothers, my brother-in-law, and thirteen knights of the house of my father all died. . . . And they took them all out to the ironsmith's like slaves to remove their irons. After they were dead my sad little brother Don Lope López asked the jailer who held us to tell Gonzalo Ruiz Bolante to do us a great kindness and a great honor for the love of God: "Sir jailer be so kind as to strike these irons from me before my soul departs, and do not let them take me out to the ironsmith's." . . . He was but one year older than I, and they took him out to the ironsmith's on a plank like a slave, and they buried him with my brothers and with my sisters, and with my brothers-in-law in San Francisco of Seville. . . .

Then the very eminent and very honorable, most illustriously and saintedly remembered Lord King Don Enrique died, and he ordered in his will that they let us out of prison and return to us all that was ours. And I stayed at the home of my lady aunt María García Carrillo, and my husband went to reclaim his property and those who held it esteemed him little, because he had no rank nor means to claim it, and you well know how rights depend on the station you have on which to base a claim. And thus was my husband lost, and he wandered seven years through the world, a wretched man, and never did he find a relative or friend who did him a good turn or had pity on him. And at the end of seven years, they told my husband, who was in Badajoz with his uncle Lope Fernández de Padilla in the War of Portugal, that I was doing very well in the house of my lady and aunt Doña María García Carrillo, that my relatives had done me much kindness. He rode on his mule, which was worth very little money, and what he wore was not worth thirty *maravedís*.[70] And he came through the doorway of my lady and aunt.

. . . After my husband came, as I have said, he went to the house of my lady aunt, which was in Córdoba next to San Hipólito, and she took me in with my husband there in some houses adjacent to hers. And seeing that we had so little peace, for thirty days I said a prayer to the Holy Virgin Mary of Bethlehem, praying every night on my knees three hundred Hail Marys, that she might put it into my lady aunt's mind to consent and open a doorway into her dwellings. And two days before I finished the prayer, I asked my aunt if she would allow me to open that passageway so that we would not have to walk through the street, among all the knights who were in Córdoba, to

---

70. *Maravedís* = Muslim coins.

come and eat at her table. And her grace responded that she would be happy to do so, and I was greatly consoled. When on the following day I tried to open the passageway, maids of hers had turned her against me, so that she would not do it, and I was so disconsolate I lost my patience, and the one who had most set my lady aunt against me died in my hands, swallowing her tongue. . . .

Then there was a raid on the Jewish quarter, and I took an orphan child who was there and had him baptized so that he might be instructed in the faith. And one day, walking back with my lady aunt from mass at San Hipólito, I saw the clerics of San Hipólito dividing up those courtyards . . . , and I begged my lady aunt Doña Mencía Carrillo that she be so kind as to buy that place for me, since I had been in her company for seventeen years. She bought them for me and gave them. . . . I believe that for the charitable act I performed in raising that orphan in the faith of Jesus Christ, God helped me in giving me the beginning of a house. . . . At this time, it pleased God that with the help of my lady aunt and of the labor of my hands I built in that courtyard two palaces and a garden and another two or three houses for the servants.

Then there came a very cruel pestilence, and my lady did not want to leave the city. I begged her for mercy to flee with my little children so that they would not die, and this did not please her, but she gave me permission, and I departed from Córdoba, and I went to Santaella with my children. The orphan I brought up lived in Santaella, and he gave me lodging in his house, and all the residents of the town were very happy with my going there, and received me very warmly because they had been servants of my lord and father. And thus they gave me the best house that there was in the place, which belonged to Fernando Alonso Mediebarba. My lady aunt arrived unexpectedly with her daughters, and I removed myself to a small apartment. And her daughters, my cousins, were never favorably disposed toward me because of the kindness their mother did me, and from then on I suffered so much bitterness that it cannot all be written down. And a pestilence came, and my lady departed with her people for Aguilar, and she took me with her, although her daughters thought that was doing too much, because she loved me greatly and had a high opinion of me. And I sent the orphan whom I had raised to Ecija.

The night we arrived in Aguilar the young man came in from Ecija with two tumors on his throat and three dark blotches on his face and a very high fever. Don Alfonso Fernandez, my cousin, was there, and his wife and all his household, and although all of them were my nieces and my friends, they came to me when they found out that my

servant had come in that state. They said to me: "Your servant Alonso
has come with pestilence, and if Don Alfonso Fernandez sees him, he
will wreak havoc being in the presence of such an illness." You who
hear this story can well understand the pain that came to my heart for
I was angered and bitter. Thinking that such great suffering had
entered the house on my account, I had a servant of the lord my father,
the Grand Master, called, whose name was Miguel de Santaella, and
I begged him to take that young man to his house, and the poor man
became afraid and said: "My lady, how shall I take him sick with the
pestilence, for it may kill me?" And I said to him, "Son, God shall not
will it so." And he took him out of shame. And because of my sins,
thirteen people, who kept vigil over him during the night, all died.
And I offered a prayer that I had heard a nun say before a crucifix. It
seems she was very devoted to Jesus Christ, and it is said that after
she heard morning prayer, she came before the crucifix and prayed
on her knees seven thousand times: "Merciful son of the Virgin, take
pity." And one night the nun heard that the crucifix answered her
and said: "You called me merciful and merciful I shall be." I place
great faith in these words and prayed this prayer every night, entreating God that he should want to free me and my children, and if
any of them had to be taken away, it should be the older one for he
was in great pain. And it was God's will that one night I could not
find anyone to watch over that suffering young man, because all those
who had watched over him up to then had died. And that son of mine
whose name was Juan Fernández de Henestrosa, after his grandfather,
and who was twelve years and four months of age, came to me and
said: "My lady, is there no one who will watch over Alonso tonight?"
And I said to him: "You watch over him for the love of God." And he
answered me: "My lady, now that the others have died, do you want
it to kill me?" And I said to him: "For the charitable act I am performing,
God will take pity on me." And my son, so as not to disobey me, went
to watch over him, and because of my sins, that night he came down
with the plague and the next I buried him. And the sick one survived,
but all those stated above died. And Doña Teresa, wife of Don Alfonso
Fernández my cousin, became very angry that my son was dying for
that reason in her house, and with death in his mouth, she ordered
him to be taken out. And I was so wrought with anguish that I could
not speak for the shame that those noble people made me bear. And
my sad little son said: "Tell my lady Doña Teresa that she not have
me cast out, for my soul will soon depart for Heaven." And that night
he died, and he was buried in Santa María la Coronada, which is in
the town. But Doña Teresa had designs against me, and I did not

know why. And she had ordered that he not be buried within the town, and thus, when they took him to be buried I went with him. And when I was going down the street with my son, the people, offended for me, came out shouting: "Come out good people and you will see the most unfortunate, forsaken and condemned woman in the world," with cries that rent the Heavens. Since the residents of that place were all liege and subject to my lord father, and although they knew it troubled their masters, they made great display of the grief they shared with me, as if I were their lady.

That night, as I came back from burying my son, they told me that I should go to Córdoba, and I approached my lady aunt to see if she would order me to do it. But she said to me: "Lady niece, I cannot fail to do so, as I have promised my daughter-in-law and my daughters, who are of one mind; since they have pressed me to remove you from my presence, I have granted it to them. I do not know what vexation you have caused my daughter-in-law, Doña Teresa, that she feels such ill will toward you." And I said to her with many tears: "My lady, may God not save me if I deserved this." And thus I came to my houses in Córdoba.

39. Christine de Pisan: Advice for Noblewomen (1405)

Christine de Pisan (1365–1430?) came from an Italian family which moved to France when her father, an astrologer and physician, went to work for the French king. At the age of 15, she married Etienne du Castel, a French nobleman and courtier. Etienne died in 1390; Christine was left a 25-year-old widow with three young children. At this point in her life she began to study seriously, and eventually she became a successful professional writer—the first woman we know of to take up such a profession. Many of her works survive, and an increasing number are becoming available in English translation. Christine is known for her defense of women in writings including *The Book of the City of Ladies*, an allegorical work published in 1404. *The Treasure of the City of Ladies, or, The Book of Three Virtues*, which is excerpted here, was published in 1405 as a sort of sequel to the earlier book. It is simply a book of advice for women. A large part of the book is addressed to queens, princesses and ladies of the royal court; a considerable portion is addressed to noblewomen of various ranks; relatively brief sections speak to townswomen and peasant women.

Source: Christine de Pizan, *A Medieval Woman's Mirror of Honor: The Treasury of the City of Ladies*, tr. Charity Cannon Willard, ed. Madeleine Pelner Cosman (New York and Tenafly, NJ: Persea Books, Inc. and Bard Hall Press, 1989).

A slightly different manner of life from that of the baronesses is suitable for ladies and demoiselles living in fortified places or on their lands outside of towns. . . . These women spend much of their lives in households without husbands. The men usually are at court or in distant countries. So the ladies will have responsibilities for managing their property, their revenues, and their lands. In order for such a woman to act with good judgment, she must know the yearly income from her estate. She must manage it so well that by conferring with her husband, her gentle words and good counsel will lead to their agreement to follow a plan for the estate that their revenues permit. This plan must not be so ambitious that at year's end they find themselves in debt to their retainers or other creditors. Surely there is no disgrace in living within one's income, however small it may be. But it is shameful to live so extravagantly that creditors daily shout and bellow outside the door, some even raising clubs and threatening violence. It is also terrible to have to resort to extortion from one's own men and tenants. The lady or demoiselle must be well informed about the rights of domain of fiefs and secondary fiefs, about contributions, the lord's rights of harvest, shared crops, and all other rights of possession, and the customs both local and foreign. The world is full of governors of lord's lands and jurisdictions who are intentionally dishonest. Aware of this, the lady must be knowledgeable enough to protect her interests so that she cannot be deceived. She should know how to manage accounts and should attend to them often, also superintending her agents' treatment of her tenants and men. If they are being deceived or harassed beyond reasonable bounds, both she and her husband would suffer. As for penalties against poor people, she should be more compassionate than rigorous.

Farming also is this good housekeeper's domain. In what weather and in what season the fields should be fertilized; whether the land is moist or dry; the best way to have furrows run according to the lay of the land; their proper depth, straightness, and parallel layout; and the favorable time for sowing with seed suited to the land—all these she must know. Likewise, she must know about vineyards if the land lies in a region where there are grapes. She requires good laborers and supervisors in these activities, and she should not hire people who change masters from season to season. It is a bad sign if workers are always on the move. Nor should she hire workers who are too old, for they will be lazy and feeble, nor too young, for they will be frivolous.

She will insist that her laborers get up early. If she is a good manager she won't depend on anyone else to see to this but will arise early herself, put on a cloak, go to the window, and watch there until she sees them go out, for laborers usually are inclined to laziness. She should often take her recreation in the fields to see just how they are working, for many willingly stop raking the ground beyond scratching the surface if they think nobody notices. There are plenty of workers capable of sleeping in the shade of a willow tree in the field, leaving the workhorses or the oxen to graze by themselves, caring only that by evening they can say they have put in their day. The good housekeeper must keep her eyes wide open.

She will not wait for the season when labor is in short supply to hire her workers. Rather, when the grain is ripening, even as early as the month of May, she will engage her workers for August, selecting good, strong, diligent fellows. She will agree to pay them either in money or grain. At harvest time she will supervise, or have others make sure that the workers do not leave grain sheaves behind them or try any of the other deceptions farm workers commonly practice on unsuspecting landholders. Just as she watched the other workers, the lady in charge at harvest time should arise early daily. Things rarely go well in a household where the mistress lies abed late. Keeping an eye on her entire domestic enterprise will give her plenty to oversee. . . .

Furthermore, she will instruct her maids to look after the animals, prepare food for the workers, take care of the milk, weed the gardens, or hunt for herbs, even though it may muddy them to the knees. It is their duty. She, her daughters, and attendants will make cloth, separating the wool, sorting it out, and putting the fine strands aside to make cloth for her husband and herself or to sell. The thick strands will be used for the small children, her servingwomen, and the workmen. She will stuff bedcovers with the large balls of wool. And she will have hemp grown by the farmers. During the long winter evenings, her maids will work and spin it into coarse linen. Many more such tasks as these would take too long to describe here. . . .

40. Household Accounts of Dame Alice de Bryene (1412–13)

Dame Alice de Bryene, a wealthy widow, lived on an estate in eastern England in the late fourteenth and early fifteenth century.

She had her steward, John, keep meticulous records of the daily consumption of the household; extracts from these accounts are printed below. In another document from her household, some of Dame Alice's servants are listed as a "lady's maid and chamberlain, squires, chaplains, grooms, clerks of the chapel and boys." There are also accounts of the purchases made for the household for the year, in which it is noted that Alice herself did some of the shopping, particularly for spices, salt, wax and candles, and some food items; her steward, however, did most such work.
Source: *The Household Book of Dame Alice de Bryene*, tr. M. K. Dale, ed. Vincent B. Redstone (Ipswich: Suffolk Institute of Archaeology and Natural History, 1931).

The account of John . . . [of the] expenses of the household of Dame Alice de Bryene . . . from the eve [of the feast of St. Michael] the Archangel, in the thirteenth year of the reign of [Henry] the fourth after the Conquest, until the eve of [the same feast] in the first year of the reign of King Henry the fifth, for one whole year [i.e., from 28 Sept. 1412 to 28 Sept. 1413].

Meals: Breakfast 8, dinner 20, supper 20. Sum 48.
Thurs., 29 Sept., the feast of St. Michael, the Lady took her meals there with her household; in addition, Agnes Sampson, a certain groom [of] Robert Louell for the whole day, two friars of Norwich, Colbrook, and one of the household of John Cok at one repast. Pantry: 40 white loaves and 6 black loaves; wine from what remained; ale from stock. Kitchen: One quarter of bacon, one joint of mutton, one lamb, and 32 pigeons. Purchases: in companage,[71] 2d. Provender: hay from stock for 7 horses of the Lady and of the company; fodder for the same one bushel of oats.
Sum of the purchases, 2d.

Meals: Breakfast 8, dinner 22, supper 10. Sum 40.
Frid., the last of Sept., the Lady took her meals with the household; in addition, Marg[aret] Sampson with her daughter, son and one of her household, Thomas Malcher'[72] at one repast, 9 of the household of Colbrook Manor and one of the household of Thomas Darbour for the whole day. Pantry: 46 white loaves and 6 black loaves; wine from what remained; ale from stock. Kitchen: half a salt fish and one

---

71. Companage = accompaniment.
72. The apostrophe at the end of a name is an abbreviation mark made by the original scribe.

stockfish. Purchases: in a hundred white herrings, 18d. Provender: hay from stock for 9 horses of the Lady and company, [fodder] one bushel one peck of oats.

Sum of the purchases, 18d.

Meals: Breakfast 6, dinner 18, supper 12. Sum 26.

Sat., the first of Oct., the Lady took her meals with the household; in addition, Colbrook for the whole day. Pantry: 44 white loaves and 6 black loaves; wine from what remained; ale from stock. Kitchen: Half a salt fish and one stockfish. Purchases: In a hundred oysters 2d. In a hundred smoked herrings 18d. In 33 merlings and 9 [plaice], 14d. In bread for [the] merchant's horse 1/2 d. Provender: hay from stock for 6 horses of the Lady and company; fodder for the same, one bushel of oats.

Sum of the purchases, 2s. 10d.

The baking: one quarter of wheat, whence came 236 white loaves and 36 black loaves.

Meals: Breakfast 6, dinner 20, supper 20. Sum 46.

Sun., 2 Oct., the Lady took her meals with the household; in addition, Thomas Sampsom with a woman of his household, John Hethe, "Jerold" the harvest-reeve of the manor at one repast. Pantry: 50 white loaves and 10 black loaves of which newly baked 10 white loaves and 2 black loaves; wine from supply; ale from stock. Kitchen: one quarter of bacon, one joint of mutton, one lamb, 20 pigeons. Purchases: in beef and pork 5s. 8d. Provender: hay from stock for 7 horses of the Lady and company; fodder for the same, one bushel of oats.

Sum of the purchases, 5s. 8d.

The brewing: 2 quarters of malt whereof one quarter drage,[73] whence came 112 gallons of ale.

Meals: Breakfast 10, dinner 21, supper 21. Sum 52.

Mon., 3 Oct., the Lady took her meals with the household; in addition, John Saltwell with 2 fellows, Robert Mose and Colbrook for the whole day, Robert Wellyng' with one of his household, Thomas Sampsom with one of his household at one repast. Pantry: 50 white loaves and 6 black loaves; wine from what remained; ale from stock. Kitchen: One quarter of bacon and 24 pigeons. Purchases: nil. Proven-

---

73. Drage = mixed grain.

der: hay from stock for 6 horses of the Lady and company; fodder for the same, one bush. of oats.

Sum of the purchases, nil.

A New Year's Banquet

Meals: Breakfast 30, dinner one hundred 160 [sic], supper 30. Sum, two hundred [sic].

Sun., 1 Jan. [Guests] William Sampsom with his wife and one of his household, Edward Peyton with one of his household, William Langham with one of his household, the wife of Robert Dynham with her son, John Teyler' with his son, Richard Sc[ri]ven[er], the bailiff of the manor with the harvest-reeve and 8 of the household of the manor, Margaret Brydbek, one harper, Agnes Whyte, the whole day, Agnes Rokwode with 2 sons, a daughter and a maidservant, the vicar of Aketon with one of his household, Richard Appylton with his wife and one of his household, Thomas Malcher' with 300 tenants and other strangers, one repast. Pantry: 314 white, and 40 black, loaves, whereof newly-baked 104 white, and 14 black, loaves; wine from what remained; ale from stock. Kitchen: 2 pigs, 2 swans, 12 geese, 2 joints of mutton, 24 capons, 17 conies. Purchases: beef 8s. 2d., veal 3s., 5 young pigs 2s. 4d., 12 gall. milk 18d. Provender: hay from stock for 18 horses; fodder for the same, 2 1/2 bush. oats.

Sum of purchases, 15s.

Lent

Meals: Breakfast 6, dinner 16, supper 8. Sum 30.

Mon., 10 Ap. [Guests] John Lytelton with one of his household to supper and extras. Pantry: 42 white, and 6 black, loaves; wine from supply; ale from stock. Kitchen: 50 red herrings, 50 white herrings, half a salt fish, one stockfish. Purchases: nil. Provender: hay from stock for 8 horses; fodder for the same one bush. one pk. oats.

Sum of purchases, nil.

Meals: Breakfast 8, dinner 18, supper 12. Sum 38.

Tues., 11 Ap. [Guests] John Lytelton with one of his household, a maidservant of the manor, the whole day. Pantry: 40 white, and 6 black, loaves; wine from supply; ale from stock. Kitchen: 50 red herrings, 60 white herrings, half a salt fish, one stockfish. Purchases: nil. Provender: hay from stock for 8 horses; fodder for the same, 1 1/2 bush. oats.

Sum of purchases, nil.

One cade of red herrings begun, 5.
Meals: Breakfast 3, dinner 22, supper 3. Sum 28.
Wed., 12 Ap. [Guests] John Lytelton with one of his household, Kendale, with his son, the whole day, 3 men of Brockeleigh, John Bande, one repast. Pantry: 60 white, and 6 black, loaves; wine from supply; ale from stock. Kitchen: 50 red herrings, 50 white herrings, half a salt fish, one stockfish. Purchases: nil. Provender: hay from stock for 10 horses; fodder for the same 2 bush. oats.
Sum of purchases, nil. . . .

Harvest Time

The baking: one qr. wheat for the boon-workers,[74] whence came 105 loaves.

Meals: Breakfast 7, dinner 19, supper 26. Sum 52.
Tues., 1 Aug. [Guests] Alice Fouler, 8 of the household of the manor, the whole day, Richard Appylton with one of his household, Maud (Matilda) Archer, the harvest-reeve of the manor with 16 boon-workers, one repast. Pantry: 54 white, and 6 black, loaves, and 6 loaves for the boon-workers; wine from supply; ale from stock. Kitchen: One quarter of beef, one quarter of bacon, one joint of mutton and 12 pigeons. Purchases: nil. Provender: hay from stock for 5 horses; fodder for the same, 3 pk. oats.
Sum of purchases, nil.

The brewing: 2 qrs. malt whereof 1 qr. drage, whence came 112 gall. ale.

Meals: Breakfast 20, dinner 40, supper 40. Sum 100.
Wed., 2 Aug. [Guests] John Scoyl with 27 boon-workers, the bailiff of the manor with the harvest-reeve, William Cowpere, the whole day. Pantry: 50 white, and 6 black, loaves, and 32 loaves for the boon-workers; wine from supply; ale from stock. Kitchen: 80 white herrings, 1 1/2 salt fish, one stockfish. Purchases: 3 thornbacks, 7 soles and 5 plaice 17d., milk and cream 5d., eggs 6d. Provender: hay from stock for 5 horses; fodder for the same, 3 pk. oats.

---

74. boon-workers = peasants legally obliged to do certain work for their lord.

Sum of purchases, 2s. 4d.

Meals: Breakfast 20, dinner 30, supper 30. Sum 80.
Thurs., 3 Aug. [Guests] the bailiff of the manor with the harvest-reeve, John Scoyl with 27 boon-workers, the whole day. Pantry: 50 white, and 6 black, loaves, and 22 loaves for the boon-workers; wine from supply; ale from stock. Kitchen: One quarter of beef, 1 1/2 quarters of bacon, 2 joints of mutton, 20 pigeons. Purchases: milk 2d. Provender: hay from stock for 5 horses; fodder for the same, 3 pk. oats.
Sum of purchases, 2d.

41. The Paston Family: Letters (15th c.)

Personal letters of this sort were relatively unusual in the Middle Ages, but we begin to find them surviving in greater numbers from the fifteenth century on. Margaret, who married John Paston in 1440, dictated most of her letters, and they are preserved in a vast family archive along with the letters and business documents of many of her relatives and their employees and business associates. The version used here is a modern paraphrase of the letters, which were written in Middle English.

The Pastons are not exactly "noble"; rather they belong to the "gentry," a class that was emerging in England in the Later Middle Ages. The gentry were descended variously from wealthy peasants or yeomen (as the Pastons were) or from merchant families that had acquired wealth, or from the knightly class, which was no longer considered "noble." But the gentry shared with the nobility a whole range of activities and concerns, including landed wealth, the status of knighthood and authority over peasants and employees.
Source: *The Paston Letters: A Selection in Modern Spelling*, ed. Norman Davis (London: Oxford University Press, 1963). Reprinted by permission of Oxford University Press.

Early Years of Marriage

14 (?) December 1441

Right reverend and worshipful husband, I recommend me to you, desiring heartily to hear of your welfare, thanking you for the token that ye sent me by Edmund Peres, praying you to [know] that my mother sent to my father to London for a gown cloth of musterdevillers[75] to [have made into] a gown for me; and he told my mother and me, when he was come home, that he charged you to buy it after that he were come out of London. I pray you, if it be not bought, that ye will vouchsafe to buy it and send it home as soon as ye may; for I have no gown to wear this winter but my black and my green a lierre, and that is so cumbrous that I am weary to wear it.

As for the girdle[76] that my father promised me, I spoke to him thereof a little before he went to London last, and he said to me that the fault was in you, that ye would not think thereupon to [have it made]; but I suppose that is not so—he said it but for an excuse. I pray you, if ye dare take it upon you, that ye will vouchsafe to [have it made before] ye come home; for I had never more need thereof than I have now, for I am grown so fat that I may not be girt in no bar of no girdle that I have but of one.

Elizabeth Peverel hath lain sick fifteen or sixteen weeks of the sciatica, but she sent my mother word by Kate that she should come hither when God sent time, even if she had be wheeled in a barrow. John of Damme was here, and my mother discovered me to him;[77] and he said by his troth that he was not gladder of nothing that he heard this twelvemonth than he was thereof. I may no longer live by my craft, I am discovered by all men that see me. Of all other things that ye desired that I should send you word of, I have sent you word of in a letter that I did write on our Lady's Day last. . . .

The Holy Trinity have you in his keeping. Written at Oxnead in right great haste on the Thursday next before Saint Thomas' Day.

I pray you that ye will wear the ring with the image of Saint Margaret that I sent you for a remembrance till ye come home. Ye have left me such a remembrance that maketh me to think upon you both day and night when I would sleep.

Yours, M. P.

28 September 1443

Right worshipful husband, I recommend me to you, desiring heartily to hear of your welfare, thanking God of your amending of the great disease that ye have had; and I thank you for the letter that ye sent me, for by my troth my mother and I were not in heart's ease from the time that we learned of your sickness till we learned verily of your amending. My mother promised another image of wax of the

---

75. musterdevillers = a type of grey woolen cloth.
76. girdle = belt.
77. discovered me to him = told him my secret.

weight of you to Our Lady of Walsingham,[78] and she sent 4 nobles[79] to the four orders of friars at Norwich to pray for you; and I have promised to go on pilgrimage to Walsingham and to Saint Leonard's for you. By my troth I had never so heavy a season as I had from the time that I learned of your sickness till I learned of your amending, and yet mine heart is in no great ease, nor shall be till I know that ye be very whole.

Your father and mine was this day sevennight at Beccles for a matter of the Prior of Bromholm, and he lay at Geldeston that night and was there till it was 9 of the clock the next day. And I sent thither for a gown, and my mother said that I should none have thence till I went there again; and so they could none get. My father Garneys sent me word that he should be here the next week, and mine uncle also, and they will play here with their hawks; and they wish to have me go home with them. And so God help me I shall excuse myself from going thither if I may, for I suppose that I shall more readily have tidings from you here than I should have there. . . .

I pray you heartily that ye will vouchsafe to send me a letter as hastily as ye may, if writing be none disease to you, and that ye will vouchsafe to send me word how your sore is doing. If I might have had my will I should have seen you ere this time. I would ye were at home, [for] your sore might be as well looked to here as it is there ye been now, more than a new gown, though it were of scarlet. I pray you, if your sore be whole and so that ye may endure to ride, when my father comes to London that ye will ask leave and come home when the horse shall be sent home again; for I hope ye should be kept as tenderly here as ye be at London.

I have no leisure to write half a quarter so much as I should say to you if I might speak with you. I shall send you another letter as hastily as I may. I thank you that ye would vouchsafe to remember my girdle, and that ye would write to me at this time, for I suppose the writing was none ease to you. Almighty God have you in his keeping and send you health. Written at Oxnead in right great haste on Saint Michael's Even.

Yours, M. Paston

My mother greeteth you well, and sendeth you God's blessing and her own; and she prayeth you, and I pray you also, that ye be well

---

78. Walsingham was the site of a famous and highly revered shrine of the Virgin Mary.
79. four nobles = 26s. 8d.

dieted of meat and drink, for that is the greatest help that ye may have now to your health. Your son fareth well, blessed be God.

Defending Family Property[80]

1448

Right worshipful husband, I recommend me to you, and pray you to get some crossbows, and windases to bend them with, and quarrels;[81] for your houses here are so low that no one can shoot out with a long bow, though we had never so much need. I suppose ye should have such things from Sir John Fastolf if ye would send to him. And also I would ye should get two or three short poleaxes to keep indoors, and as many jacks,[82] if ye may. . . .

28 February 1449

Right worshipful husband, I recommend me to you, desiring heartily to hear of your welfare, beseeching you that ye be not displeased though I have left that place that ye left me in; for by my troth there were brought me such tidings by diverse persons which are your well-wishers and mine that I dared no longer abide there, of which persons I shall let you have knowledge when ye come home. I was told that divers of the Lord Moleyns' men said that if they might get me they should steal me and keep me within the castle, and then they said they would that ye should fetch me out; and they said it should be but a little heart-burning to you. And after I heard these tidings I could have no rest in mine heart till I was here, nor dared I go out of the place that I was in till that I was ready to ride; nor was there anyone in the place who knew that I should leave, save the goodwife, not an hour before I came thence. And I told her that I should come hither to order such gear as I would have made for me and for the children, and said I supposed that I should be here a fortnight or three weeks. I pray you that the cause of my coming away may been secret till I speak with you, for they that let me have warning thereof do not wish it known.

---

80. In 1448, a dangerous rivalry had arisen between the Paston family and their neighbor Lord Moleyns. Margaret had written to John in May describing the outbreak of violence between the servants and followers of the two households and threats to herself and her mother.

81. quarrels = bolts fired by cross-bows.

82. jacks = sturdy leather jackets.

I spake with your mother as I came hitherwards, and she offered, if ye wished, to let me abide in this town. She would with right good will that we should abide in her place, and deliver me such gear as she might forbear, to keep with household till ye might be provided with a place and stuff of your own to keep with household. I pray you send me word by the bringer of this how ye wish that I act. I would be right sorry to dwell so near Gresham as I did, till the matter were fully determined betwixt the Lord Moleyns and you. . . .

Mourning[83]

24 December 1459

Right worshipful husband, I recommend me unto you. May it please you to know that I sent your eldest son to my Lady Morley to have knowledge what sports were used in her house in Christmas next following after the decease of my lord her husband. And she said that there were no disguisings nor harping nor luting nor singing, nor any loud disports, but playing at the tables and chess and cards; such disports she gave her folks leave to play, and none other.

Your son did his errand right well, as ye shall hear after this. I sent your younger son to the Lady Stapleton, and she said according to my Lady Morley's saying. . . .

I am sorry that ye shall not at home be for Christmas. I pray you that ye will come as soon as ye may; I shall think myself half a widow because ye shall not be at home, etc. God have you in his keeping. Written on Christmas Eve.

By your M. P.

42. A Manor House: Ightham Mote (ca. 1340)

Manor houses were the typical dwellings of the medieval nobility. Ightham Mote, in southeast England, dates from the fourteenth century and is still standing today, though it has been modified many times over the centuries. The reconstructed drawings here show the building as it probably appeared in the fourteenth century; the floor plan shows surviving parts in black and conjectural parts in dashed lines. The building was made partly of stone and partly of timber. The Great Hall, used for dining and gathering,

---

83. A close business associate of Margaret's husband had died the previous month, leaving his lands to the Pastons.

was apparently heated by a central hearth; smoke would have escaped through louvres in the roof. The solars were used as living and sleeping space.

Source: *The Development of Igthham Mote: An Architectural Handbook* (The National Trust, 1988). Drawings by Allan T. Adams, by kind permission of the National Trust.

Plan of the Building

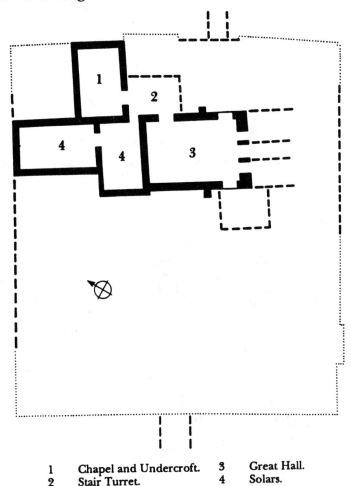

1	Chapel and Undercroft.	3	Great Hall.
2	Stair Turret.	4	Solars.

Exterior View

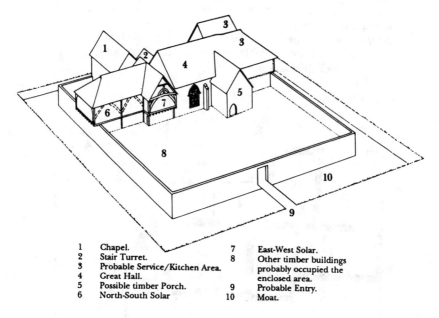

1	Chapel.	7	East-West Solar.
2	Stair Turret.	8	Other timber buildings
3	Probable Service/Kitchen Area.		probably occupied the
4	Great Hall.		enclosed area.
5	Possible timber Porch.	9	Probable Entry.
6	North-South Solar	10	Moat.

Interior Views

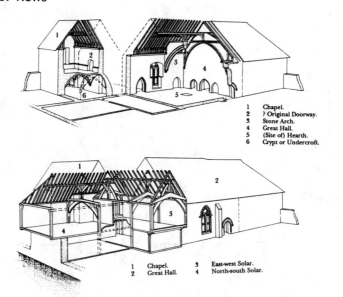

1	Chapel.		
2	? Original Doorway.		
3	Stone Arch.		
4	Great Hall.		
5	(Site of) Hearth.		
6	Crypt or Undercroft.		

1	Chapel.	3	East-west Solar.
2	Great Hall.	4	North-south Solar.

Part IV

The Working Life: Agricultural, Domestic, and Commercial

The vast majority of the medieval population worked for a living, and by far the greatest number belonged to the rural peasantry. As peasants were normally illiterate, they have left few records, except when they came into contact with officialdom on the manor or in the legal system. Such records are very scarce before the thirteenth century, when the use of written documents became more common throughout Europe. We are fortunate that the official records sometimes give us vivid glimpses of peasant lives and even echoes of their voices.

A much smaller but very important group in medieval society was the urban population, consisting of workers in crafts and the merchants, who lived by buying and selling. As the documents in this section reveal, women played a vital role in the urban as well as the agrarian economy. A few women even held the special legal status of *femme sole*, "single woman"—a woman who regardless of her marital status was regarded as an independent person for business purposes. More common were townswomen who worked as day laborers or alongside their husband in the family business.

A. Agricultural and Domestic

43. Gregory of Tours:
Frankish Working Women (6th c.)

This episode from a sixth-century chronicle describes the fate of a woman who became involved in a plot against the queen mother and the king's wife. As nurse to the royal family, Septimina held a position of prestige and responsibility; her subsequent demotion was part of her punishment.
Source: Gregory of Tours, *The History of the Franks*, tr. O. M. Dalton (Oxford: Oxford University Press, 1927). Reprinted by permission of Oxford University Press.

. . . Septimina, nurse of the royal children, . . . and Droctulf, who had been associated with Septimina to aid her in bringing up the young princes . . . confessed [under torture] to all the charges. . . . Septimina was severely flogged, together with Droctulf, and her face was seared with red-hot irons; all that she had was taken from her, and she was sent to the domain of Marlenheim to turn the mill and daily prepare the flour for the food of the women in the gynaeceum.[84]

44. Carolingian Laws:
Women's Work on Royal Estates
(Late 8th c.)

Among the laws issued by one late Frankish ruler[85] were detailed instructions for the stewards who ran the royal estates, including the following references to women's work and the general conditions in which the workers there lived. Women laborers might live in such workshops instead of with their families. The term "household" here refers to all the people who depended on or worked for the ruler.
Source: M. Guérard, *Explication du Capitulaire De Villis* (Paris: Bibliothèque de l'École des Chartes, 1853). Tr. E.M.A.

---

84. Gynaeceum = women's workshop.
85. Probably the emperor Charlemagne, but perhaps his son Louis the Pious, ruling Aquitaine under his father.

2. Let the members of our household be well cared for, and let no one impoverish them.

31. Let [our stewards] set apart each year what is necessary for the workers and for the women's workshops, and let them supply this fully at the proper time. . . .

43. Let [our stewards] give materials to our women's workshops at the proper time, as is usual, that is, linen, wool, woad, vermilion, madder,[86] wool-combs, teazles,[87] soap, oil, vessels, and any other small items which are necessary for their work.

49. Let our women's workshops be well ordered, with houses, heated rooms and cottages; and let them be enclosed by good fences and strong doors, such that they may do our work well.

53. Let each steward see to it that our people on his estate are not thieves or criminals.

54. Let each steward see to it that the members of our household do their work well, and do not spend their time idly in the market-place.

56. Let each steward hold audiences and dispense justice frequently on his estate, and let him see to it that the members of our household live rightly.

45. Freeing of a Serf (1050)

The majority of medieval peasants were serfs (or "villeins"); they were not slaves owned by other people, but they were unfree, legally bound to the land on which they lived, and they were obliged to serve the owner or holder of that land. Like slaves, serfs could be freed by their masters. This document was issued by the Holy Roman Emperor Henry III in 1050.
Source: Oliver J. Thatcher and Edgar H. McNeal, *A Source Book for Mediæval History* (New York: Charles Scribner's Sons, 1907).

Henry, etc. Let all our faithful Christian subjects, both present and future, know that we, at the request of a certain nobleman, named Richolf, have freed a certain one of his female serfs, named Sigena, by striking a penny out of her hand. We have freed her from the yoke of servitude, and have decreed that the said Sigena shall in future

---

86. Woad = a blue dye; vermilion and madder = red dyes.
87. Teazles = prickly plant heads, dried and used to raise a nap on cloth.

have the same liberty and legal status as all other female serfs who have been freed in the same way by kings or emperors. . . .

46. Descriptions of Maidservants' Work (12th–13th c.)

Here the duties (and appearance) of female servants are prescribed in works addressed to those hiring servants and running households. The first piece is by Alexander Neckham (see Part III above); the second is from an anonymous work on estate management.

Chambermaid and Serving Maid (12th c.)

Source: U. T. Holmes, *Daily Living in the Twelfth Century, Based on the Observations of Alexander Neckham in London and Paris* (Madison: University of Wisonsin Press, 1952).

. . . and let there be also a chambermaid whose face may charm and render tranquil the chamber, who, when she finds time to do so may knit or unknit silk thread, or make knots of [gold lace], or may sew linen garments and woolen clothes, or may mend. Let her have gloves with the finger tips removed; she should have a leather case protecting the finger from needle pricks, which is vulgarly called a "thimble." She must have scissors and a spool of thread and various sizes of needles—small and thin for embroidery, others not so thin for feather stitching, moderately fine ones for ordinary sewing, bigger ones for the knitting of a cloak, still larger ones for threading laces. . . . Now let her exclude the intemperate air with a cote. A band or a hair net should restrain her flowing hair. She should have a necklace, and a brooch by which she can fasten the neck opening of her cote, or fustian, or shirt. She may have bracelets and earrings.

There should be also a serving maid who will place eggs under the sitting hens and will give maslin [mixed rye and wheat] to the geese, and who will feed the ailing lambs with milk from a ewe other than the mother, in her gentleness. She will keep the calves to be weaned, whose teeth are few, in an enclosure near the barn. On holidays her clothing should be a cast-off pellice and a wimple. It is her practice to give the swineherd, plowmen, and other herdsmen whey, but to the master and his friends, clabber in cups, and to offer in the evening bran bread to the dogs in the pen.

Dairymaid (13th c.)

Source: *Fleta*, Vol. II, ed. and tr. H. G. Richardson and G. O. Sayles, (London: Selden Society, 1955). Reprinted by permission of the Selden Society.

The dairymaid should be modest and honest, faithful and hard-working, knowledgeable and experienced in the tasks of the dairy, careful and not extravagant. She should not allow any man or woman to visit her in the dairy who will take away something that might result in a deficiency in her account. It is her duty to receive from the reeve, by written indenture, the utensils belonging to her office and, when she leaves, to return them by the same indenture, in which the date of her commencing work is stated. Further, it is her business to receive milk, against a tally, by the number of gallons, and to make cheese and butter, and to take charge of the poultry, and frequently to render account and to answer to the bailiff and the reeve for the produce resulting therefrom: and some auditors of the accounts will not pass a smaller yearly yield than twelvepence for a goose and fourpence for a hen. And when she can reasonably find leisure for such things, it is her business to winnow, to cover the fire and do similar odd jobs.

47. Survey of Alwalton: Obligations of Peasants (1279)

The manorial survey was a census, taken by the lord of the manor to determine the identities, status and obligations of the peasants who lived on his land and under his authority, and whose labor supported him. These extracts are from a thirteenth-century survey of an English manor. Only the heads of households are recorded.
Source: *Translations and Reprints from the Original Sources of European History*, vol. III, ed. Edward P. Cheyney (Philadelphia: University of Pennsylvania, 1896).

The abbot of Peterborough holds the manor of Alwalton and vill[88] from the lord king directly. . . .

---

88. Vill = village.

Villeins. Hugh Miller holds 1 virgate[89] of land in villeinage[90] by paying thence to the said abbot 3s. 1d. Likewise the same Hugh works through the whole year except 1 week at Christmas, 1 week at Easter, and 1 at Whitsuntide, that is in each week 3 days, each day with 1 man, and in autumn each day with 2 men, performing the said works at the will of the said abbot as in plowing and other work. Likewise he gives 1 bushel of wheat for benseed and 18 sheaves of oats for fodder-corn. Likewise he gives 3 hens and 1 cock yearly and 5 eggs at Easter. Likewise he does carrying to Peterborough and to Jakele and nowhere else, at the will of the said abbot. Likewise if he sells a brood mare in his court for 10s. or more, he shall give to the said abbot 4d., and if for less he shall give nothing to the aforesaid. He gives also merchet[91] and heriot,[92] and is tallaged[93] at the feast of St. Michael, at the will of the said abbot. There are also 17 other villeins, viz. John of Ganesoupe, Robert son of Walter, Ralph son of the reeve, Emma at Pertre, William son of Reginald, Thomas son of Gunnilda, Eda widow of Ralph, Ralph Reeve, William Reeve, Thomas Flegg, Henry Abbot, William Hereward, Serle son of William Reeve, Walter Palmer, William Abbot, Henry Serle; each of whom holds one virgate of land in villein-age, paying and doing all things, each for himself, to the said abbot yearly just as the said Hugh Miller. . . .

Cotters. Henry, son of the miller, holds a cottage with a croft[94] which contains 1 rood,[95] paying thence yearly to the said abbot 2s. Likewise he works for 3 days in carrying hay and in other works at the will of the said abbot, each day with 1 man and in autumn 1 day in cutting grain with 1 man.

[The obligations of three more male cotters are listed.]

Likewise Sara, widow of Matthew Miller, holds a cottage and a croft which contains half a rood, paying to the said abbot 4 d.; and she works just as the said Henry.

Likewise Sara, widow of William Miller, holds a cottage and a croft which contains half a rood, paying to the abbot 4 d.; and she works just as the said Henry.

---

89. Virgate = a measure of land, between 20 and 40 acres.
90. Villein = serf (unfree peasant).
91. Merchet = payment due to a peasant woman's lord when she married. In this case the father is said to owe merchet.
92. Heriot = payment due to a peasant's lord when the peasant died leaving an inheritance.
93. Tallage = a kind of land tax.
94. Croft = small holding of land.
95. Rood = one quarter acre.

[The similar obligations of 18 more cotters, including four women, are enumerated.]

Likewise each of the said cottagers, except the widows, gives yearly after Christmas a penny which is called head-penny.

48. Manorial Court Rolls (14th c.)

> The lord of a manor had wide jurisdiction over the lives of the peasants living there, and the manor court was the place where many of those powers were exercised. At the sessions of the manor court, disputes between peasants were settled, payments due to the lord were collected, and minor infractions of the law were dealt with. The records kept of these proceedings therefore show a wide range of peasant activities and problems. The documents here come from English manors.

Durham Court Rolls

> Source: *Translations and Reprints from the Original Sources of European History*, vol. III, ed. Edward P. Cheyney (Philadelphia: University of Pennsylvania, 1896).

First Tourn of the [manorial courts] of the Priory of Durham, beginning at Fery, July 6th A.D. 1345, before lords William of Chareton and Robert of Benton, Terrar and Bursar, and Simon Esshe, Steward.

Spen, 1345. Agnes widow of Adam de Mora has taken a house and 50 acres of land which her husband Adam formerly held, paying annually for her life 33s. 4d. And there is remitted to her 16s. 8d. a year from the old rent on account of her age and weakness of mind.

Billingham, 1345. Agnes daughter of William Nouthird has taken a cottage with the curtilage, which the said William her father formerly held, to be held on payment of 6d. a year and 20 autumn works in the manor of Billingham, provided she has food. Fine, 2s.; pledges[96] J. of Stokton and Alexander son of Gilbert. . . .

Billingham, 1364. It is enjoined upon all the tenants of the vill that none of them grind his grain outside of the domain so long as the mill of the lord prior is able to grind, under penalty of 20s. . . .

West Raynton, 1365. A day is given to all the tenants of the vill to

---

96. Pledge = someone who guarantees one's appearance in court, payment of debt, etc.

make a law that neither they nor their wives nor their servants shall cut down anything within the woods, not carry anything green away from the woods. . . .

Coupon, 1365. From Agnes Postell and Alice of Belasis, for bad ale, 12d. From Alice de Belasis, for bad ale, and moreover because the ale which she sent to the Terrar was of no strength, as was proved in court, 2s. . . .

Newton Bewley, 1368. From Alice, servant of Adam of Marton, for leyr 6d. . . .[97]

East Raynton, 1370. From Margaret daughter of Robert Wright for merchet, pledge, Alice her mother, 2s.

Fery, 1370. From Margaret Ferywoman for leyr, 6d. . . .

Bradford Court Rolls

Source: *English Economic History: Select Documents*, eds. A. E. Bland, P. A. Brown and R. H. Tawney (London, 1914).

Court of Bradford holden on Saturday, the eve of St. Lucy the Virgin, 23 Edward III [12 Dec. 1349].

. . . Amice, daughter and heir of Roger de Oulesnape, came here into the Court and took a cottage and 4 acres of poor bondage land in the town of Stanbury after the death of the aforesaid Roger, to hold to her and her heirs according to the custom of the manor by the services, etc., saving the right, etc. And she gives to the lord 2s., of fine for entry.[98] Pledge, Roger son of Jordan. . . .

John Barne of Manningham, who held a messuage and a bovate of bondage land there, is dead. And hereupon came Margery his wife and took those tenements, to hold according to the custom of the manor for the term of her life by the services, etc. And she gives to the lord 2s. of fine. Pledge, John atte Yate.

Margaret and Agnes, daughters and heirs of Hugh Browne, Alice, Joan and Juliana, daughters and heirs of John Kyng, Juliana, who was the wife of Hugh Kyng of Thornton, Robert son of John Bollyng and Elizabeth his wife, Alice, daughter and heir of Robert de Manyngham, and Thomas her husband, William, son and heir of Ellen Coke, and John (dead), son and heir of John de Wyndhill, came here into Court and did their fealties, and they have a day at the next Court to acknowl-

---

97. Leyr, leyrwite = fine for fornication or for bearing an illegitimate child.
98. Fine for entry = fee paid to the lord to obtain one's inheritance.

edge their tenements and services, etc. and also to show their deeds etc.

Agnes Chapman came here into Court and took a small house in Bradford called the Smythhouse, to hold at the will of the lord by the services. And she gives to the lord 18d. of fine to have such an estate, etc. . . .

William Wilkynson, who held [in Manningham] in like manner a messuage and a bovate of land, is dead, and Alice his daughter and heir is of the age of half a year. And hereupon came John Magson, her next friend, to whom [the inheritance cannot descend] and took full wardship of the aforesaid land and heir until her full age, etc., by the services, etc. And he gives to the lord 2s. of fine for entry. Pledges Hugh Barne and Thomas de Chellowe.

Thomas Neucomen, who held a messuage and a bovate of land in Bradford, is dead. And hereupon came Margery, daughter and heir of the same Thomas, and took the aforesaid tenements, to hold to her and her heirs according to the custom of the manor by the services, etc., saving the right, etc. And the fine for entry is put into respite until the next court. . . .

It is presented . . . that Alice Geldoghter and Adam Notebroun are bakers and sell bad bread contrary to the assize. Therefore they are [in mercy]. . . .

Court of Bradford holden on Thursday next before the feast of St. Gregory the Pope, 24 Edward III [11 March 1350].

. . . Alice Chilyonge of Manningham, the lord's bondwoman, came here in Court and made fine of 12d. with the lord for her leyrwite; pledge, William Walker; and the fine is not more because she is very poor and has nothing. . . .

Roger son of Roger de Manynghame has made a fine of 1/2 mark for the merchet of Cecily his wife, the lord's bondwoman; pledge, Thomas de Manynghame.

Thomas Gabriell has made the fine of 1/2 mark in like manner for the merchet of Maud his wife, the lord's bondwoman; pledge, Thomas de Tiresale. . . .

Agnes daughter of Adam atte Yate, the lord's bondwoman, has made fine for her chevage,[99] for license to dwell wheresoever she will, to wit, 6d. to be paid yearly at Michaelmas and Easter in equal portions; pledge, Robert atte Yate.

It is presented by Roger Judson, Thomas son of Roger, Thomas

---

99. Chevage = annual payment by serf for privilege of living elsewhere.

Gabriel, Adam del Oldfeld, Robert de Oldfeld, and John atte Yate, that Cecily de la More, the lord's bondwoman, has been violated by John Judson; therefore let her be distrained to make fine therefor with the lord.

Further, it is presented that Isabel daughter of William Childyong, the lord's bondwoman, has married one William Cisson, a free man, without license. And Alice daughter of John Gepson, the lord's bondwoman, has married one William del Hale, a free man, at Beston, without license; therefore let them be distrained to make fine with their lord for their merchet, etc.

Let inquest be made touching the sons and daughters of William del Munkes, who dwell at Darthington and are the lord Duke's bondmen and bondwomen of Bradford, etc.

Further, it is presented that Alice daughter of William Childyong, the lord's bondwoman, dwells at York; therefore let her be taken, etc. . . .

Court holden at Bradford on Wednesday, 12 December, 32 Edward III [1358].

Again Anabel del Knoll has a day,[100] as above,[101] to rebuild a house on a plot of land which she holds of the lord at will, and under the same penalty as in the Court preceding.

It is ordered, as many times before, to take William son of Richard Gilleson, Roger son of William del Mersh, dwelling with John de Bradlay, Thomas son of John atte Yate, William son of William Childyong (in Pontefract), Alice daughter of John atte Yate (in Selby), Alice daughter of William Childyong (in Methelay), and William son of William Childyong, the lord's bondmen and bondwomen of his lordship here, etc., who have withdrawn without license, and to bring them back hither until [they make fine for their chevage]. . . .

Roger son of Roger makes plaint of Alice de Bollyng [in a plea] of trespass, pledge to prosecute, William Walker, to wit, that she has not made an enclosure which she is bound to make between his holdings and her own holding in Mikelington, so that for lack of enclosure there divers cattle entered and fed off his corn, to wit, his rye and oats and grass, to his damages of 10s. And the aforesaid Alice defends and says that the aforesaid Roger, and not she, is bound to make an enclosure there, and hereon she puts herself upon the country. But the jurors hereupon elected, tried and sworn, say on their oath that the aforesaid

---

100. To have a day = to be summoned to court at a future date.

101. This is a continuing case, in which Anabel has been ordered several times to rebuild the house, but has not complied.

Roger is bound to make the aforesaid enclosure between the aforesaid holdings. And therefore it is awarded that the aforesaid Roger be in mercy[102] for his false claim, and that the said Alice go without a day.

49. Coroners' Rolls: Violent Incidents (13th–14th c.)

The following are extracts from the rolls kept by the coroners, English public officials whose duties included (and still include) the investigation of any unexpected death. These documents provide us with two kinds of information. Their main concern is with death and crime, and so they tell us much about law enforcement. But in the course of describing the events being investigated, the rolls record incidental information about daily life. Most of the people appearing in these rolls are peasants. (The eventual outcomes of most of these cases are not included here. When the inquest itself is described, the four towns named are those required by law to provide the members of the inquest jury.) Source: *Bedfordshire Coroners' Rolls*, ed. R. F. Hunnisett (Bedfordshire Historical Record Society, 1961). Reprinted with the permission of the Controller of Her Britannic Majesty's Stationery Office.

9. On 14 Jan. 1267 Sabillia, an old woman, went into Colmworth to beg bread. At twilight she wished to go to her house, fell into a stream and drowned by misadventure. The next day her son Henry searched for her [and] found her drowned . . .

13. Soon after nones on 22 July 1267 Emma, Christine de Furnevall's washerwoman, tried to draw water from a leaden vat full of boiling water with a bowl in Cadbury and by misadventure fell into it. Richard the Brewer of Christine's house was present, tried to drag her from the vat, lost his foothold and fell in. Gregory de Canmori arrived, saw them lying in the vat, raised the hue[103] and called his servant Richard, who dragged them both out. Emma died about vespers on 24 July, having had the rites of the church.

14. On 12 Aug. 1267 William Blaunche's daughters, Muriel aged almost 6 and Beatrice aged almost 3, were in his house in Great Barford, William and his wife Muriel being in the field, when a fire broke out in the house and burned it together with Beatrice.

---

102. To be in mercy = to be convicted.
103. Raise the hue = notify others about a crime or sudden death.

30. On 24 Sept. Margery wife of Simon Daffe [of] Great Barford went between Great Barford and Roxton by the river Ouse looking for her husband, who had earlier been drowned there, and, coming by a ditch near "Lytlemade" meadow, found a poor woman, a stranger, lying dead there, raised the hue and ran to Great Barford, which followed the hue.

Inquest before the same coroner by Great Barford, Roxton, Wilden and Renhold, who knew nothing of this death, the woman having no wound or injury, but they believed that she died of cold and because she was weak. Margery found pledges,[104] Robert the Carpenter and Jordan of Seaton, both of Great Barford.

35. About nones on 2 Oct. 1270 Amice daughter of Robert Belamy of Staploe and Sibyl Bonchevaler were carrying a tub full of grout between them in the brewhouse of Lady Juliana de Beauchamp in the hamlet of Staploe in Eaton Socon, intending to empty it into a boiling leaden vat, when Amice slipped and fell into the vat and the tub upon her. Sibyl immediately jumped towards her, dragged her from the vat and shouted; the household came and found her scalded almost to death. A chaplain came and Amice had the rites of the church and died by misadventure about prime the next day.

58. After nones on 24 May 1270 Emma daughter of Richard Toky of Southill went to "Houleden" in Southill to gather wood. Walter Garglof of Stanford came, carrying a bow and a small sheaf of arrows, took hold of Emma and tried to throw her to the ground and deflower her, but she immediately shouted and her father came. Walter immediately shot an arrow at him, striking him on the right side of the forehead and giving him a mortal wound. He struck him again with another arrow under the right side and so into the stomach. Seman of Southill immediately came and asked him why he wished to kill Richard, and Walter immediately shot an arrow at him, striking him in the back, so that his life was despaired of. Walter then immediately fled. Later Emma, Richard's wife, came and found her husband wounded to the point of death and shouted. The neighbours came and took him to his house. He had the rites of the church, made his will and died at twilight on the same day.

73. About prime on 27 March 1270 Mariot, formerly the wife of Richard the Reeve of Pertenhall, who was infirm, feeble and old, lay in her bed in Pertenhall while Maud Mody, John Spayne and Richard's son Henry were about the affairs of the house, at the plough and

---

104. Pledge = someone who guarantees one's appearance in court.

elsewhere. She rose from her bed, took a pitcher in her hand, went to a well in her court-yard and tried to draw water, but, because she was feeble, she slipped and fell into the well and drowned by misadventure. Maud Mody came to the house and into the court-yard, saw Mariot lying in the well and raised the hue. John Spayne came to the hue and sprang to Mariot, because he thought to save her, but could not because she was dead.

103. About prime on 16 Feb. 1271 Alexander le Gardiner of Potton, Lady Christine de Fornival's servant, was digging under the walls of an old dovecote in the garden in Lady Christine's court-yard in Sutton to demolish them and, as he dug, the wall by misadventure fell upon him and broke his head so that he immediately died there. His wife Alice came with his breakfast, looked for him, saw his surcoat and cap and the spade with which he dug and so found him dead and his whole body broken.

106. After midday on 16 June 1271 Annora daughter of Agnes Oter, aged 3, went out of the south side of her mother's house in Edworth, while her mother was seeking fuel, by misadventure fell into a ditch outside a wood and drowned. Agnes first found her dead and shouted; the neighbours came.

116. Well into the night of 30 March 1270 Simon and Richard, sons of Hugh the Fisher of Radwell, came from the house of Hugh's daughter Alice towards that of their father in Radwell and wished to cross the court-yard of Robert Ball of Radwell, in which Simon son of Agnes of Radwell and Juliana daughter of Walter the Fisher of Radwell were lying under a haystack. Simon immediately arose and struck Simon the Fisher on the top of the head to the brain apparently with an axe, so that he immediately died. Richard, seeing this, raised the hue and fled. Simon the felon immediately fled and Juliana with him. The township came and the hue was followed. Robert Ball found pledges, Robert de la More and Simon the Reeve of Radwell. Richard found pledges, his father and Richard Tappe of Radwell. . . . It was ordered that Simon and Juliana be arrested. . . .

[At the eyre[105] it was ordered that Simon son of Agnes, who was suspected, be exacted and outlawed, but that Juliana, who was not suspected, could return if she wished. Simon's chattels,[106] worth 21d., were forfeited; Juliana had no chattels.]

228. About prime on 28 Feb., while William Sagar of Sutton was at

---

105. Eyre = court dealing with criminal cases.
106. Chattels = moveable goods. The chattels of a convicted felon were forfeited.

the plough, his wife Emma took a bundle of straw inside the court-yard of his house in Sutton, intending to go to heat an oven. She came to a part of the court-yard which was near their dwelling-house and near a well on the north of the house, and by misadventure fell into the well and drowned. Maud daughter of Ellis Batte of Sutton was sitting in William's house guarding Emma's child Rose, who was lying in a cradle, heard the noise made by Emma as she sank, immediately went outside [and] found Emma drowned. . . .

251. About midnight on 12 Aug., when John Clarice was lying near his wife Joan daughter of Richard le Freman, as was his custom, in his bed in the chamber of his house at Houghton Regis in the liberty of Eaton Bray, madness took possession of him, and Joan, thinking that he was seized by death, took a small scythe and cut his throat. She also took a [bill-hook] and struck him on the right side of the head, so that his brain flowed forth and he immediately died. The next day Joan fled to Houghton Regis church. About prime on that day John's son Ralph was troubled that his father was lying in bed so late, entered the chamber, called him [and] found him dead. . . .

On 15 Aug. Joan was asked about this felony in the said church before the same coroner and townships. She openly confessed that she had committed it alone without any help. The port of Dover was assigned to her by the road called "le Kokevey", which enters into the king's highway. She then abjured the realm according to the custom of England.

Inquiry was made about the felon's chattels by the same townships, who said that on the day of the felony John and Joan jointly had 2 horses worth 5s., a mare with a foal worth 5s., a stirk worth 20d., a calf worth 12d., 3 pigs worth 4s., 3 young pigs worth 18d., household goods worth 18d., 3 acres of wheat worth 4s. 6d. an acre, 3 acres of maslin worth 4s. an acre and 11 acres of dredge worth 4s. an acre, total £4. 9s. 2d. . . .

[At the eyre . . . Joan was found to have no chattels. John's were distributed among his boys.]

255. At twilight on 4 Sept. 1300 Nicholas le Swon of Bedford came to his house there, when his wife Isabel was at Robert Asplon's house giving milk to Robert's son, and asked his daughter where her mother was. She said: at Robert Asplon's house; whereupon he immediately went after her because she stayed there too much. As he left his house he met his wife and told her to come home to sleep, saying that he wanted to go to his bed. While Isabel was making his bed, Nicholas drew his sword and struck her in the back so that she immediately

died. He immediately fled. His chattels were 3 bushels of corn worth
15d., 2 bushels of oats worth 4d., 8 lbs. of wool worth 2s., wood worth
4d., 2 pigs worth 3d. and a chest worth 4d. . . .

259. On 10 Sept. 1301 William son of Peter of Bromham, nephew of
the vicar of Wootton, Stephen de Rivers, William the Cobbler and
Margery le Wyte came together from a tavern in Bedford towards
Wootton, and as they came into Cauldwell road a quarrel arose between them. William the vicar's nephew, seeing John Hokerynge,
who was following them but with no ulterior motive, drew his bow
and shot at him with a barbed arrow. Margery went between them in
order to stop the quarrel and by misadventure received a blow from the
arrow in her throat so that she immediately died. William immediately
fled. . . .

50. Peasant Dwellings

The construction of peasant houses varied widely across Europe,
but such dwellings were generally small and simple in layout.
Many peasants shared their roof with animals, as can be seen in
the floor plan below. The reconstructed drawing shows what the
interior of a fairly large peasant home might have looked like.

Floor Plan (Saxony, 13th c.)

Source: Jean Chapelot and Robert Fossier, *The Village and House in
the Middle Ages*, tr. Henry Cleere (London: B. T. Batsford Ltd.,
1985).

. . . in northern Germany [the "Lower German House"] appeared
in the thirteenth century. . . . Medieval and post-medieval examples
show the main characteristics of this type: the central passage was
enlarged to accommodate vehicles, and the doorway in one of the
short walls, giving access to the byre section, becomes the main en-
trance, and even the only means of access.

The section reserved for human occupation is usually central within
the building, sometimes on one side, especially in post-medieval examples. The hearth is, as a general rule, placed centrally.

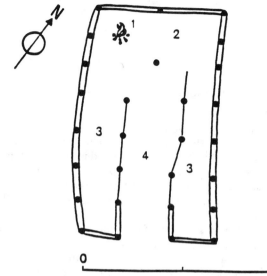

1   hearth

2   living space

3   byre [for animals]

4   central aisle

Reconstructed Drawing (England)

Source: Maurice Barley, *Houses and History* (London and Boston: Faber & Faber, 1986).

B. Commercial

51. Parisian Guild Regulations (13th c.)

The craft guilds were important institutions in medieval European towns from the eleventh and twelfth centuries onward; the regulations printed here provide a good idea of the scope of their activities and authority. In about 1270 Etienne de Boileau compiled his *Livre des métiers*, or *Book of Crafts*, a collection of the regulations of Parisian craft guilds. The statutes of most of the guilds are couched in purely masculine terms, but some speak of female apprentices and workers; a few refer to "mistresses" as well as "masters" of the craft; and a handful are those of exclusively female guilds, concerned with various aspects of the silk industry. Many male guilds made provision for widows who wished to continue in the trade of their late husbands.
Source: *Le Livre des Métiers, XIIIe Siècle*, eds. René de Lespinasse and François Bonnardot (Paris, 1879; repr. Geneva: Slatkine Reprints, 1980). Tr. E.M.A.

The Craft of Silk Fabric

1. No journeywoman maker of silk fabric may be a mistress of the craft until she has practiced it for a year and a day, after she has done her apprenticeship, because she will be more competent to practice her craft and observe the regulations.

2. No mistress of this craft may take an apprentice for fewer than six years with a fee of four livres, or for eight years with forty sous, or for ten years with no fee; and she may have no more than two apprentices at the same time, and she may not take another until their apprenticeships are completed.

3. No mistress or journeywoman may work at night or on a feast day observed by the whole town.

4. No mistress of the craft may weave thread with silk, or foil with silk, because the work is false and bad; and it should be burned if it is found.

5. No mistress or journeywoman of the craft may make a false hem or border, either of thread or of foil, nor may she do raised work of thread or foil. And if such work is found, it should be burned, because it is false and bad.

6. No mistress or journeywoman of the craft, after she has done her apprenticeship, may hire anyone who is not a mistress of the craft, but she may take work to do from whomever she likes.

7. It is ordered that all the mistresses of the said craft who send their work outside the town to be done must show it to those who are designated to watch over the craft, along with the work of their own house, to make sure that it is up to standard.

8. And anyone who infringes on any of the above regulations must pay eight Parisian sous, each time she is found at fault; of which the king will have five sous, and the craft guild twelve deniers, and the masters who oversee the craft two sous for their pains and for the work they do in overseeing the craft.

9. To safeguard this craft in the manner described above, there should be established three masters and three mistresses, who will swear by the Saints that they will make known to the provost of Paris or to his representative all the infringements of the regulations of the said craft, to the best of their ability.

The Craft of Weavers of Silk Kerchiefs at Paris

1. Any woman who wishes to weave silk kerchiefs in Paris may do so, provided she knows how to practice the craft well and truly, according to the following usage and customs.

2. First: it is ordered that no journeywoman of the craft may work on a feast day which the commune of the city celebrates and which is commanded by the holy Church.

3. No one may work at night, because one cannot do as good work at night as during the day.

4. It is ordered that no one may have more than one apprentice in the craft who is not related to her and one who is a relative; and she may not take an apprentice for fewer than seven years with a fee of twenty sous, or eight years without a fee. And if it happens that any mistress sells her apprentice for her need, she may not take another before her term is up; and if it happens that the apprentice buys her own freedom, the mistress may not take another apprentice before the term of the one who bought her freedom is up.

5. It is ordered that no mistress or journeywoman of the craft may buy silk from Jews, from spinsters or from any others, but only from the proper merchants.

6. No woman may work on the premises of a man or woman, if she does not know the craft.

7. Whoever infringes any of these regulations, she must pay six

sous as a fine for each time that she is found at fault: of which four sous are for the king, and two sous are for those who oversee the craft, for their pains therein.

8. It is ordered that no mistress or hired woman of the aforesaid craft may put the work which she does, whether warped or not warped, or whether finished or unfinished, in pawn to any Jew or Lombard or any other kind of person. And if she does this, every time she does it and is discovered, she will pay a fine of ten sous: of which the king will receive six sous and the mistresses who oversee the craft four sous.

9. No one may sell woven scraps, if they are not worked in the craft.

10. The aforesaid craft has three good women and true who will oversee the craft on behalf of the king, sworn and pledged at Chastelet, who will make known all the infringements against the craft, whenever they discover them.

The Craft of the Fullers of Paris

1. Whoever wishes to be a fuller[107] in Paris may do so freely without buying the privilege of the craft from the king.

2. Master fullers may have no more than two apprentices who are not their sons or their brothers, born of legal marriages.

3. The apprentice or apprentices should and may do everything in the craft which their master commands.

4. Master fullers may teach their craft to the children of their wives, and to their brothers born of legal marriages, and may have them with their apprentices, just as they may their own children and brothers.

5. If a master dies, his wife may practice the craft and keep the apprentices, freely, in the manner described above; and with the two apprentices she may teach the children of her husband and her brothers born of a legal marriage.

6. If a widowed woman practicing the aforesaid craft of fullers marries a man who is not a member of the aforesaid craft, she may not practice the craft; and if she marries a man who is a member of the craft, even if he is an apprentice or a worker, she may practice it freely. . . .

13. No woman may lay a hand on the cloth, to do things belonging to the craft of fullers, before the cloth has been sheared. . . .

---

107. Fulling was an important step in the cloth-making process, involving the cleaning and thickening of the cloth.

The Trade of Bathhouse-Keepers

1. Whoever wishes to be a bathhouse-keeper in the city of Paris may freely do so, provided he works according to the usage and customs of the trade, made by agreement of the commune, as follow.

2. Be it known that no man or woman may cry or have cried their baths until it is day, because of the dangers which can threaten those who rise at the cry to go to the baths.

3. No man or woman of the aforesaid trade may maintain in their houses or baths either prostitutes of the day or night, or lepers, or vagabonds, or other infamous people of the night.

4. No man or woman may heat up their baths on Sunday, or on a feast day which the commune of the city keeps.

And every person should pay, for a steam-bath, two deniers; and if he bathes, he should pay four deniers.

And because at some times wood and coal are more expensive than at others, if anyone suffers, a suitable price shall be set by the provost of Paris, through the discussion of the good people of the aforesaid trade, according to the situation of the times.

The male and female bathhouse-keepers have sworn and promised before us to uphold these things firmly and consistently, and not to go against them.

5. Anyone who infringes any of the above regulations of the aforesaid trade must make amends with ten Parisian sous, of which six go to the king, and the other four go to the masters who oversee the trade, for their pains.

6. The aforesaid trade shall have three good men of the trade, elected by us unanimously or by a majority, who shall swear before the provost of Paris or his representative that they will oversee the trade well and truly, and that they will make known to the provost of Paris or his representative all the infringements that they know of or discover, and the provost shall remove and change them as often as he wishes. . . .

52. Alexander Neckham: Descriptions of Crafts (12th c.)

The writer describes two of the crafts which women practiced. Women provided much of the labor in the weaving industry

(though they were even more frequently employed as spinners), and in some cities they were allowed to be goldsmiths.
Source: U. T. Holmes, *Daily Living in the Twelfth Century, Based on the Observations of Alexander Neckham in London and Paris* (Madison: University of Wisonsin Press, 1952).

A Goldsmith's Work

The goldsmith should have a furnace with a hole at the top so that the smoke can get out by all exits. One hand should operate the bellows with a light pressure and the greatest diligence, so that the air inside the bellows, being pressed through the tubes, may blow up the coals and that the constant spread of it may feed the fire. Let there be an anvil of extreme hardness on which iron and gold may be softened and may take the required form. They can be stretched and pulled with the tongs and the hammer. There should be a hammer also for making gold leaf, as well as sheets of silver, tin, brass, iron, or copper. The goldsmith must have a very sharp chisel by which he can engrave in amber, diamond, or *ophelta*, or marble, or jacinth, emerald, sapphire, or pearl, and form many figures. He should have a hardness stone for testing metals, and one for comparing steel with iron. He must also have a rabbit's-foot for smoothing, polishing, and wiping the surface of gold and silver, and the small particles of metal should be collected in a leather apron. He must have small boxes, flasks, and containers, of pottery, and a toothed saw and a gold file, as well as gold and silver wire, by which broken objects can be mended or properly constructed. The goldsmith should be skilled in feathery work as well as in bas-relief, in fusing as well as in hammering. His apprentice must have a waxed or painted table, or one covered with clay, for portraying little flowers and drawing in various ways. That he may do this conveniently let him have litharge[108] and chalk. He must know how to distinguish solid gold from brass and copper, that he may not purchase brass for gold. . . .

A Weaver's Work

The weaver has a [breast] roller to which the cloth to be rolled up is fastened. Let there be beamlike strips marked with holes and facing each other from opposing sides, with wires shaped like a shepherd's crook and the strips going the same way as the warp threads, also [let

---

108. Litharge = lead monoxide (commonly used in various industries).

there be] linen threads as slender as those that are properly associated with fringes [tied to] rods in the heddles, these threads at set intervals; let the weaver draw the warp threads [with such a heddle], the upper series of threads and then the lower. When the weft has been passed through by means of a shuttle, let him beat down the work accomplished, and let the shuttle have an iron or wooden bobbin between open spaces. The bobbin should be filled from a spool, and this spool should be covered in the manner of a clew of yarn with a weight. Let the material of the weft thread be pulled from this weighted spool, so that the one hand of the weaver tosses the shuttle to the other, to be returned vice versa.

But in vain does one weave a cloth unless previously iron combs, working upon the wool, to be softened by flame, have carded the strands in long and reciprocal endeavor. Thus the better and finer parts of the combed wool may be reserved for the thread, with the woolly dregs like coarse tow being left over. Afterwards let the wool thread be aided by the application of madder or woad such as is done in Beauvais, or let the material to be dyed be saturated with frequent dipping in *graine*. Then let the weaver reclaim it; but before it makes its appearance in the form of clothing, it should be subjected to the care of the fuller, demanding frequent washing.

53. Lawsuit: Women Moneylenders (1281)

> The medieval church forbade "usury," or money-lending for profit, and many secular governments also prohibited it officially, although there were various legal ways to charge interest. Some medieval Christians engaged in money-lending, but it was the Jews who were famous as bankers in medieval Europe. In the court case below, two Jewish women, Bona and Belasez, are engaged in small-scale money-lending, and another woman, Matilda, is their customer.
>
> Source: *Select Pleas, Starrs, and Other Records from the Rolls of the Exchequer of the Jews, A.D. 1220–1284*, ed. J. M. Rigg (London: Selden Society, 1902). Tr. E.M.A.

Moses of Dog Street and Bona, his wife, are required to respond to Matilda La Megre in a case of unjust detention of pledges. Matilda complains that she gave seven ells of burnet,[109] worth three shillings

---

109. Ell = measure of length, equal to 45 inches in England; burnet = brown cloth.

per ell, in pledge to them and Belasez for six shillings, on the Tuesday after the feast of St. Benedict in the ninth year of the reign of King Edward, on the following condition: that whenever, within fifteen days after this transaction, she might pay the said six shillings to the aforesaid Jews, they would deliver the aforesaid pledge [i.e., the cloth] to her for the said six shillings; and within those fifteen days the aforesaid Matilda did go to the house of the said Jews, and offered them the aforesaid six shillings, and the aforesaid Belasez accepted three shillings for the three shillings which she had lent to Matilda for the aforesaid pledge, but the aforesaid Moses and Bona refused to accept the other three shillings, demanding from her ten shillings in principal and interest for the aforesaid three shillings, in contravention of the king's statutes, and they said they would not return her pledge, unless she wished to give them the said ten shillings for it; and to this day they unjustly retain the said pledge, to her damage to the amount of forty pounds, and against the king's statute. And she offers to prove this.

The aforesaid Moses and Bona . . . say that they have received nothing from the said Matilda, and that they have no goods of hers handed over by her, but that the aforesaid Belasez gave them a certain measure of burnet in pledge for 8s. 9d.; and that they would have been willing to return the cloth to Matilda for the aforesaid 8s. 9d., for which the cloth had been pledged. And they ask that the justices inquire of Belasez whether the said cloth was pledged for such a sum of money. . . .

Belasez says that the said Matilda once asked her to lend her five shillings on pledge of the aforementioned cloth, but that she did not have the money, so she asked Bona, wife of the said Moses, to go in with her and lend Matilda half of this sum of five shillings for the aforesaid pledge, and that Bona then did lend Matilda 2s. 6d. for the aforesaid pledge, and Belasez herself lent her 2s. 6d. And another time the same Bona and Belasez lent the same Matilda twelve pence on the same pledge, so that she received from them six shillings in all, three shillings belonging to Bona and three shillings belonging to Belasez, for which she had pledged the said cloth to both of them. And Belasez says that she told Moses and Bona to deliver the aforesaid cloth to Matilda for the three shillings which they had lent to Matilda, because she had paid Belasez her three shillings; but they refused to give back the said cloth, unless Matilda gave them ten shillings for it. And because it is disproved by Belasez's testimony, on which the said Moses and Bona relied, that the said Matilda owed them 8s. 9d. on the said cloth, because she borrowed only three shillings from them, for which they demanded ten shillings in usury, against the king's statutes, therefore the said Moses and Bona are committed to the Tower of London, to be held in safe custody, until they have made satisfaction to the king for this offense, and until the said cloth is delivered to the said Matilda for three shillings, as said above.

54. Infractions of Commercial Regulations (13th–14th c.)

Commercial life was regulated by guild regulations such as those of Paris, and also by municipal codes and royal decrees. The excerpts below are from the records of the city of London; women are in the minority among the offenders in these records, but they are found committing almost every kind of commercial misdemeanor.

Source: *Memorials of London and London Life in the XIIIth, XIVth, and XVth Centuries*, ed. and tr. Henry Thomas Riley (London: Longmans, Green and Co., 1868).

Lightweight Bread (1298)

Be it remembered, that on Wednesday next after the Feast of St. Laurence [10 August] . . . Juliana la Pestour [i.e., Baker] of Nuetone, brought a cart laden with six shillings'[110] worth of bread into West Chepe: of which bread, that which was light bread was wanting in weight, according to the assize[111] of the halfpenny loaf, to the amount of 25 shillings. And of the said six shillings' worth, three shillings' worth was brown bread; which bread was of the right assize. It was therefore adjudged, that the same should be delivered to the aforesaid Juliana, by Henry le Galeys, Mayor of London, Thomas Romeyn, and other Aldermen. And the other three shillings' worth, by award of the said Mayor and Aldermen, was ordered to be given to the prisoners in the Neugate.

---

110. Shilling is used here both as an amount of money (12 pence) and as a measure of weight (3/5 of an ounce).

111. Assize = "law"; in this case a regulation concerning product standards.

Lightweight Bread (1310)

On the Monday next before the Feast of St. Hilary [13 January] . . .
the bread of Sarra Foting, Christina Terrice, Godiyeva Foting, Matilda
de Bolingtone, Christina Prichet, Isabella Sperling, Alice Pegges, Johanna de Cauntebrigge, and Isabella Pouveste, bakeresses of Strat-
ford, was taken by Roger le Paumer, Sheriff of London, and weighed
before the Mayor and Aldermen; and it was found that the halfpenny
loaf weighed less than it ought by eight shillings.

But seeing that the bread was cold, and ought not to have been
weighed in such a state, by the custom of the City, it was agreed that
it should not be forfeited this time. But in order that such an offense
as this should not pass unpunished, it was [decided] as to bread so
taken, that three-halfpenny loaves should always be sold for a penny;
but that the bakeresses aforesaid should this time have such penny.

Bakers Stealing Dough (1327)

John Brid, baker, was attached to make answer as to certain falsehood, malice, and deceit, by him committed, to the nuisance of the
common people; as to which, . . . [it was alleged that] the same John
. . . did skilfully and artfully cause a certain hole to be made upon a
certain table of his, called a "moldingborde," pertaining to his bake-
house, after the manner of a mouse-trap, in which mice are caught;
there being a certain wicket warily provided for closing and opening
such hole.

And when his neighbours and others, who were wont to bake their
bread at his oven,[112] came with their dough or material for making
bread, the said John used to put such dough or other material upon
the said table, called a "moldingborde," as aforesaid; and . . . the
same John had one of his household . . . sitting in secret beneath such
table; which servant of his, so seated beneath the hole, and carefully
opening it, piecemeal and bit by bit carefully [collected] some of the
dough aforesaid, frequently collecting great quantities from such
dough, falsely, wickedly, and maliciously; to the great loss of all his
neighbours and other persons living near. . . .

William atte Sele, John atte Barnet, Robert de Bertone, John de
Polberowe, Robert de Brokesbourne, Roger de Milton, and Richard

---

112. People brought their own dough to be baked (for a fee) in the baker's oven.
Thus it is his neighbors' dough, not his own, that John is accused of stealing.

de Honesdone, bakers, and Alice de Brightenoch, and Lucy de Pyker-inge, bakeresses, in whose houses, also, like tables, called "mold-ingbordes," were found, with like holes, and with like dough beneath, as aforesaid, fraudulently and maliciously collected, were attached in like manner as to the fraud, malice, and deceit aforesaid . . . . Who appeared; and each of them being singly arraigned as to the matters aforesaid, they say that they are in no way guilty . . . . And hereupon, . . . [the jurors] say upon their oath that the aforesaid John and all the others are guilty of all, as well as to the hole so suspected, and the dough drawn through the hole, as the other things charged against them; and that for long they have been wont to commit the said falsehood and deceit. Therefore it was adjudged that the said John and all the others should be committed to the Gaol of Neugate . . . [until sentencing].

Afterwards, . . . it was agreed and ordained, that all those of the bakers aforesaid, beneath whose tables with holes dough had been found, should be put upon the pillory, with a certain quantity of such dough hung from their necks; and that they should so remain upon the pillory until Vespers at St. Paul's in London should be ended.

And as to the two women aforesaid, because they allege that they have husbands, namely, Alice [has] William de Brechenoke for her husband, and Lucy aforesaid [has] Hugh de Pykerynge for her hus-band, and this same has by their neighbours been attested; seeing too that the same Alice and Lucy allege that the said deed was not their deed;—it was agreed and ordained that they should be sent back to the prison of Neugate, there to remain until as to them it should have been otherwise ordained; and that all such tables with holes, as aforesaid, should be thrown down and utterly destroyed, and from thenceforth not allowed to be made; and that if any one of the said bakers should in future be found acting with such deceit, falsehood, and malice, he should stand upon the pillory for one whole day, and afterwards abjure the City, so as at no future time to return thereto. . . .

It should also be known, that the women aforesaid remained in the said Prison of Neugate, in the custody of the Sheriffs before-mentioned.

Rotten Meat (1348)

At a congregation of Thomas Leggy, the Mayor, the Aldermen, Sheriffs, and an immense number of the Commonalty, on [6 May] . . . John, son of John Gylessone, of Refham, and Agnes le Ismongere, were questioned for that on that day they had exposed for sale, in divers places in the City of London, putrid and stinking meat; in deceit, and to the peril of the lives, of persons buying the same, and to the scandal and disgrace of the Mayor, Aldermen, Sheriffs, and all the Commonalty, of the city aforesaid.

And the said Agnes for herself said, that she bought meat of the aforesaid John, son of John Gylessone, to the value of 4 pence, supposing that the same was good and proper, and without any default; and which meat she, Agnes, with such belief, exposed for sale. And the said John in full court acknowledged that he had sold the meat aforesaid to the said Agnes, for the price before mentioned; further acknowledging, of his own accord, that shortly before he sold [it to her], he had found a certain dead sow, thrown out near the ditch [outside] Alegate, in the suburb of London; which sow he then flayed, and the flesh of the same, cooked as well as raw, he exposed for sale to the aforesaid Agnes, and to others who chose to buy it.

And [it was decided that] . . . the skin of the said sow . . . should be carried by the Sheriffs of the City in public before him, the said John, to the pillory on Cornhulle; and that he, the said John, should be first upon the pillory there, and the said flesh be burnt beneath him, while upon the pillory.

And seeing that the said Agnes thought that the said meat, so sold to her, was good and proper, when she bought the same, it was awarded that she should go acquitted thereof.

Fraudulent Measure (1364)

On the 23rd day of November, . . . Alice, wife of Robert de Caustone, appeared before Adam de Bury, the Mayor, and the Aldermen, and before them acknowledged that she had sold ale in a measure called a "quart," that was not sealed; and also, that in the same measure there was put pitch, one inch and a half in depth, and that rosemary was laid upon it, so as to look like a bush, in the sight of the common people.

Which measure was assayed by the standard of London; whereby it was found that six such quarts as this would not make one proper gallon of ale. And for the falsehood and deceit aforesaid, it was adjudged by the Mayor and Aldermen, that the said Alice should undergo the punishment of the pillory for women ordained, called the "thewe" . . . . And the same false measure was divided into two equal parts; one of which was tied to the pillory, in sight of the common people, and the other part remained in the Chamber of the Guildhall.

Rotten Fish (1372)

On Saturday next after the Feast of St. Giles the Abbot [1 September], . . . Margery Hore, fishwife, was brought here, before the Mayor and Aldermen, with certain fish called "soles," stinking and rotten, and unwholesome for the use of man, which she had exposed for sale at the Stokkes on the day aforesaid, in deceit of the common people, and against the Ordinance published thereon, and to the scandal of the City. . . .

Which Margery being questioned thereupon, did not deny the same, etc. Therefore it was awarded that she should have the punishment of the pillory ordained for women, called the "thewe", for her fraud and deceit aforesaid; and that the said fish should there be burnt etc., and the cause of her punishment there proclaimed.

Deceptive Tapestry (1374)

On Monday next after the Feast of St. Valentine [14 February], . . . Henry Clerke, John Dyke, William Tanner, and Thomas Lucy, tapicers, and Masters of the trade of Tapicers, in London, caused to be brought here a coster[113] of tapestry, wrought upon the loom after the manner of the work of Arras, and made of false work, by Katherine Duchewoman, in her house at Fynkeslane, being 4 yards in length, and 7 quarters in breadth; seeing that she had made it of linen beneath, but covered with wool above, in deceit of the people, and against the Ordinance of the trade aforesaid; and they asked that the coster might be adjudged false, and for that reason burnt, according to the form of the Articles of their trade, as here in the Chamber enrolled etc.

And whereas the said Katherine was warned to be here on the morrow, to shew if she had aught to say why the same coster should not be burnt, for the reason aforesaid, she did not afterwards appear etc.

Therefore, after due examination thereof by the Masters aforesaid, and other reputable men of the same trade, by assent of the Mayor, Recorder, and certain of the Aldermen, it was ordered that the said coster, as being false work, should be burnt, according to the form of the Articles of the trade of Tapicers aforesaid.

---

113.   Coster = hanging.

55. Business Contracts (14th–15th c.)

Business deals which involved precious objects, large sums of
money or long-term arrangements might be set out in writing. In
the first three cases below, the parties had their agreements copied
into the municipal records of the city of London, so as to ensure
an official record of the transaction. It is interesting to note that
luxurious goods like those described here were often forbidden
by sumptuary laws to people of the relatively low status of pepper-
ers and spicers (see Part II above). In the fourth document, the
government of the German city of Cologne makes a contract with
a woman who agrees to teach her craft to a number of men.
Source: First three documents from *Memorials of London and London
Life in the XIIIth, XIVth, and XVth Centuries*, ed. and tr. Henry
Thomas Riley (London: Longmans, Green and Co., 1868). Fourth
document reprinted with permission from *The Legend of Good
Women: Medieval Women in Towns & Cities*, by Erika Uitz, published
by Moyer Bell Limited, Colonial Hill/RFD 1, Mt. Kisco, NY 10549.

Arrangement about an Embroidered Cloth (1304)

To all those who this letter shall see and hear, Thomasin Guydichon
of Lucca, greeting in God. Whereas I had in time past granted, released, and quitclaimed[114] unto Aleyse Darcy, who was the daughter
of Messire Thomas Darcy, all my share, and all the right and claim
that I ever had, or could have, in one piece of cloth, embroidered with
divers works in gold and silk, which she is now preparing, eight ells
in length, and six ells in breadth, for ever; in consideration of 300
marks sterling which I lately received for the aforesaid Aleyse from
Messire Henry de Lacy, Earl of Lincoln, and Sir John de Sandale, clerk,
for another embroidered cloth which the aforesaid Aleyse and myself
sold to the Earl of Lincoln aforesaid,—as by a letter of quitclaim, sealed
with my seal, the which was made at London, on the Monday next
after Christmas Day in the year of Grace 1302, more fully appears;—
be it known unto all of you that I, the aforesaid Thomasin, do . . .
release and quitclaim unto the aforesaid Aleyse, by the present letter,
all the action, and the right and claim, which I ever had, or in any
manner ought to have, in the cloth of gold aforesaid; in such manner
that neither I . . . nor my heirs, nor my executors, nor any other man,
by us, for us, or in our name, may or can, from this day forth, claim,

---

114. Quitclaim = to give up all legal claim to a thing.

challenge, or demand, at any time whatsoever, any right or claim whatsoever against the aforesaid Aleyse, against her heirs, or her executors, by reason of the said embroidered cloth which she is now preparing. In witness of which thing I have to this letter set my seal. . . .

A Sale of Precious Items (1338)

To all those who this letter shall see or hear, Walter Adryan, pepperer, of London, greeting in God. Know ye, that I have sold and granted unto Margery Randolf, of the same city, jewels and other things below written, that is to say—; a circlet, a [handled cup] of silver with a foot, a [buckle] of gold, a girdle of silver, 12 silver spoons, a [cup] on a foot, and silver covercle,[115] a silver cup and covercle, a [handled cup] of mazer,[116] with an impression of St. Thomas of Lancaster thereon, and with a covercle, a [handled cup] of mazer with an impression of a head, 2 chaplets of pearls and of prayer-beads, a table-cloth of 5 1/2 ells, and 4 linen sheets; all for 10 marks sterling, which the said Margery has paid me in the City of London beforehand, for all such jewels and the other things before named. . . .

A Sale of Jewels (1363)

To all who this letter shall see or hear, Agneys Chalke, spicer, of London, greeting in God. Know that I have sold and delivered for a certain sum of silver, by me received on the day of the making hereof, to Master John Caumbrugge, executor of the will of Master Michael de Northburghe, late Bishop of London, whom may God assoil, a coronal of gold, wrought with stones, that is to say, with *rubyes*, *saphirs*, emeralds, and pearls; and a [brooch] of gold, in the fashion of an eagle, wrought with stones, that is to say, with *rubyes, saphirs*, emeralds, and pearls, with one great ruby in the breast thereof; and two rings of gold, the one with a *dyamaunt*, and the other enamelled; and one mazer, bound with silver gilt; to have and to hold all the said jewels well and freely, to him and to his assigns forever. In witness of the truth whereof, to this letter of true sale I have set my seal. Given at London, on the Eve of St. Michael [29 September], in the 37th year of the reign of King Edward, after the Conquest the Third.

---

115. Covercle = lid.
116. Mazer = a hardwood, or a cup made of such wood.

Agreement to Train Brewers (1420)

. . . Thus that I, the aforementioned Fygin with the knowledge, approval and permission of my aforementioned husband have agreed with the honourable wise gentlemen mayors and town council of Cologne . . . that I shall loyally and industriously and to the best of my ability teach two men to make good *grut*. These two men shall be appointed by them. They have appointed a man by the name of Hermann von Aiche, the brewer upstream near Airsbuch, whom I have already begun to teach and whom I shall continue to teach and another, whom they still have to appoint . . . without dishonestly withholding any of my knowledge of the making of the aforementioned *grut*. With this document I have obliged and committed myself to do this for the aforementioned gentlemen and the town of Cologne for eight consecutive years, beginning with the date of this document. And whenever they let me know that they need me for their *grut*making I shall, unless I am ill, come to their town of Cologne to instruct and teach. And for every day that I leave my house and live in Cologne for this reason they shall give me one mark of the Cologne currency to cover my labour and my upkeep. . . .

56. Guardians' Accounts: Raising Girls (14th c.)

These extracts from the municipal records of London reveal some of the details of arrangements made for the guardianship of orphaned girls. Isabel in particular obviously came from a very wealthy urban family.
Source: *Memorials of London and London Life in the XIIIth, XIVth, and XVth Centuries*, ed. and tr. Henry Thomas Riley (London: Longmans, Green and Co., 1868).

Isabel de Hakeneye (1350)

The wardship of Isabel, daughter of Richard de Hakeneye, late Alderman of London, was delivered and granted to Richard, son of the aforesaid Richard de Hakeneye, brother of the said Isabel, on the Monday next after the Feast of St. Valentine . . . ; with divers silver plate and jewels, in weight and value to the amount of £20 10s. 3d. sterling, which had been left to the said Isabel by the will of Alice, the wife of the aforesaid Richard de Hakeneye, and mother of the same Isabel; as also, with £43 sterling in ready money; in full payment of the whole portion of the said Isabel, left to her as well by the will of the said Richard, her father, as by the said will of her mother, Alice aforesaid. Also with one messuage[117] and three shops in the Parish of St. Agnes within Aldresgate, in London, which are of no value beyond the reprises upon them.—On the understanding that he shall answer unto the aforesaid Isabel, when she reaches full age, as to the silver plate aforesaid, [and jewels], £20 10s. 3d. in weight and value, and as to the said £43 . . . ; together with all the profit from the said £43 in the meantime arising; saving to the aforesaid Richard his reasonable outlays and expenses, upon the maintenance of the said Isabel in the meantime dispersed. And further, it shall not be lawful for the said Richard to marry the aforesaid Isabel to any one in the meantime, without the assent of the Mayor and Aldermen for the time being.

And well and faithfully to do the same the said Richard bound himself, his heirs and executors, and all his goods, moveable and immoveable, wheresoever they might be. . . .

The particulars as to the silver plate and jewels, left to the said Isabel in the will of Alice aforesaid, are set forth as follow, namely.—

First, two silver pots, in weight and value, 100s. One enamelled pot, with covercle, weight £4 5s. One enamelled cup, with a covercle, weight and value, 68s. 4d. One other enamelled cup, with a covercle, weight and value, 100s. Three cups plated with silver, with three covercles, weight and value, 38s. One silver water-pot, weight and value, 28s. 4d. One silver foot for a cup, weight 10s. 7d. Twelve silver spoons, weight and value, 13s. Three silver [buckles], with two [brooches], weight 12s. Five rings, value 5s. Sum total, £20 10s. 3d.

Alice Reigner (1380)

Account of John Bryan, citizen and fishmonger, delivered on the first day of December . . . in the Chamber of the Guildhall of London, before the auditors by William Walworthe, the then Mayor, assigned; for the time that he was guardian of the body and chattels of Alice, daughter of John Reigner, blader, an orphan of the said city; at the instance of Richard Fraunceys, fishmonger, her husband, then present.

He charges himself with 100 marks received to the use of the said Alice; and with profit thereupon for five years, at 4 shillings in the pound yearly, according to the custom of the said city, amounting to 100 marks.—Sum total, 200 marks.

---

117. Messuage = piece of land.

He claims allowance of one half of such increase, namely 2 shillings
in the pound yearly for five years, for his trouble as to the same,
according to the custom of the City, making 50 marks. For the board
of the said Alice, at 8 pence per week, making 34s. 8d. yearly, in the
whole, £8 13s. 4d. For her clothes, linen and woolen, and bed, 13s.
4d. yearly, making in the whole, £3 6s. 8d. For dressing and doctoring
the head of the same Alice, and for her teaching, shoes, and other
small necessaries, 13s. 4d. yearly, making in the whole, £3 6s. 8d. For
his expenses upon a plea in the Courts of the Bishop of London and
of the Archbishop, for the marriage contract of the said Alice, £4 13s.
4d.—Sum total, £53 6s. 8d.

57. London Prostitutes (14th c.)

Prostitution was usually regarded by medieval society as a sinful
but necessary occupation. Procuring or pimping, however, was
less likely than prostitution to be tolerated, and prostitutes themselves were regulated in ways designed to set them apart from
other people and to limit the damage which they were perceived
as doing to the community. The extracts below are from the municipal records of London.
Source: *Memorials of London and London Life in the XIIIth, XIVth,
and XVth Centuries*, ed. and tr. Henry Thomas Riley (London:
Longmans, Green and Co., 1868).

Regulation of Prostitutes' Clothing (1382)

On the 13th day of February, . . . it was ordered by the Mayor, and
Aldermen, and Common Council, that all common harlots, and all
women commonly reputed as such, should have and use hoods of
ray[118] only; and should not wear any manner of budge, or *perreie*, or
revers,[119] within the franchise of the City. And if anyone should be
found doing to the contrary thereof, she was to be taken and brought
to the Compter, and the Sheriffs were to have the coloured hoods,
budge, *perreie*, or *revers*, to the contrary of this Ordinance found upon
her.

---

118. Ray = striped cloth.
119. Budge, perreie and revers = types of fur.

A Procuress (1385)

On the 27th day of July . . . Elizabeth, the wife of Henry Moring, was brought before Nicholas Brebre, Knight, the Mayor, the Aldermen, and the Sheriffs of London, in the Guildhall, for that, as well at the information of divers persons, as upon the acknowledgment and confession of one Johanna, her serving-woman, the same Mayor, Aldermen, and Sheriffs, were given to understand that the said Elizabeth, under colour of the craft of embroidery, which she pretended to follow, took in and retained the same Johanna and divers other women, as her apprentices, and bound them to serve her after the manner of apprentices in such art; whereas the truth of the matter was, that she did not follow that craft, but that, after so retaining them, she incited the same Johanna and the other women who were with her, and in her service, to live a lewd life, and to consort with friars, chaplains, and all other such men as desired to have their company, as well in her own house, in the Parish of All Hallows near the Wall, in the Ward of Bradstreet, in London, as elsewhere; and used to hire them out to the same friars, chaplains, and other men, for such stipulated sum as they might agree upon, as well in her own house as elsewhere, she retaining in her own possession the sum so agreed upon.

And in particular, on Thursday the 4th day of May last past, by the compassing and procuring of the said Elizabeth, and of a certain chaplain, whose name is unknown, she sent the same Johanna, and ordered her to accompany the said chaplain at night, that she might carry a lantern before him to his chamber—but in what Parish is likewise unknown;—it being her intention that the said Johanna should stay the night there with the chaplain; of their own contriving, while the said Johanna herself, as she says, knew nothing about it. Still, she remained there with such chaplain the whole of that night; and when she returned home to her mistress on the morrow, this Elizabeth asked her if she had brought anything with her for her trouble that night; to which she made answer that she had not. Whereupon, the same Elizabeth used words of reproof to her, and ordered her to go back again to the chaplain on the following night, and whatever she should be able to lay hold of, to take the same for her trouble, and bring it with her. Accordingly, Johanna by her command went back on the following night to the said chaplain, at his chamber aforesaid, and again passed the night there: and on the morrow she rose very early in the morning, and bearing in mind the words of her mistress, and being afraid to go back without carrying something to her said mistress, she took a Portifory[120] that belonged to the chaplain, and carried it off, the chaplain himself knowing nothing about it; which Portifory she delivered to the said Elizabeth, who took it, well knowing how and in what manner the same Johanna had come by it. And after this, the said Elizabeth pledged this Portifory for eight pence, to a man whose name is unknown.

And many other times this Elizabeth received the like base gains from the same Johanna, and her other serving-women, and retained the same for her own use; living thus abominably and damnably, and inciting other women to live in the like manner; she herself being a common harlot and procuress.

Whereupon, on the same day, the said Elizabeth was asked by the Court, how she would acquit herself thereof; to which she made answer, that she was in no way guilty, and put herself upon the country to the same. Therefore the Sheriffs were instructed to summon twelve good men of the venue aforesaid to appear here on the 28th day of the same month, to make a Jury thereon; and the said Elizabeth was in the meantime committed to prison.

Upon which day the good men of the venue aforesaid appeared . . . [and] declared upon their oath, the same Elizabeth to be guilty of all the things above imputed to her; and that she was a common harlot, and a common procuress. And because that through such women and the like deeds many scandals had befallen the said city, and great peril might through such transactions in future arise; therefore, according to the custom of the City of London in such and the like cases provided, and in order that other women might beware of doing the like; it was adjudged that the said Elizabeth should be taken from the Guildhall aforesaid to the Cornhulle, and be put upon the *thewe*,[121] there to remain for one hour of the day, the cause thereof being publicly proclaimed. And afterwards, she was to be taken to some Gate of the City, and there be made to foreswear the City, and the liberty thereof, to the effect that she would never again enter the same; on pain of imprisonment for three years, and the said punishment of the thewe, at the discretion of the Mayor and Aldermen for the time being, so often as it should please them that she should suffer such punishment.

Restriction of Prostitutes (1393)

. . . whereas many and divers affrays, broils, and dissensions, have arisen in times past, and many men have been slain and murdered,

---

120. Portifory = type of prayer book.
121. Thewe = pillory for women. It was different in design from the men's pillory, and may have been chair-shaped.

by reason of the frequent resort of, and consorting with, common harlots, at taverns, brewhouses of *huksters*,[122] and other places of ill-fame, within the said city, and the suburbs thereof; and more especially through Flemish women, who profess and follow such shameful and dolorous life: —we do by our command forbid, on behalf of our Lord the King, and the Mayor and Alderman of the City of London, that any such women shall go about or lodge in the said city, or in the suburbs thereof, by night or by day; but they are to keep themselves to the places thereunto assigned, that is to say, the Stews[123] on the other side of [the River] Thames, and Cokkeslane; on pain of losing and forfeiting the upper garment that she shall be wearing, together with her hood, every time that any one of them shall be found doing to the contrary of this proclamation. And every officer and serjeant of the said city shall have power to take such garments and hoods, in manner and form aforesaid: the which they shall bring to the Guild-hall, and shall have the half thereof for their trouble.

58. Carpenter's Specifications: A Town House (1308)

The building being planned here can be usefully compared to those shown in the drawings below.
Source: *Memorials of London and London Life in the XIIIth, XIVth, and XVth Centuries*, ed. and tr. Henry Thomas Riley (London: Longmans, Green and Co., 1868).

Simon de Canterbury, carpenter, came before the Mayor and Aldermen on the Saturday next after the Feast of St. Martin the Bishop [11 October], . . . and acknowledged that he would make at his own proper charges, down to the locks, for William de Hanigtone, a pelterer, before the Feast of Easter then next ensuing, a hall and a room with a chimney, and one larder between the said hall and room; and one sollar[124] over the room and larder; also, one oriole [window] at the end of the hall, beyond the high bench, and one step with an oriole [porch], from the ground to the floor of the hall aforesaid, outside of that hall; and two enclosures as cellars, opposite to each other, beneath the hall; and one enclosure for a sewer, with two pipes

---

122. Hukster = peddlar.
123. Stews = bathhouses.
124. Sollar (solar) = "sun-room," used as a sitting room.

leading to the said sewer; and one stable, [blank] in length, between the said hall and the old kitchen, and twelve feet in width, with a sollar above such stable, and a garret above the sollar aforesaid; and at one end of such sollar, there is to be a kitchen with a chimney; and there is to be an oriole [window-room] between the said hall and the old chamber, eight feet in width. . . .

59. A Town Building

Town buildings often served as both dwellings and commercial establishments, with the owners of a business living on the premises, along with servants, apprentices and possibly employees. The plan and reconstructed drawing below are are based on the archaeological remains of a building in the English town of Lincoln.

Source: Helen Clarke, *The Archaeology of Medieval England* (London: The British Museum, 1984). (After R. H. Jones, 1980.)

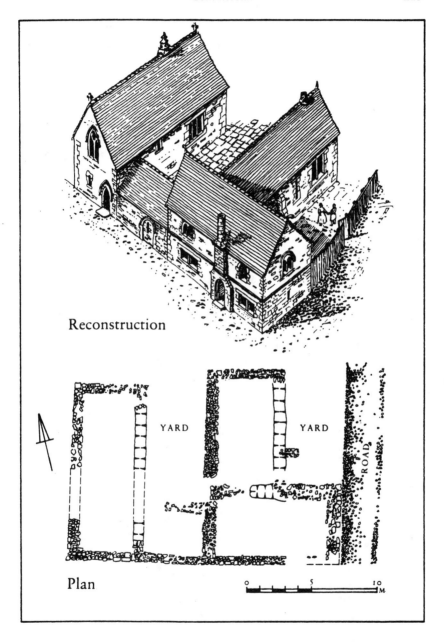

Reconstruction

Plan

YARD   YARD

ROAD

o   5   10
M

Part V

The Religious Life

Women living the religious life were a tiny minority, but they loom large in the written source material. Writers who were churchmen themselves were more interested in writing about nuns—either to praise or to blame them—than about other kinds of women. The religious achievements of female saints and other renowned holy women were the female accomplishments that medieval writers were most likely to recognize. Moreover, nuns were (somewhat tenuously) part of the literate network of the church; thus convents turn up in ecclesiastical documents. More importantly, nuns and mystics were almost the only women who did any writing themselves—though it was unusual even for a nun to write, especially in the Later Middle Ages.

A life dedicated to religion was in some ways a narrow and restricted one, but it did offer an alternative to the usual path of marriage and motherhood, and it might well be an opportunity for a woman to exercise considerable responsibility as an abbess or other monastic official. Many women became nuns because their families dedicated them to religion at a youthful age, but others chose the convent out of genuine piety or an affinity for a life of study or service. Religious impulses could also find an outlet in less permanent activities such as pilgrimages.

60. Church Council Decrees (5th–7th c.)

Church councils, which were gatherings of bishops and other important churchmen, decided the church's official stance on many issues, including the position of women in the church, whether as wives of clergymen or in their own right. The following decrees come from councils held in Gaul (later called France) and applied to the church there, but they are in line with similar decisions by more general councils. The practice of ordaining deaconesses died out relatively quickly, but it took many centuries for the church to enforce clerical celibacy widely.

Source: *Corpus Christianorum, Series Latina*, Vol. 148: *Concilia Galliae, A. 314-A. 506*, ed. C. Munier; and Vol. 148A: *Concilia Galliae, A. 511-A. 695*, ed. Charles de Clercq (Turnholt, 1963). Tr. E.M.A.

Ancient Statutes of the Church (ca. 475)

36. Young widows who are frail in body shall be supported at the expense of the church whose widows they are.

37. A woman, however learned and holy, shall not presume to teach men in the assembly.

38. A layman shall not dare to teach when clergy are present, unless they are examining him.

39. A man who is put in charge of religious women shall be examined by the bishop of the place.

41. A woman shall not presume to baptize.

99. A holy virgin who offers herself to the bishop for consecration shall be dressed in the sort of garments she shall always wear, suitable to her profession and chastity.

100. Widows or nuns who are chosen for ministry to women who are to be baptized shall be so instructed in this office that they can, by clear and sound speech, teach ignorant and rustic women how they should answer the questions of the baptizer at the time when they are baptized, and how they should live after they have received baptism.

102. Widows who are supported by a stipend from the church should be so assiduous in the work of God that they delight the church with their good works and their prayers.

Council of Orange (441)

25. Deaconesses of any sort shall not be ordained. If any now exist, they shall bow their heads for the same blessing which is given to the people.

26. The profession of consecrated widowhood made before a bishop in his chamber is to be shown by the vidual garments bestowed by the bishop. And the abductor of such women, or the woman who deserts such a profession, deserves to be eternally damned.

Council of Arles (442–506)

2. He who is to be received into the priesthood may not be bound by the tie of marriage, unless a conversion is promised.

3. If any clergyman from the rank of the diaconate shall presume to have a woman for his comfort, other than his grandmother, mother, sister, daughter or niece, or his wife who has converted with him, he shall be excommunicated. And this penalty shall equally affect the woman too, if she does not wish to separate herself from him.

4. No deacon or priest or bishop shall bring a girl, whether freeborn or slave, into his personal chamber.

Council of Orange (533)

17. Women who have until now received the diaconal blessing, against the prohibitions of the canons, shall be excommunicated if they are shown to have fallen again into marriage. But if, warned by their bishop and recognizing their error, they dissolve such a marriage and do penance, they shall return to the grace of communion.

18. It was also pleasing [to the council] that the diaconal blessing be given to no woman from now on, on account of the frailty of the [female] condition.

Council of Epaone (517)

21. We utterly annul in this whole region the consecration of widows who are called deaconesses, and only the blessing of penitence, if they agree to be converted, is to be given them.

32. If any widow of a priest or deacon remarries, let her be expelled from the church, until she shall be separated from the unlawful union, and her husband too shall be punished with similar severity until he has been corrected.

61. Caesarius of Arles:
Rule for Nuns (ca. 512–534)

A monastic "rule" is the collection of regulations under which a particular community or a whole "order" of monks or nuns lives. Caesarius, a sixth-century bishop of Arles in Gaul, wrote the first rule specifically for nuns. Drawing on other monastic rules, and in turn influencing some which came after him, Caesarius' rule was adopted in various forms by a number of prominent convents in early medieval Europe.
Source: *Sancti Caesarii Episcopi Arelatensis Opera Omnia*, Vol. II: *Opera Varia*, ed. D. G. Morin (Maretioli, 1942). Tr. E.M.A.

1. To his holy and very venerable sisters in Christ, living in the monastery which we established with God's aid and inspiration, Bishop Caesarius.

Because the Lord in his mercy has deigned to inspire and aid us in establishing a monastery for you, we have also established for you spiritual and holy precepts as to how you ought to live in that monastery, in accordance with the statutes of the ancient fathers; and in order that with God's help you may be able to keep them, you must, while living perpetually in the cells of your monastery, invoke the presence of the Son of God with assiduous prayers, so that afterwards you may say with confidence: "I found him whom my soul loveth" [Cant. 3:4]. And therefore I ask you, sacred virgins and souls dedicated to God, who with your lamps shining await with clear conscience the coming of the Lord, that, because you know that I labored to establish a monastery for you, you with your prayers might ask that I be made a companion on your journey; and that, when you shall enter joyfully into the kingdom with the wise and holy virgins, you might obtain by your plea that I not remain outside with the foolish ones. May divine favor grant blessings in the present life to your sanctity, which is praying for me and shining among the precious gems of the church, and make it worthy of eternal blessings.

2. And because many things in monasteries of maidens seem to be different from those of monks, we have chosen a few things out of the many, by which the older and the younger ones shall live according to the Rule, and strive to fulfill spiritually what they have seen to be especially suitable to their sex.

These principal things are suited to your holy souls:

If anyone, having left her parents, wishes to renounce the world and enter the holy fold, in order to evade, with God's help, the jaws of spiritual wolves, let her never leave the monastery until her death, not even into the church, where the door can be seen.

3. Let her strive to shun and avoid oaths and curses like the venom of the devil.

4. And she, who at God's inspiration has converted,[125] is not permitted to assume the clothing of a religious immediately, unless her determination has already been proved in many tests; but, under the care of one of the seniors, let her persist in the clothing in which she came for a whole year. As to whether she may change that clothing, and whether she may have a bed in the community, let her be in the power of the prior; and just as he considers her person and her conscience, so much more quickly or slowly shall he allow her to progress.

5. Those who have come to the monastery as widows, or leaving their husbands behind, or having changed their clothing, are not exempted from this, unless they have previously deeded or given or sold all their resources to whomever they wish, so that they retain in their power nothing which they control or possess for themselves, according to the Lord's command: "If thou wilt be perfect, go and sell that thou hast" [Matt. 19:21]; and, "If anyone does not leave everything, and follow me, he cannot be my disciple." This I say, therefore, venerable daughters, because nuns who have possessions cannot achieve perfection. Even those who enter the religious life as virgins, if they do not fulfill this condition, either shall not be received, or shall not be permitted to put on the clothing of religion, until they have freed themselves of all the impediments of this world.

6. Those who do not control their own wealth, because their parents are still living, or who are still minors, shall be required to draw up charters when they gain control over their parents' property, or when they reach the age of majority. Therefore we give this order to your holy souls, mindful of the example of Ananias and Saphiras, who, although they said they had offered everything to the apostles, had offered only a part, and had deceitfully kept a part for themselves, which is neither fitting, nor permissible, nor useful.

7. None, not even the abbess, may have her own maid serving her; but if they have a need, let them receive some assistance from the younger ones.

And, if it can be done, even with difficulty, no little girl shall ever be taken into the monastery, until she is six or seven years old, able

---

125. Convert = to become a nun.

to learn to read and write and to obey the rules. Girls, whether they are the daughters of nobles or of commoners, are definitely not to be received for the purpose of raising or teaching them.

8. No one shall choose for herself what work or task she shall do; but it shall be up to the superior to order what seems useful.

9. No one shall be permitted to choose separate accommodations, nor to have a bedroom or a chest or anything of this sort, which can be closed up privately; but all shall stay in one room, in separate beds. Nor may those who are old or sick, so that it is suitable for them to be deferred to or to be cared for, have single cells, but let all be housed in one, and let them remain there.

Let them never speak in a loud voice, according to the Apostle's command: "Let all clamor be put away from you" [Eph. 4:31]; such is not at all fitting or useful.

10. Similarly, during hymns, talking and working are not permitted.

11. No one whosoever shall presume to serve as godmother to any girl, whether rich or poor; for she who has disregarded her own liberty for the love of God ought not to seek or have the love of others, so that without any impediment she may always devote herself to God.

12. She who when the signal is sounded comes late to worship or to work, shall be subject to rebuke, as is fitting. If she has not improved in this at the second or third admonition, let her be separated from the community and from communal meals.

13. She who is admonished, corrected or reproved for any fault shall not presume to respond to her accuser at all; she who does not wish to fulfill any one of these things which are commanded shall be sequestered from the communion of prayer or from the table, depending on the gravity of her fault.

14. . . . In all physical service, whether in the kitchen, or whatever daily living requires, each of them, except the mother and the prioress, ought to take a turn in the duties.

15. In vigils, so that no one becomes sleepy through idleness, let there be such work as does not distract the mind from hearing the reading. If anyone grows sleepy, let her be commanded to stand while the others are sitting, so that she may drive away from herself the faintness of sleep, lest she be found either unenthusiastic or negligent in the work of God.

16. Let them accept their daily task of wool-working with humility and strive to complete it with great industriousness.

17. Let no one consider anything her own, whether clothing, or any other thing. . . .

18. Let all obey the mother after God; let them defer to the prioress.

Let them be silent while they sit at table, and direct their thoughts to the reading. When the reading is finished, the holy meditation of the heart is not to cease. If there is need of anything, she who is at the head of the table should take care of it, and what is necessary should be sought with a nod rather than by voice. Let not only your throats take in nourishment for you, but let your ears also hear the word of God.

All should learn to read.

19. They should always devote themselves to reading for two hours, that is, from daybreak until the second hour. For the rest of the day let them do their work, and not occupy themselves in conversation. . . .

20. When, however, it is necessary for their work, then let them speak. When the rest are working together, let one of the sisters read until the third hour; for the rest of the time, meditation on God's word and prayer from the heart should not cease. . . .

21. Let those who had something in the world, when they enter the monastery, humbly offer it to the mother, to be used for the common good. And those who had nothing should not seek in the monastery that which they could not have outside it. But let those who are known to have had something in the world not despise their sisters who have come to this holy fellowship from poverty; nor should they take pride in the riches which they have presented to the monastery, just as they enjoyed them in the world. What does it benefit you to disperse your wealth, and to be made poor by giving to the poor, if your wretched soul is filled with diabolical pride? You should all therefore live harmoniously and peacefully, and honor God, whose temples you are worthy to be, in each other.

Apply yourselves to your prayers without pause, in accordance with the Evangelist's saying: "Pray always, that ye may be accounted worthy" [Luke 21:36]; and the Apostle: "Pray without ceasing" [I Thess. 5:17].

22. When you pray to God with psalms and hymns, let that which is offered in your voice be pondered in your heart. Whatever work you are doing, when reading is not being done, ruminate always on something from the holy scriptures.

The sick are to be treated in such a way that they recover quickly; but when they have regained their good health, let them return to the more beneficial practice of abstinence.

Let not your apparel be notable, nor should you aspire to please in your clothing, but in your morals, which is fitting for your purpose.

23. Let no desire for the gaze of men spring up in you at the devil's urging; nor should you say that you have chaste souls if you have

unchaste eyes: for the unchaste eye is the messenger of the unchaste heart. Nor should she who gazes immodestly on a man think that she is not seen by others when she does this: she is certainly seen, by those she supposes do not see her. But behold, even if she is hidden, so that she is seen by no man, what about that overseer, from whom nothing at all can be hidden? Let her fear therefore to displease God; let her avoid sinfully pleasing man. When therefore you stand together, if the provider of the monastery arrives there, or any other man with him, guard each other's modesty; for God, who lives in you, also guards you in this way.

24. If you see anyone behaving more freely than is proper, correct her privately as your sister; if she does not heed you, bring it to the attention of the mother. Nor should you think it malicious, when you give such evidence with a holy spirit: for you are no more innocent, and you become a partner in her sin, if you permit your sister to perish by being silent when you could save her by rebuking her. For if she had a wound in her body, or had been bitten by a snake, and wished to hide this because she was afraid to be operated on, would it not be cruel to keep such a thing quiet, and merciful to make it known? How much more, then, ought you to reveal the counsel of the devil and his plans, so that the wound of sin in her heart is not worsened, or the evil of concupiscence nourished longer in her breast! And you must do this with the love of a sister and with hatred of vice.

25. Whoever—God forbid—has fallen into such evil that she secretly receives letters or any instructions or presents from someone, if she has voluntarily confessed this, let her be forgiven, and prayers be said for her; if, however, she is accused or convicted while concealing it, let her be punished more severely, according to the statutes of the monastery. Let her be subject to similar punishment if, by a sacrilegious daring, she has presumed to send letters or presents to anyone. If, however, anyone wishes, in fondness for her parents or in friendship for anyone, to send a gift of bread, let her discuss it with the mother; and, if the mother permits it, let the sister give it via the porteresses, and they shall send it on, by name, to whomever she wishes; let her not presume to give or receive anything herself, without the prioress or the porteress.

26. And although it ought not to be thought or believed that holy virgins hurt each other with harsh words or invective, nevertheless if by chance and human frailty, any of the sisters at the devil's urging should happen to break out into such sin, so that they either commit theft, or strike each other, it is right that they, by whom the statutes of the rule were broken, should receive the legitimate punishment.

For it is necessary that in these matters, that which the Holy Spirit taught through Solomon regarding disobedient children should be fulfilled: "He who loves his son will not spare the whip" [Ecclus. 30:1]; and also, "Thou shalt beat him with the rod, and shalt deliver his soul from hell" [Prov. 23:14]. And let them receive that punishment in the presence of the congregation, according to the Apostle: "Them that sin, rebuke before all" [1 Tim. 5:20].

27. And because the mother of the monastery must be concerned for the health of souls, and for the resources of the monastery which are necessary for the sustenance of the body, and must always meditate, and must offer affection to those who call on her, and must answer letters from the faithful, therefore all responsibility for woolworking, whence the clothing of the holy sisters is supplied, belongs to the prioress or to the wool-mistress. Through their industry let whatever garments are needed be prepared so faithfully, with zeal and love of God, that however often the holy sisters have a need, they can meet it with holy discretion.

28. Let them make clothing in the monastery with such industriousness that the abbess never needs to procure it from outside the monastery. And such clothing as is offered to you for a suitable time does not belong to you. But if contention and murmuring arise among you because some of you have perhaps received something of lesser quality than you had before, test yourselves in this: for how much is lacking to you in that inner holy habit of the heart, if you are murmuring on account of the bodily habit? Nevertheless if your weakness is indulged, so that you have more than daily use requires, put what you have in one place under communal custody, and let the registrar hold the keys to your boxes or chests.

29. No one is to work on anything of her own, unless the abbess has given her an order or permission; but let all your work be done in common, with such holy zeal and such fervent alacrity as you would give to it if it were your own.

30. Let such women be appointed by the superior to the offices of cellaress and porteress and wool-mistress, not as the wishes of any, but such as the needs of all, decide, in the fear of God; and therefore let none of the sisters have or keep around her bed anything that pertains to eating and drinking. And whoever does this shall undergo very strict correction. Above all, before God and his angels, I entreat you: let none of the sisters secretly buy wine or in any way obtain it; but if any does receive some wine, let the porteresses receive it in the presence of the abbess or the prioress, and let them hand it over to the wine-mistress; and let it be dispensed to her to whom it was sent,

in accordance with the statutes of the rule, and as is proper for her infirmity, by the wine-mistress's dispensation. And because it is normal for the cells of the monastery not always to have good wine, it will be the concern of the holy abbess to provide such wine as shall soothe those who are ill or who were raised more delicately.

31. Baths should not be denied to those whose infirmities require them; but let what is needed for her health be done without murmuring, according to medical advice and at the command of the superior, even if she who is sick does not wish to bathe. If, however, it is not required by any infirmity, her desire shall not be indulged.

32. The care of those who are ill or otherwise laboring under any weakness should be entrusted to one who is sufficiently faithful and responsible, who will seek from the cellar whatever she sees to be necessary. And someone ought to be chosen who will both keep the monastic rigor and serve the sick faithfully. And if the needs of the sick require it, and it seems right to the mother of the monastery, the sick ones may even have their own small cellar and common kitchen. . . .

33. You should have no quarrels, . . . and if they happen, let them be ended as quickly as possible, lest anger grow into hatred, and a rod turn into a beam, and the soul be made murderous. For thus you read: "Whosoever hateth his brother is a murderer" [I John 3:15]; and: "Lifting up holy hands, without wrath and doubting" [I Tim. 2:8]. Whoever injures her sister with invective or cursing or even by accusing her of faults, let her remember to make amends for her sin. If she presumes to repeat this vice, let her suffer the most severe punishment, until through her penance she deserves to be received again. Let the younger ones especially defer to the elders.

34. If anyone is excommunicated for any reason, removed from the congregation, let her reside in the place which the abbess has ordered, with one of her spiritual sisters, until humbly penitent she receives forgiveness. If, however, as frequently happens, at the urging of the devil, sisters injure each other, they should seek each other's pardon and forgive their debts, because of the prayers, and the more frequent your prayers are, the purer they ought to be. If she whose pardon is sought does not wish to forgive her sister, let her be removed from the community, and she should fear this, for if she will not forgive, she will not be forgiven. And she who never wishes to seek pardon, or does not seek it from the heart, or who is asked but does not forgive, has no place in the monastery. Therefore refrain from harsh words, and if they have been uttered, you should not hesitate to offer healing from that same mouth by which the wounds were made.

35. And when the need for discipline compels you, as prioress, to say harsh words in order to restrain evil behavior, and if you feel that you have perhaps been excessive in this, it is not required of you to ask for forgiveness, lest in preserving your humility too well, you damage your authority over those who ought to be subject to you. But all should seek forgiveness from the Lord, who knows with how much kindness you love even those whom you have very properly reproved.

Let the mother, who bears responsibility for all of you, and the prioress be obeyed without murmuring, lest charity be saddened in them. And let those who lead you take care to observe discretion and the rule with charity and true piety. Let them set an example of good works to all around them; let them reprove the restless, comfort the fearful, and support the frail, always remembering that they will have to account to God for you. Wherefore even you, who more piously subject yourselves, ought to pity not only yourselves but also them, for as they seem to be superior among you in rank, so much greater is the danger in which they live. For which reason you ought humbly to obey not only the mother, but also the prioress, the chancelloress and the infirmaress with reverence.

36. Above all, for the safeguarding of your reputation, let no man come into the private part of the monastery or into the oratory, with the exception of bishops, the provider and a priest, deacon, subdeacon and one or two readers, commended by their age and life, who must celebrate masses from time to time. And when the buildings must be remodeled, or doors or windows must be constructed, or any repairs of this sort are needed, such artisans and workers as are necessary to do the work may come in with the provider, but not without the knowledge and permission of the mother. And the provider may never enter the inner part of the monastery except for those reasons which we have explained above, and never without the abbess or at least some other very respectable witness, so that the holy women have their private place as is fitting and expedient.

37. Secular matrons and girls and widows still in lay clothing similarly are prohibited from entering.

38. This is to be observed: that the abbess, for her proper dignity, not go to meet callers in the parlor without two or three sisters. Bishops, abbots or other religious, whose good life commends them, may enter the oratory to pray if they ask. This should also be observed: that the door of the monastery be open to callers at suitable hours.

39. You are never to prepare any banquet, either in the monastery or outside it, even for these persons, that is, for bishops, abbots, monks, clerks, secular men, women in secular clothing, or the parents

of the abbess, or of any nun; nor may a banquet be prepared for the bishop of this city or for the provider of this monastery, nor for any religious woman from the diocese, unless they happen to be of very holy life, and do sufficient honor to the monastery; and let this be done very rarely.

40. If any woman comes from another city to inquire after her daughter or to visit the monastery, if she is a religious, and it seems right to the abbess, she ought to be invited to a banquet, but others must never be at all, for holy virgins who are dedicated to God ought to pray for all people, devoting themselves to Christ, rather than prepare worldly feasts. If anyone wishes to see her sister or daughter or any relative or kinswoman, let her not be denied a conversation in the presence of the infirmaress or some other senior nun.

41. The abbess is not to dine outside the congregation unless required to do so by some indisposition, infirmity or business.

42. In this above all I remind you and call you to witness, holy mother, and venerable prioress, whoever you are, and also you to whom the care of the sick is entrusted, and the chancelloress and the infirmaress; that you consider most carefully whether any of the sisters, either because they were raised more delicately, or perhaps because they frequently suffer a weakness of the stomach, cannot abstain as the rest do, or at least find it very difficult to fast, and if in their modesty they do not presume to ask, you are to order that they be given what they need by the cellaress, and that they accept it. And they may be very sure that whatever they have consumed by dispensation or order of the superior, at whatever hour, they have received Christ in that repast. And the cellaress, and she who cares for the sick, shall be proclaimed before God and his angels for all their solicitude, for their care and diligence toward the sick.

And I also advise this: to avoid excessive noise, alms should not be given daily or continually at the door of the monastery; but let the abbess arrange to have what God has given, such as remains to the use of the monastery, distributed to the poor through the provider.

43. Above all, this is to be observed: if any man or woman, because of their close relationship, gives or sends clothing or anything else to his or her daughter, it is not to be received secretly; wherefore I call all who watch at the gate to witness before God and his angels, that they permit nothing to be given from the monastery, and that they let nothing be received into the monastery from outside, without the knowledge and approval of the abbess. But if the abbess, as is common, is busy with callers, the porteresses shall show whatever has arrived to the prioress. If they neglect to do this, both the porteresses

who permitted and those who received shall not only suffer the most severe punishment of the monastery, but they also know that because of their transgression of the holy Rule they will have to plead their case with me before God. And as for that which was sent, if it is necessary for her, let her have it; but if she needs nothing, let it be given back and offered to one who needs it, because of the Lord's command: "He that hath two coats, let him impart to him who hath none" [Luke 3:11]. And when new clothes are received, if they do not need the old ones, let them give them back to the abbess, to be distributed to the poor or to those just beginning or to the younger ones.

44. Let them have all their clothing only in a simple and respectable color, never black, never bright white, but only natural or milky-white; let it be made in the monastery by the industry of the prioress and the care of the wool-mistress, and distributed by the mother of the monastery, to each reasonably, according to her needs. Let there be no other colors in the monastery, except natural and milky-white, as said above: for anything else is not fitting for the the humble state of the virgins. Let your bedding also be simple: for it is not proper for worldly covers or patterned hangings to decorate the bed of a religious. You are not to use silver, except when worshiping in the oratory.

45. There is never to be anything covered or decorated with embroidery or needlework or fine weaving in the monastery. Even the ornaments in the oratories ought to be simple, never embroidered, never silken; and let nothing be added to these other than crosses, either black or white, and only of plain work from scraps of cloth or linens. For no waxed curtain should be hung, no figured plaque should be set up, nor should any painting be done on the walls or in the rooms, because that which pleases not the spiritual eyes, but the human ones, ought not to be in the monastery. And if any ornament is given to the monastery, by you or by any of the faithful, let it either be sold for the benefit of the monastery, or let it be assigned, if necessary, to the Church of St. Mary. Needlework is never to be done, except in small napkins and face-towels, as the abbess orders.

46. None of you shall presume to receive the clothes of clerks or laymen, nor of your relatives, nor of any man or woman from outside, whether to wash them, or to sew them, or to mend them, or to dye them, except at the command of the abbess, lest the good name of the monastery be harmed through this careless familiarity which is the enemy of reputation. Whoever does not observe this, let her be struck with the punishment of the monastery, just as if she had committed a crime.

47. You, holy and venerable mother of the monastery, and you, prioress of the holy congregation, I admonish and adjure before God and his angels, that no threats or arguments or blandishments shall ever so soften your spirit that you relax any part of the institution of this holy and spiritual Rule. I believe that according to the mercy of God you shall not incur any charge of negligence, but that for your holy obedience which pleases God you shall happily attain to eternal bliss.

62. Simeon of Durham: Segregated Churches (7th–11th c.)

The following narrative illustrates the attitudes of many churchmen toward women and the consequences this could have for female religious life. The prohibition against women within the church grounds is an unusual one, but the ideas behind it are not. In the Early Middle Ages there were quite a few double monasteries housing both monks and nuns, and these were gradually abandoned, sometimes because of the kind of problems described here. St. Cuthbert was a seventh-century Anglo-Saxon bishop; Simeon's account was written in the late eleventh or early twelfth century.
Source: Simeon of Durham, *A History of the Church of Durham*, tr. J. Stevenson in *The Church Historians of England* (1858).

It is a well-known fact, that into scarce one of the churches which the blessed [St. Cuthbert] illustrated with the presence of his body . . . has permission to enter been granted to a woman. How this custom originated, we will now show. . . .

During the period of his episcopate, the monastery of Coldingham was consumed by a fire, which, though happening accidentally, yet was admitted by all who were acquainted with the circumstances to have had its foundation in the wickedness of the inmates. In this place resided congregations of monks as well as nuns, which, however, were separated from each other, and resided in distinct dwellings; but they grew lax, and receded from their primitive discipline, and, by their improper familiarity with each other, afforded to the enemy[126] an opportunity of attacking them. For they changed into resorts for feasting, drinking, conversation, and other improprieties, those very

---

126. The enemy = Satan.

residences which had been erected as places to be dedicated to prayer and study. The virgins also, who had been dedicated to God, despising the sanctity of their profession, devoted themselves to the sewing of robes of the finest workmanship, in which they either adorned themselves like brides, thereby endangering their own estate of life and profession, or they gave them to men who were strangers, for the purpose of thereby securing their friendship. It was no wonder, then, that a heavy punishment from heaven consigned this place and its inhabitants to the devouring flames. . . . [T]hey were for a short time induced to abandon their evil deeds, and to chastise themselves. But, after the death of the religious abbess Ebba, they returned to their former pollutions, or rather they did worse than hitherto; and while they were saying, "Peace, peace," the heavy wrath of God came upon them. Not long after this, Cuthbert, that man of God, being elevated to the episcopal throne, careful that an example of this sort should no longer provoke the anger of God against themselves or their successors, entirely secluded [the monks] from the society of women, apprehensive that the incautious use of that familiarity should endanger the purpose which they had in hand, and their ruin should afford the enemy cause for rejoicing. Men and women alike assented to the arrangement, by means of which they were mutually excluded from each other's society, not only for the present, but for all future time; and thus the entry of a woman into the church became a matter which was entirely forbidden. Wherefore he caused a church to be erected in the island on which was his episcopal see, and this the inhabitants called "Grene Cyrice," that is, The green church, because it was situated upon a green plain; and he directed that the women who wished to hear masses and the word of God should assemble there, and that they should never approach the church frequented by himself and his monks. This custom is so diligently observed, even unto the present day, that it is unlawful for women to set foot even within the cemetaries of those churches in which his body obtained a temporary resting-place, unless, indeed, compelled to do so by the approach of an enemy or the dread of fire. . . .

There have been some women, however, who in their boldness have ventured to infringe these decrees; but the punishment which has speedily overtaken them, gave proof of the magnitude of their crime. One of these, named Sungeova, the wife of the son of Bevo, who was named Gamel, as she was one night returning home from an entertainment, was continually complaining to her husband that there was no clean piece of the road to be found, in consequence of the deep puddles with which it was everywhere studded. So at last they determined that they would go through the churchyard of this church, (that is, of Durham,) and that they would afterwards make an atonement for this sin by almsgiving. As they were going on together, she was seized with some kind of indefinite horror, and cried out that she was gradually losing her senses. Her husband chid her, and urged her to come on, and not be afraid; but as soon as she set foot outside the hedge which surrounds the cemetary of the church, she immediately fell down; and being carried home, she that very night ended her life. . . .

Here follows another narrative of the same kind. A certain rich man—who afterwards resided amongst us in this church, wearing the dress of a monk—had a wife; and she, having heard many persons talk of the beauty of the ornaments of the church, was inflamed, woman-like, with the desire of seeing these novelties. Unable to bridle her impetuous desires, for the power of her husband had elevated her above her neighbours, she walked through the cemetary of the church. But she did not go unpunished; for presently she was deprived of her reason,—she bit out her own tongue; and in her madness she ended her own life by cutting her throat with her own hand. For, as it was no easy matter to keep her at home, she wandered from place to place; and one day she was found lying dead under a tree, her throat all bloody, and holding in her hand the knife with which she had committed suicide.

Many other instances might easily be added to these, showing how the audacity of women was punished from heaven; but let these suffice, since we must proceed to other matters.

63. Hildegard of Bingen:
Letter to Her Nuns (12th c.)

Hildegard of Bingen (d. 1178) was one of the foremost women of her day. An abbess who corresponded with powerful churchmen and secular leaders, she was also a learned author and a respected mystic. In this letter she recounts the history of her convent at Rupertsberg for the nuns living there and exhorts them in their spiritual life. More of Hildegard's works, including songs and mystical, moral and scientific writings, can be found in the list of Further Readings.

Source: Reprinted from *Hildegard of Bingen's Book of Divine Works*, edited by Matthew Fox, Copyright Bear & Co. 1987, by permission of Bear & Co., Inc., PO Drawer 2860, Santa Fe, NM 87504.

O daughters, who out of your love for charity are following the footsteps of Christ and who for the sake of spiritual improvement have chosen me, poor creature that I am, in humble submissiveness to be your mother, I have something to say to you from my maternal heart, something that doesn't originate with me but comes from godly vision: this spot, the resting place for the earthly remains of the holy confessor Rupert, to whose patronage you have taken refuge, is the site I have recognized according to God's will and with the evidence of miracles as a place for the sacrifice of praise. I came here with the approval of my superiors and with God's aid I have freely taken possession of it for myself and all of those who follow me. After that I went back by God's direction to Disibodenberg, the community I had left with permission, and I presented before all who lived there this proposal—namely, that not only our place of residence, but all the real estate added to it as gifts, should not be attached to them but should be released. But in all of this practical business I had nothing else in mind but the salvation of souls alone and concern for the discipline commanded in our rule.

I then shared with the Abbot [Kuno], the superior at this site, what I had received in a true vision: "The bright streaming light speaks, 'You should be the father over the provost [Volmar] and over the spiritual care of this mystical plant-nursery for my daughters. The gifts made to them belong neither to you nor to your brothers. On the contrary, your monastery should be their shelter.' But if you want to grow stubborn in your opposition and gnash your teeth against us, you will be like the hated Amalekites in the Bible and like Antiochus, of whom it is written that he robbed the temple of the Lord (I Maccabees 1:21). Some of you have said in your unworthiness, 'We want to diminish your possession.' Here is the response of the Divine: 'You are the worst thieves! But if you should try to take away the shepherd of the sisters' spiritual healing [Provost Volmar], then I further say to you: You are like the sons of Belial and you don't have the justice of God before your eyes. Therefore, God's judgment will destroy you!'"

When in these words, I, poor creature that I am, demanded from the abbot named above the freedom of the place and the possessions of my daughters (as I explained above), all these things were granted to me through a written contract in a legal codex. All who saw, heard, and perceived these things, great and lowly alike, took a favorable view of them, so that it was surely God's will that this was all pinned down in writing. And all who depend on God, experience God, and listen to God's word, should favorably certify, enforce, and defend this legal transaction, so that they might receive that blessing which God gave to Jacob and Israel.

Alas, what a great lament my daughters will raise after the death of their mother, when they will drink no more at their mother's breast and when they will speak with sighs and sorrow and often with tears: "Oh, how gladly we would drink at the breast of our mother, if only we now had her in our midst."

And therefore, daughters of God, I advise you and I have advised you from my youth that you love one another, so that because of your goodwill towards others you might be like the angels as a bright shining light strong in your powers, as your father Benedict taught.

May the Holy Spirit grant you its gifts, for after my death you will no longer hear my voice. But may my voice never fall into forgetfulness among you; may it rather be heard often in your midst in love. Now my daughters blush in their hearts because of the sorrow that they feel because of their mother. They sigh and long for heaven. But later through God's grace they will be radiant in bright, shining light and they will be staunch champions in the House of God.

But if any in the flock of my daughters should want to sow discord or bring about the abandonment of this convent and its spiritual discipline, then I pray that the gift of the Holy Spirit may drive such thoughts out of their hearts. But if someone, God forbid, should nevertheless go ahead and act in this way, then may the hand of the Lord strike such a one down before all the people, for such a person would merit being put to shame.

And so, my daughters, live in this place you have chosen for yourselves, so that you may fight for God with total dedication and constancy and thus gain for yourselves here a heavenly reward.

64. The Rule of St. Clare (1253)

Clare of Assisi was born in 1193 into a well-off urban family. Interested in the ideas of the radical preacher Francis of Assisi, she refused to marry, and in 1212 she became a follower of Francis; he eventually established her as the leader of a community of religious women at the church of San Damiano. Like the members of Francis' male order, known as the Friars Minor, the "Damianites," as the women were called, lived a rigorous life of spiritual poverty and charitable works. The rule Clare wrote for her convent was the first religious rule written by a woman. It was finally

approved in 1253, the year of her death. Franciscan nuns are
known today as "Poor Clares," after their founder.
Source: Reprinted from *Clare of Assisi: Early Documents*, edited and
translated by Regis J. Armstrong, O.F.M., Cap. © 1988 by The
Province of St. Mary of the Capuchin Order. Used by permission
of Paulist Press.

[I. In the Name of the Lord Begins
the Form of Life of the Poor Sisters]

The form of life of the Order of the Poor Sisters that Blessed Francis
established is this: to observe the Holy Gospel of our Lord Jesus Christ,
by living in obedience, without anything of one's own, and in chastity.

Clare, the unworthy servant of Christ and the little plant of the most
blessed Francis, promises obedience and reverence to the Lord Pope
Innocent and his canonically elected successors, and to the Roman
Church. And, just as at the beginning of her conversion, together with
her sisters she promised obedience to the Blessed Francis, so now she
promises his successors to observe the same obedience inviolably, and
the other sisters shall always be obliged to obey the successors of
Blessed Francis and Sister Clare and the other canonically elected
Abbesses who succeed her.

[II. Those Who Wish to Accept This Life
and How They Are To Be Received]

If, by divine inspiration, anyone should come to us desiring to
accept this life, the Abbess is required to seek the consent of all the
sisters; and if the majority have agreed, she may receive her, after
having obtained the permission of the Lord Cardinal Protector. If
she judges [the candidate] acceptable, [the Abbess] should carefully
examine her, or have her examined, concerning the Catholic faith and
the sacraments of the Church. And if she believes all these things and
is willing to profess them faithfully and to observe them steadfastly
to the end; and if she has no husband, or if she has [a husband] who
has already entered religious life with the authority of the Bishop of
the diocese and has already made a vow of continence, and if there is
no impediment to her observance of this life, such as advanced age or
ill-health or mental weakness, let the tenor of our life be thoroughly
explained to her.

If she is suitable, let the words of the holy Gospel be addressed to
her that she should go and sell all that she has and take care to
distribute the proceeds to the poor (Matt. 19:21). If she cannot do this,

her good will suffices. Let the Abbess and the sisters take care not to be concerned about her temporal affairs, so that she may freely dispose of her possessions as the Lord may inspire her. However, if some counsel is required, let them send her to some discerning and God-fearing men, according to whose advice her goods may be distributed to the poor.

Afterwards, once her hair has been cut off round her head and her secular clothes set aside, she may be permitted three tunics and a mantle. Thereafter, she may not go outside the monastery except for a useful, reasonable, evident, and approved purpose. When the year of probation is ended, let her be received into obedience, promising to observe perpetually our life and form of poverty.

No one is to receive the veil during the period of probation. The sisters may also have little mantles for convenience and propriety in serving and working. In fact, the Abbess should with discernment provide them with clothing according to the diversity of persons, places, seasons and cold climates, as it shall seem expedient to her by necessity.

Young girls who are received into the monastery before the age established by law should have their hair cut round [their heads]; and, putting aside their secular clothes, they should be clothed in a religious garb, as the Abbess sees fit. However, when they reach the age required by law, they may make their profession clothed in the same way as the others. The Abbess shall carefully provide a Mistress from among the more discerning sisters of the monastery both for these and the other novices. She shall form them diligently in a holy way of life and proper behavior according to the form of our profession.

The same form described above should be observed in the examination and reception of the sisters who serve outside the monastery. These sisters may wear shoes. No one may live with us in the monastery unless she has been received according to the form of our profession.

I admonish, beg, and exhort my sisters to always wear cheap garments out of love of the most holy and beloved Child Who was wrapped in such poor little swaddling clothes and laid in a manger and of His most holy Mother.

[III. The Divine Office and Fasting, Confession and Communion]

The sisters who can read shall celebrate the Divine office according to the custom of the Friars Minor. They may have breviaries for this, but they should read it without singing. Those who, for some reasonable cause, occasionally are not able to recite their hours by reading them, may, like the other sisters, say the *Our Father's*.

Those who do not know how to read shall say twenty-four *Our Father's* for Matins; five for Lauds; seven for each of the hours of Prime, Terce, Sext, and None; twelve, however, for Vespers; seven for Compline. Let them also say for the dead seven *Our Father's* with the *Requiem aeternam* at Vespers; twelve for Matins, because the sisters who can read are obliged to recite the office of the Dead. When a sister of our monastery shall have departed this life, however, they should say fifty *Our Father's*.

The sisters shall fast at all times. They may eat twice on Christmas, however, no matter on what day it happens to fall. The younger sisters, those who are weak, and those who are serving outside the monastery may be mercifully dispensed as the Abbess sees fit. But the sisters are not bound to corporal fasting in time of manifest necessity.

They shall go to confession, with the permission of the Abbess, at least twelve times a year. They shall take care not to introduce other talk unless it pertains to the confession and the salvation of souls. They should receive Communion seven times [a year], that is, on Christmas, Thursday of Holy Week, Easter, Pentecost, the Assumption of the Blessed Virgin, the feast of Saint Francis, and the Feast of All Saints. The Chaplain may celebrate inside [the enclosure] in order to give Communion to the sisters who are in good health or to those who are ill.

[IV. The Election and Office of the Abbess:
The Chapter, and the Officials and the Discreets[127]]

The sisters are bound to observe the canonical form in the election of the Abbess. They should quickly arrange to have the Minister General or the Minister Provincial of the Order of Friars Minor present. Let him dispose them, through the Word of God, to perfect harmony and the common good in the election that is to be held. No one should be elected who is not professed. And if a non-professed is elected or somehow given them, she should not be obeyed unless she first professes our form of poverty.

At her death the election of another Abbess shall take place. If at any time it should appear to the entire body of sisters that she is not competent for their service and common welfare, the sisters are bound

---

127. Discreets = advisers to the abbess.

as quickly as possible to elect another as abbess and mother according to the form described above.

Whoever is elected should reflect upon the kind of burden she has undertaken and to Whom she must render an account of the flock committed to her. She should strive as well to preside over the others more by her virtues and holy behavior than by her office, so that, moved by her example, the sisters may obey her more out of love than out of fear. Let her avoid particular friendships, lest by loving some more than others she cause scandal among all. Let her console those who are afflicted. Let her also be the last refuge for those who are troubled, lest the sickness of despair overcome the weak should they fail to find in her the remedies for health.

Let her preserve common life in everything, especially in whatever pertains to the church, the dormitory, refectory, infirmary, and clothing. Let her vicaress be bound to serve in the same way.

The Abbess is bound to call her sisters together at least once a week in the Chapter, where both she and her sisters should humbly confess their common and public offenses and negligences. Let her consult with all her sisters there concerning whatever pertains to the welfare and good of the monastery, for the Lord frequently reveals what is best to the least [among us].

Let no heavy debt be incurred except with the common consent of the sisters and by reason of manifest necessity, and let this be done by the procurator. Let the Abbess and her sisters, however, be careful that nothing is deposited in the monastery for safekeeping; for such practices often give rise to troubles and scandals.

Let all who hold offices in the monastery be chosen by the common consent of all the sisters to preserve the unity of mutual love and peace. Let at least eight sisters be elected from the more discerning ones in the same way, whose counsel the Abbess should be always bound to use in those matters which our form of life requires. Moreover the sisters can and should, if it seems useful and expedient, remove the officials and discreets and elect others in their place.

[V. Silence, the Parlor, and the Grille]

Let the sisters keep silence from the hour of Compline until Terce, except those who are serving outside the monastery. Let them also continually keep silence in the church, the dormitory, and the refectory, only while they are eating. They may speak discreetly at all times, however, in the infirmary for the recreation and service of the sick. Nevertheless, they can communicate always and everywhere, briefly and in a low tone of voice, whatever is necessary.

The sisters may not speak in the parlor or at the grille without the permission of the Abbess or her Vicaress. Let those who have permission not dare to speak in the parlor unless they are in the presence and hearing of two sisters. Let them not presume to go to the grille, moreover, unless there are at least three sisters present [who have been] appointed by the Abbess or her Vicar from the eight discreets who were elected by all the sisters for the council of the Abbess. Let the Abbess and her Vicaress be themselves bound to observe this form of speaking. [Let the sisters speak] very rarely at the grille and, by all means, never at the door.

Let a curtain be hung inside the grille which may not be removed except when the Word of God is preached or when a sister is speaking with someone. Let the grille have a wooden door which is well provided with two distinct iron locks, bolts, and bars, so that it can be locked, especially at night, by two keys, one of which the Abbess should keep and the other the sacristan. Let it always be locked except when the Divine Office is being celebrated and for the reasons given above. Under no circumstance whatever, may a sister speak to anyone at the grille before sunrise or after sunset. Let there always be a curtain on the inside of the parlor, which may not be removed.

No one may speak in the parlor during the Lent of Saint Martin and the Greater Lent, except to a priest for Confession or for some other manifest necessity, which is left to the prudence of the Abbess or her Vicaress.

[VI. The Lack of Possessions]

After the Most High Heavenly Father saw fit by His grace to enlighten my heart to do penance according to the example and teaching of our most blessed Father Saint Francis, shortly after his own conversion, I, together with my sisters, willingly promised him obedience.

When the Blessed Father saw we had no fear of poverty, hard work, trial, shame, or contempt of the world, but, instead, regarded such things as great delights, moved by compassion he wrote a form of life for us as follows:

> Because by divine inspiration you have made yourselves daughters and servants of the Most High King, the heavenly Father, and have taken the Holy Spirit as your spouse choosing to live according to the perfection of the holy Gospel, I resolve and promise for myself and for my brothers to always have that same loving care and solicitude for you as [I have] for them.

As long as he lived he diligently fulfilled this and wished that it always be fulfilled by his brothers.

Shortly before his death he once more wrote his last will for us that we—or those, as well, who would come after us—would never turn aside from the holy poverty we had embraced. He said:

> I, little brother Francis, wish to follow the life and poverty of our most high Lord Jesus Christ and of His holy mother and to persevere in this until the end; and I ask and counsel you, my ladies, to live always in this most holy life and poverty. And keep most careful watch that you never depart from this by reason of the teaching or advice of anyone.

Just as I, together with my sisters, have ever been solicitous to safeguard the holy poverty which we have promised the Lord God and blessed Francis, so, too, the Abbesses who shall succeed me in office and all the sisters are bound to observe it inviolably to the end: that is to say, by not receiving or having possession or ownership either of themselves or through an intermediary, or even anything that might reasonably be called property, except as much land as necessity requires for the integrity and proper seclusion of the monastery, and this land may not be cultivated except as a garden for the needs of the sisters.

[VII. The Manner of Working]

Let the sisters to whom the Lord has given the grace of working work faithfully and devotedly after the Hour of Terce at work that pertains to a virtuous life and the common good. They must do this in such a way that, while they banish idleness, the enemy of the soul, they do not extinguish the Spirit of holy prayer and devotion to which all other things of our earthly existence must contribute.

At the Chapter, in the presence of all, the Abbess or her Vicaress is bound to assign the work of her hands that each should perform. Let the same be done if alms have been sent by someone for the needs of the sisters, so that a prayer may be offered for them in common. Let all such things be distributed for the common good by the Abbess or her vicaress with the advice of the discreets.

[VIII. The Sisters Shall Not Acquire Anything as Their Own; Begging Alms; The Sick Sisters]

Let the sisters not appropriate anything, neither a house nor a place nor anything at all; instead, as pilgrims and strangers in this world who serve the Lord in poverty and humility, let them confidently send for alms. Nor should they be ashamed, since the Lord made Himself poor in this world for us. This is that summit of the highest poverty which has established you, my dearest sisters, heiresses and queens of the kingdom of heaven; it has made you poor in the things [of this world] but exalted you in virtue. Let this be your portion which leads into the land of the living. Clinging totally to this, my most beloved sisters, do not wish to have anything else forever under heaven for the name of our Lord Jesus Christ and His most holy mother.

Let no sister be permitted to send letters or to receive or give away anything outside the monastery without the permission of the Abbess. Let it not be permitted to have anything that the Abbess has not given or allowed. Should anything be sent to a sister by her relatives or others, let the Abbess give it to the sister. If she needs it, the sister may use it; otherwise, let her in all charity give it to a sister who does need it. If, however, money is sent to her, the Abbess, with the advice of the discreets, may provide for the needs of the sister.

Concerning the sick sisters, let the Abbess be strictly bound to inquire diligently, by herself and through other sisters, what their illness requires both by way of counsel as well as food and other necessities. Let her provide for them charitably and kindly according to the resources of the place. [Let this be done] because all are bound to serve and provide for their sisters who are ill just as they would wish to be served themselves if they were suffering from any illness. Let each one confidently manifest her needs to the other. For if a mother loves and nourishes her child according to the flesh, should not a sister love and nourish her sister according to the Spirit even more lovingly?

Those who are ill may lie on sacks filled with straw and may use feather pillows for their head; those who need woolen stockings and quilts may use them.

When the sick sisters are visited by those who enter the monastery, they may answer them with brevity, each responding with some good words to those who speak to them. But the other sisters who have permission [to speak] may not dare to speak to those who enter the monastery unless in the presence and hearing of the two sister-discreets assigned by the Abbess or her Vicaress. Let the Abbess and her Vicaress, as well, be bound to observe this manner of speaking.

[IX. The Penance To Be Imposed on the Sisters Who Sin;
The Sisters Who Serve outside the Monastery]

If any sister, at the instigation of the enemy, has sinned mortally against the form of our profession, and if, after having been admonished two or three times by the Abbess or other sisters, she does not amend, let her eat bread and water on the floor before all the sisters in the refectory for as many days as she shall have been obstinate. If it seems advisable to the Abbess, let her be subjected to even greater punishment. Meanwhile, as long as she remains obstinate, let the prayer be that the Lord will enlighten her heart to do penance. The Abbess and her sisters, however, should beware not to become angry or disturbed on account of anyone's sin, for anger and disturbance prevent charity in oneself and in others.

If it should happen—may it never be so—that an occasion of trouble or scandal should arise between sister and sister through a word or gesture, let her who was the cause of the trouble, before offering her gift of prayer to the Lord, not only prostrate herself humbly at once at the feet of the other and ask pardon, but also beg her simply to intercede for her to the Lord that He might forgive her. Let the other sister, mindful of that word of the Lord—"If you do not forgive from the heart, neither will your heavenly Father forgive you" (Matt. 6:15; 18:35)—generously pardon her sister every wrong she has done her.

Let the sisters who serve outside the monastery not linger outside unless some manifest necessity requires it. Let them conduct themselves virtuously and say little, so that those who see them may always be edified. Let them strictly beware of having suspicious meetings and dealings with others. They may not be godmothers of men or women lest gossip or trouble arise because of this. Let them not presume to repeat the gossip of the world inside the monastery. Let them be strictly bound not to repeat outside the monastery anything that was said or done within which could cause scandal.

If anyone should innocently offend in these two matters, let it be left to the prudence of the Abbess mercifully to impose a penance on her. But if a sister does this through a vicious habit, let the Abbess, with the advice of her discreets, impose a penance on her according to the nature of the fault.

[X. The Admonition and Correction of the Sisters]

Let the Abbess admonish and visit her sisters, and humbly and charitably correct them, not commanding them anything that is against their soul and the form of our profession. Let the sisters, however, who are subjects, remember that they have renounced their wills for God's sake. Let them, therefore, be firmly bound to obey their Abbess in all the things they have promised the Lord to observe and which are not against their soul and our profession.

Let the Abbess, on her part, be so familiar with them that they can speak and act with her as ladies do with their servant. For this is the way it should be: the Abbess should be the servant of all the sisters.

In fact, I admonish and exhort the sisters in the Lord Jesus Christ to beware of all pride, vainglory, envy, avarice, care and anxiety about this world, detraction and murmuring, dissension and division. Let them be always eager to preserve among themselves the unity of mutual love which is the bond of perfection.

Let those who do not know how to read not be eager to learn. Let them rather devote themselves to what they should desire to have above all else: the Spirit of the Lord and His holy manner of working, to pray always to Him with a pure heart, and to have humility, patience in difficulty and infirmity, and to love those who persecute, blame, and accuse us, for the Lord says: Blessed are those who suffer persecution for the sake of justice, for theirs is the kingdom of heaven (Matt. 5:10). But whoever perseveres to the end will be saved.

[XI. The Custody of the Enclosure]

Let the portress be mature in her manner of acting, discerning, and of a suitable age. Let her remain in an open cell without a door during the day.

Let a suitable companion be assigned to her who may take her place in everything whenever necessary.

Let the door be well secured by two different iron locks, with bars and bolts, so that, especially at night, it may be locked with two keys, one of which the portress may have, the other the Abbess. Let it never be left without a guard and securely locked with one key.

Let them most diligently take care to see that the door is never left open, except when this can hardly be conveniently avoided. Let it never be opened to anyone who wishes to enter, except to those who have been given permission by the Supreme Pontiff or our Lord Cardinal. The sisters may not allow anyone to enter the monastery before sunrise or to remain within after sunset, unless a manifest, reasonable, and unavoidable cause demands otherwise.

If a bishop has permission to offer Mass within the enclosure, either for the blessing of an Abbess or for the consecration of one of the sisters as a nun or for any other reason, let him be satisfied with both as few and virtuous companions and assistants as possible.

Whenever it is necessary for other men to enter the monastery to do some work, let the Abbess carefully post a suitable person at the door, who may only open it to those assigned for work and to no one else. Let the sisters be extremely careful at such times not to be seen by those who enter.

[XII. The Visitator, the Chaplain, and the Cardinal
Protector]

Let our Visitator always be taken from the Order of the Friars Minor
according to the will and command of our Cardinal. Let him be the
kind of person who is well known for his integrity and good manner
of living. His duty shall be to correct any excesses against the form of
our profession, whether these be in head or in the members. Taking
his stand in a public place, that he can he seen by others, let him speak
with several and with each one concerning the matters that pertain to
the duty of the visitation as he sees best.

We ask as a favor of the same order a chaplain and a clerical companion of good reputation, of prudent discernment and two lay brothers,
lovers of a holy and upright way of life, in support of our poverty, as
we have always mercifully had from the aforesaid Order of Friars
Minor, in light of the love of God and our blessed Francis.

Let the chaplain not be permitted to enter the monastery without a
companion. When they enter, let them remain in an open place, in
such a way that they can always see each other and be seen by others.
They may enter the enclosure for the confession of the sick who cannot
go to the parlor, for their Communion, for the Last Anointing and the
Prayers of the Dying.

Suitable and sufficient outsiders may enter, moreover, according to
the prudence of the Abbess, for funeral services and on the solemnity
of Masses for the Dead, for digging or opening a grave, or also for
making arrangements for it.

Let the sisters be strictly bound always to have that Cardinal of the
Holy Roman Church, who has been delegated by the Lord Pope for
the Friars Minor, as Governor, Protector, and Corrector, that always
submissive and subject at the feet of that holy Church and steadfast
in the Catholic faith, we may always observe the poverty and humility
of our Lord Jesus Christ and of His most holy Mother and the Holy
Gospel we have firmly promised. Amen.

65. Eudes of Rouen: Visitations of Nunneries (13th c.)

As archbishop of Rouen, Eudes had the duty of visiting and
inspecting the religious houses in his archdiocese in northern
France. Like many bishops, he kept a "register" of his activities,
including these visitations. Eudes' register has been taken by some

historians to indicate that monasticism was in a particularly poor
condition in thirteenth-century Normandy, but similar records
can be found in other places. One reason for the negative impression given here is the tendecy of a bishop's register, like court
records, to record the problems and to ignore the areas in which
all is well. Still, the excerpts below provide a very different view
of monasticism from that given by the rules which nuns were
supposed to follow.
Source: *The Register of Eudes of Rouen*, tr. Sydney M. Brown, ed.
Jeremiah F. O'Sullivan, 1964, Columbia University Press, New
York. Used by permission.

1248

August 7. We visited the monastery at Bival and found some of the
nuns defamed[128] of the vice of incontinence. This day the abbess
resigned the government of the abbey into our hands, and we gave
the nuns permission to elect another. They appointed the day after
tomorrow for the election.

August 9. This day the prioress of Bival and certain other nuns
presented their elect to us through a letter from the community in the
following form:

"Clemence of Appetot, prioress of Bival, and its entire community,
to the reverend father in Christ, Eudes, by the grace of God archbishop
of Rouen, greetings and due and dedicated obedience. When a va-
cancy occurred in our monastery through the resignation of Sister
Eleanor, our former abbess, a fact which we believe does not escape
your watchfulness, we chose with your permission the Saturday before the Assumption of the Blessed Virgin as the time to elect a suitable
person for the monastery. Convening that day in chapter,[129] and invok-
ing the grace of the Holy Spirit, we treated this business. At length,
with the common consent and will of the whole chapter, we agreed
to give our sisters Matilda of Les Andelys, Joan of Bec, and Matilda
of Hoqueville power to provide our monastery with a head and to
chose an abbess. They, taking counsel together have canonically with
one heart and one mind provided Marguerite of Aunay [as abbess]
for our monastery. Wherefore with care and devotion we beg Your
Paternity to confirm the provision made in respect to this worthy

---

128. Defamed = accused by rumor.
129. Chapter = the regular meeting of nuns or monks to conduct the business of
their house, so called because the meeting generally opened with the reading of a
chapter from the monastic Rule followed by the order.

person and to bestow the gift of benediction, when it shall seem good to you. Given the Sunday following in the year of our Lord 1248." We confirmed this election. . . .

1249

January 4. We visited the monastery of St-Amand-de-Rouen, where we found forty-one veiled nuns and six due to take the veil.[130] They make profession only when they receive the archbishop's blessing. We ordered that when they had reached the age for taking the vows, they should wait yet another year before making profession. Sometimes they sing the hours of the Blessed Mary and the Suffrages with too much haste and jumbling of the words; we enjoined them to sing these in such a way that those beginning a verse should wait to hear the end of the preceding verse, and those ending a verse should hear the commencement of the following verse. Item, the monastery has one priory,[131] to wit, at Saane[-St-Just], where there are four professed nuns. Item, they have the patronage of ten churches.[132] There are three priests in perpetual residence. [The nuns] confess five times a year. They do not keep the rule of silence very well; we enjoined them to correct this. They eat meat freely in the infirmary, to wit, three times a week. Sometimes the healthy ones eat with the sick in the infirmary, two or three with one sick sister. They have chemises, use feather beds and sheets, and wear cloaks of rabbits, hares, cats, and foxes; we utterly forbade the use of rabbit skins. The nuns sleep cinctured and in their chemises.[133] Each nun receives a measure of wine, but more is given to one than to another; we ordered that wine should be given to each according to her needs and in equal measure, and if one of them should without permission give a portion of her wine to another outside the house she should be compelled by the abbess to go without wine the next day. The monastery has debts amounting to two hundred pounds and an income of one thousand pounds. The abbess does not give detailed accounts to the community at large; we ordered her to cast her accounts each quarter.

---

130. Nuns due to take the veil = novices, or nuns not yet fully professed.
131. Priory = a daughter house, presided over by its own prioress, but ruled by the abbess of the mother house.
132. Patronage of a church = the right to "present," or appoint, a priest for the church.
133. Sleeping "cinctured," or belted, was correct practice, but having chemises (linen undergarments) was not.

March 17. We were at La Salle-aux-Puelles near Rouen, and we found during our visitation that they do not hold their chapter twice a week, as . . . ordered. Item, lay folk constantly enter the cloisters, the kitchens, and the workrooms; they mingle with the sisters and talk with them without permission. Item, there is overmuch talking in the refectory. The prioress does not audit the accounts with the chapter. The measure of bread has been decreased. We ordered them to hold a chapter twice a week. We prohibited the entry of lay folk into the cloisters or workrooms, and we forbade the sisters to talk with any lay folk without receiving permission from the prioress. We forbade talking in the refectory or in the dormitory after Compline unless in a low voice, and briefly. . . .

July 9. We visited the priory at Villarceaux. There are twenty-three nuns and three lay sisters in residence. They confess and receive Communion six times a year. They have an income of about one hundred pounds, and they owe about fifty pounds. The prioress casts her accounts only once a year. We ordered them to be cast every month by the prioress, by the priest and by two of the nuns especially elected by the community for this purpose. Item, because of their poor financial condition, we forbade them to receive any nun, even should the abbess [of St-Cyr] send one. There are four nuns who are professed only; namely, Eustacia, Comtesse, Ermengarde and Petronilla. Many have pelisses of the furs of rabbits, hares, and foxes. They eat meat in the infirmary when there is no real need; silence is not well observed anywhere, nor is the cloister closed off. Joan of l'Aillerie at one time left the cloister and went to live with a certain man and had a child by him, and sometimes she goes out to see the said child; item, she is ill famed of a certain man called Gaillard. Isabelle la Treiche is always complaining about the prioress and finding fault with other sisters. . . . Joan of Hauteville wanders beyond the priory alone with Gaillard, and last year she had a child by him. The sister in charge of the cellars is ill famed of Philip of Villarceaux and of a certain priest of her own neighborhood. Item, the subprioress [is ill famed] with Thomas the carter; Idonia, her sister [is ill famed] of Crispin, and this ill fame has arisen within the year. Item, the prior of Gisors often comes to this priory to see the said Idonia. Philippa of Rouen [is ill famed] of the priest at Chèrence, in the diocese of Chartres. Marguerite, the treasurer, is ill famed of Richard of Genainville, cleric. Agnes of Fontenay is ill famed of the priest at Guerreville, in the diocese of Chartres. La Toolière is ill famed of Sir Andrew of Mussy, knight. All of them let their hair grow down to the chin, and put saffron on their veils. Jacqueline left the priory pregnant as a result of her relations with one of the chaplains, who was expelled because of this. Item, Agnes of Mont-Secours is ill famed of the same man. Ermengarde of Gisors and Joan of Hauteville came to blows. The prioress is drunk nearly every night. They manage their own affairs as best they can. The prioress does not get up for Matins, does not eat in the refectory, and does not correct excesses. We considered that an order should be drawn up concerning these things, and we despatched [a] letter to the prioress and to the community. . . .

1250

May 14. We visited the monastery of nuns at St-Sauveur-d'Evreux. There are sixty-one nuns in residence. The nuns occasionally drink in rooms other than the refectory and the infirmary. Item, they have small dogs, squirrels, and birds; we decreed that all such things be taken away. They do not observe the Rule. They have an income of nine hundred pounds; they owe about six hundred pounds. They eat meat when there is no need for it. They have locked coffers; we enjoined the abbess to make frequent and unannounced inspection of these coffers or else have the locks removed. They owe about forty pounds in pensions. Their stock of provisions is low. We enjoined the abbess to cast her accounts at least twice a year in the presence of some sisters elected by the community. Item, we decreed that they were to put away their metaled belts and their unseemly purses. Item, we decreed that the abbess should visit the sisters more frequently and take away the purses and pillows which they make unless they have her permission to possess them.

1251

May 25. At Montivilliers, at the expense of the monastery. May 26. At the same, and we visited the abbess in chapter. We found everything there to be in good condition.

1253

September 18. We visited the nuns of St-Saëns. In residence are fifteen nuns, two lay sisters, and one lay brother. One nun is dwelling alone at St-Aubert. We enjoined that another nun be sent to her. When they leave the priory the nuns sometimes stay away for two weeks or even longer, and by themselves. Since the one was stolen from the chapter, they have no French copy of the Rule. They sometimes eat meat when there is no need, but this is because of their poverty. They have keys, but they say that they keep what is under key with the permission of the prioress. They owe about one hundred pounds. They have four carucates[134] of land and one hundred pounds in rents. A nun assists the priest at Mass.[135] We enjoined them to correct all of these things. Their priest is incontinent; we enjoined them to get another. Dom Luke, the priest, is their confessor. The prioress eats in the infirmary more often than she does in the refectory. We enjoined them to correct all of these matters.

1256

July 23. We visited the priory at St-Aubin, where there are fifteen nuns. . . . We, at the time, took the veil away from Alice of Rouen and from Eustasia of Etrépagny because of their fornications. We sent Agnes of Pont to the leper house at Rouen, because she had connived at Eustasia's fornication, and indeed had even arranged it, as the rumor goes; further, she gave the said Eustasia, as report has it, some herbs to drink in order to kill the child already conceived within the said Eustasia. We removed the prioress from her office. Until a new prioress shall be instituted, we have suspended punishment of Anastasia, the subprioress, who is ill famed of incontinence.

1260

March 5. This very day we visited the nuns' priory at St-Aubin, after we had pronounced God's Word. Sixteen nuns were there. The prioress was away. At our last visitation we forbade them to receive or give the veil to anyone without our special mandate. However, despite our command, they had received as a nun and bestowed the veil upon a certain girl, to wit, the daughter of Sir Robert, called Malvoisin, knight. When we asked them why they had presumed to do this, they replied that urgent necessity and poverty had so compelled them, and that in consideration of their consent, the father of this girl had given and endowed them with an annual income of one hundred shillings, and they had a letter to prove this. They added that they had done this without the consent or wish of the prioress. We, realizing and considering that they had not done this without the

---

134. Carucate = measurement of land: the amount that one plow can till.
135. This was forbidden by canon law. See Church Council Decrees above, Part V.

vice of greed and of depraved simony,[136] subsequently ordered the dean of Bray, by letter patent, to admonish, as the law requires, the said nuns to remove this girl from their house before Ascension Day and, having taken away the veil from her, to return her to her father's house. Upon the prioress we enjoined and caused to have enjoined a penance which seemed expedient because she had allowed such a crime, and likewise upon the nuns for their boldness in undertaking such a matter. . . .

1264

October 18. With God's grace we visited the nuns' priory at St-Aubin, where twelve nuns were in residence. Beatrice of Beauvais was a rover, and it was said that she had had several children. The houses badly needed repair, especially the roof of the main monastery where they could hardly stay when the weather was rainy. They did not chant their Hours, especially Matins, because many of them had been sick for a long time. Because of the absence of the prioress, who was then lying ill in bed, we could not obtain complete information concerning the state of the house.

1265

March 28. With God's grace we visited Bondeville priory. Thirty nuns, four lay sisters, and two lay brothers were there. They should confess and receive Communion once a month. They complained that doves flew through the choir and chancel and created a tumult there which, as they said, disturbed the Divine Office; wherefore we ordered them to block up or plaster most of the windows, for several of them were superfluous. They owed one hundred twenty pounds. With God's grace we found other things to be in good condition. In truth, recognizing the feebleness of Comtesse who had long been prioress there, and wishing to make provision for her comfort, we felt that we should remove her from office, although she was worthily acquitting herself of this position and had done so for many years. We gave the community permission to elect another.

------

136. Simony = the buying and selling of positions in the church, forbidden by canon law.

1268

May 16. With God's grace we came to the priory at Villarceaux, where there were nineteen nuns. According to the certain and statutory number there should be twenty nuns, four lay sisters, and four general maidservants. . . . Eustasia, a former prioress, had a certain bird which she kept to the annoyance and displeasure of some of the older nuns, wherefore we ordered it removed. She, because of this, spoke somewhat indiscreetly and irreverently to us, which much displeased us. They did not have wheat and oats to last until the new harvest. They owed seventy pounds.

66. The Ancrene Riwle (13th c.)

> Anchoresses and anchorites (often known as "recluses" or "hermits") were women and men who lived a life recognized as "holy" but usually did not belong to a regulated monastic community— although the church did officially require a would-be recluse to obtain permission from the local bishop. Some recluses lived in groups; some lived in complete isolation, either in the wilderness or in cells where they were fed by other people but had no contact with them. The "Ancrene Riwle" is an early thirteenth-century English text, probably written for a group of three anchoresses and then adapted for a community of twenty. In places it is greatly influenced by monastic rules, but the life it prescribes, especially in the excerpts below, is a less stringently monastic one—since, indeed, anchoresses were not nuns.
> Source: James Morton, *The Nun's Rule, Being the Ancren Riwle Modernised* (London: De La More Press, 1905; Chatto & Windus, 1924).

Preface

Do you now ask what rule you anchoresses should observe? Ye should by all means, with all your might and all your strength, keep well the inward rule, and for its sake the outward. The inward rule is always alike. The outward is various, because every one ought so to observe the outward rule as that the body may therewith best serve the inward. Now then, is it so that all anchoresses may well observe one rule? "All may and ought to observe one rule concerning purity of heart," that is, a clean unstained conscience, without any reproach of sin that is not remedied by confession. This the lady rule effects, which governs and corrects and smoothes the heart and the conscience of sin, for nothing maketh it rugged but sin only. To correct it and smooth it is the good office and the excellent effect of all religion and of every religious order. This rule is framed not by man's contrivance, but by the command of God. Therefore, it ever is and shall be the same, without mixture and without change; and all men ought ever invariably to observe it. But all men cannot, nor need they, nor ought they to keep the outward rule in the same unvaried manner, "that is to say, in regard to observances that relate to the body." The external rule, which I called the handmaid, is of man's contrivance; nor is it instituted for any thing else but to serve the internal law. It ordains fasting, watching, enduring cold, wearing haircloth, and such other hardships as the flesh of many can bear and many cannot. Wherefore, this rule may be changed and varied according to every one's state and circumstances. For some are strong, some are weak, and may very well be excused, and please God with less; some are learned, and some are not, and must work the more, and say their prayers at the stated hours in a different manner; some are old and ill favoured, of whom there is less fear; some are young and lively, and have need to be more on their guard. Every anchoress must, therefore, observe the outward rule according to the advice of her confessor, and do obediently whatever he enjoins and commands her, who knows her state and her strength. He may modify the outward rule, as prudence may direct, and as he sees that the inward rule may thus be best kept.

No anchorite, by my advice, shall make profession, that is, vow to keep any thing as commanded, except three things, that is, obedience, chastity, and constancy as to her abode; that she shall never more change her convent, except only by necessity, as compulsion and fear of death, obedience to her bishop or superior; for, whoso undertaketh any thing, and promises to God to do it as his command, binds herself thereto, and sinneth mortally in breaking it, if she brake it wilfully and intentionally. If, however, she does not vow it, she may, nevertheless, do it, and leave it off when she will, as of meat and drink, abstaining from flesh or fish, and all other such things relating to dress, and rest, and hours, and prayers. Let her say as many, and in such a way, as she pleases. These and such other things are all in our free choice, to do or to let alone whenever we choose, unless they are vowed. But charity or love, and meekness and patience, truthfulness, and keeping the ten old commandments, confession, and penitence, these and such others, some of which are of the old law, some of the new, are not of man's invention, nor a rule established by man, but they are the commandments of God, and, therefore, every man is bound and obliged to keep them, and you most of all; for they govern the heart, and its government is the main point concerning which I have to give directions in this book, except in the beginning and in the concluding part of it. As to the things which I write here concerning the external rule, ye, as my dear sisters, observe them, our Lord be thanked, and through his grace ye shall do so, the longer the better; and yet I would not have you to make a vow to observe them as a divine command; for, as often thereafter as ye might break any of them it would too much grieve your heart and frighten you, so that you might soon fall, which God forbid, into despair, that is, into hopelessness and distrust of your salvation. Therefore, my dear sisters, that which I shall write to you in the first, and especially in the last part of your book, concerning your service, you should not vow it, but keep it in your heart, and perform it as though you had vowed it. . . .

Now, my dear sisters, this book I divide into eight distinctions, which ye call parts, and each part treats separately, without confusion, of distinct matters, and yet each one falleth in properly after another, and the latter is always connected with the former.

The first part treats entirely of your religious service.

The next is, how you ought, through your five senses, to keep your heart, wherein is order, religion, and the life of the soul. In this part there are five chapters or sections concerning the five senses, which guard the heart as watchmen when they are faithful, and which speak concerning each sense separately in order.

The third part is of a certain kind of bird, to which David, in the Psalter, compares himself, as if he were an anchorite, and how the nature of those birds resembles that of anchorites.

The fourth part is of fleshly, and also of spiritual temptations, and of comfort against them, and of their remedies.

The fifth part is of confession. The sixth part is of penitence. The seventh part is of a pure heart, why men ought and should love Jesus Christ, and what deprives us of his love, and hinders us from loving him.

The eighth part is entirely of the external rule; first, of meat and drink and of other things relating thereto; thereafter, of the things that ye may receive, and what things ye may keep and possess; then of your clothes and of such things as relate thereto; next of your tonsure, and of your works, and of your bloodletting; lastly, the rule concerning your maids, and how you ought kindly to instruct them. . . .

Speech and Visitors

. . . Wherefore, my dear sisters, love your windows as little as possible; and see that they be small,—the parlour's smallest and narrowest. Let the cloth upon them be twofold; black cloth; the cross white, within and without. . . .

First of all, when you have to go to your parlour window, learn from your maid who it is that is come; for it may be some one whom you ought to shun; and, when you must needs go forth, make the sign of the cross carefully on your mouth, ears, and eyes, and on your breast also, and go forth in the fear of God to a priest. Say first, "Confiteor," and then "Benedicite,"[137] which he ought to say; hear his words and sit quite still, that, when he parteth from you, he may not know either good or evil of you, nor know any thing either to praise or to blame in you. Some one is so learned and of such wise speech, that she would have him to know it, who sits and talks to him and gives him word for word, and becomes a preceptor, who should be an anchoress, and teaches him who is come to teach her; and would, by her own account, soon be celebrated and known among the wise.— Known she is well; for, from the very circumstance that she thinketh herself to be reputed wise, he understands that she is a fool; for she hunteth after praise and catches reproach. For, at last, when he is gone away he will say, "This anchoress is a great talker." . . .

Without a witness, of man or of woman, who may hear you, speak not with any man often or long; and even though it be of confession, in the same house, or where he may look at you, let there be a third person present; except the same third person upon another occasion should fail thee. This is not said in respect of you, dear sisters, nor of any such as you; —no, but because the truth is disbelieved, and the innocent often belied, for want of a witness. Men readily believe the evil, and the wicked gladly utter falsehoods against the good. . . .

Hold no conversation with any man out of a church window, but respect it for the sake of the holy sacrament which ye see therein, and sometimes take your woman to the window of the house; the other men and women to the window of the parlour, to speak when necessary; nor ought ye but at these two windows. . . .

Silence always at meals; for if other religious persons do so, as you well know, ye ought before all; and if any one hath a guest whom she

---

137. *Confiteor* = "I confess"; *Benedicite* = "Say a blessing."

holds dear, she may cause her maid, as in her stead, to entertain her friend with glad cheer; and she shall have leave to open her window once or twice, and make signs to her of gladness at seeing her. The courtesy of some is nevertheless converted into evil to her. Under the semblance of good, sin is often hidden. An anchoress ought to be very different from the mistress of a family. Every Friday of the year keep silence, unless it be a double feast; and then keep it on some other day in the week. In Advent and in the Ember days, Wednesdays and Fridays; in Lent, three days; and all the holy week until noon in Easter eve. To your maid, however, you may say, in few words, what you please, and if any good man is come from a distance, listen to his speech, and answer, in a few words, what he asks.

. . . You must not, upon any account, imprecate evil upon any one; nor take an oath, except ye be able to speak from clear or certain knowledge of the fact, or in some such way; nor are you to preach to any man; nor must any man ask of you, or give you advice or counsel. Consult with women only. St. Paul forbade women to preach, "Mulieres non permitto docere."[138] Rebuke no man, nor reprove him for his fault; but, if he be very forward, holy aged anchoresses may do it in some manner; but it is not a safe thing, and belongeth not to the young. It is their business who are set over the rest and have to take charge of them. An anchoress hath only to take heed to herself and her maidens. Let every one attend to his own business and not meddle with that which is another's. Many a man thinketh that he doeth that well which he doeth very ill; for, as I said before, sin is oft concealed under the appearance of good; and, by means of such rebukes, an anchorite has raised between her and her priest, either a treacherous love or a great quarrel.

Wherefore, my dear sisters, if any man requests to see you, ask him what good might come of it; for I see many evils in it, and no good; and if he insists immoderately, believe him the less; and if any one becometh so mad and so unreasonable that he puts forth his hand toward the window cloth, shut the window quickly and leave him; and as soon as any man falls into evil discourse that tends towards impure life, close the window directly and give him no answer at all, but go away with this verse, that he may hear it, "The wicked have told me foolish tales, but not according to thy law;" and go forth before

---

138. "I do not permit women to teach." I Timothy 2:12. See selections from St. Paul's writings in Part I above, and Church Council Decrees, "Ancient Statutes of the Church," number 37, in Part V.

your altar, with the Miserere.[139] Do not reprove any man of such a character in any way but this, for, with the reproof, he might answer in such a way and blow so gently that a spark might be quickened into a flame. No seduction is so perfidious as that which is in a plaintive strain; as if one spoke thus: "I would rather suffer death, than indulge an impure thought with regard to you; but had I sworn it, I could not help loving you; and yet I am grieved that you know it. But yet forgive me that I have told you of it; and, though I should go mad, thou shalt never after this know how it is with me." And she forgives him, because he speaks thus fair, and then they talk of other matters. But, "the eye is ever toward the sheltering wood, wherein is that I love." The heart is ever upon what was said before; and still, when he is gone, she often revolves such words in her thoughts, when she ought to attend diligently to something else. He afterwards seeketh an opportunity to break his promise, and swears that necessity forces him to do it; and thus the evil grows, the longer the worse; for no enmity is so bad as false friendship. An enemy who seems a friend is of all traitors the most treacherous. . . .

Chapter VIII: Domestic Matters

I said before, at the commencement, that ye ought not, like unwise people, to promise to keep any of the external rules. I say the same still; nor do I write them for any but you alone. I say this in order that other anchoresses may not say that I, by my own authority, make new rules for them. Nor do I command that they observe them, and ye may even change them, whenever ye will, for better ones. In regard to things of this kind that have been in use before, it matters little.

Of sight, and of speech, and of the other senses enough was said. Now this last part, as I promised you at the commencement, is divided and separated into seven small sections.

Men esteem a thing as less dainty when they have it often, and therefore ye should be, as lay brethren are, partakers of the holy communion only fifteen times a-year: at Mid-winter; Candlemas; Twelfthday; on Sunday half-way between that and Easter, or our Lady's day, if it is near the Sunday, because of its being a holiday; Easter-day; the third Sunday thereafter; Holy Thursday; Whitsunday; and Midsummer day; St. Mary Magdalen's day; the Assumption; the

---

139. Miserere = "Have mercy," i.e., a prayer for forgiveness.

Nativity; St. Michael's day; All Saints' day; St. Andrew's day. And before all these days, see that ye make a full confession and undergo discipline; but never from any man, only from yourselves. And forego your pittance for one day. And if any thing happens out of the usual order, so that ye may not have received the sacrament at these set times, ye may make up for it the Sunday next following, or if the other set time is near, ye may wait till then.

Ye shall eat twice every day from Easter until the Holyrood day, the later, which is in harvest, except on Fridays, and Ember days, and procession days and vigils. In those days, and in the Advent, ye shall not eat any thing white, except necessity require it. The other half year ye shall fast always, except only on Sundays.

Ye shall eat no flesh nor lard except in great sickness; or whosoever is infirm may eat potage without scruple; and accustom yourselves to little drink. Nevertheless, dear sisters, your meat and your drink have seemed to me less than I would have it. Fast no day upon bread and water, except ye have leave. There are anchoresses who make their meals with their friends outside the convent. That is too much friendship, because, of all orders, then is it most ungenial, and most contrary to the order of an anchoress, who is quite dead to the world. We have often heard it said that dead men speak with living men; but that they eat with living men, I have never yet found. Make ye no banquetings, nor encourage any strange vagabond fellows to come to the gate; though no other evil come of it but their immoderate talking, it might sometimes prevent heavenly thoughts.

It is not fit that an anchoress should be liberal of other men's alms. Would we not laugh loud to scorn a beggar who should invite men to a feast? . . . [An] anchoress ought to take sparingly only that which is necessary for her. Whereof, then, may she make herself liberal? She must live upon alms, as frugally as ever she can, and not gather that she may give it away afterwards. She is not a housewife, but a church anchoress. If she can spare any fragments for the poor, let her send them quite privately out of her dwelling. Sin is oft concealed under the semblance of goodness. And how shall those rich anchoresses that are tillers of the ground, or have fixed rents, do their alms privately to poor neighbours? Desire not to have the reputation of bountiful anchoresses, nor, in order to give much, be too eager to possess more. Greediness is the root of bitterness: all the boughs that spring from it are bitter. To beg in order to give away is not the part of an anchoress. From the courtesy of an anchoress, and from her liberality, sin and shame have often come in the end.

Make women and children who have laboured for you to eat whatever food you can spare from your own meals; but let no man eat in your presence, except he be in great need; nor invite him to drink any thing. Nor do I desire that ye should be told that ye are courteous anchoresses. From a good friend take whatever ye have need of when she offereth it to you; but for no invitation take any thing without need, lest ye get the name of gathering anchoresses. Of a man whom ye distrust, receive ye neither less nor more—not so much as a race of ginger. It must be great need that shall drive you to ask any thing; yet humbly shew your distress to your dearest friend.

Ye shall not possess any beast, my dear sisters, except only a cat. An anchoress that hath cattle appears . . . a better housewife than anchoress. . . . For then she must think of the cow's fodder, and of the herdsman's hire, flatter the heyward, defend herself when her cattle is shut up in the pinfold, and moreover pay the damage. Christ knoweth, it is an odious thing when people in the town complain of anchoresses' cattle. If, however, any one must needs have a cow, let her take care that she neither annoy nor harm any one, and that her own thoughts be not fixed thereon. An anchoress ought not to have any thing that draweth her heart outward. Carry ye on no traffic. An anchoress that is a buyer and seller selleth her soul to the chapman of hell. Do not take charge of other men's property in your house, nor of their cattle, nor their clothes, neither receive under your care the church vestments, nor the chalice, unless force compel you, or great fear, for oftentimes much harm has come from such caretaking. Let no man sleep within your walls. If, however, great necessity should cause your house to be used, see that, as long as it is used, ye have therein with you a woman of unspotted life day and night.

Because no man seeth you, nor do ye see any man, ye may be well content with your clothes, be they white, be they black; only see that they be plain, and warm, and well made—skins well tawed; and have as many as you need, for bed and also for back.

Next your flesh ye shall wear no flaxen cloth, except it be of hards and of coarse canvas. Whoso will may have a stamin,[140] and whoso will may be without it. Ye shall sleep in a garment and girt.[141] Wear no iron, nor haircloth, nor hedgehog-skins; and do not beat yourselves therewith, nor with a scourge of leather thongs, nor leaded; and do not with holly nor with briars cause yourselves to bleed without leave of your confessor; and do not, at one time, use too many flagellations. Let your shoes be thick and warm. In summer ye are at liberty to go

---

140. Stamin = garment made of a linen-wool blend.
141. In a garment and girt = clothed and belted.

and to sit barefoot, and to wear hose without vamps, and whoso liketh may lie in them. A woman may well enough wear drawers of haircloth very well tied, with the strapples[142] reaching down to her feet, laced tightly. If ye would dispense with wimples, have warm capes, and over them black veils. She who wishes to be seen, it is no great wonder though she adorn herself; but, in the eyes of God, she is more lovely who is unadorned outwardly for his sake. Have neither ring, nor broach, nor ornamented girdle, nor gloves, nor any such thing that is not proper for you to have.

I am always the more gratified, the coarser the works are that ye do. Make no purses, to gain friends therewith . . . ; but shape, and sew, and mend church vestments, and poor people's clothes. Ye shall give nothing away without leave from your father confessor. Assist with your own labour, as far as ye are able, to clothe yourselves and your domestics, as St. Jerome teacheth. Be never idle; for the fiend immediately offers his work to her who is not diligent in God's work; and he beginneth directly to talk to her. For, while he seeth her busy, he thinketh thus: It would avail nothing if I were now to accost her, nor would she take time to listen to my teaching. From idleness ariseth much temptation of the flesh, "All the wickedness of Sodom came of idleness, and of a full belly." Iron that lieth still soon gathereth rust; and water that is not stirred soon stinketh. An anchoress must not become a schoolmistress, nor turn her anchoress-house into a school for children. Her maiden may, however, teach any little girl concerning whom it might be doubtful whether she should learn among boys, but an anchoress ought to give her thoughts to God only.

Ye shall not send, nor receive, nor write letters without leave. Ye shall have your hair cut four times a-year to disburden your head; and be let blood as oft, and oftener if it is necessary; but if any one can dispense with this, I may well suffer it. When ye are let blood, ye ought to do nothing that may be irksome to you for three days; but talk with your maidens, and divert yourselves together with instructive tales. Ye may often do so when ye feel dispirited, or are grieved about some worldly matter, or sick. Thus wisely take care of yourselves when you are let blood, and keep yourselves in such rest that long thereafter ye may labour the more vigorously in God's service, and also when ye feel any sickness, for it is great folly, for the sake of one day, to lose ten or twelve. Wash yourselves wheresoever it is necessary, as often as ye please.

---

142. Strapples = coverings for the lower leg, made of bands wrapped around the leg.

When an anchoress hath not her food at hand, let two women be employed, one who stays always at home, another who goes out when necessary; and let her be very plain, or of sufficient age; and, by the way, as she goeth let her go singing her prayers; and hold no conversation with man or with woman; nor sit, nor stand, except the least possible, until she come home. Let her go nowhere else, but to the place whither she is sent. Without leave, let her neither eat nor drink abroad. Let the other be always within, and never go out of the gate without leave. Let both be obedient to their dame in all things, sin only excepted. Let them possess nothing unknown to their mistress, nor accept nor give any thing without her permission. They must not let any man in; nor must the younger speak with any man without leave; nor go out of town without a trusty companion, nor sleep out. If she cannot read her hours in a book, let her say them with Paternosters and Ave Marias; and do the work that she is commanded to do, without grudging. Let her have her ears always open to her mistress. Let neither of the women either carry to her mistress or bring from her any idle tales, or new tidings, nor sing to one another, nor speak any worldly speeches, nor laugh, nor play, so that any man who saw it might turn-it to evil. Above all things, they ought to hate lying and ribaldry. Let their hair be cut short, their headcloth sit low. Let each lie alone. Let their hesmel[143] be high pointed: none to wear a broach. Let no man see them unveiled, nor without a hood. Let them look low. They ought not to kiss, nor lovingly embrace any man, neither of their acquaintance nor a stranger, nor to wash their head, nor to look fixedly on any man, nor to romp nor frolic with him. Their garments should be of such a shape and all their attire such that it may be easily seen to what life they are dedicated. Let them observe cautiously their manners, so that nobody may find fault with them, neither in the house nor out of the house. Let them, by all means, forbear to vex their mistress; and, whenever they do so, let them before they either eat or drink make obeisance on their knees bending to the earth before her and say, "Mea culpa;"[144] and accept the penance that she layeth upon them, bowing low. And let not the anchoress ever again thereafter upbraid her with the same fault, when vexed, except she soon afterwards fall into the same, but drive it entirely out of her heart. And if any strife ariseth between the women, let the anchoress cause them to make obeisance to each other kneeling to the earth, and the one to raise up the other, and finally to kiss each other;

---

143. Hesmel = collar.
144. Mea culpa = "My fault," i.e., the words of confession.

and let the anchoress impose some penance on both, but more upon her who is most in fault. Be ye well assured, this is a thing most pleasing to God—peace and concord—and most hateful to the fiend; and, therefore, he is always endeavouring to stir up some strife. . . .

Though the anchoress impose penance on her maidens for open faults, let them nevertheless confess often to the priest; but always, however, with permission. And if they cannot say the graces at meals, let them say, instead of them, Paternoster and Ave Maria, before and also after meat, and the Creed over and above; and in conclusion say thus, "May the Father, Son, and Holy Ghost, one God Almighty, give our mistress his grace, always more and more, and grant to her and us both to have a good ending, and reward all who do us good, and be merciful to the souls of them who have done us good—to the souls of them and of all Christians. Amen." Between meals, do not munch either fruit or any thing else; and drink not without leave; but let the leave be easily granted in all those matters where there is no sin. At meat let there be no talking, or little, and then be still. Also, neither do nor say any thing after the anchoress' compline, until prime next morning, whereby her silence might be disturbed. No servant of an anchoress ought, properly, to ask stated wages, except food and clothing, with which, and with God's mercy, she may do well enough. Let her not disbelieve any good of the anchoress, whatever betide, as that she may deceive her. The maidens out of doors, if they serve the anchoress in such a manner as they ought, shall have their reward in the eternal blessedness of heaven. Whoso hath any hope of so high a reward will gladly serve, and easily endure all grief and all pain. With ease and abundance men do not arrive at heaven.

Ye anchoresses ought to read these little concluding parts to your women once every week until they know it well. And it is very necessary for you both that ye take much care of them, for ye may be much benefited by them; and, on the other hand, made worse. If they sin through your negligence, ye shall be called to give account of it before the Supreme Judge; and, therefore, it is very necessary for you, and still more for them, that ye diligently teach them to keep their rule, both for your sake and for themselves; in a gentle manner, however, and affectionately; for such ought the instructing of women to be—affectionate and gentle, and seldom stern. It is right that they should both fear and love you; but that there should be always more of love than of fear. Then it shall go well. Both wine and oil should be poured into the wounds, according to divine instruction; but more of the soft oil than of the biting wine; that is, more of gentle than of vehement words; for thereof cometh that which is best—love-fear.

Mildly and kindly forgive them their faults when they acknowledge them and promise amendment.

As far as ye can, in regard to drink, and food, and clothing, and other things which the wants of the flesh require, be liberal to them, though ye be the more strict and severe to yourselves; for so doth he that bloweth well: He turneth the narrow end of the horn to his own mouth, and the wide end outward. And do ye the like, as ye would that your prayers may resound like a trumpet, and make a sweet noise in the ears of the Lord; and not to your own salvation only, but to that of all people; which may our Lord grant through the grace of himself, that so it may be. Amen.

In this book read every day, when ye are at leisure—every day, less or more; for I hope that, if ye read it often, it will be very beneficial to you, through the grace of God, or else I shall have ill employed much of my time. God knows, it would be more agreeable to me to set out on a journey to Rome, than to begin to do it again. And, if ye find that ye do according to what ye read, thank God earnestly; and if ye do not, pray for the grace of God, and diligently endeavour that ye may keep it better, in every point, according to your ability. May the Father, and the Son, and the Holy Ghost, the one Almighty God, keep you under his protection! May he give you joy and comfort, my dear sisters, and for all that ye endure and suffer for him may he never give you a less reward than his entire self. May he be ever exalted from world to world, for ever and ever. Amen.

As often as ye read any thing in this book, greet the Lady with an Ave Mary for him who made this rule, and for him who wrote it, and took pains about it. Moderate enough I am, who ask so little.

67. Description of the Beguines of Ghent (1328)

The term "Beguine" was used to describe any member of a widespread and heterogeneous female religious movement which arose in northern Europe in the thirteenth century. Its members were women who wished to live a religious life without actually becoming nuns. Some Beguines lived in "Beguinages," while others lived on their own or with their families. Beguines generally supported themselves through manual labor, and they did not take permanent vows as nuns did. Some Beguines engaged in teaching, preaching and writing, and this often led to condemnation from the ecclesiastical authorities, but many others, especially those who lived in well-regulated communities, were praised by churchmen. The following document, written during a church inquiry into Beguine activities in Flanders, seeks to assure the investigators that the Beguines of Ghent are orthodox and respectable in every way.

Source: *Cartulaire du Beguinage de Sainte-Elisabeth à Gand*, ed. Jean Béthune (Bruges, 1883). Tr. E.M.A.

Why the Beguinage Was Founded

Those ladies of good memory, Joanna and her sister Margaret, successive countesses of Flanders and Hainault, noticed that the region was greatly abounding in women for whom, because of their own position or that of their friends, suitable marriages were not possible, and they saw that the daughters of respectable men, both nobles and commoners, wished to live chastely, but could not easily enter a monastery because of the great number of these girls and the poverty of their parents,[145] and that respectable and noble but impoverished damsels had to go begging or shamefully support themselves or seek support from their friends, unless some solution could be found. Then by divine inspiration, as it is piously believed, having first obtained the advice and consent of respectable men of the diocese and elsewhere, in various parts of Flanders they set up certain spacious places which are called Beguinages, in which the aforesaid women, girls and damsels were received, so that living in common therein, they might preserve their chastity, with or without taking vows, and where they might support and clothe themselves by suitable work, without shaming themselves or their friends.

The Beguinage of Saint Elizabeth

Among these Beguinages, they founded one in Ghent, which is called the Beguinage of Saint Elizabeth, which is encircled by ditches and walls. In the middle of it is a church, and next to the church a cemetery and a hospital, which the aforesaid ladies endowed for the weak and infirm of that same Beguinage. Many houses were also built there for the habitation of the said women, each of whom has her own garden, separated from the next by ditches or hedges; and two chaplains were established in this place by the same ladies.

---

145. Although the practice was officially forbidden by the church, most convents required a money payment or "dowry" before accepting a new nun.

The Manual Work Which They Do

In these houses, indeed, many dwell together communally and are very poor, having nothing but their clothing, a bed and a chest, nor are they a burden to anyone, but by manual work, washing the wool and cleaning the pieces of cloth sent to them from the town, they earn enough money daily that, making thereby a simple living, they also pay their dues to the church and and give a modest amount in alms. And in each convent there is one who is called the mistress of work, whose duty is to supervise the work and the workers, so that all things are faithfully carried through according to God's will.

Their Way of Working and Praying

On work days they hold to the practice of rising early in the morning and coming together in the church, each going to her own place, which she has specially assigned to her, so that the absence of anyone may thereby be more easily noticed. After they have heard the Mass and said their prayers there, they return to their houses, working all day in silence, in which thing they are considered very useful to the whole country. And while working thus, they do not cease from prayer, for in each convent the two women who are best suited for this recite clearly the psalm "Miserere" and other psalms which they know, and the "Ave Maria," one singing one verse, the other the next, and the rest recite silently with them, or diligently listen to those who are reciting. Late at night, after Vespers, they go into the church, devoting themselves to prayers and meditations, until the signal is given and they go to bed. On Sundays and holy days, with masses and sermons, prayers and meditations, they devote themselves to the Lord's service in all things; nor may anyone leave the Beguinage on these days without special permission from the principal mistress.

The Severity of Their Life

We shall not say much of their abstinence from food and drink but this: that many of them are satisfied for the whole day with the coarse bread and pottage which they have in common in each convent, and with a drink of cold water they lessen their thirst rather than increase their appetite. And many among them are accustomed to fast frequently on bread and water, and many of them do not wear linen on their bodies, and they use straw pallets instead of beds.

Their Training in Manners

And in all these things, they have such respectable manners and are so learned in domestic affairs that great and respectable persons often send them their daughters to be raised, hoping that, to whatever estate they may later be called, whether in the religious life or in marriage, they may be found better trained than others. Their way of living, in fear of God and in obedience to the holy Mother Church, has been such that nothing unusual or suspect has ever been heard concerning their congregation.

Their Prayers for the Dead

When any one of them dies, each member of the convent visits the corpse individually, with devout prayers and intercessions, and each, according to her obligation, devoutly performs fasts, vigils, psalms and prayers for the one who has died.

The Color and Form of Their Clothing

All wear the same color and style of clothing, so that they may thereby very strictly avoid anything that might distinguish them from the others or be suspect. For they wear a habit which is grey in color, humble, and of a coarse shape, and none may have anything which is unusual or suspect in its shape, sewing, or belting, or in the way of nightcaps, hoods, gloves, mitts, straps, purses and knives.

Government and Correction

One woman, nominated by the conventual mistresses, rules the previously mentioned hospital. She is called the principal mistress of the Beguinage, or the great mistress, and each year, after the accounts are rendered, it is customary for her to be retained in or removed from this office according to the will of the aforementioned conventual mistresses. And she appoints the mistresses in the individual convents, with the advice and consent of the convents and of respectable men; and only with the permission and at the will of the said principal mistresses is anyone permitted to build or to tear down in that place, or to give or assign a place in the convent. To her also falls the correction of those who transgress against the praiseworthy rules of the said place, so that she may combat vices through restraint within the Beguinage, or by the transfer of a person from one convent to another, or by other similar penalties, or she may, through the complete expulsion of the rotten member from the Beguinage, preserve the body of the rest from shame and decay. And no one may be away from the Beguinage for long or spend the night in the town without her permission. Nor may anyone leave the Beguinage for an hour, without the special permission of the conventual mistress; and she who has that permission may not go alone but must have one or more companions, taken only from her own convent. Those who go out are required to avoid anything suspect in all their movements, and in the places they go, and in the persons they meet; those who do otherwise are warned about these matters, and unless they immediately desist they are deprived of the consolation of the Beguinage.

The Fame of the Place

That benevolent confessor, the most pious king Saint Louis,[146] personally visited this place in devotion, and, pleased with the zeal of these women, arranged with the venerable father, the lord bishop of Tournai, that a church should be consecrated for them, and acquired and conferred on them many privileges and liberties for their devotion, and he established and endowed a Beguinage like this one at Paris, and others in various places. There is also another Beguinage in Ghent, which is called "Oya," and many houses throughout the town where women dwell in a similar situation.

68. The Book of Margery Kempe: Pilgrimage to the Holy Land (15th c.)

Margery Kempe was born into a wealthy merchant family of the town of King's Lynn, in England, in about 1373; she married a local merchant at the age of twenty and bore him many children. Margery is famous because she underwent a long and emotional religious conversion experience and then, near the end of her life, had a priest write down the story of her life. Her autobiography is worth reading in full for the firsthand account it gives us of many aspects of Margery's experiences. The extract printed here is the story of Margery's pilgrimage to Jerusalem; although Margery was an unusual woman (and an unusual pilgrim), many men and women went on pilgrimages to places both near and far, so this is an account of a common religious activity.

---

146. Louis IX, King of France 1226–70.

Note that Margery always refers to herself in the third person, as "this creature."
Source: *The Book of Margery Kempe*, tr. B. A. Windeatt (Harmondsworth: Penguin Books, 1985).

Chapter 26

When the time came that this creature should visit those holy places where Our Lord was quick and dead, as she had by revelation years before, she prayed the parish priest of the town where she was dwelling, to say for her in the pulpit, that, if any man or woman claimed any debt from her husband or herself, they should come and speak with her ere she went, and she, with the help of God would make a settlement with each of them, so that they should hold themselves content. And so she did.

Afterwards, she took her leave of her husband. . . . Then she went forth to Norwich, and offered at the Trinity, and afterwards she went to Yarmouth and offered at an image of Our Lady, and there she took her ship.

And next day they came to a great town called Zierikzee,[147] where Our Lord of His high goodness visited this creature with abundant tears of contrition for her own sins, and sometime for other men's sins also. And especially she had tears of compassion in mind of Our Lord's Passion. And she was [given communion] each Sunday where there was time and place convenient thereto, with great weeping and boisterous sobbing, so that many men marvelled and wondered at the great grace that God had wrought in His creature.

This creature had eaten no flesh and drunk no wine for four years ere she went out of England, and so now her ghostly father[148] charged her, by virtue of obedience, that she should both eat flesh and drink wine. And so she did a little while; afterwards she prayed her confessor that he would hold her excused if she ate no flesh, and suffer her to do as she would for such time as pleased him.

And soon after, through the moving of some of her company, her confessor was displeased because she ate no flesh, and so were many of the company. And they were most displeased because she wept so much and spoke always of the love and goodness of Our Lord, as much at the table as in other places. And therefore shamefully they reproved her, and severely chid her, and said they would not put up with her as her husband did when she was at home and in England.

---

147. In Flanders.
148. Ghostly father = confessor.

And she answered meekly to them:—"Our Lord, Almighty God, is as great a Lord here as in England, and as good cause have I to love Him here as there, blessed may He be."

At these words, her fellowship was angrier than before, and their wrath and unkindness to this creature was a matter of great grief, for they were held right good men and she desired greatly their love, if she might have it to the pleasure of God.

And then she said to one of them specially:—"Ye cause me much shame and great grievance."

He answered her anon:—"I pray God that the devil's death may overcome thee soon and quickly," and many more cruel words he said to her than she could repeat.

And soon after some of the company in whom she trusted best, and her own maiden[149] also, said she could no longer go in their fellowship. And they said that they would take away her maiden from her, so that she should no strumpet be, in her company. And then one of them, who had her gold in keeping, left her a noble[150] with great anger and vexation to go where she would and help herself as she might, for with them, they said, she should no longer abide; and they forsook her that night.

Then, on the next morning, there came to her one of their company, a man who loved her well, praying her that she would go to his fellows and meeken herself to them, and pray them that she might go still in their company till she came to Constance.[151]

And so she did, and went forth with them till she came to Constance with great discomfort and great trouble, for they did her much shame and much reproof as they went, in divers places. They cut her gown so short that it came but little beneath her knee, and made her put on a white canvas, in the manner of a sacken apron, so that she should be held a fool and the people should not make much of her or hold her in repute. They made her sit at the table's end, below all the others, so that she ill durst speak a word.

And, notwithstanding all their malice, she was held in more worship than they were, wherever they went.

And the good man of the house where they were hostelled, though she sat lowest at the table's end, would always help her before them all as well as he could, and sent her from his own table such service as he had, and that annoyed her fellowship full evil.

---

149. Maiden = maidservant.
150. Noble = a gold coin worth 6s. 8d.
151. In Germany.

As they went by the way Constance-ward, it was told them that they would be robbed and have great discomfort unless they had great grace.

Then this creature came to a church and went in to make her prayer, and she prayed with all her heart, with great weeping and many tears, for help and succour against their enemies.

Then Our Lord said to her mind:—"Dread thee naught, daughter, thy fellowship shall come to no harm whilst thou art in their company."

And so, blessed may Our Lord be in all His works, they went forth in safety to Constance.

Chapter 27

When this creature and her fellowship had come to Constance, she heard tell of an English friar, a master of divinity, and the Pope's legate, who was in that city. Then she went to that worshipful man and shewed him her life from the beginning till that hour, as nigh as she might in confession, because he was the Pope's legate and a worshipful clerk.

And afterwards she told him what discomfort she had with her fellowship. . . . He full benignly and kindly received her as though she had been his mother, and received her gold, about twenty pounds, and yet one of them withheld wrongfully about sixteen pounds.

And they withheld also her maiden, and would not let her go with her mistress, notwithstanding that she had promised her mistress and assured her that she would not forsake her for any need.

And the legate made arrangements for this creature and made her his charge as if she had been his mother.

Then this creature went into a church and prayed Our Lord that He would provide her with a leader.

And anon Our Lord spoke to her and said:—

"Thou shalt have right good help and a good leader."

Immediately afterwards there came to her an old man with a white beard. . . .

Then they went forth day by day and met with many jolly men. And they said no evil word to this creature, but gave her and her man meat and drink, and the good wives where they were housed, laid her in their own beds for God's love, in many places where they came.

And Our Lord visited her with great grace of ghostly comfort as she went by the way. And so God brought her forth till she came to

Bologna.[152] And after she had come there, there came thither also her other fellowship, which had forsaken her before. And when they heard say that she had come to Bologna ere they had, then had they great wonder, and one of their fellowship came to her praying her to go to his fellowship and try if they would receive her again into their fellowship. And so she did.

"If ye will go in our fellowship, ye must make a new covenant, and that is this—ye shall not speak of the Gospel where we are, but shall sit still and make merry, as we do, both at meat and at supper."

She consented and was received again into their fellowship. Then went they forth to Venice and dwelt there thirteen weeks; and this creature was [given communion] every Sunday in a great house of nuns, and had great cheer among them, where Our Lord Jesus Christ visited this creature with great devotion and plenteous tears, so that the good ladies of the place were much marvelled thereof.

Afterwards, it happened, as this creature sat at meat with her fellowship, that she repeated a text of the Gospel that she had learnt beforetime with other good words, and then her fellowship said she had broken covenant. And she said:—

"Yea, sirs, forsooth I may no longer keep your covenant, for I must needs speak of My Lord Jesus Christ, though all this world had forbidden it me."

Then she took to her chamber and ate alone for six weeks, unto the time that Our Lord made her so sick that she weened to have been dead, and then suddenly He made her whole again. And all the time her maiden let her alone and made the company's meat and washed their clothes, and, to her mistress, under whom she had taken service, she would no deal attend.

Chapter 28

Also this company, which had put the aforesaid creature from their table, so that she should no longer eat amongst them, engaged a ship for themselves to sail in. They bought vessels for their wine, and obtained bedding for themselves, but nothing for her. Then she, seeing their unkindness, went to the same man where they had been, and bought herself bedding as they had done, and came where they were and shewed them what she had done, purposing to sail with them in that ship which they had chartered.

Afterwards, as this creature was in contemplation, Our Lord warned

---

152. In Italy.

her in her mind that she should not sail in that ship, and He assigned her to another ship, a galley, that she should sail in. Then she told this to some of the company, and they told it forth to their fellowship, and then they durst not sail in the ship they had chartered. So they sold away their vessels which they had got for their wines, and were right fain to come to the galley where she was, and so, though it was against her will, she went forth with them in their company, for they durst not otherwise do.

When it was time to make their beds, they locked up her clothes, and a priest, who was in their company, took away a sheet from the aforesaid creature, and said it was his. She took God to witness that it was her sheet. Then the priest swore a great oath, by the book in his hand, that she was as false as she might be, and despised her and strongly rebuked her. . . .

So they went forth into the Holy Land till they could see Jerusalem. And when this creature saw Jerusalem, riding on an ass, she thanked God with all her heart. . . .

Then went they to the temple in Jerusalem and they were let in on the same day at evensong time, and abode there till the next day at evensong time. Then the friars lifted up a cross and led the pilgrims about from one place to another where Our Lord suffered . . . His Passion, every man and woman bearing a wax candle in one hand. And the friars always, as they went about, told them what Our Lord suffered in every place. . . . And when they came up on to the Mount of Calvary, she fell down because she could not stand or kneel, and rolled and wrested with her body, spreading her arms abroad, and cried with a loud voice as though her heart would have burst asunder. . . .

Chapter 30

Another time, this creature's fellowship would go to the Flood of Jordan[153] and would not let her go with them. Then this creature prayed Our Lord that she might go with them, and He bade that she should go with them whether they would or not. Then she went forth by the grace of God, and asked no leave of them.

When she came to the Flood of Jordan, the weather was so hot that she thought her feet would have burnt for the heat that she felt.

Afterwards she went with her fellowship to Mount Quarentyne. There Our Lord fasted forty days, and there she prayed her fellowship

---

153. Flood of Jordan = Jordan River.

to help her up on to the Mount. And they said, "Nay", for they could not well help themselves. Then had she great sorrow, because she might not come on to the hill. And anon, happed a Saracen,[154] a well-favoured man, to come by her, and she put a groat into his hand, making him a sign to bring her on to the Mount. And quickly the Saracen took her under his arm and led her up on to the high Mount, where Our Lord fasted forty days.

Then was she sore athirst, and had no comfort in her fellowship. Then God, of His great goodness, moved the Grey Friars with compassion, and they comforted her, when her countrymen would not know her. . . .

Afterwards, when this creature came down from the Mount, as God willed, she went forth to the place where Saint John the Baptist was born. And later she went to Bethania, where Mary and Martha dwelt, and to the grave where Lazarus was buried and raised from death into life. And she prayed in the chapel where Our Blessed Lord appeared to His blissful Mother on Easter Day at morn, first of all others. And she stood in the same place where Mary Magdalene stood when Christ said to her:—

"Mary, why weepest thou?"

And so she was in many more places than be written, for she was three weeks in Jerusalem and the country thereabout, and she had ever great devotion as long as she was in that country.

The friars of the Temple made her great cheer and gave her many great relics, desiring that she should have dwelt still amongst them if she would, for the faith they had in her. Also the Saracens made much of her, and conveyed her, and led her about the country wherever she would go; and she found all people good to her and gentle, save only her own countrymen.

Then Our Lord commanded her to go to Rome and, so, forth home into England. . . . When Our Lord had brought them again to Venice in safety, her countrymen forsook her and went away from her, leaving her alone. And some of them said that they would not go with her for a hundred pound.

When they had gone away from her, then Our Lord Jesus Christ, Who ever helpeth at need, and never forsaketh His servants who truly trust in His mercy, said to this creature:—

"Dread thee not, daughter, for I will provide for thee right well, and bring thee in safety to Rome and home again into England without

---

154. Saracen = Muslim.

any villainy to thy body, if thou wilt be clad in white clothes, and wear them as I said to thee whilst thou wert in England."

69. Plans of Religious Communities (12th–13th c.)

The first plan below represents the remains and conjectural original state of the nunnery of Lacock in Wiltshire, England. This Augustinian community was founded in 1232 by Ela, countess of Salisbury. The second plan is of Watton Priory in Yorkshire, founded in 1150 as a house of the English Gilbertine order. Double monasteries, housing both male and female religious in separate buildings but as a single community (often headed by a woman), had been fairly common in many parts of Europe and the Mediterranean world in the Early Middle Ages, but the practice had generally died out by the ninth century. The Gilbertines revived the custom briefly with houses such as this one, where 140 nuns lived in one half of the complex and 70 canons in the other; there were also lay brothers and sisters who acted as servants. Both the architecture and the regulations of the community prevented communication and fraternization between the men and the women. Although many of the earlier double houses had been under the direction of an abbess, Gilbertine double houses were headed by male priors.

Lacock (13th c.)

Source: Anthony New, *A Guide to the Abbeys of England and Wales* (London: Constable, 1985).

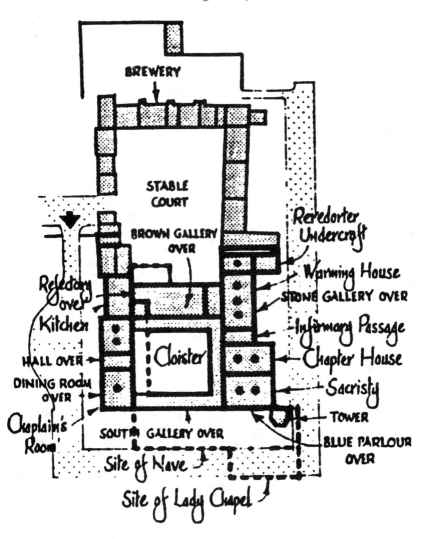

BREWERY

STABLE COURT

BROWN GALLERY OVER

Reredorter Undercroft

Warming House

STONE GALLERY OVER

Infirmary Passage

Chapter House

Refectory over

Kitchen

HALL OVER

DINING ROOM OVER

Cloister

Sacristy

Chaplain's Room

SOUTH GALLERY OVER

TOWER

BLUE PARLOUR OVER

Site of Nave

Site of Lady Chapel

Watton Priory (12th c.)

Source: Raymonde Foreville, *Saint Gilbert of Sempringham: His Life and Achievement*, tr. Kathleen F. Dockrill (Lincoln: Honywood Press, 1986). (Drawn by Max Maschner from a plate in the *Archaeological Journal*, 58 (1901).)

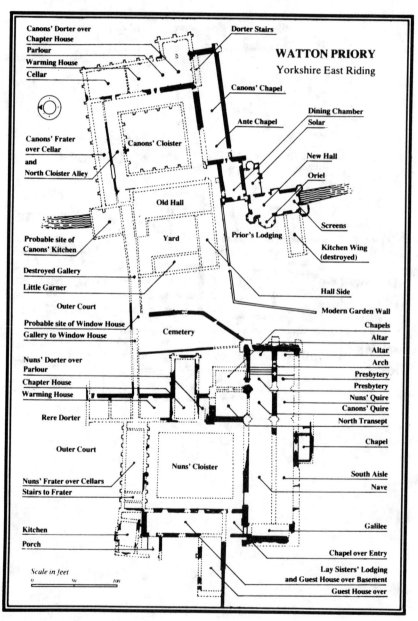

Part VI

Outsiders: Jewish, Muslim, and Heretic Women

The readings in the preceding chapters have all described the lives of women of the Christian and largely Germanic majority; there were also minorities in medieval Europe. The Jews, whose religion was rejected by Christians, were nevertheless officially tolerated by the church and protected by governments; they were forbidden to own land, but Jewish communities flourished in many medieval towns, profiting from trade and often practicing money-lending, which was forbidden for Christians. Blamed for the death of Christ and resented for their relative wealth, the Jews were regarded by Christian society with suspicion, and from the time of the First Crusade on they were often the victims of persecution, massacres and expulsions.

The Muslims came to the Iberian peninsula (modern Spain and Portugal) in the early eighth century, during the great era of Arabic expansion which followed the death of Mohammed, the founder of Islam, in 632. For several centuries they ruled that region and even made incursions into Gaul. In the eleventh century the Christians to their north regained the offensive, and over the following centuries Spain was gradually wrested from Muslim control. In the meantime, Christian, Jewish and Muslim society rubbed shoulders there, sometimes in hostility, sometimes in relative tolerance. The island of Sicily was the site of another ethnically and religiously diverse society, being inhabited by European Christians, by Muslims and by Byzantine Greeks. On the eastern frontiers of Europe, too, lived many pagan peoples who were only slowly converted to Christianity, or whose particular brand of Christianity made them seem alien to the Catholics of the west.

Finally, there were within Christian society groups of people who rejected religious truth as defined by the Roman Catholic church and practiced religions which differed in minor or major ways from that of the majority. Such divergent beliefs were called "heresy" by the church, and a heretic could be punished in various ways, including death. The heretics are included here because some of the larger groups formed distinct communities within society, and because the role of women in the heretical sects was sometimes very different from that of women in the Catholic church.

A. Jewish Women

70. Hebrew Chronicles:
Massacres of Jews during the First Crusade (1096)

Beginning in the eleventh century, the small communities of European Jews faced increasing intolerance and persecution from the Christian majority. With the First Crusade, Christian hostility broke out into large-scale violence, and from this point on pogroms against the Jews became fairly common. The following is a Jewish account of the first of the mass killings. The more prominent biblical quotations are italicized.
Source: Robert Chazan, *European Jewry and the First Crusade* (Berkeley: University of California Press, 1987).

Events at Speyer

It came to pass that, when [the crusaders] traversed towns where there were Jews, they said one to another: "Behold we journey a long way to seek the idolatrous shrine and to take vengeance upon the Muslims. But here are the Jews dwelling among us, whose ancestors killed [Jesus Christ] and crucified him groundlessly. Let us take vengeance first upon them. *Let us wipe them out as a nation; Israel's name will be mentioned no more.* Or else let them be like us and acknowledge the son born of menstruation."

Now when the [Jewish] communities heard their words, they reverted to the arts of our ancestors—repentance, prayer and charity. The hands of the holy people fell weak and their hearts melted and their strength flagged. They hid themselves in innermost chambers before *the ever turning sword.* They afflicted themselves with fasting. They fasted three consecutive days—both night and day, in addition to daily fasts, until *their skin shriveled on their bones and became as dry wood.* They cried out and gave forth a loud and bitter shriek. But their Father did not answer them. . . .

That year Passover fell on Thursday and the new moon of Iyyar on Friday. On the eighth of Iyyar, on the Sabbath,[155] the enemy arose

---

155. May 3, 1096.

against the [Jewish] community of Speyer and killed eleven saintly souls who sanctified their Creator on the holy Sabbath day and refused to be baptized. There was a notable and pious woman who slaughtered herself for the sanctification of the [Divine] Name. She was the first of those who slaughtered themselves in all the communities. . . .

Events at Worms

On the twenty-third of Iyyar, they rose up against the [Jewish] community of Worms. The community divided into two groups. Some stayed in their homes and some fled to the bishop. Then *the wolves of the steppes* rose up against those that were in their homes and pillaged them—men, women, and children; young and old. They tore down the stairways and destroyed the houses. They plundered and ravaged. They took the Torah and trampled it in the mud and tore it and burned it. *They devoured Israel with a greedy mouth.*

Seven days later, on the new moon of Sivan, the day of the arrival of Israel at Sinai in order to receive the Torah, those who still remained in the chambers of the bishop[156] were subjected to terror. The enemy assaulted them, as they had done to the earlier group, and put them to the sword. They [the Jews] held firm to the example of their brethren and were killed and sanctified the [Divine] Name publicly. They stretched forth their necks, so that their heads might be cut off for the Name of their Creator. There were some of them that took their own lives. They fulfilled the verse: *Mothers and babes were dashed together.* Indeed fathers also fell with their children, for they were slaughtered together. They slaughtered brethren, relatives, wives, and children. Bridegrooms [slaughtered] their intended and merciful mothers their only children. All of them accepted the heavenly decree unreservedly. As they commended their souls to their Creator, they cried out: "Hear O Israel! The Lord is our God; the Lord is one." The enemy stripped them and dragged them about. There remained only *a small number* whom they converted forcibly and baptized against their will in their baptismal waters. Approximately eight hundred was the number killed, who were killed on these two days. . . .

There was a certain young man, named R. Meshullam ben R. Isaac. He called out loudly to all those standing there and to Zipporah his helpmate: "Listen to me both great and small. This son God gave me.

---

156. Christian bishops frequently tried to protect Jews during this period, sometimes giving them sanctuary in the episcopal residence, or "palace."

My wife Zipporah bore him in her old age and his name is Isaac. Now I shall offer him up as did our ancestor Abraham with his son Isaac." Zipporah replied: "My lord, my lord. Wait a bit. Do not stretch forth your hand against the lad whom I have raised and brought up and whom I bore in my old age. Slaughter me first, so that I not witness the death of the child." He then replied: "I shall not delay even a moment. He who gave him to us will take him as his portion. He will place him in the bosom of Abraham our ancestor." He then bound Isaac his son and took in his hand the knife with which to slaughter his son and made the benediction for slaughtering. The lad answered amen. He then slaughtered the lad. He took his screaming wife. The two of them departed together from the chamber and the crusaders killed them. . . .

There was also a respected woman there, named Minna, hidden in a house underground, outside the city. All the men of the city gathered and said to her: "Behold you are *a capable woman.* Know and see that God does not wish to save you, for [the Jews] *lie naked at the corner of every street,* unburied. Sully yourself [with the waters of baptism]." They fell before her to the ground, for they did not wish to kill her. Her reputation was known widely, for all the notables of the city and the princes of the land were found in her circle. She responded and said: "Heaven forfend that I deny the God on high. For him and his holy Torah kill me and do not tarry any longer." There the woman *whose praises were sung at the gates* was killed. All of them were killed and sanctified the Divine Name unreservedly and willingly. All of them slaughtered one another together—young men and young women, old men and old women, even infants slaughtered themselves for the sanctification of the [Divine] Name.

Events at Mainz

Now I shall recount and tell the great wonders that were done that day by these saintly ones. Behold has such a thing ever happened before, from the earliest days? For they jostled one another saying: "I shall sanctify first the Name of the King of kings the Holy One, blessed be he." The pious women, the daughters of kings, threw coins and silver out the windows at the enemy, so that they be occupied with gathering the money in order to impede them slightly until they might finish slaughtering their sons and daughters. The hands of merciful mothers slaughtered their children, in order to do the will of their Creator. . . .

Subsequently the saintly women threw stones through the windows against the enemy. The enemy threw stones against them. They took the stones until their flesh and faces became shredded. They cursed and blasphemed the crusaders in the name of the Crucified the impure and foul, the son of lust: "Upon whom do you trust? Upon a rotting corpse!" The crusaders advanced to break down the door.

Who has seen anything like this; who has heard anything like that which the saintly and pious woman, Rachel daughter of R. Isaac ben R. Asher wife of R. Judah, did? She said to her companions: "I have four children. On them as well have no mercy, lest these uncircumcised come and seize them alive and they remain in their pseudofaith. With them as well you must sanctify the Name of the holy God." One of her companions came and took the knife to slaughter her son. When the mother of the children saw the knife she shouted loudly and bitterly and smote her face and breast and said: "Where is your stead-fast love, O Lord?" Then the woman said to her companions in her bitterness: "Do not slaughter Isaac before his brother Aaron, so that he not see the death of his brother and take flight." The women took the lad and slaughtered him—he was small and exceedingly comely. The mother spread her sleeve to receive the blood; she received the blood in her sleeves instead of in the [Temple] vessel for blood. The lad Aaron, when he saw that his brother had been slaughtered, cried out: "Mother, do not slaughter me!" He went and hid under a bureau. She still had two daughters, Bella and Matrona, comely and beautiful young women, the daughters of R. Judah her husband. The girls took the knife and sharpened it, so that it not be defective. They stretched forth their necks and she sacrificed them to the Lord God of Hosts, who commanded us not to renounce pure awe of him and to remain faithful to him, as it is written: *You must be wholehearted with the Lord your God.* When the saintly one completed sacrificing her three children before the Creator, then she raised her voice and called to her son: "Aaron, Aaron, where are you? I shall not have mercy nor pity on you as well." She pulled him by the leg from under the bureau where he was hidden and she sacrificed him before the sublime and exalted God. She placed them under her two sleeves, two on each side, near her heart. They convulsed near her, until the enemy seized the chamber and found her sitting and mourning them. They said to her: "Show us the moneys which you have in your sleeves." When they saw the children and saw that they were slaughtered, they smote her and killed her along with them. With regard to her it is said: *Mothers and babes were dashed to death together.* She [died] with her four children. . . . The father wailed and cried out when he saw the death of his four children, *comely and beautiful.* He went and threw himself on the sword in his hand. His innards flowed forth and he writhed in blood on the roadway along with those who had been killed, who had been convulsing and writhing in their blood. The enemy killed all those that remained in the chamber and stripped them naked. *See, O Lord, how abject I have become.* . . .

There were many women who sanctified the Name of the Creator to the death and did not wish to exchange him for the crucified bastard. Rachel, the companion of the deceased Rabbi Elazar and the companion of R. Judah ben R. Isaac, the great guide, was killed for the sanctification of his Name. Likewise other saintly women who were with them sanctified the [Divine] Name. These pious ones were brought before the courtyard of the church and they entreated them to immerse themselves in the waters of baptism. When they reached the church, they did not wish to enter a shrine of idolatry and their feet were mired, against their will, on the threshhold. They did not wish to enter the shrine of idolatry. . . . When the crusaders saw that they would not accept baptism—rather that they trusted mightily in the living God with all their heart, then the enemy leaped upon them and struck them with axes and blows. There the pious ones were killed for the sanctification of the [Divine] Name. There were in addition two pious women. One was Guta, the wife of Rabbi Isaac ben R. Moses, who had been killed at the outset, and the second was Scholaster, the wife of R. Isaac who was [subsequently] burned for the sanctification of the [Divine] Name. They likewise sanctified the sacred and unique Name, whose uniqueness is celebrated by all the living, at the time when the saintly ones were killed in the courtyard of the archbishop. They were in the courtyard of a certain burgher. The enemy forced him out of his house, and the crusaders and burghers gathered against them and urged them to be baptized with their evil waters. They put their trust in the Holy One of Israel and stretched forth their necks. The crusaders struck them without mercy. There the holy ones were killed for the sanctification of the awesome and unique Name.

Events near Cologne

The women likewise greatly sanctified the [Divine] Name publicly. When Sarit the young lady, the bride, saw that they had killed themselves with their swords and had slaughtered one another—she was *beautiful and comely* and exceedingly lovely in the eyes of those who beheld her—she wished to flee, out of fear of what she saw through the window. When her father-in-law Judah ben R. Abraham the pious saw that this was the intention of his daughter-in-law, he called to her and said: "My daughter, since you were not permitted to be wed to my son Abraham, you will not be wed to any other, to the foreigners." He seized her and held her outside the window and kissed her on the mouth and raised his voice in weeping along with the lass. He cried out loudly and very bitterly and said to all those standing there: "Behold, all of you. This is the bridal canopy of my daughter, my bride, that I make this day." They all wept with great weeping and wailing and *mourning and moaning*. The pious Judah said to her: "My daughter, come and lie in the bosom of Abraham our ancestor. For in one moment you shall acquire your future and shall enter the circle of the saintly and pious." He took her and placed her in the bosom of his son Abraham, her betrothed, and cut her with his sharp sword into two pieces. Subsequently he also slaughtered his son. . . .

Events at Trier

After [many killings in Trier], the enemy saw those remaining in the [bishop's] palace—that they were as firm in their faith as at the outset and that their hands had not been weakened by what had been done to these first [martyrs]. They said to one another: "All this the women do—they incite their husbands, strengthening their hands to rebel. . . ." Then all the ministers came and each grasped forcefully the hands of the women, smiting and wounding them, and led them to the church in order to baptize them. Afterward they sent and took forcefully children from the bosoms of their mothers and took them with them, to fulfill what is said: *Your sons and daughters shall be delivered to another people*. The women raised their voices and wept. Three days prior to informing them of this forced conversion, the ministers came to the palace and closed the pit in which water was held in the palace, for they feared lest they throw their children there to kill them. They did not permit them to ascend the wall, so that they not throw themselves from the wall. All night they guarded them that they not kill one another, until dawn. All this they planned because they did not wish to kill them—rather they labored to seize them and to forcibly convert them.

There was a young woman in front of the gateway of the palace. She stretched her neck outside and said: "Anyone who wishes to cut off my head for the fear of my Rock[157] let him come and do so." The uncircumcised did not wish to touch her, because the young lady was

---

157. "My Rock" = "my God."

comely and charming. But many times they wished to take her and carry her off with them. They intended [to do so] but could not, for she threw herself to the ground and made herself dead weight. Thus she remained in the palace. Then her aunt came and said to her: "Do you wish to die with me for the fear of our Rock?" She answered and said to her: "Yes, gladly." They went and bribed the guard of the gate. They left and went to the bridge and threw themselves into the water out of fear of the eternal King. Thus also did two young girls from Cologne. . . . Praise to the Lord that they were accorded burial. May the Avenger avenge in our days and before our eyes the blood of his servants that has been spilled. May their virtue and saintliness serve for our merit and protect us on a day of evil.

71. Maimonides: The Book of Women (12th c.)

The rabbi Maimonides (1135–1204), one of the greatest Jewish philosophers of medieval Europe, lived in Spain, in a region ruled by Muslims. He collected in this book the traditions of Jewish law concerning the family, from ancient times to his own.
Source: Isaac Klein, tr., *The Code of Maimonides, Book Four: The Book of Women,* Yale University Press, copyright 1972. Used by permission.

Chapter XII. 1. When a man marries a woman, whether virgin or non-virgin, whether adult or minor, whether a daughter of Israel, a proselyte, or an emancipated bondswoman, he obligates himself to her for ten things, and is in turn entitled to four things from her.

2. Of the ten, three are found in the Torah: *her food, her raiment, and her conjugal rights* (Exod. 21:10). *Her food* signifies her maintenance; *her raiment,* what the term implies; *her conjugal rights,* sexual intercourse with her, according to the way of the world.

The other seven are of Scribal origin, and all of them are conditions laid down by the court. The first of them is the statutory ketubbah;[158] the rest are called "conditions contained in the ketubbah." They are the following: to treat her if she falls ill; to ransom her if she is captured; to bury her if she dies; to provide for her maintenance out of his estate; to let her dwell in his house after his death for the duration of her widowhood; to let her daughters sired by him receive their mainte-

---

158. Ketubbah = the written document containing the terms of the marriage contract; by extension, the share of the husband's property assigned to the wife in the document.

nance out of his estate after his death, until they become espoused; to let her male children sired by him inherit her ketubbah, in addition to their share with their half-brothers in his estate.

3. And the four things he is entitled to are all of Scribal origin, namely the following: he is entitled to her earnings, to anything she finds, and to the usufruct of her estate during her lifetime. And should she die in his lifetime, he is her heir, with precedence over anyone else as to her estate.

Chapter XIII. 1. How much raiment is the husband obligated to provide for his wife? Clothes to the amount of fifty zuz per annum, in the coin current at that time, when fifty zuz equaled six and a quarter silver denar.

The new garments should be given to her in the rainy season, so that they would be well worn when she wears them in the dry season; as for worn-out garments, meaning what remains of the original clothes, they are hers to cover herself therewith during her menstrual period. She is also to be given a girdle for her loins, a cap for her head, and shoes from one festival to the other.

2. When does this apply? In those days and in the Land of Israel. At other times, however, and in other places, the specified value is not the determinant. There are places where clothing may be very expensive or very cheap. The principle to be observed is that the husband is obligated to give her garments suitable for the rainy season and for the dry season, worth not less than what any housewife in that country would require for her wearing apparel.

3. Included with the garments that he is obligated to give her are the house furnishings and the dwelling itself in which she resides.

What are the house furnishings? A spread couch, and a mattress or mat to sit on; and eating and drinking utensils such as a pot, a platter, a cup, a bottle, and the like. As for the dwelling, he must lease for her a house at least four cubits by four, with a yard outside for her use. It should also have a separate lavatory.

4. He is likewise obligated to give her toilet articles, such as colored fabrics to wind around her head and forehead, eye-paint, rouge, and the like, so that she might not seem unattractive to him.

5. To whom does this apply? To the poor in Israel. As for the wealthy, everything should be commensurate with his wealth. Even if he can afford to buy her silken and embroidered garments and gold jewelry, he should be compelled to do so.

The same applies to the dwelling, which should likewise be commensurate with his wealth; and so should the toilet articles and the house furnishings—everything should be according to his wealth. . . .

14. If a man says to his wife, "I do not wish to have your father, your mother, your brothers, or your sisters come to my house," his wish is to be honored, and she should visit them instead when anything happens to them. She should also visit her father's house once a month, and on each pilgrimage festival. They, however, should not visit her, unless something has happened to her, such as illness or a delivery, for no man may be compelled to let others enter his premises.

Thus, also, if she says, "I do not wish to have your mother or your sisters visit me, nor do I wish to reside in the same courtyard with them, because they cause me harm and annoyance," her wish is to be honored. . . .

Chapter XIV. 2. A wife may restrict her husband in his business journeys to nearby places only, so that he would not otherwise deprive her of her conjugal rights. Hence he may not set out except with her permission.

8. The wife who prevents her husband from having intercourse with her is called "a rebellious wife," and should be questioned as to the reason for her rebelliousness. If she says, "I have come to loathe him, and I cannot willingly submit to his intercourse," he must be compelled to divorce her immediately, for she is not like a captive woman who must submit to a man that is hateful to her. She must, however, leave with forfeiture of all of her ketubbah. . . .

9. If she rebels against her husband merely in order to torment him, and says, "I am going to make him suffer in this way, because he has done thus-and-so to me," or "because he has cursed me," or "because he quarrels with me," or anything similar, the court should send her a message stating as follows: "Be it known unto you that if you persist in your rebellion, your ketubbah . . . will stand forfeited." After that an announcement should be made about her in the synagogues and the houses of study, every day for four consecutive weeks, to the effect that "So-and-so has rebelled against her husband."

10. After the announcement the court should send her a second message, saying, "If you persist in your rebellion, you will forfeit your ketubbah." If she persists in her rebellion and does not repent, a consultation should be held with her. Whereupon she is to forfeit her ketubbah and lose her title to any ketubbah at all. . . .

Chapter XXI. 1. Anything a woman may find and her handiwork belong to her husband. And what is she required to do for him? It all depends on the custom of the country. Where the custom is for wives to weave, she must weave; to embroider, she must embroider; to spin wool or flax, she must spin. If it is not the custom of the women of that town to do all these kinds of work, he cannot compel her to do any of them, except spinning wool only—because flax injures the mouth and lips—for spinning is a kind of work that is characteristic of women, as it is said, *And all women that were wise-hearted did spin with their hands* (Exod. 35:25).

2. If she exerts herself to perform more work than is proper for her, the surplus belongs to her husband.

If he has a great deal of money, and even if she herself has many maidservants, she should not sit idle, without work, because idleness leads to immorality. She should not, however, be compelled to work all day long, but may reduce her work in proportion to their wealth.

3. . . . Every wife must likewise wash her husband's face, hands, and feet, pour his cup for him, spread his couch, and wait on him, for example, by handing him water or a vessel, or removing these from before him, and the like. She is not obligated, however, to wait on his father or his son.

5. There are other kinds of work that a wife must perform for her husband when they are poor. These are the following: She must bake bread in the oven—Ezra ordained that a wife should rise early to do her baking, so that bread might be available for the poor—cook food, wash clothes, nurse her child, put fodder before her husband's mount—but not before his cattle—and attend to the grinding of corn. How should she attend to the grinding? By sitting at the flour mill and watching the flour, not by doing the grinding herself; or by driving the beast, so that the mill would not stand idle. If, however, the local custom is for wives to do their grinding with a hand mill, she must do the grinding herself.

11. As long as the wife is nursing her child, the amount of her work should be reduced, while her maintenance should be augmented with wine and other things that are beneficial for lactation.

Chapter XXIII. 11. There are many customs regarding the dowry. . . .

13. If a man and a woman are negotiating with a view to matrimony, he saying to her, "How much will you bring me?", to which she replies, "So-and-so much. And how much will you give me," or "write for me?", to which he replies, "So-and-so much"; and similarly, if the two fathers are negotiating in behalf of the son and the daughter, respectively, the one asking, "How much are you giving in behalf of your son?", and the other replying, "So-and-so much. And how much are you giving in behalf of your daughter?", "So-and-so much"—once the two parties perform the betrothal, each is entitled to the property stipulated in the negotiation, even if no symbolic act of barter had taken place between them. . . .

Chapter XXIV. 11. The following acts, if committed by a woman, render her guilty of transgressing the law of Moses: going out into the street with the hair of her head uncovered, making vows or swearing oaths and not fulfilling them, indulging in sexual intercourse during menstruation, failing to set aside her dough offering, or serving her husband prohibited food, that is, not only such food as swarming and creeping creatures or carrion, but also untithed food. . . .

15. How is a woman to be dismissed on the ground of ill repute? For example, if witnesses testify that she has done something exceedingly unseemly, indicating that a transgression has been committed, even though there is no clear evidence of harlotry.

How so? If, for example, she is alone in the courtyard, and people seeing a spice-peddlar come out, immediately at the moment of his exit enter and find her rising from the couch and putting on her trousers or tying her belt, or find moist saliva above the canopy; or if both of them come out of a dark place, or help one another to ascend from a pit, or the like; or if they see him kiss her at the opening of her chemise, or see them kiss or hug each other, or if the two of them enter a place one after the other and shut the doors, or act in a similar manner. In any case such as these, if the husband wishes to dismiss her, she may be dismissed without her ketubbah, and no warning is required.

72. Judah Asheri: Family History (13th–14th c.)

Judah Asheri (d. 1349) was a German Jew who migrated to Spain early in his life. In his will he recounts episodes of family history which remind us of the precarious conditions under which Jews lived in medieval Europe. The first paragraph below is included for its description of a female medical practitioner.
Source: *Hebrew Ethical Wills*, tr. Israel Abrahams (Philadelphia: The Jewish Publication Society of America, 1926).

. . . When I was an infant about three months old, my eyes were affected, and were never completely restored. A certain woman tried to cure me when I was about three years of age, but she added to my blindness, to the extent that I remained for a year unable to see the road on which to walk. Then a Jewess, a skilled oculist, appeared on the scene; she treated me for about two months, and then died. Had she lived another month, I might have received my sight fully. As it was, but for the two months' attention from her, I might never have been able to see at all. . . .

One of the good methods which I desired for maintaining the family record was the marriage of my sons to members of my father's house. I had many reasons for this. First, it is a fair and fit thing to join fruit of vine to fruit of vine. It is indeed an important duty, for as our Sages said: He who loves his relatives, he who marries his sister's daughter, and he who lends to the poor in the hour of his distress—to him applies the text: "Then shalt thou call, and the Lord will answer; thou shalt cry and He will say, Here I am." Furthermore, the women of our family have grown accustomed to the ways of students, and the love of the Torah has entered their hearts, so that they are a help to their husbands in their scholarly pursuits. Moreover, they are not used to extravagant expenditure; they do not demand luxuries, the provision of which disturbs a man from his study. Then again, children for the most part resemble the mother's family. Finally, if with changing times a man see fit to seek his livelihood in another city, there will be none to place obstacles in the way of the wife accompanying her husband.

The second plan is for me to write something of the history of my saintly progenitors, for the edification of those that come after us. . . . As I left Germany when about thirteen years of age, I did not acquire exact information as to our fathers' righteous lives, except the little which I heard from my lord, my father of blessed memory, and from his sister and my grandmother, who related to me some of the family history. . . .

Six months after [my grandfather's] death, at midnight on the Sabbath night, he appeared to his wife and said to her: "Haste and rise, take thy sons and thy daughters, and remove them hence, for tomorrow all the Jews of this place will be slain. So it was decreed against the whole neighborhood, but we prayed and our petition was successful except as regards this place." She rose and obeyed, but returning to save her belongings, she was killed with the congregation. She had previously rescued my lord, my father, R. Asher of blessed memory, and his brother, R. Hayyim . . . . They had another brother . . . [and] six sisters, the whole family saintly—all bearing deservedly high reputations among their contemporaries. The nine of them escaped on the day and under the circumstances narrated above. All of them had large families of sons and daughters, and I have heard that one of the sons of my uncle, R. Hayyim, of blessed memory, married in Germany, and that there were at his wedding about five hundred men and women, all relatives, the relationship reaching to that of third cousins. . . .

73. Eleazar of Mainz:
Moral Instruction for His Family (14th c.)

Eleazar (d. 1357) left a will which is largely devoted to moral instructions for his sons and daughters. Like a code of law, this sort of source must be read not only for what it prescribes but also for the clues it may contain about life as it was actually lived.
Source: *Hebrew Ethical Wills*, tr. Israel Abrahams (Philadelphia: The Jewish Publication Society of America, 1926).

. . . My daughters must obey scrupulously the rules applying to women; modesty, sanctity, reverence, should mark their married lives. They should carefully watch for the signs of the beginning of their periods and keep separate from their husbands at such times. Marital intercourse must be modest and holy, with a spirit of restraint and delicacy, in reverence and in silence. They shall be very punctilious and careful with their ritual bathing,[159] taking with them women friends of worthy character. They shall cover their eyes until they reach their home, on returning from the bath, in order not to behold anything of an unclean nature. They must respect their husbands, and must be invariably amiable to them. Husbands, on their part, must honor their wives more than themselves, and treat them with tender consideration.

If they can contrive it, my sons and daughters should live in communities, and not isolated from other Jews, so that their sons and daughters may learn the ways of Judaism. Even if compelled to solicit from others the money to pay a teacher, they must not let the young, of both sexes, go without instruction in the Torah. Marry your children, O my sons and daughters, as soon as their age is ripe, to members of respectable families. Let no child of mine hunt after money by making a low match for that object; but if the family is undistinguished only on the mother's side, it does not matter, for all Israel counts descent from the father's side.

Every Friday morning, they shall put themselves in careful trim for honoring the Sabbath, kindling the lamps while the day is still great, and in winter lighting the furnace before dark, to avoid desecrating the Sabbath (by kindling fire thereon). For due welcome to the Sabbath, the women must prepare beautiful candles. As to games of chance, I entreat my children never to engage in such pastimes. During

---

159. Jews were required by their religion to bathe regularly, reciting certain prayers before and after; this was usually done at public bathhouses.

the leisure of the festival weeks they may play for trifling stakes in kind, and the women may amuse themselves similarly on New Moons, but never for money. In their relation to women, my sons must behave continently, avoiding mixed bathing and mixed dancing and all frivolous conversation, while my daughters ought not to speak much with strangers, nor jest nor dance with them. They ought to be always at home, and not gadding about. They should not stand at the door, watching whatever passes. I ask, I command, that the daughters of my house be never without work to do, for idleness leads first to boredom, then to sin. But let them spin, or cook, or sew. . . .

Now, my sons and daughters, eat and drink only what is necessary, as our good parents did, refraining from heavy meals, and holding the gross liver in detestation. The regular adoption of such economy in food leads to economy in expenditure generally, with a consequent reluctance to pursue after wealth, but the acquisition of a contented spirit, simplicity in diet, and many good results. Concerning such a well-ordered life the text says: "The righteous eateth to the satisfaction of his desire." Our teachers have said: "Method in expenditure is half a sufficiency." Nevertheless, accustom yourselves and your wives, your sons and your daughters, to wear nice and clean clothes, that God and man may love and honor you. In this direction do not exercise too strict a parsimony. But on no account adopt foreign fashions in dress. After the manner of your fathers order your attire, and let your cloaks be broad without buckles attached. . . .

Be very particular to keep your houses clean and tidy. I was always very scrupulous on this point, for every injurious condition, and sickness and poverty, are to be found in foul dwellings. . . .

74. Jewish Sumptuary Laws (15th c.)

"Sumptuary" laws regulating the dress and other aspects of material consumption were common in medieval Europe. The following examples were enacted by the Jewish authorities themselves; the Christian majority also sometimes imposed certain restrictions of dress on Jews.
Source: *The Jew in the Medieval World: A Sourcebook*, ed. Jacob R. Marcus (Cincinnati: The Union of American Hebrew Congregations, 1938).

Forli, Italy, 18 May 1418

In order also to humble our hearts, and to walk modestly before our God, and not to show off in the presence of the Gentiles, we have agreed that from today, until the termination of the time already mentioned [1426], no Jew or Jewess of the above recorded Jewish communities, towns, or villages shall be so arrogant as to wear a fur-lined jacket, unless, of course, it is black. Also the sleeves must not be open, nor be lined with silk, for that would be arrogant. These fur-lined jackets, however, other than black, may still be worn, provided that the sleeves and the garments themselves are closed at the sides and at the back. . . .

Likewise no woman shall openly wear any girdle or belt if its silver weighs more than ten ounces.

Valladolid, Spain, 2 May 1432

No son of Israel of the age of fifteen or more shall wear any cloak of gold-thread, olive-colored material or silk, or any cloak trimmed with gold or olive-colored material or silk, nor a cloak with rich trimmings nor with trimmings of olive-colored or gold cloth.

This prohibition does not include the clothes worn at a time of festivity or at the reception of a lord or lady, nor at balls or similar social occasions.

Because of the diversity of custom among the communities in regard to the wearing apparel, we find it impracticable to make a general ordinance which shall provide for all the details that ought to be included, and we therefore ordain that each community shall make such ordinances on the subject so long as this Ordinance endures, as will keep before their minds that we are in Dispersion because of our sins, and if they desire to establish more rigorous rules than this they have the power to do so.

75. A Marital Question: An Innkeeper's Wife Leaves Home (ca. 1470)

> The narrator here is Hakkym ben Jehiel Cohen Falcon, a Jewish innkeeper in the Italian city of Pavia. His wife, having left him, is under technical suspicion of sexual misconduct, and thus Hakkym must appeal to the Jewish authorities for permission to take her back as his wife.
> Source: *The Jew in the Medieval World: A Sourcebook*, ed. Jacob R.

Marcus (Cincinnati: The Union of American Hebrew Congregations, 1938).

[Hakkym writes his story to Rabbi Joseph Colon:]

In order to relate everything that has happened to me I shall tell
you in detail what my business is and I shan't hide a thing from you,
sir. Now this is the matter concerning which I make inquiry of my
master:

For the past several years I have made my living as an innkeeper in
Pavia, and this was my business up to the year 230 [1469] when my
wife began to trouble me saying: "You've got to leave this business,"
and she gave me some good reasons for it. After she had kept hammering away at me every day for about six months and I had paid no
attention to her—I kept pushing her off—the quarrel between us
regarding this affair reached its climax about the beginning of Adar
230 [February 1470]. While I was in the house teaching my daughter,
my wife picked herself up right at noon, took all the silver vessels and
her jewelry, and repaired to the house of a Gentile woman, a neighbor,
to whom my wife went frequently. This woman used to sew linen
clothes for me, for my household, and for the guests who used to
come to my place. She was also my laundress.

My wife was in the house of this Gentile woman about half an hour
before I inquired of my daughters where she had gone—for I was
intent on teaching my daughter. Suddenly, however, my thoughts
rose up and stirred me to ask my daughters: "Girls, where is your
mother?" They told me that she had gone outside and that my four
year old little girl, holding her right hand, had gone with her. I
thereupon went after her, seeking her in Jewish homes unsuccessfully,
till my heart told me: "Go to the house of the Gentile; perhaps she's
staying there." So I turned in her direction and came to the house of
the Gentile woman but found the door locked. I knocked and the
husband of the woman opened the door at once, but when he saw
that it was I, the husband of the woman who had just come into his
home, he was distressed and tried to close the door, but he couldn't,
for I entered by force. When the auxiliary bishop, who was there,
heard my voice, he said to me: "Come on in and don't be afraid."

There were present there, in addition to the auxiliary bishop, two
citizens, the bishop's chaplain, and two Gentile women seated beside
my wife, who was on a bench with her daughter in her arms. As I
came into the house the auxiliary bishop said to me: "Is this your
wife?" and I answered: "Yes, my lord."

"According to what we now observe," he said again, "another spirit has clothed your wife, who wishes to change her religion; therfore are we come to encourage her to turn to the Christian religion if she has really set her heart on it. If not, we advise her to return to her people and to her God."

I then asked his permission to have an earnest talk with her in German, and he gave me permission to speak with her in any kindly way as long as I did not scold her. Now this is what I said to her: "Why have you come here and why don't you return home?" To which she answered: "I'm going to stay here and I don't care to return, for I don't want to be the mistress of a tavern." "Come on, come on back," I said to her, "I have already promised you, you can do whatever your heart desires in this matter."

"You can't fool me again," she responded. "You've lied to me ten times and I don't trust you." And as she was speaking to me after this fashion I said to her: "Why have you your little daughter in your arms?" "Take your daughter and go," she answered, and I took her in my arms. Then as I turned to go my way the auxiliary bishop said to me: "Look here, Falcon, don't be disturbed about your wife. No pressure will be brought to bear on her. Nothing will be done in haste, but quietly, calmly, and with her consent. Before we make a decision in this matter we will place her in a cloistered spot, among virtuous nuns, where no man may enter. She'll have to stay there forty days until she completes the period of her isolation and reflection—for this practice has been established by the founder of Christianity that one may determine what is in the heart of those who come to change their religion, and also in order to prevent confusion to Christianity."[160]

When I heard this I turned homeward weeping as I went. My oldest daughter came out to meet me, and I told her all about the unseemly affair that had happened to me. She ran to her mother to find out what she had in mind. "Go back to the house and don't be concerned, and don't bother about me," her mother told her. Whereupon the girl ran to a prominent Jewess. Then the both of them came to the girl's mother, and the Jewess spoke to her. Behold, the entire conversation of this Jewess is recorded in a deposition that has been forwarded to you.

Within half an hour after this had happened the bishop ordered the woman to be taken to a convent in which a very rigorous Christian discipline prevailed and which, of all the convents, was the most isolated from man. Such convents are shut off so completely that no

---

160. The period of reflection for a person preparing to be baptized was actually established by Pope Gregory I (590–604), not by Jesus.

man can enter there except on rare occasions or in case of emergency. For instance, the bishop would go there when there was an absolute need, or the physician, who was assigned to them, would come there with the permission of the bishop if one of the nuns took sick. When my wife went to the convent she was accompanied by seven Gentile women and two citizens, and she remained there all that day and all that night.

However, her spirit was moved for good, and when the morning came she sent word to the bishop that she earnestly desired to return to her home saying: "I am the wife of a *cohen*, and if I stay here a day or two more I can no more return to the shelter of his home, for he must divorce me." . . .[161]

The bishop then sent for me and came to meet me—for he had gone to the convent—and he repeated to me all the things that had been said and done, and said further: "Look here, your wife wants to return to your home, but I fear you may vex her with words and reproaches. Don't do it. For wherein has she sinned against you? And although she says that she has no cause to fear, nevertheless I beg of you, please do not reprove her or oppress her. Return to her as of old and I'll do this for you: I'll cross-question her in the presence of witnesses, as is meet to be done in such a case," and so he did.[162] Toward evening God's light shone on that bishop, for he restored my wife to her home, and she is there now, weeping for her sin, imploring my forgiveness and pardon and condonation, and afflicting her soul, and may God forgive her.

Therefore your humble servant, here undersigned, requests my lord to be so kind as to inform me—if I have found favor in your learned sight—whether my wife is permitted to live with me or not. And this is the inquiry which I make of you, even as I might bring my case before a divine oracle, and I shall adhere closely to whatever you command me. It will be ascribed to you as an act of righteousness if you clarify this distressing situation, and may God be kind and gracious unto you and give you opportunities greater even than your ancestors' to spread Torah and to impart knowledge to the people, for your ways are ways of pleasantness.

---

161. Normally a Jewish husband need not have divorced his wife even if she admitted to adultery, but *cohen*s, the descendants of the Jewish priestly caste, were held to a higher standard of purity than other Jews.

162. The bishop is attempting to establish her innocence of adultery in order to allow her to return home.

B. Muslim Women

76. The Koran (7th c.)

The holy book of Islam was compiled in the early seventh century in Arabia; Muslims believe that it was dictated by Allah to Mohammed. The Muslim faith was spread by the Arab conquests of the Middle East, Northern Africa and Spain (by the early eighth century), and Islamic law, based on the Koran, spread along with it. The passages below are addressed to men but prescribe the place of women in Islamic society.

Source: *Quran, The Final Testament: Authorized English Version, with the Arabic Text*, tr. Rashad Khalifa (Tucson: Islamic Productions, 1989). Selections below are from the following suras and verses: 2:221–3, 226–31, 233–7, 240–1, 282; 4:1, 3, 7, 11–12, 15–16, 19–25, 32, 34–5; 24:32–3, 60; 33:35–59.

The Place of Women

O people, observe your Lord; the One who created you from one being and created from it its mate, then spread from the two many men and women. . . .

You shall not covet the qualities bestowed on each other by God; the men enjoy certain qualities, and women enjoy certain qualities. . . .

The men are made responsible for the women, since God endowed them with certain qualities, and made them the bread earners. The righteous women will cheerfully accept this arrangement, and observe God's commandments, even when alone in their privacy. If you experience opposition from the women, you shall first talk to them, then [you may use such negative incentives as] deserting them in bed, then you may beat them. If they obey you, you are not permitted to transgress against them. . . .

The Muslim men, the Muslim women, the believing men, the believing women, the obedient men, the obedient women, the truthful men, the truthful women, the steadfast men, the steadfast women, the reverent men, the reverent women, the charitable men, the charitable women, the fasting men, the fasting women, the chaste men, the chaste women, and the men who commemorate God frequently, and the commemorating women; God has prepared for them forgiveness and a great recompense. . . .

Women in Law

. . . if you transact a loan . . . [you] shall have two witnesses from among your men. If two men are not available, then choose two women whose testimony is acceptable to all parties. Thus, if one woman becomes biased, the other will remind her. . . .

Inheritance

The men get a share of what the parents and the relatives leave behind. The women too shall get a share of what the parents and relatives leave behind. Whether it is a small or a large inheritance, [the women must get] a definite share. . . .

God decrees a will for the benefit of your children; the male gets twice the share of the female. If the inheritors are only women, more than two, they get two-thirds of what is bequeathed. If only one daughter is left, she gets one-half. . . .

You get half of what your wives leave behind, if they had no children. If they had children, you get one-fourth of what they leave. All this, after fulfilling any will they had left, and after paying off all debts. They get one-fourth of what you leave behind, if you had no children. If you had children, they get one-eight of the inheritance you leave behind. All this, after fulfilling any will you had left, and after paying off all debts. . . .

O you who believe, it is not lawful for you to inherit what the women leave behind, against their will. You shall not force them to give up anything you had given them, unless they commit a proven adultery. You shall treat them nicely. If you dislike them, you may dislike something wherein God has placed a lot of good.

Marriage

Do not marry idolatress women unless they believe; a believing woman is better than an idolatress, even if you like her. And do not give your daughters to idolaters, unless they believe. A believer is better than an idolater, even if you like him. Those people invite to Hell, while God invites to Paradise and forgiveness by His leave. . . .

If you deem it best for the orphans, you may marry their mothers— you may marry two, three, or four of them. If you fear lest you become unfair, then you shall be content with only one, or with what you already have. This way, you are more likely to avoid inequality. . . .

Prohibited for you [in marriage] are your mothers, your daughters, your sisters, the sisters of your fathers, the sisters of your mothers, the daughters of your brother, the daughters of your sister, your nursing mothers, the girls who nursed from the same woman as you, the mothers of your wives, the daughters of your wives, with whom you have consummated the marriage—if the marriage has not been consummated, you may marry the daughter. Also prohibited for you are the women who were married to your genetic sons. Also, you shall not be married to two sisters at the same time—but do not break up existing marriages. . . .

Also prohibited are the women who are already married, unless their husbands are disbelievers at war with you. . . . All other categories are permitted for you in marriage, so long as you pay them their due dowries.[163] . . .

Those among you who cannot afford to marry free believing women, may marry believing slave women. . . . You shall obtain permission from their guardians before you marry them, and pay them their due dowry equitably. . . . Once they are freed through marriage, if they commit adultery, their punishment shall be half of that for the free women. Marrying a slave shall be a last resort for those unable to wait. To be patient is better for you. . . .

You shall encourage those of you who are single to get married. They may even marry the righteous among your male and female servants; if they are poor, God will enrich them from His grace. God is Bounteous, Knower. Those who cannot afford to get married shall maintain morality until God provides for them from His grace. Those among your slaves who wish to be freed in order to marry, you shall grant them their wish, once you realize that they are honest. And give to them from God's money that He has bestowed on you. You shall not force your girls to commit prostitution, seeking the materials of this world, if they wish to be chaste. If anyone forces them, then God, seeing that they are forced, is Forgiver, Merciful.

Divorce

Those who intend to estrange their wives shall wait four months [for cooling off]; if they reconcile, then God is Forgiver, Most Merciful. If they go through with the divorce, then God is Hearer, Knower. The divorced women shall wait three menstruations [before marrying

---

163. "Dowry" is used here to mean a marriage payment to the wife by the husband, similar to the medieval European dower rather than the medieval European dowry.

another man]. It is not lawful for them to conceal what God has created in their wombs, if they believe in God and the Last Day. [In case of pregnancy,] the husband's wishes shall supersede the wife's wishes if he wants to remarry her. The women have rights, as well as obligations, equitably. Thus, the men's wishes prevail [in case of pregnancy]. God is Almighty, Most Wise.

Divorce may be retracted twice. . . . If he divorces her for the third time, it is not lawful for him to remarry her, unless she marries another man, and he divorces her. The first husband can then remarry her, so long as they observe God's laws. . . .

If you divorce the women, once they shall fulfill their interim [three mentruations], you shall allow them to live in the same home amicably, or let them leave amicably. Do not force them to stay, as a revenge. Anyone who does this wrongs his own soul. . . .

Divorced mothers shall nurse their infants two full years, if the father so wishes. The father shall provide the mother's food and clothing, equitably. No one shall be burdened beyond capacity. . . . If the father dies, his inheritor shall assume these responsibilities. If the parents mutually agree to part, after due consultation, they commit no sin by doing so. You commit no sin by hiring nursing mothers, so long as you pay them equitably. . . .

You commit no error if you divorce the women before touching them, or before setting the dowry for them. In that case, you shall compensate them—the rich as he can afford and the poor as he can afford—an equitable compensation. This is a duty upon the righteous. If you divorce them before touching them, but after you had set the dowry for them, the compensation shall be half the dowry, unless they voluntarily forfeit their right, or the responsible party chooses to forfeit the whole dowry. To forfeit is closer to righteousness. Do not abandon amicable relations among you. . . .

The divorcees also shall be provided for, equitably. This is a duty upon the righteous. . . .

If you wish to marry another wife, in place of your present wife, and you had given the latter a great deal, you shall not take back anything you had given her. Would you take it fraudulently, maliciously, and sinfully? How could you take it back, after you have been intimate with each other, and after they have taken from you a solemn pledge? . . .

If a couple fears separation, you shall appoint an arbitrator from his family and an arbitrator from her family; if they decide to reconcile, God will help them get together. . . .

Menstruation

They ask you about menstruation: say, "It is harmful. Therefore, avoid sexual intercourse with the women during menstruation, and do not approach them until they are over it. Once they are over it, you may have intercourse with them in the manner designed by God. God loves the repenters, and he loves those who are clean." Your women are the bearers of your seed. Thus, you may enjoy them however you wish, so long as you maintain righteousness. . . .

Adultery

Those who commit adultery among your women, you must have four witnesses against them. If they do bear witness, then you shall keep such women in their homes until they die, or until God creates an exit for them. The couple who commit adultery shall be punished. If they repent and reform, you shall leave them alone. . . .

Widows

Those who die and leave wives, their widows shall wait four months and ten days [before remarriage]. Once they fulfill their interim, you commit no sin by letting them do whatever they wish, equitably. . . . You commit no sin if you declare your engagement to the women, or keep it secret. But do not meet them secretly, unless you have something righteous to discuss. Do not consummate the marriage until the interim is fulfilled. . . .

For those who die and leave wives, a will shall provide their wives with support for one year, provided they stay within the same household.

Women's Dress

The elderly women who do not expect to get married commit nothing wrong by relaxing their dress code, provided they do not reveal too much of their bodies. To maintain modesty is better for them. . . .

O prophet, tell your wives, your daughters, and the believing women to lengthen their garments. Thus, they will be recognized [as righteous women] and avoid being insulted. . . .

77. Rules for Muslim Government:
Exclusion of Women (11th c.)

Although the jurist al-Mawardi, from whose writings the following piece is taken, lived in the Middle East, rather than in Europe,
his views were on government were widely respected and may
be taken as typical of medieval Muslim authorities.
Source: From *Islam: From the Prophet Muhammed to the Capture of
Constantinople, Volume II: Religion and Society*, edited and translated
by Bernard Lewis. Copyright (c) 1974 by Bernard Lewis. Reprinted
by permission of Oxford University Press, Inc.

Nobody may be appointed to the office of qadi[164] who does not
comply fully with the conditions required to make his appointment
valid and his decisions effective. . . . The first condition is that he
must be a man. This condition consists of two qualities, puberty
and masculinity. As for the child below puberty, he cannot be held
accountable, nor can his utterances have effect against himself; how
much less so against others. As for women, they are unsuited to
positions of authority, although judicial verdicts may be based on
what they say. Abu Hanifa said that a woman can act as qadi in matters
on which it would be lawful for her to testify, but she may not act as
qadi in matters on which it would not be lawful for her to testify. Ibn
Jarir al-Tabari, giving a divergent view, allows a woman to act as qadi
in all cases, but no account should be taken of an opinion which is
refuted by both the consensus of the community and the word of God.
"Men have authority over women because of what God has conferred
on the one in preference to the other" [Koran 4: 38], meaning by this,
intelligence and discernment. He does not, therefore, permit women
to hold authority over men.

78. Market Regulations at Seville (12th c.)

Much of Spain was still Muslim in the twelfth century, when the
writer Ibn 'Abdun recorded the following rules for public behavior
in the Muslim-ruled city of Seville. (For Spanish Christian laws,
see Part II.)
Source: From *Islam: From the Prophet Muhammed to the Capture of
Constantinople, Volume II: Religion and Society*, edited and translated

---

164. Qadi = judge.

Women should be forbidden to do their washing in the gardens, for these are dens for fornication. . . .

Women should not sit by the river bank in the summer if men appear there.

No barber may remain alone with a woman in his booth. He should work in the open market in a place where he can be seen and observed. . . .

No one may be allowed to claim knowledge of a matter in which he is not competent, especially in the craft of medicine, for this can lead to loss of life. The error of a physician is hidden by the earth. Likewise a joiner. Each should keep to his own trade and not claim any skill of which he is not an acknowledged master—especially with women, since ignorance and error are greater among them. . . .

The lime stores and [other] empty places must be forbidden, because men go there to be alone with women.

Only good and trustworthy men, known as such among people, may be allowed to have dealings with women in buying and in selling. The tradespeople must watch over this carefully. The women who weave brocades must be banned from the market, for they are nothing but harlots.

On festival days men and women shall not walk on the same path when they go to cross the river. . . .

Muslim women shall be prevented from entering [the Christians'] abominable churches, for the priests are evil-doers, fornicators, and sodomites. Frankish[165] women must be forbidden to enter the church except on days of religious services or festivals, for it is their habit to eat and drink and fornicate with the priests, among whom there is not one who has not two or more women with whom he sleeps. This has become a custom among them, for they have permitted what is forbidden and forbidden what is permitted. The priests should be ordered to marry, as they do in the eastern lands. If they wanted to, they would.

No women may be allowed in the house of a priest, neither an old woman nor any other, if he refuses marriage. . . .

The contractor of the bathhouse should not sit there with the women, for this is an occasion for license and fornication. The contrac-

---

165. Frankish = European non-Muslim.

tor of hostelries for traders and travelers should not be a woman, for this is indeed fornication. The broker of houses shall not be a young man, but a chaste old man of known good character. . . .

Prostitutes must be forbidden to stand bareheaded outside the houses. Decent women must not bedeck themselves to resemble them. They must be stopped from coquetry and party making among themselves, even if they have been permitted to do this [by their husbands]. Dancing girls must be forbidden to bare their heads.

C. Heretic Women

79. Descriptions of Heretics:
Waldensian Women's Activities (13th c.)

The twelfth and thirteenth centuries saw an upsurge in "heresy"—
religious beliefs and practices which were contrary to the teachings
of the Catholic church. Several heretical sects, including the Wal-
densian movement, became widespread. As we see here, women
sometimes found a larger role in these heretical groups than they
were allowed in the orthodox church. The writers of the following
selections were all concerned with describing heresy in order to
combat it.

Source: *Heresy and Authority in Medieval Europe: Documents in Translation*, ed and tr. Edward Peters (Philadelphia: University of Pennsylvania Press, 1980); Margaret Deanesly, *The Lollard Bible and
Other Medieval Biblical Versions* (Cambridge University Press, 1920).
Reprinted by permission of the University of Pennsylvania Press
and Cambridge University Press.

Rainier Sacconi (1254)

[The Poor Men of Lyons] also say that a simple layman may consecrate the body of the Lord.[166] And I believe that they say that even a
woman may do this, since they have never denied this to me. . . .

The Poor of Lombardy agree with [the statements above] concerning
the swearing of oaths and temporal justice. Concerning the body of
the Lord, however, they believe even worse things than the other
group, saying that it may be consecrated by any person as long as he
is without mortal sin.

Etienne de Bourbon

A certain rich man of the city [of Lyons], called Waldo, . . . sold all
his goods, and despising the world, he gave all his money to the poor,
and usurped the apostolic office by preaching the gospel . . . in the
villages and open places, and by calling to him many men and women
to do the same thing, and teaching them the gospel by heart, . . .

---

166. Consecrate the body of the Lord = officiate at the sacrament of the Eucharist.

who indeed, being simple and illiterate men and women, wandered through villages and entered houses and preached in open places, and even in churches, and provoked others to the same course.

David of Augsburg (Bavaria, 1270)

They give all their seal to lead others astray with them: they teach even little girls the words of the Gospels and Epistles, so that they may be trained in error from their childhood. . . .

The Passau Anonymous (Germany, the 1260s)

The second cause [of heresy] is that men and women, greater and lesser, day and night, do not cease to learn and teach; the workman who labors all day teaches or learns at night. They pray little, on account of their studies. They teach and learn without books. . . .

. . . They also say that the clergy are full of . . . envy, because they alone wish to be teachers; Matthew [23:13]: "Woe unto you, you scribes who hold the key of knowledge, and close up the kingdom of heaven before all men." From which they claim that all men, and even women, are allowed to preach. . . . Against this, [the church cites] . . . Corinthians [I Cor. 14:34]: "Women should keep silence in Church, for it is not permitted for them to speak."

80. Inquisition Records of Jacques Fournier: Life of a Cathar Woman (1320)

One of the best-known heresies of the Middle Ages was that of the Albigensians or Cathars, in the south of France, who were bloodily persecuted by the church and by northern French nobles and eventually wiped out. The Cathars were dualists, believing in a strict dichotomy between good (which included all purely spiritual things) and evil (which included all material and earthly things). They rejected the incarnation of Christ, the sacrament of the Eucharist and the doctrine of purgatory, believing instead that individuals are reincarnated until they reach a perfect state and can become purely spiritual.

The inquisitor Jacques Fournier (later a pope) recorded in detail his interviews with suspected Cathar heretics, many of whom were condemned to death for their beliefs. The following is one of many personal accounts preserved in Fournier's text; it is the story of one woman of the lesser nobility and her dealings with the Cathar community.

Source: *Readings in Medieval History*, ed. Patrick J. Geary (Lewiston, NY: Broadview Press, 1989). Adapted.

Testimony of Béatrice de Planissoles

(August 7, 1320, in the chamber before the bishop and Gaillard de Pomiès)

Béatrice: Twenty-six years ago during the month of August (I do not recall the day), I was the wife of the late knight Bérenger de Roquefort, castelain of Montaillou. The late Raimond Roussel, of Prades, was the . . . steward of our household which we held at the castle of Montaillou. He often asked me to leave with him and to go to Lombardy with the good Christians[167] who are there, telling me that the Lord had said that man must quit his father, mother, wife, husband, son and daughter and follow him, and that he would give him the kingdom of heaven. When I asked him, "How could I quit my husband and my sons?" he replied that the Lord had ordered it and that it was better to leave a husband and sons whose eyes rot than to abandon him who lives for eternity and who gives the kingdom of heaven.

When I asked him "How is it possible that God created so many men and women if many of them are not saved?" he answered that only the good Christians will be saved and no others, neither religious nor priests, nor anyone except these good Christians. Because, he said, just as it is impossible for a camel to pass through the eye of a needle, it is impossible for those who are rich to be saved. This is why the kings and princes, prelates and religious, and all those who have wealth, cannot be saved, but only the good Christians. They remained in Lombardy, because they did not dare live here where the wolves and the dogs would persecute them. The wolves and the dogs were the bishops and the Dominicans, who persecute the good Christians and chase them from this country.

He said that he had listened to some of these good Christians. They were such that once one had heard them speak one could not do without them and if I heard them one time, I would be one of theirs for ever.

When I asked how we could flee together and go to the good Christians, because, when my husband found out, he would follow

---

167. Good Christians = Cathars.

us and kill us, Raimond answered that when my husband would take a long trip and be afar from our country, we could leave and go to the good Christians. I asked him how we would live when we were there. He answered that they would take care of us and give us enough with which to live. "But," I told him, "I am pregnant. What could I do with the child that I am carrying when I leave with you for the good Christians?" [He said:] "If you give birth to it in their presence, it will be an angel. With the help of God they will make a king and a holy thing of him because he will be born without sin, not having frequented the people of this world, and they would be able to educate him perfectly in their sect, since he would know no other."

He also told me that all spirits sinned at the beginning with the sin of pride, believing that they could know more and be worth more than God, and for that they fell to earth. These spirits later take on bodies, and the world will not end before all of them have been incarnated into the bodies of men and women. Thus it is that the soul of a new born child is as old as that of an old man.

They also said that the souls of men and women who were not good Christians, after leaving their bodies, enter the bodies of other men and women a total of nine times. If in these nine bodies they do not find the body of a good Christian, the soul is damned. If on the contrary, they find the body of a good Christian, the soul is saved.

I asked him how the spirit of a dead man or woman could enter the mouth of a pregnant woman and from there into the mouth of the fruit that she carries in her womb. He answered that the spirit could enter the fruit of the woman's womb by any part of her body. When I asked him why children do not speak from birth, since they have the old souls of other persons, he answered that God does not wish it. He also told me that the spirits of God which sinned lived wherever they could.

Thus he urged me to leave with him so that we could go together to the good Christians, mentioning various noble women who had gone there.

Alesta and Serena, women of Châteauverdun, painted themselves with colors which made them appear foreign so that they could not be recognized and went to Toulouse. When they arrived at an inn, the hostess wanted to know if they were heretics and gave them live chickens, telling them to prepare them because she had things to do in town, and left the house.

When she had returned she found the chickens still alive and asked them why they had not prepared them. They responded that if the hostess would kill them, they would prepare them but that they would not kill them. The hostess heard that and went to tell the inquisitors that two heretics were in her establishment. They were arrested and burned. When it was time to go to the stake, they asked for water to wash their faces, saying that they would not go to God painted thusly.

I told Raimond that they would have done better to abandon their heresy than to allow themselves to be burned, and he told me that the good Christians did not feel fire because fire with which they are burned cannot hurt them.

Raimond also told me that one of these two women, when she was leaving her house at Châteauverdun, had a child in a crib that she wanted to see before leaving. She kissed it, the child smiled, and as she was beginning to move away from the place where it lay, she returned toward it. The child began to laugh and this process began again so that she could not leave. Finally she ordered its nurse to take it, which she did. Thus she was able to leave.

And Raimond told me this to encourage me to do the same!

About 21 years ago, a year after the death of my husband, I wanted to go to the church of Montaillou to confess during Lent. When I was there, I went to Pierre Clergue, the rector, who was hearing confessions behind the altar of Saint Mary. As soon as I had knelt before him, he embraced me, saying that there was no woman in the world that he loved as much as me. In my surprise, I left without having confessed.

Later, around Easter, he visited me several times, and he asked me to give myself to him. I said one day that he so bothered me in my home that I would rather give myself to four men than to a single priest because I had heard it said that a woman who gave herself to a priest could not see the face of God. To which he answered that I was an ignorant fool because the sin is the same for a woman to know her husband or another man, and the same whether the man were husband or priest. It was even a greater sin with a husband he said, because the wife did not think that she had sinned with her husband but realized it with other men. The sin was therefore greater in the first case.

I asked him how he, who was a priest, could speak like that, since the church said that marriage had been instituted by God, and that it was the first sacrament instituted by God between Adam and Eve, as a result of which it was not a sin when spouses know each other. He answered, "If it was God who instituted marriage between Adam and Eve and if he created them, why didn't he protect them from sin?" I understood then that he was saying that God did not create Adam and Eve and that he had not instituted marriage between them. He added that the Church taught many things which were contrary to truths. Ecclesiastics said these things because without them it would inspire neither respect nor fear. Because, except for the Gospels and the Lord's Prayer, all of the other texts of Scripture were only "affitil-has," a word in the vernacular which designates what one adds on one's own to what one has heard.

I answered that in this case ecclesiastics were throwing the people into error.

(August 8, 1320, in the Chamber of the bishop before the bishop and Gaillard de Pomiès)

Béatrice: Speaking of marriage, he told me that many of the rules concerning it do not come from divine will who did not forbid people to marry their sisters or other persons related by blood, since at the beginning brothers knew their sister. But when several brothers had one or two pretty sisters, each wanted to have her or them. The result was many murders among them and this is why the Church had forbidden brothers to know their sisters or blood relatives carnally. But for God the sin is the same whether it is an outside woman, a sister, or another relative, because the sin is as great with one woman as with another, except that it is a greater sin between a husband and wife, because they do not confess it and they unite themselves without shame.

He added that the marriage was complete and consummated as soon as a person had promised his faith to the other. What is done at the church between spouses, such as the nuptial benediction, was only a secular ceremony which had no value and had been instituted by the Church only for secular splendor.

He further told me that a man and a woman could freely commit any sort of sin as long as they lived in this world and act entirely according to their pleasure. It was sufficient that at their death they be received into the sect or the faith of the good Christians to be saved and absolved of all the sins committed during this life. . . .

And with these opinions and many others he influenced me to the point that in the octave of Saints Peter and Paul I gave myself to him one night in my home. This was often repeated and he kept me like this for one and one half years, coming two or three times each week to spend the night in my house near the chateau of Montaillou.

I myself came two nights to his house so that he could unite himself with me. He even knew me carnally Christmas night and still this priest said the mass the next morning although there were other priests present.

And when, on this night of the Nativity, he wanted to have relations with me, I said to him, "How could you want to commit so great a sin on so holy a night?" He answered that the sin was the same to have intercourse with a woman on any other night or on Christmas night. Since this time and many others he said mass the morning after having known me the night before without having confessed since there was no other priest, and since I often asked him how he could celebrate the mass after having committed such a sin the night before, he answered that the only valid confession is one which one makes to God, who knows the sin before it is committed, and who alone can absolve it. But the confession that one makes to a priest who is ignorant of the sin until it is revealed to him and who does not have the power to absolve sin has no value and is only made for the ostentation and the splendor of this world. Because only God can absolve sins, man cannot. . . .

He told me all this and what will follow in my home, sometimes near a window that looked out on the road, while I was delousing his head, sometimes near the fire, sometimes when I was in bed. We avoided being overheard by others as much as possible when we broached this subject. I do not recall if Sibille my maid servant, the daughter of Arnaud Teisseyre of Montaillou, who became the concubine of Raimond Clergue, heard anything.

The priest told me that God only made the spirits and that which did not decay or corrode, because the works of God endure for ever. But all of the body which one sees and which one feels, that is to say the heaven and the earth and all that is in them, except only the spirits, were the work of the devil, who rules the world, who made them. . . .

These heretical conversations continued between us for around two years and this priest taught me all of this.

Inquisitor: Did you believe and do you still believe these heresies that this rector of the church of Montaillou, Pierre Clergue, told you and in which he instructed you?

Béatrice: The last year, when I left the region of Alion from Easter until the following August, I completely and fully believed these errors to the point that I would not have hesitated to undergo any suffering to defend them. I believed that they were truth taught by the priest whom, because he was a priest, I believed. . . . But when I was at Crampagna with my second husband and I heard the preaching of the Dominicans and Franciscans and I visited with faithful Christians, I abandoned these errors and heresies and I confessed at the penitential court of a Franciscan of the convent of Limoux in the Church of Notre Dame de Marseille where I had gone to see my sister Gentille, who lived at Limoux and who was the wife of the late Paga de Post. I made this confession fifteen years ago and I remained around five years without confessing heretical opinions that I had heard and believed although I confessed my other sins during these five years.

At the time when I believed these heresies, I did not see (nor did I see before or after) any heretics that I knew to be heretics, although I believed that they were good men because they suffered martyrdom for God and this priest had taught me that it was only in their sect that one could be saved.

I greatly regret having ever heard these heretical opinions and even more for having believed these heresies, and I am ready to accept the penance that my lord the bishop may wish to impose on me for them.

(August 22, in the episcopal chamber, before the bishop and Brother Gaillard de Pomiès)

. . . I had said to [Pierre Clergue] at the beginning of our relations, "What will I do if I become pregnant by you? I will be dishonored and lost." He answered that he had a good herb which, if a man wears it when he is with a woman, he cannot engender nor can a woman conceive. I said to him, "What is this herb? Is it not the one that the cheese makers put on their pots of milk into which they have put rennet and which prevents the milk from curdling as long as it is on the pot?" He told me not to bother trying to know what kind of herb it was but that it was a herb that had this power and that he had some.

Since that time when he wanted to take me, he wore something rolled up and tied in a piece of linen the thickness and length of an ounce or of the first digit of my little finger, with a long thread which he passed around my neck. And this thing which he said was this herb hung down between my breasts to the base of my stomach. He always placed it thus when he wanted to know me and it remained on my neck until he rose. And if sometimes during the same night this priest wanted to know me two or more times, he asked me, before we coupled, where this herb was. I would take it by finding it by the thread which I had at my neck and place it in his hand. He took it and placed it before the base of my stomach with the thread passing between my breasts. This is how he coupled with me and no other way. I asked him one day to leave this herb with me. He refused because he said that then I could give myself to another man without becoming pregnant. He would not give it to me so that I would refrain from so doing out of fear of the consequences. He did this in particular thinking of his cousin Raimond Clergue, alias Pathau, who had first kept me before this priest, his fraternal cousin, had me, because they were jealous of each other.

He again told me that he did not want me to have a child from him while my father, Philippe de Planissoles was alive, because the latter would have been too ashamed, but that after his death his wanted me to have his child.

Inquisitor's Judgment on Béatrice

After this [testimony], the same year [1320], on the 25th of the month of August, the above named Béatrice swore juridically before the bishop of Pamiers before my lord bishop, assisted by Brother Gaillard of Pomiès, substitute of my lord the inquisitor of Carcassonne, in presence of the religious person Brother Guillaume Séguier, prior of the convent of Preachers (Dominicans) of Pamiers, the discreet person master Bernard Gaubert, jurist, and me, the undersigned notary. Because she was very ill and in bed and her death was expected, my lord bishop told her that if she had hidden anything concerning heresy in the confession that she had made above about herself or others, or if she had accused a person against truth and justice, she should admit it and reveal it, or she should exonerate the persons she had unjustly accused. And my lord the bishop commanded this at the peril of her soul. . . .

And my lords the bishop and the inquisitor assigned to the above named Béatrice a day to hear the definitive sentence on the preceding, that is, the following Sunday, March 8, before the third hour, in the house of the Preachers (Dominicans) of Pamiers. . . .

And the Sunday assigned to the above named Béatrice, she appeared in the cemetery of Saint-Jean-Martyr of Pamiers and was given the sentence by my lords the bishop and the inquisitor which reads as follows, "Know all ye, etc." See this sentence in the book of sentences of the Inquisition.[168]

And I, Rainaud Jabbaud, cleric of Toulouse, sworn in the matter of the Inquisition, on the order of my lord the bishop, have faithfully corrected this confession against the original.

---

168. The death sentence for heresy is commuted to wearing a double cross, the sign of a convicted heretic.

Part VII

Manual for a Wife

81. The Householder of Paris: Manual for His Wife (c. 1392)

The anonymous author of this work is known as the *Ménagier* ("householder" or "goodman") of Paris. The book is addressed to his young wife, and is a guide for her good behavior and housekeeping; much of the material in it which is not reproduced here consists of moral advice and illustrative stories. It is one of the most famous and widely used sources for the lives of medieval women. Like any prescriptive work, it presents an idealized picture—things the way they *should* be. But it was written with practical problems in mind and was intended to be of real use in guiding a woman in her day-to-day life. The author was a wealthy, middle-aged member of urban society; his wife came from the lower nobility. The work also tells us something about the lives of women other than the young wife herself; the day-to-day activities of Dame Agnes the Beguine (who served as their housekeeper) and various female employees are also described. We can only speculate on the author's sources of information, especially for the practical aspects of housekeeping, which would hardly have been within his own realm of experience; perhaps we hear Dame Agnes' voice in these parts.

Source: Adapted from the translation by Eileen Power, *The Goodman of Paris* (London: George Routledge & Sons, 1928); Old French text in *Le Ménagier de Paris*, eds. Georgine E. Brereton and Janet M. Ferrier (Oxford: The Clarendon Press, 1981).

Prologue

Dear Sister,

At the age of fifteen years, in the week that you and I were wed, you asked me to be indulgent to your youth and to your small and ignorant service, until you had seen and learned more; to this end you promised that you would give me all heed and would be very careful and diligent to keep my love; you spoke full wisely, and, I am sure, with other wisdom than your own, beseeching me humbly in our bed, I remember, for the love of God, not to correct you harshly before strangers or before our own people, but rather each night, or from day to day, in our chamber, to remind you of unseemly or foolish things done in the day or days past, and chastise you, if it pleased me, and then you would strive to amend yourself according to my teaching and correction, and to serve my will in all things, as you said. And your words were pleasing to me, and won my praise and thanks, and I have often remembered them since. And know, dear sister, that all that I know you have done since we were wed until now and all that you shall do hereafter with good intent, was and is to my liking, pleases me, and has well pleased me, and will please me. For your youth excuses your unwisdom and will still excuse you in all things as long as all you do is with good intent and not displeasing to me. And know that I am pleased rather than displeased that you tend rose-trees, and care for violets, and make chaplets, and dance, and sing: nor would I have you cease to do so among our friends and equals, and it is good and seemly so to pass the time of our youth, so long as you neither seek nor try to go to the feasts and dances of lords of too high rank, for that does not become you, nor is it compatible with your rank or mine.

And as for the greater service that you say you would willingly do for me, if you were able and I taught it to you, know, dear sister, that I am well content that you should do me such service as your good neighbors of similar rank do for their husbands, and as your kinswomen do unto their husbands. Ask their advice in private, and then follow it either more or less as you please. For I am not so overwhelming in my attitude to you and your good intent that I am not satisfied with what you do for me therein, nor with all other services, provided there be no disorder or scorn or disdain, and that you are careful. For although I know well that you are of gentler birth than I, nevertheless that would not protect you, for, by God, the women of your lineage are good enough to correct you harshly themselves, if I did not, if they were to learn of your error from me or from another source; but I have no worry for you; I have confidence in your good intent. Yet although, as I have said, you owe me only the lesser service, I want you to know how to give good will and service and honor in greater measure and abundance than is fit for me, either so that you may serve another husband, if you have one, after me, or to be able to teach greater wisdom to your daughters, friends or others, if you choose and have such a need. For the more you know the greater your honor and the greater the praise belonging to your parents and to me and to others around you, by whom you have been nurtured. And for your honor and love, and not for my service (for I deserve only the common service, or less), since I had pity and loving compassion on you who for so long have had neither father not mother, nor any of your kinswomen near you to whom you might turn for counsel in your private needs, but only myself, for whom you were brought from your kin and the country of your birth—for these reasons I have often wondered how I might find a simple general introduction to teach you the things which you might already have known how to introduce into your work and care, had you not had these difficulties. And lastly, it seems to me that if your love is as it has appeared in your good words, it can be accomplished in this way, namely in a general instruction that I will write for you and present to you, in three sections containing nineteen principal articles.

The first section of the three is necessary to gain the love of God and the salvation of your soul, and also to win the love of your husband and to give you in this world that peace which should be in marriage. And because these two things, namely the salvation of your soul and the comfort of your husband, are the two things most necessary, therefore are they here placed first. And this first section contains nine articles.

The first article speaks of worshipping and thanking our Savior and his Blessed Mother at your waking and your rising, and of apparelling yourself suitably. The second article speaks of fit companions, and of going to church, and of choosing your place, of hearing mass and of making confession. The third article is that you should love God and his blessed Mother and serve them continually and set and keep yourself in their grace.

The fourth article is that you should dwell in continence and chastity, after the example of Susanna, of Lucretia, and others. The fifth article is that you should love your husband (whether myself or another) after the example of Sarah, Rebecca and Rachel. The sixth article is that you should be humble and obedient to him after the example of Griselda [and others]. . . . The seventh that you be careful and heedful of his person. The eighth that you be silent in hiding his secrets. . . . The ninth and last article shows that if your husband should try to act foolishly or does act so, you must wisely and humbly draw him away from such action. . . .

The second section is necessary to increase the profit of the household, gain friends and save one's possessions; to succor and aid oneself against the ill fortunes of age to come, and it contains six articles.

The first article is that you take care of your household with diligence and perseverance and respect for work; take pains to find pleasure therein and I will do likewise on my part. . . . The second article is that at the least you take pleasure and have some little skill in the care and cultivation of a garden, grafting in due season and keeping roses in winter. The third article is that you know how to choose menservants, doorkeepers, handymen or other strong folk to perform the heavy work that from hour to hour must be done, and likewise laborers etc. And also tailors, shoemakers, bakers, pastry-makers, etc. And in particular how to set the household menservants and chambermaids to work, to sift and winnow grain, clean dresses, air and dry, and how to order your folk to take thought for the sheep and horses and keep and amend wines. The fourth article is that you, as sovereign mistress of your house, know how to order dinners, suppers, dishes and courses, and be wise in that which concerns the butcher and the poulterer, and have knowledge of spices. The fifth article is that you know how to order, ordain, devise and have made all manner of pottages,[169] civeys, sauces and all other meats, and the same for sick folk.

The third section tells of games and amusements that are pleasant enough to keep you in countenance and give you something to talk about in company, and contains three articles. The first article is concerned with amusing questions, which are set out and answered in strange fashion by the chance of dice and by rooks and kings. The second article is how to feed and fly the falcon. The third article tells of certain other riddles concerning counting and numbering, which are subtle to find out and guess.

Section 1, Article 7

The seventh article of the first section shows how you should be careful and thoughtful of your husband's person. So, fair sister, if you have another husband after me, know that you should think much of his person, for after a woman has lost her first husband and marriage, she commonly finds it hard to find a second to her liking, according to her rank, and she remains lonely and disconsolate for a long time, and the more so if she loses the second. So love your husband's person carefully, and I pray you keep him in clean linen, for that is your business, and because the trouble and care of outside affairs lies with men, so must husbands take heed, and go and come, and journey hither and thither, in rain and wind, in snow and hail, now drenched, now dry, now sweating, now shivering, ill-fed, ill-lodged, ill-warmed and ill-bedded. And nothing harms him, because he is upheld by the hope which he has of the care which his wife will take of him on his return, and of the ease, the joys and the pleasures which she will do

---

169. Pottage = soup or stew.

to him, or cause to be done to him in her presence; to be unshod before a good fire, to have his feet washed and fresh shoes and hose, to be given good food and drink, to be well served and well looked after, well bedded in white sheets and nightcaps, well covered with good furs, and assuaged with other joys and amusements, intimacies, loves and secrets whereof I am silent. And the next day fresh shirts and garments.

Certainly, fair sister, such services make a man love and desire to return to his home and to see his good wife, and to be distant with others. So I advise you to make such cheer to your husband at all his comings and stayings, and to persevere in this; and also be peaceable with him, and remember the rustic proverb, which says there are three things which drive the goodman from home: a leaking roof, a smoky chimney and a scolding woman. And therefore, dear sister, I beseech you that, to keep yourself in the love and good favor of your husband, you be unto him gentle, and amiable, and good-tempered . . . and beware of roofless house and of smoky fire, and scold him not, but be unto him gentle and amiable and peaceable. Have a care that in winter he has a good fire and smokeless and let him rest well and be well covered between your breasts, and thus bewitch him. And in summer take heed that there be no fleas in your chamber, nor in your bed, the which you may do in six ways, I have heard. For I have heard from several that if the room is strewn with alder leaves, the fleas will be caught on them. And I have heard that if you have at night one or two bread trenchers slimed with glue or turpentine and set about the room, with a lighted candle in the midst of each trencher, they will come and be stuck to them. Another way, which I have tried and which works, is to take a rough cloth and spread it about your room and over your bed, and all the fleas that hop onto it will be caught, so that you may carry them away with the cloth wherever you want. And also sheepskins. And I have seen blankets set on the straw [on the floor] and on the bed, and when the black fleas hopped onto them, they were more easily found on the white, and killed. But the best way is to guard oneself against those inside the coverlets and the furs, and the material of the dresses with which one is covered. For that I have tried this: when the coverlets, furs or dresses, in which there are fleas, are folded and shut tightly up, for instance in a chest tightly bound with straps, or in a bag well tied up and pressed, or otherwise put and pressed so the the aforesaid fleas are without light and air and are kept imprisoned, then they will perish forthwith and die. And I have sometimes seen in diverse chambers, that when one had gone to bed they were so full of mosquitoes, which at the smoke of the breath came to sit on the faces of those that slept, and stung them so hard, that they had to get up and light a fire of hay, in order to make a smoke so that they had to fly away or die. And this may be done by day if they are suspected. And likewise he who has a mosquito net may protect himself with that.

And if you have a chamber or a passage where there are a great many flies, take little sprigs of fern and tie them to threads like tassels, and hang them up, and all the flies will settle on them at eventide; then take the tassels down and throw them out. . . . [Several more remedies for flies follow.]

And thus shall you preserve and keep your husband from all discomforts and give him all the comforts you can bethink of, and serve him and have him served in your house, and you shall rely on him for outside things, for if he is good he will take even more pains and labor in them than you would wish, and by doing what I have said you will cause him to miss you all the time and have his heart with you and your loving service, and he will shun all other houses, all other women, all other services and households. . . .

But there are certain old hags, who are sly and play the wise woman and pretend great love by way of showing their heart's great service, and nothing else; and be sure, fair sister, that the husbands are fools if they do not notice it. And when they do notice it, and the husband and wife grow silent, and pretend with each other, it is an ill beginning and will lead to a worse end. And there are some women who serve their husbands very well in the beginning, and then they find that their husbands are then so loving to them and so good-tempered, that they think those husbands will scarcely dare to be angry with them, if they do less, so they slacken and little by little they try to show less respect and service and obedience, but—what is more—they take upon themselves authority, command and lordship, first in a small thing, then in a larger, and a little more every day. Thus they attempt and advance and rise, they think, and they think that their husbands, who say nothing about this because they are so good-tempered or perhaps because they are setting a trap, do not notice it, because they permit it thus. And certainly, it is an ill thought and deed, for when the husbands see that they cease their service, and climb to domination, and that they do it too much, and that by enduring ill, good may come, then those women are all at once, by their husband's rightful will, cast down even as Lucifer was. . . . Wherefore you should be obedient in the beginning and ever persevere therein, according to this example.

Section 2, Article 3

Which tells how to choose serving men, servants and chamber-maids, etc.

Concerning which matter, dear sister, if perchance you should desire to become a good housewife, or to help thereto some lady among your friends, know that serving folk be of three kinds. There are some who are hired as workmen for a fixed time, to perform some short piece of work, as porters who carry burdens on their backs, wheelbarrow men, packers and the like; or for one day or two, a week or a short season, to perform some necessary, or difficult, or laborious work, as reapers, mowers, threshers, vintagers, basket bearers, wine pressers, coopers and the like. Others are hired for a time and for a special craft, as dressmakers, furriers, bakers, butchers, shoemakers and the like, who work by the piece upon a particular task. And others are taken to be domestic servants, serving by the year and dwelling in the house. And of all these there is none who does not full readily seek work and a master.

As for the first, they are necessary for the unloading and carrying of burdens and the doing of heavy work; and these are commonly tiresome, rough and prone to answer back, arrogant, haughty (except on pay day), and ready to break into insults and reproaches if you do not pay them what they ask when the work is done. So I pray you, dear sister, that when you need such things done, you bid master Jehan the Dispenser[170] or other of your folk to seek out, choose and take, or cause to be sought out, chosen and taken, the peaceable ones; and always bargain with them before they set hand to the work, that there may be no dispute afterwards. Still, most often they wish not to bargain, but desire to fall upon the task without bargain made, and they say nicely: "Milord, it is nothing—there is no need; you will pay me well, and I shall be content with what you think fit." And if Master Jehan takes them thus, when the work is finished they will say, "Sir, there was more to do than I thought; there was this and that to do, and here and there to go," and they will not take what is given and will break out into shouting and foul words. So bid Master Jehan not to set them to work, not allow them to be set to work, without first making terms with them, for those that desire to earn are your subjects before the work is begun, and for the need that they have to earn they

---

170. Dispenser = household official similar to a butler.

fear lest another should take it before them and fear to lose the work and the wage thereof to another. Wherefore they bear themselves more reasonably. And if perchance Master Jehan were to believe in them and put too great faith in their fair words, and it happened therefore that he allowed them to begin work without bargaining, they know well that after they have set their hand to it, none other for shame will meddle with it, and so you will be in their power afterwards and they will ask more; and if then they are not paid according to their will, they will cry and shout foul and outrageous blame upon you; and they have no shame and spread abroad evil report concerning you, which is worst of all. Wherefore it is better to bargain with them plainly and openly before the work, to avoid all argument. And certainly, this I do beg of you, that if need be you cause enquiry to be made, how those whom you would set to work have borne themselves toward others, and also that you have nothing to do with folk who answer back and are arrogant, proud and scornful, or give foul answers, however great profit or advantage it seems to be and however cheaply they are willing to come; but graciously and quietly send them away from you and from your work, for if once they begin thereon, you shall not escape without slander and wrangling. Wherefore cause your people to engage servants and workmen who are peaceful and good-humored, and pay them more, for peace and rest lie entirely in having worthy servants to deal with; for which reason there is a saying: "He that hath to do with good servants, he hath peace," and likewise one might well say that he that has to deal with grumblers stores up sorrow for himself.

And concerning others, such as vintagers, threshers, laborers and the like, or such as tailors, clothmakers, shoemakers, bakers, farriers, tallow-candlemakers, spicers, blacksmiths, wheelwrights, and others like unto them, dear sister, I counsel and pray you ever to bear in mind that you bid your people to have quiet folk to work for them and to make bargain beforehand and to reckon and make payment often, without long credit by tally or on paper. Nevertheless, it is better to keep tally and paper than to keep all things in the memory, for creditors think ever that the sum is more and debtors that it is less, and thereby is born wrangling, hatred and foul reproach; and cause your good creditors to be paid readily and often that which is owing to them and bear yourself lovingly towards them, that they change not towards you; for it is not always possible to find others that are peaceable folk.

And as to chambermaids and house servants, who are called domestics, know, dear sister, that in order that they may obey you better and fear the more to anger you, I leave you the rule and authority to have them chosen by Dame Agnes the Beguine, or whichever other of your women you please, to receive them into our service, to hire them at your pleasure, to pay and keep them in our service as you please, and to dismiss them when you will. Nevertheless you should speak privately with me about it and act according to my advice, because you are too young and might be deceived by your own people. And know that of those chambermaids who are unemployed, there are many who offer themselves and clamor and seek urgently for masters and mistresses; and of these take none until you first know where their last place was, and send some of your people to get their character, that is whether they chattered or drank too much, how long they were in the place, what work they have been wont to do and know how to do, whether they have homes or friends in the town, from what manner of folk and what part of the country they come, how long they were there and why they left; and by their work in the past you shall find out what hope or expectation you may have of their work in the future. And know that often such women from distant parts of the country have been blamed for some vice in their own district and this is what brings them into service at a distance. For if they were without fault they would be mistresses and not servants; and of men I say the same. And if you find from the report of her master and mistress that a girl is what you need, find out from her and cause Master Jehan to register in his account book in her presence, on that same day whereon you engage her, her name and the names of her father and mother and some of her kinfolk, and the place where they live and her birthplace and references. For servants will fear the more to do wrong if they know that you are recording these things, and that if they leave you without permissions, or are guilty of any offense, you will write and complain to the justice of their country and to their friends. And notwithstanding bear in mind the saying of the philosopher called Bertram the Old, who says that if you engage a maid or man of high and proud answers, you shall know that when she leaves she will miscall you if she can; and if, on the contrary, she is flattering and full of blandishments, trust her not, for she seeks to trick you in some other way; but if she blushes and is silent and ashamed when you correct her, love her as your daughter.

Next, dear sister, know that after your husband you should be mistress of the house, the giver of orders, visitor, ruler and sovereign administrator, and it is for you to keep your maidservants in subjection and obedience to you, teaching, correcting and chastising them; wherefore forbid them all excess and gluttony of life.

Also forbid them to quarrel with each other or with your neighbors; forbid them to speak ill of others, save only to you and in secret, and only in so far as the misdeed concerns your profit, and to save harm from befalling you and not otherwise; forbid them to lie, to play at forbidden games, to swear foully and to utter words that smell of villainy, unseemly words and ribald, as do certain evil or ill-bred persons, who curse about "bloody bad fevers, the bloody bad week, the bloody bad day." . . . Forbid revenge to them and teach them in all patience by the example of Melibeus, of whom I have told you. And as for you yourself, dear sister, be such in all that you do, that in you they may find an example of all goodness.

Now we must speak of setting your folk and your servants to work at times suitable for work and of giving them rest likewise at due times. Concerning the which matter, dear sister, know that you and Dame Agnes the Beguine (who is with you to teach you wise and ripe behavior and to serve and train you, and to whom in particular I give the charge of this matter) must devise and order and lay one duty upon one and another upon the other, according to the work which has to be done and the fitness of your folk to one sort of labour or another. And if you bid them to do something now and these your servants answer, "There is plenty of time," "It shall be done soon," or "It shall be done early tomorrow morning," consider it to be forgotten; all must be done again; it goes for nothing. And likewise concerning that which you order all in general to do, know that each waits for the other to do it, and it is as before.

So be warned, and bid Dame Agnes the Beguine to see that what you desire to be done at once is begun before her eyes; at first, let her bid the chambermaids very early to sweep out and clean the entrances to your house, that is the hall and other places whereby people enter and stay to speak in the house, and let them dust and shake out the covers and cushions which are on the benches; and afterwards let the other rooms be likewise cleaned and tidied for the day, and so daily, as is fitting for our rank.

And through the same Dame Agnes you should chiefly and carefully and diligently take thought for your chamber animals, such as little dogs and birds; and you and the Beguine should also take thought for other domestic birds, for they cannot speak, and therefore you must speak and think for them, if you have any.

And also I bid Dame Agnes the Beguine, when you are in the country, to order those whose business it is to take thought for the other beasts; such as Robin the shepherd, to look to his sheep, ewes and lambs, and Josson the oxherd to his oxen and bulls, Arnould the cowherd and Jehanneton the dairymaid to take thought for the cows, the heifers and the calves, the sows, pigs and piglets, Eudeline the farmer's wife to look to the geese, goslings, cocks, hens, chickens, doves and pigeons, and the carter or the farmer to take thought for our horses, mares and the like. And the said Beguine and you yourself likewise, ought to show your folk that you know about it all and care about it, for so will they be the more diligent. And, if you remember, cause your people to remember to feed these beasts and birds, and Dame Agnes ought to lay this work upon those men and women who are best suited to it. And hereupon, let it be observed that it behooves you to cause Dame Agnes to inform you of the number of your sheep, ewes and lambs, and to have them constantly visited and to make enquiry concerning their increase and decrease and how or by whom they are cared for, and she should report it to you, and between the two of you, you should cause it to be written down. . . .

Now let me return to the subject of how you and the Beguine shall set your folk to work at fit times and shall cause your women to air and go over your sheets, coverlets, dresses and furs, fur coverlets and other things of the sort. Concerning which, know and tell your women that in order to preserve your fur coverlets and your stuffs, it is good to air them often, in order to prevent the damage which moths may do to them; and because such vermin gather when the cold weather of autumn and winter grows milder and are born in the summer, at such time it behooves you to set out furs and stuffs in the sun in fair and dry weather; and if there comes a dark damp mist that clings to your dresses, and you fold them in such a condition, that mist folded and wrapped up in your dresses will shelter and breed worse vermin than before. Wherefore choose a fine dry day, as soon as you see heavier weather coming, before it reaches you, have your dresses hung up under cover and shaken to get rid of most of the dust, then cleaned by beating them with rods. And the Beguine knows well that if there be any spot of oil or other grease, this is the remedy: Take wine and heat it until it is warm, and set the stain to soak in it for two days, and then wring out the stuff in which the stain is, without squeezing it too hard, and if the stain is not gone, let Dame Agnes the Beguine have more wine prepared and mix oxgall with it, and do as before. . . . [Several more stain removers are described, and other household hints given.]

And after this and with this, fair sister, bid Master Jehan the Dispenser to order Richart of the kitchen to air, wash and clean and do all things that pertain to the kitchen, and see that Dame Alice the Beguine for the women and Master Jehan the Dispenser for the men

set your folk to work on all sides: the one upstairs, the other down-
stairs, the one in the fields, the other in the town, the one in the
chamber, the other in the solar,[171] or the kitchen, and send one here,
the other there, each according to his place and his skill, so that these
servants all earn their wages, men and women according to what they
know and have to do; and if they do so, they will do well, for laziness
and idleness are the root of all evil.

Nevertheless, fair sister, at suitable times have them all seated at
table, and give them to eat one kind of meat only, but plenty of it,
and not several varieties, not dainties and delicacies; and order them
one drink, nourishing but not intoxicating, whether it is wine or
something else, but not several kinds. And bid them to eat well and
drink well and deeply, for it is reasonable that they should eat at a
stretch, without sitting too long over their food and without lingering
over their meat, or staying with their elbows on the table. And as soon
as they begin to tell tales and to argue and to lean upon their elbows,
order the Beguine to make them rise and remove their table, for the
common folk have a saying, "When a servant holds forth at table and
a horse grazes in the ditch, it is time to take them away, for they have
had their fill." Forbid them to get drunk, and never allow a drunken
person to serve you nor approach you, for it is perilous; and after they
have taken their midday meal, when it is due time, cause your folk to
set them to work again. And after their afternoon's work, upon feast
days, let them have another meal, and after that, in the evening, let
them be fed abundantly and well as before, and if the weather is cold
let them warm themselves and take their ease.

After this, let your house be closed and shut up by Master Jehan
the Dispenser or by the Beguine, and let one of them keep the keys,
so that none may go in or out without leave. And every evening before
you go to bed, cause Dame Agnes the Beguine or Master Jehan the
Dispenser to go round with a lighted candle, to inspect your wines,
verjuice[172] and vinegar, to see that none has been taken away, and bid
your farmer to find out from his men whether your beasts have fodder
for the night. And when you have made sure from Dame Agnes or
Master Jehan that the fires on your hearths are all covered, give your
folk time and space for the repose of their limbs. And make certain
before bedtime that each of them has, at a distance from his bed, a
candlestick with a large foot in which to put his candle, and that they
have been wisely taught how to extinguish it with mouth or hand

---

171. Solar = "sun room," used here as a sitting room.
172. Verjuice = bitter juice from green or unripe fruit.

before getting into bed, and by no means with their shirts. And you should also have them admonished and told, each separately, what he must begin to do on the morrow, and how each must rise up on the morrow and set to work on his own task, and let each be informed thereon. And still there are two things I would say to you: the one is that if you have girls or chambermaids of fifteen to twenty years, since they are foolish at that age and have seen nothing of the world, have them sleep near you, in a closet or chamber, where there is no dormer window or low window looking onto the road, and let them go to bed and arise at your own time, and you yourself (who, if God please, will be wise by this time) should be near to guard them. The other thing is that if one of your servants falls ill, lay all your concerns aside, and take care of him yourself full lovingly and kindly, and visit him and think of him or her very carefully, seeking to bring about his cure. And thus you will have fulfilled this article. . . .

Section 2, Article 4

Which teaches you how, as sovereign mistress of your household, you must know how to order and devise dinners and suppers with Master Jehan, and how to devise dishes and courses.

. . . without spending or paying out your money every day you may send Master Jehan to the butcher and order meat by tally.

Now I will tell and speak of certain general terms that are used in the feat of cookery, and afterwards show how you may know and choose the foods with which the cook works, as follows:

First, in all sausages and thick pottages, in which there are pounded spices and bread, you should first pound the spices and take them out of the mortar, because the bread which you pound afterwards absorbs that which remains from the spices; thus nothing is lost that would be lost it were done the other way round.

Item: spices and bindings put into pottages ought not to be strained; but do so for sauces, that the sauces may be clearer and likewise the more pleasant.

Item: know that pea or bean pottages or others burn easily, if the burning brands touch the bottom of the pot when it is on the fire.

Item: before your pottage burns and in order that it not burn, stir it often in the bottom of the pot, and turn your spoon in the bottom so that the pottage may not take hold there. And note as soon as you see that your pottage is burning, do not move it, but straightaway take it off the fire and put it in another pot.

Item: note that commonly all pottages on the fire boil over, and fall onto the said fire, until salt and grease are put into the pot, and afterwards they do not.

Item: note that the best caudle[173] there is, is beef's cheek washed twice in water, then boiled and well skimmed. . . .

Item: fresh shad comes into season in March.

Item: carp should be very well cooked, or otherwise it is dangerous to eat.

Item: plaice should be soft to the touch and dab the contrary. . . . [More tips for selecting food follow.]

I. Dinner for a Meat Day
Served in Thirty-one Dishes and Six Courses

First course. [Wine of] Grenache and roasts, veal, pasties, pimpernel pasties, black-puddings and sausages.

Second course. Hares in civey[174] and cutlets, strained peas, salt meat and great joints, a soringue of eels and other fish.

Third course. Roast coneys,[175] partridges, capons etc., luce, bar, carp and a quartered pottage.

Fourth course. River fish à la dodine, savory rice, a [dish] with hot sauce and eels reversed.

Fifth course. Lark pasties, rissoles, larded milk, sugared flawns.[176]

Sixth course. Pears and comfits, medlars[177] and peeled nuts. Hippocras and wafers.

. . .

[More menus of varying complexity follow, all with fewer dishes than the first.]

---

173. Caudle = a type of warm drink for an invalid.
174. Civey = a sauce of wine, vinegar, herbs and spices.
175. Coneys = rabbits.
176. Flawns = flat cakes or pies.
177. Medlars = apple-like fruit of the medlar tree, eaten after it begins to decay.

Further Reading

General Works on Medieval Women

Primary Sources

Bell, Susan G., ed. *Women from the Greeks to the French Revolution*. Belmont, CA, 1973.

Moriarty, Catherine, ed. *The Voice of the Middle Ages In Personal Letters, 1100–1500*. Oxford, 1989.

O'Faolain, Julia and Lauro Martines, eds. *Not in God's Image: Women in History from the Greeks to the Victorians*. New York, 1973.

Petroff, Elizabeth Alvilda, ed. *Medieval Women's Visionary Literature*. Oxford, 1986.

Thiébaux, Marcelle, ed. and tr. *The Writings of Medieval Women*. New York, 1987.

Wilson, Katharina M., ed. *Medieval Women Writers*. Athens, GA, 1984.

Secondary Works

Anderson, Bonnie S. and Judith P. Zinser. *A History of their Own: Women in Europe from Prehistory to the Present*. New York, 1989. 2 vols.

Baker, Derek, ed. *Medieval Women. Studies in Church History, Subsidia, I*. Oxford, 1978.

Bechtold, Joan, Julia Bolton Holloway and Constance S. Wright, eds. *Equally in God's Image: Women in the Middle Ages*. New York, 1990.

Bennett, Judith M., Elizabeth A. Clark, Jean F. O'Barr, B. Anne Vilen and Sarah Westphal-Wihl, eds. *Sisters and Workers in the Middle Ages*. Chicago, 1990.

Bridenthal, Renate and Claudia Koonz. *Becoming Visible: Women in European History*. Boston, 1977.

Bullough, Vern L., Brenda Shelton and Sarah Slavin. *The Subordinated Sex: A History of Attitudes Toward Women*. Rev. edn. Athens, GA, 1988.

Dillard, Heath. *Daughters of the Reconquest: Women in Castilian Town Society, 1100–1300*. Cambridge, 1984.

Dronke, Peter. *Women Writers of the Middle Ages: A Critical Study of Texts from Perpetua († 203) to Marguerite Porete († 1310)*. Cambridge, 1984.

Echols, Anne and Marty Williams, eds. *Women in Medieval Times: An Annotated Index of Medieval Women*. New York and Princeton, 1991.

Ennen, Edith. *The Medieval Woman.* Tr. Edmund Jephcott. Oxford, 1990.

Erler, Mary and Maryane Kowaleski, eds. *Women and Power in the Middle Ages.* Athens, GA, 1988.

Fell, Christine, with Cecily Clark and Elizabeth Williams. *Women in Anglo-Saxon England and the Impact of 1066.* Oxford, 1986.

Gies, Frances and Joseph. *Women in the Middle Ages.* New York, 1978.

Jesch, Judith. *Women in the Viking Age.* Woodbridge, Suffolk, 1991.

Kirshner, Julius and Suzanne F. Wemple, eds. *Women of the Medieval World.* Oxford, 1985.

Labalme, Patricia H., ed. *Beyond Their Sex: Learned Women of the European Past.* New York, 1984.

Labarge, Margaret Wade. *A Small Sound of the Trumpet: Women in Medieval Life.* Boston, 1986.

Levin, Carole and Jeanie Watson, eds. *Ambiguous Realities: Women in the Middle Ages and Renaissance.* Detroit, 1987.

Lucas, Angela. *Women in the Middle Ages: Religion, Marriage and Letters.* New York, 1983.

Morewedge, Rosemarie Thee, ed. *The Role of Women in the Middle Ages.* Albany, 1975.

Power, Eileen. *Medieval People.* London, 1924.

Power, Eileen. *Medieval Women.* Ed. M. M. Postan. Cambridge, 1975.

Rose, Mary Beth, ed. *Women in the Middle Ages and the Renaissance.* Syracuse, NY, 1986.

Rosenthal, Joel T., ed. *Medieval Women and the Sources of Medieval History.* Athens, GA, 1990.

Shahar, Shulamith. *The Fourth Estate: A History of Women in the Middle Ages.* New York, 1983.

Stenton, Doris Mary. *The English Woman in History.* London, 1957.

Stuard, Susan Mosher. *Women in Medieval History and Historiography.* Philadelphia, 1987.

Stuard, Susan Mosher. *Women in Medieval Society.* Philadelphia, 1976.

Uitz, Erica. *The Legend of Good Women: Medieval Women in Towns and Cities.* Tr. Sheila Marnie. Mt. Kisco, NY, 1990.

Wemple, Suzanne Fonay. *Women in Frankish Society: Marriage and the Cloister, 500 to 900.* Philadelphia, 1985.

Williams, Marty and Anne Echols. *Between Pit and Pedestal: Women in the Middle Ages.* Princeton, 1992.

I. The Heritage of Ideas

Primary Sources

Ambrose, Bishop of Milan. *On Virginity*. Tr. Daniel Callam. Toronto, 1980.

Augustine of Hippo. *St. Augustin: Anti-Pelagian Writings*. Tr. Peter Holmes, Robert Ernest Wallace and Benjamin B. Warfield. *Select Library of Nicene and Post-Nicene Fathers*, Ser. 1, Vol. V. Grand Rapids, MI, 1971.

The Burgundian Code. Tr. Katherine Fischer Drew. Philadelphia, 1972.

The Civil Law. Ed. S. P. Scott. Cincinnati, 1932.

Clark, Elizabeth and Herbert Richardson, eds. *Women and Religion: A Feminist Sourcebook of Christian Thought*. New York, 1977.

Jerome. *Select Letters of St. Jerome*. Tr. F. A. Wright. Loeb Classical Library. Cambridge, MA, 1963.

Jerome. *St. Jerome: Letters and Select Works* . Tr. W. H. Fremantle. *Select Library of Nicene and Post-Nicene Fathers*, Ser. 2, Vol. VI. Edinburgh, 1892; repr. Grand Rapids, MI, 1989.

Laws of the Alamans and Bavarians. Tr. Theodore John Rivers. Philadelphia, 1977.

The Laws of the Salian and Ripuarian Franks. Tr. Theodore John Rivers. New York, 1986.

Lefkowitz, Mary R. and Maureen Fant. *Women's Life in Greece and Rome*. Baltimore, 1982.

The Lombard Laws. Tr. Katherine Fischer Drew. Philadelphia, 1973.

Miller, Robert P., ed. *Chaucer: Sources and Backgrounds*. New York, 1977.

Shelton, Jo-Ann. *As the Romans Did: A Sourcebook in Roman Social History*. Oxford, 1988.

The Theodosian Code and Novels and the Sirmondian Constitutions. Tr. Clyde Pharr. Princeton, 1952.

Three Medieval Views of Women: La Contenance des Fames, Le Bien des Fames, Le Blasme des Fames. Ed. and tr. Gloria K. Fiero, Wendy Pfeffer and Mathé Allain. New Haven, 1989.

The Visigothic Code (Forum Judicum). Tr. S. P. Scott. Boston, 1910.

Secondary Works

Cantarella, Eva. *Pandora's Daughters: The Role and Status of Women in Greek and Roman Society*. Tr. Maureen B. Fant. Baltimore, 1987.

Fell, Christine, with Cecily Clark and Elizabeth Williams. *Women in Anglo-Saxon England and the Impact of 1066*. Oxford, 1986.

Gardner, Jane F. *Women in Roman Law and Society*. Bloomington, IN, 1986.

Geary, Patrick J. *Before France and Germany: The Creation and Transformation of the Merovingian World*. Oxford, 1988.

James, Edward. *The Origins of France From Clovis to the Capetians, 500–1000*. London, 1982.

Pomeroy, Sarah B. *Goddesses, Whores, Wives and Slaves: Women in Classical Antiquity*. New York, 1975.

Wemple, Suzanne Fonay. *Women in Frankish Society: Marriage and the Cloister, 500 to 900*. Philadelphia, 1985.

Wiedemann, Thomas. *Adults and Children in the Roman Empire*. New Haven, 1989.

Wolfram, Herwig. *History of the Goths*. Berkeley, 1988.

II. The Conditions of Life

Primary Sources

Bateson, M., ed. *Borough Customs*. London, 1966.

The Coutumes de Beauvaisis of Philippe de Beaumanoir. Tr. F.R.P. Akehurst. Philadelphia, 1992.

Medieval Woman's Guide to Health: The First English Gynecological Handbook. Tr. Beryl Rowland. Kent, OH, 1981.

Tractatus de legibus et consuetudinibus regni Anglie qui Glanvilla vocatur: The Treatise on the Laws and Customs of the Realm of England Commonly Called Glanvill. Ed. and tr. G.D.G. Hall. Nelson Medieval Texts. London, 1965.

Trotula of Salerno. *The Diseases of Women*. Tr. Elizabeth Mason-Hohl. The Ward-Ritchie Press, 1940.

The Welsh Law of Women. Ed. Dafydd Jenkins and Morfydd E. Owen. Cardiff, 1980.

Secondary Works

Atkinson, Clarissa W. *The Oldest Vocation: Christian Motherhood in the Middle Ages*. Ithaca, NY, 1991.

Boswell, John. *The Kindness of Strangers: The Abandonment of Children in Western Europe from Late Antiquity to the Renaissance*. New York, 1988.

Brooke, Christopher, ed. *The Medieval Idea of Marriage*. Oxford, 1989.

Duby, Georges. *The Knight, the Lady and the Priest: The Making of Modern Marriage in Medieval France*. Tr. Barbara Bray. Harmondsworth, 1983.

Duby, Georges. *Medieval Marriage: Two Models from Twelfth-Century France.* Tr. Elborg Forster. Baltimore, 1986.

Dyer, Christopher. *Standards of Living in the Later Middle Ages: Social Change in England, c. 1200–1520.* Cambridge, 1989.

Gies, Frances and Joseph Gies. *Marriage and the Family in the Middle Ages.* New York, 1987.

Herlihy, David. *Medieval Households.* Cambridge, MA, 1985.

Hughes, Muriel Joy. *Women Healers in Medieval Life and Literature.* New York, 1943.

Shahar, Shulamith. *Childhood in the Middle Ages.* London and New York, 1990.

Stone, Marilyn. *Marriage and Friendship in Medieval Spain: Social Relations According to the Fourth Partida of Alfonso X.* New York, 1990.

III. The Noble Life

Primary Sources

Barber, Richard. *The Pastons: A Family in the Wars of the Roses.* Harmondsworth, 1981.

Christine de Pizan. *Christine's Vision.* Tr. Glenda McLeod. New York, 1990.

Christine de Pizan. *The Epistle of the Prison of Human Life.* Tr. Josette A. Wisman. New York, 1984.

Dhuoda. *Handbook for William: A Carolingian Woman's Counsel for Her Son.* Tr. Carol Neel. Lincoln, NB, and London, 1991.

Gregory of Tours. *The History of the Franks.* Tr. Lewis Thorpe. Harmondsworth, 1974.

Guibert de Nogent. *The Autobiography of Guibert, Abbot of Nogent-sous-Coucy.* Tr. C. C. Swinton Bland. London and New York, 1925.

Guibert de Nogent. *Self and Society in Medieval France: The Memoirs of Abbot Guibert of Nogent.* Ed. John F. Benton. New York, 1970.

Secondary Works

Bennet, H. S. *The Pastons and Their England.* Cambridge, 1932.

Bogin, Meg. *The Women Troubadours.* New York, 1980.

Gies, Joseph and Frances Gies. *Life in a Medieval Castle.* New York, 1974.

Holmes, Urban Tigner. *Daily Living in the Twelfth Century: Based on the Observations of Alexander Neckham in London and Paris.* Madison, WI, 1952.

Labarge, Margaret Wade. *A Baronial Household of the Thirteenth Century*. To-towa, NJ, 1980.

Mirrer, Louise. *Upon My Husband's Death: Widows in the Literature and Histories of Medieval Europe*. Ann Arbor, MI, 1991.

Rosenthal, Joel T. *Patriarchy and Families of Privilege in Fifteenth-Century England*. Philadelphia, 1991.

Stenton, Doris Mary. *The English Woman in History*. London, 1957.

Willard, Charity Cannon. *Christine de Pizan, Her Life and Letters: A Biography*. New York, 1984.

IV. The Working Life

Primary Sources

Bedfordshire Coroners' Rolls. Ed. R. F. Hunnisett. Bedfordshire Historical Record Society, 1961.

Memorials of London and London Life. Ed. H. T. Riley. 2 vols. London, 1868.

Secondary Works

Bennett, H. S. *Life on the English Manor: A Study of Peasant Conditions, 1150–1400*. Cambridge, 1937.

Bennet, Judith M. *Women in the Medieval English Countryside*. Oxford, 1989.

Charles, Lindsey and Lorna Duffin. *Women and Work in Preindustrial England*. London, 1985.

Gies, Joseph and Frances Gies. *Life in a Medieval City*. New York, 1969.

Gies, Joseph and Frances Gies. *Life in a Medieval Village*. New York, 1990.

Hanawalt, Barbara. *The Ties that Bound: Peasant Families in Medieval England*. New York, 1986.

Hanawalt, Barbara, ed. *Women and Work in Preindustrial Europe*. Bloomington, IN, 1986.

Hanham, Alison. *The Celys and Their World: An English Merchant Family of the Fifteenth Century*. Cambridge, 1985.

Herlihy, David. *Opera Muliebria: Women and Work in Medieval Europe*. Philadelphia, 1990.

Howell, Martha C. *Women, Production and Patriarchy in Late Medieval Cities*. Chicago, 1988.

Nicholas, David *The Domestic Life of a Medieval City: Women, Children, and the Family in Fourteenth-Century Ghent*. Lincoln, NB, 1988.

Origo, Iris. *The Merchant of Prato: Francesco di Marco Datini, 1335–1410.* Boston, 1957.

Otis, Leah Lydia. *Prostitution in Medieval Society: The History of an Urban Institution in Languedoc.* Chicago, 1985.

Rossiaud, Jacques. *Medieval Prostitution.* Tr. Lydia G. Cochrane. Oxford, 1988.

Thrupp, Sylvia. *The Merchant Class of Medieval London, 1300–1500.* Chicago, 1948.

V. The Religious Life

Primary Sources

Ancrene Riwle: Introduction and Part I, tr. Robert W. Ackerman and Roger Dahood. Binghamton, NY, 1984.

Augustine of Hippo. *St. Augustine: Select Letters.* Tr. J.H. Baxter. Loeb Classical Library. London, 1930.

The Bishop's Register. Ed. Clifford J. Offer. London, 1929.

Brunn, Emilie Zum and Georgette Epiney-Burgard, eds. *Women Mystics in Medieval Europe.* New York, 1989.

Cazelles, Brigette. *The Lady as Saint: A Collection of French Hagiographic Romances of the Thirteenth Century.* Philadelphia, 1991.

Clare of Assisi: Early Documents, ed. Regis J. Armstrong. Mahwah, NJ, 1988.

Donatus of Besançon. *The Ordeal of Community, and The Rule of Donatus of Besançon.* Tr. Jo Ann McNamara and John Halborg. Toronto, n.d.

Dreyer, Elizabeth. *Passionate Women: Two Medieval Mystics.* Mahwah, NJ, 1989.

Eudes of Rouen. *The Register of Eudes of Rouen.* Tr. Sydney M. Brown, ed. Jeremiah F. O'Sullivan. New York and London, 1964.

Hallborg, John E., Jo Ann McNamara and Gordon Whatley, eds. *Sainted Women of the Dark Ages.* Durham, NC, 1992.

Hildegarde of Bingen. *Book of Divine Works, with Letters and Songs.* Ed. Matthew Fox. Santa Fe, NM, 1987.

Hildegarde of Bingen. *Explanation of the Rule of Benedict.* Tr. Hugh Feiss. Toronto, 1990.

Hildegarde of Bingen. *Illuminations.* Ed. Matthew Fox. Santa Fe, NM, 1985.

Hrotswitha of Gandersheim. *The Plays of Hrotsvit of Gandersheim.* Tr. Katharina M. Wilson. New York, 1989.

Hrotswitha of Gandersheim. *The Plays of Hrotswitha of Gandersheim.* Tr. Larissa Bonfante with Alexandra Bonfante-Warren. Oak Park, IL, 1986.

Julian of Norwich. *Revelations of Divine Love.* Ed. Halcyon Backhouse with Rhona Pipe. London, 1987.

Kempe, Margery. *The Book of Margery Kempe.* Tr. Barry Windeatt. Harmondsworth, 1985.

The Letters of Abelard and Heloise. Ed. Betty Radice. Harmondsworth, 1974.

The Life of Christina of Markyate, A Twelfth-Century Recluse. Tr. C. H. Talbot. Oxford, 1987.

Millett, Bella and Jocelyn Wogan-Browne, eds. *Medieval English Prose for Women: The Katherine Group and Ancrene Wisse.* Oxford, 1990.

The Nun's Rule, Being the Ancren Riwle Modernised. Ed. James Morton. London, 1905.

Ward, Benedicta. *Harlots of the Desert: A Study of Repentance in Early Monastic Sources.* Kalamazoo, MI, 1987.

Secondary Works

Bynum, Caroline Walker. *Holy Feast, Holy Fast: The Religious Significance of Food to Medieval Women.* Berkeley, 1987.

Chervin, Ronda De Sola. *Treasury of Women Saints.* Ann Arbor, MI, 1991.

Collis, Louise. *Memoirs of a Medieval Woman: The Life and Times of Margery Kempe.* New York, 1964.

Elkins, Sharon K. *Holy Women of Twelfth-Century England.* Chapel Hill, NC, 1988.

Finnegan, Mary Jeremy. *The Women of Helfta: Scholars and Mystics.* Athens, GA, 1991.

Flanagan, Sabina. *Hildegarde of Bingen: A Visionary Life.* New York, 1989.

Haight, Anne Lyon, ed. *Hroswitha of Gandersheim: Her Life, Times, and Works, and a Comprehensive Bibliography.* New York, 1965.

Johnson, Penelope D. *Equal in Monastic Profession: Religious Women in Medieval France.* Chicago, 1991.

McDonnell, Ernest W. *The Beguines and Beghards in Medieval Culture with Special Emphasis on the Belgian Scene.* New Brunswick, NJ, 1954 and 1969.

Newman, Barbara. *Sister of Wisdom: St. Hildegarde's Theology of the Feminine.* Berkeley, 1987.

Nichols, John A. and Lillian Thomas Shank, eds. *Distant Echoes: Medieval Religious Women I.* Kalamazoo, MI, 1984.

Nichols, John A. and Lillian Thomas Shank, eds. *Peace Weavers: Medieval Religious Women II.* Kalamazoo, MI, 1987.

Power, Eileen. *Medieval English Nunneries.* Cambridge, 1922.

Ruether, Rosemary and Eleanor McLaughlin, eds. *Women of Spirit: Female Leadership in the Jewish and Christian Traditions.* New York, 1979.

Salisbury, Joyce E. *Church Fathers, Independent Virgins.* New York, 1991.

Thurston, Bonnie Bowman. *A Women's Ministry in the Early Church.* Minneapolis, 1989.

Wilson, Katharina M. *Hrotsvit of Gandersheim: Rara Avis in Saxonia?* Ann Arbor, MI, 1987.

VI. Outsiders

Primary Sources

The Code of Maimonides. Book Four: The Book of Women. Tr. Isaac Klein. New Haven and London, 1972.

Henry, Sondra and Emily Taitz. *Written Out of History: A Hidden Legacy of Jewish Women Revealed Through Their Writings and Letters.* New York, 1978.

The Koran. Tr. N. J. Dawood. Harmondsworth, 1990.

Lewis, Bernard, ed. and tr. *Islam from the Prophet Muhammad to the Capture of Constantinople.* New York, 1974. 2 vols.

Maitland, S. R., ed. *Facts and Documents Illustrative of the History, Doctrine, and Rites of the Ancient Albigenses and Waldenses.* London, 1832.

Malleus Maleficarum. Tr. Montague Summers. London, 1928 and 1948.

Marcus, Jacob R., ed. *The Jew in the Medieval World: A Sourcebook, 315–1791.* Cincinnati, 1938.

Peters, Edward, ed. *Heresy and Authority in Medieval Europe: Documents in Translation.* Philadelphia, 1980.

Secondary Works

Baskin, Judith R. *Jewish Women in Historical Perspective.* Detroit, 1991.

Ladurie, Emmanuel Le Roy. *Montaillou: Cathars and Catholics in a French Village, 1294–1324.* London, 1980.

Rabinowitz, Louis. *The Social Life of the Jews of Northern France in the XII-XIVth Centuries.* London, 1938.

Richards, Jeffrey. *Sex, Dissidence, and Damnation: Minority Groups in the Middle Ages.* New York, 1991.

VII. Manual for a Wife

Primary Sources

Christine de Pisan. *The Book of the City of Ladies*. Tr. Earl Jeffrey Richards. London, 1983.

Christine de Pisan. *The Treasure of the City of Ladies, or, The Book of the Three Virtues*. Tr. Sarah Lawson. Harmondsworth, 1985.

Christine de Pizan. *A Medieval Woman's Mirror of Honor: The Treasury of the City of Ladies*. Tr. Charity Canon Willard, ed. Madeleine Pelner Cosman. New York, 1989.

The Goodman of Paris. Tr. Eileen Power. London, 1928.

A Medieval Home Companion: Housekeeping in the Fourteenth Century. Tr. Tania Bayard. New York, 1991.

Index